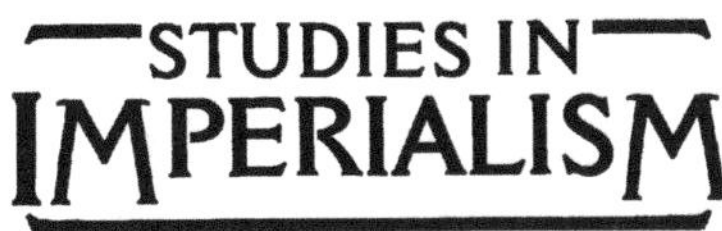

general editor John M. MacKenzie

When the 'Studies in Imperialism' series was founded more than twenty-five years ago, emphasis was laid upon the conviction that 'imperialism as a cultural phenomenon had as significant an effect on the dominant as on the subordinate societies'. With more than eighty books published, this remains the prime concern of the series. Cross-disciplinary work has indeed appeared covering the full spectrum of cultural phenomena, as well as examining aspects of gender and sex, frontiers and law, science and the environment, language and literature, migration and patriotic societies, and much else. Moreover, the series has always wished to present comparative work on European and American imperialism, and particularly welcomes the submission of books in these areas. The fascination with imperialism, in all its aspects, shows no sign of abating, and this series will continue to lead the way in encouraging the widest possible range of studies in the field. 'Studies in Imperialism' is fully organic in its development, always seeking to be at the cutting edge, responding to the latest interests of scholars and the needs of this ever-expanding area of scholarship.

Oceania under steam

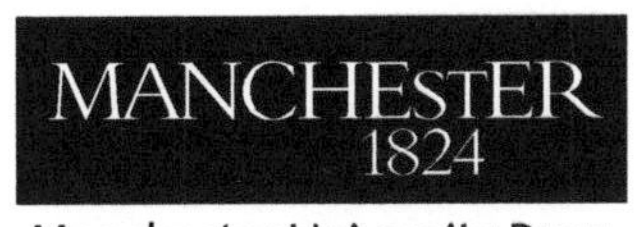

Manchester University Press

Oceania under steam

SEA TRANSPORT AND THE CULTURES OF COLONIALISM, c.1870–1914

Frances Steel

MANCHESTER
UNIVERSITY PRESS

Published by Manchester University Press
Altrincham Street, Manchester M1 7JA, UK
www.manchesteruniversitypress.co.uk

British Library Cataloguing-in-Publication Data is available

Library of Congress Cataloging-in-Publication Data is available

ISBN 978 1 5261 0656 8 *paperback*

First published by Manchester University Press in hardback 2011

This edition first published 2016

The publisher has no responsibility for the persistence or accuracy of URLs for any external or third-party internet websites referred to in this book, and does not guarantee that any content on such websites is, or will remain, accurate or appropriate.

Printed by Lightning Source

For my parents

CONTENTS

LIST OF FIGURES

ACKNOWLEDGEMENTS

This book has a lot to say about ships and the people who owned, worked on and travelled by them, yet it was inspired by time in the archives rather than time at sea. I grew up in Dunedin, at the sometimes chilly south-western edge of the vast Pacific Ocean, but only over the course of this research did I begin to think seriously about the historical significance of the surrounding oceanic world. Along the way I have had the very good fortune to be supported and encouraged by many people and institutions in Oceania and beyond. I have a number of debts to acknowledge here.

This book developed from my doctoral research undertaken at the Australian National University. My supervisor, Margaret Jolly, has been an inspiring mentor. Margaret prompted me to place New Zealand history in its Pacific context, guided me through the challenges and complexities of writing about the colonial past, and kept me alert to the colonial legacies in the contemporary Pacific. Her creative energy, spirit of enquiry, compassion and sense of fun demonstrated to me the rich rewards of an academic career. I am also indebted to other members of my doctoral committee. Tony Ballantyne offered many perceptive comments, insights and suggestions. I have been greatly influenced by the work Tony has done to reframe and locate New Zealand history in the context of imperial networks and exchanges. I appreciate his ongoing intellectual generosity. Paul D'Arcy showed ceaseless enthusiasm for this project. His formative work on the maritime dimensions of Pacific history influenced my own turn to the sea. I am grateful to Vicki Luker for her thoughtful engagement with and careful critiques on my many chapter drafts, and Ann McGrath for her ongoing interest in my research. The Gender Relations Centre in the Research School of Pacific and Asian Studies was a wonderfully supportive and productive place to pursue this research and I am thankful for the collective friendship and collegiality of all the academic and administrative staff and fellow graduate students who worked in the Centre between 2004 and 2007.

I have appreciated the opportunity to present my ideas at a number of conferences and seminars. Graduate workshops hosted by the Australian National University's History Program, Humanities Research Centre and Centre for Cross-Cultural Research were invaluable in the early stages of my research. I was privileged to participate in the final 'Challenges to Perform' workshop held in September 2004, where Greg Dening, Donna Merwick and Carolyn Strange inspired all participants to embrace the essential creativity of the scholarly writing life. Greg's legacy continues to inspire.

The transition from dissertation to book was aided by the comments of my doctoral examiners, Miles Ogborn and Sugata Bose. I am grateful for their insight and encouragement, pressing me to articulate the wider significance of the Pacific lives narrated in the following pages. The book took final shape at the University of Otago and the University of Wollongong. I thank colleagues at both institutions for their support and interest, and Georgine Clarsen, Julia Martinez and members of the Faculty of Arts Writing Group for offering valuable criticisms and comments on various chapters. I also thank Jenny Newell at the National Museum of Australia who made many thoughtful suggestions on aspects of my work.

Others have offered invaluable advice as I got to grips with the book-writing process and I would particularly like to thank Barbara Brookes, Angela McCarthy and Brian Martin. As my honours supervisor at Otago, Barbara was the one who encouraged me to pursue a PhD and to move countries to do so. I appreciate her continued support, advice and friendship. Special thanks are also due to my auntie, Valerie O'Reilly, for her interest in this project and for reading each chapter as I slowly revised it and emailed it through to her. Nicky Page also read the whole manuscript and offered many helpful editorial suggestions.

Research in Australia, New Zealand, Fiji and England was only possible through funding provided by a doctoral scholarship associated with the project funded by the Australian Research Council, 'Oceanic Encounters: Colonial and Contemporary Transformations of Gender and Sexuality in the Pacific', and through supplementary grants from the Research School of Pacific and Asian Studies and the University of Wollongong. Helpful service provided by staff at the Hocken Collections, the Alexander Turnbull Library, the Wellington City Council Archives, and the National Archives of Fiji made archival research such a pleasure. I also thank for their assistance the Wellington Museum of City and Sea, Archives New Zealand (Wellington), the Special Collections at the University of Auckland Library, the Auckland City Library, the National Library of Australia, the Fiji Museum, the Caird Library and the Port Chalmers Museum. I am also grateful to Ian Farquhar for his kind and prompt assistance with my jumble of questions about the Union Steam Ship Company's operations.

I have enjoyed working with Manchester University Press and thank staff for their assistance, advice and hard work throughout the production process. I am also grateful to the Press's anonymous

ACKNOWLEDGEMENTS

reviewers whose suggestions and critiques have helped to sharpen my analysis.

Some aspects of this book previously appeared in my article 'Women, men and the Southern Octopus: shipboard gender relations in the age of steam', *International Journal of Maritime History*, Forum 'Women and the Sea in the Pacific', 20:2 (2008), 285–306; my chapter 'Suva under steam: mobile men and a colonial port capital, 1880s–1910s,' in Tony Ballantyne and Antoinette Burton (eds), *Moving Subjects: Gender, Mobility and Intimacy in an Age of Global Empire* (Urbana and Chicago: University of Illinois Press, 2008), 110–26; and 'Via New Zealand around the world: The Union Steam Ship Company and the trans-Pacific mail lines, 1870s–1910s', in Prue Ahrens and Chris Dixon (eds), *Coast to Coast: Case Histories of Modern Pacific Crossings* (Newcastle: Cambridge Scholars Publishing, 2010), 59–76.

Many family members and friends in Australia and New Zealand have offered encouragement and welcome distractions over the years: thank you to my sisters, Amelia, Renee, Hannah and Gabrielle, and to Diana Brown, Emma Dolan, Kirsty Douglas, Greg Dvorak, Susan Engel, Willy Flockton, Dave Haines, Aimee Jephson, Emily O'Gorman, Kumiko Kawashima, Katherine Lepani, Greg Rawlings, Tiffany Shellam and Heather Wilson. In Canberra I shared much domestic bliss with Alison and Mia McCaskie, Anna Paice and Anita Reynolds. Many people were very hospitable and generous of their time and space during my research trips: I would like to thank Katherine and John Dolan, Amelia and family, Renee and Chris, Sione Makasiale, Arieta Rasiga and the Wainaloka community on Ovalau.

I have dedicated this book to my parents, Janis and David, who have supported my research interests and endeavours in so many ways over the years. My father has recently embraced the hunt for steamship company ephemera in junk shops and online with an enthusiasm that appears to rival my own for the textual traces of the maritime world. And, finally, I owe a great debt of gratitude to Tom Bond of Shrimp Lodge for his patience and good humour, for making sure I stepped out of the archives to rediscover the beauty of the Otago coast, and for simply believing in what I do.

LIST OF ABBREVIATIONS

AJHR	*Appendices to the Journals of the House of Representatives*
ASNCo.	Australasian Steam Navigation Company
AUSNCo.	Australasian United Steam Navigation Company
CSO	Colonial Secretary's Office (Fiji)
FSU	Federated Seamen's Union of New Zealand
NZPD	*New Zealand Parliamentary Debates*
P&O	Peninsula and Oriental Steam Navigation Company
USSCo.	Union Steam Ship Company of New Zealand

Archives

ANZ	Archives New Zealand Wellington (branch)
ATL	Alexander Turnbull Library, Wellington
HC	Hocken Collections, Uare Taoka o Hakena, University of Otago, Dunedin
NAF	National Archives of Fiji, Suva
UASC	University of Auckland Library Special Collections
WCCA	Wellington City Council Archives

MAPS

NEW ZEALAND

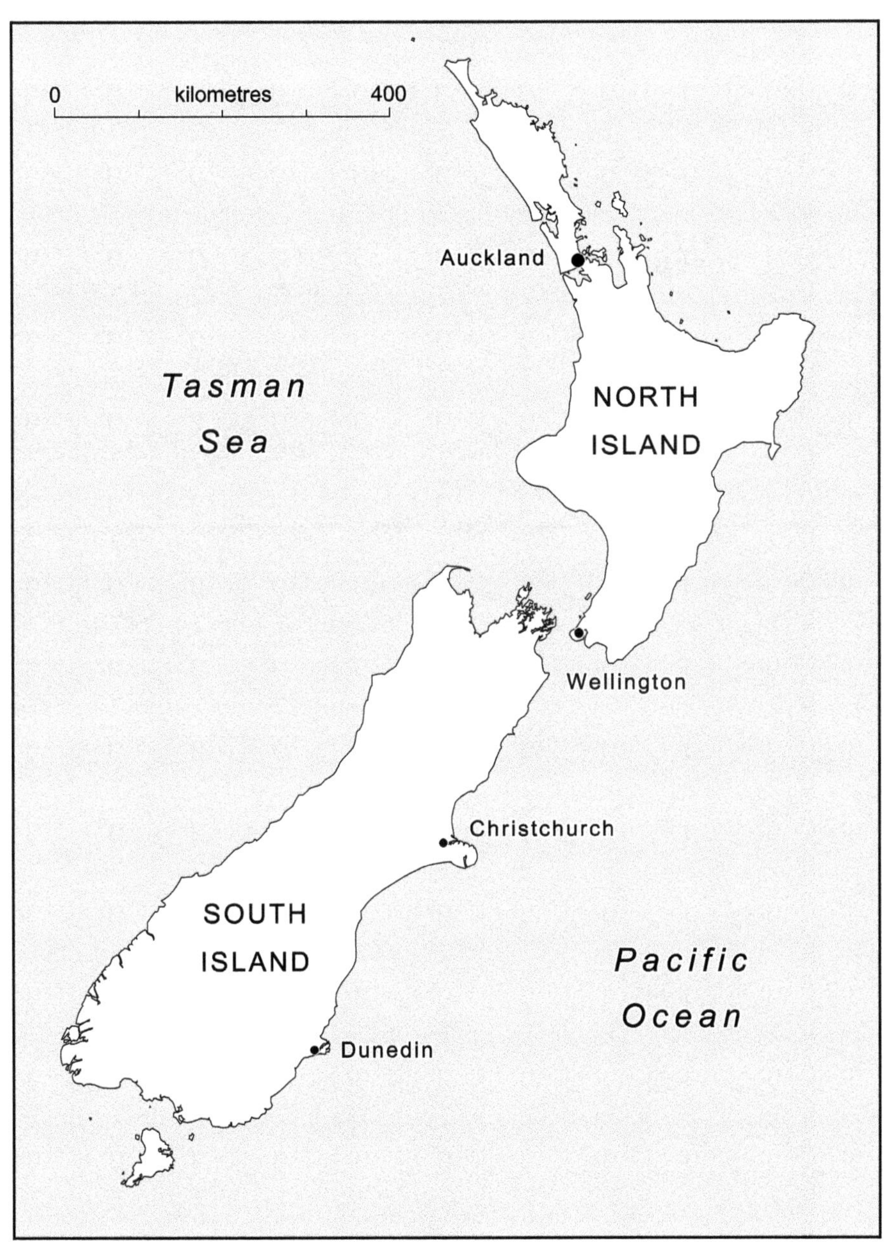

FIJI

0 kilometres 100
VANUA LEVU
YASAWA GROUP
TAVEUNI
OVALAU
Levuka
VITI LEVU
Koro Sea
REWA
LAU GROUP
Suva
KADAVU GROUP

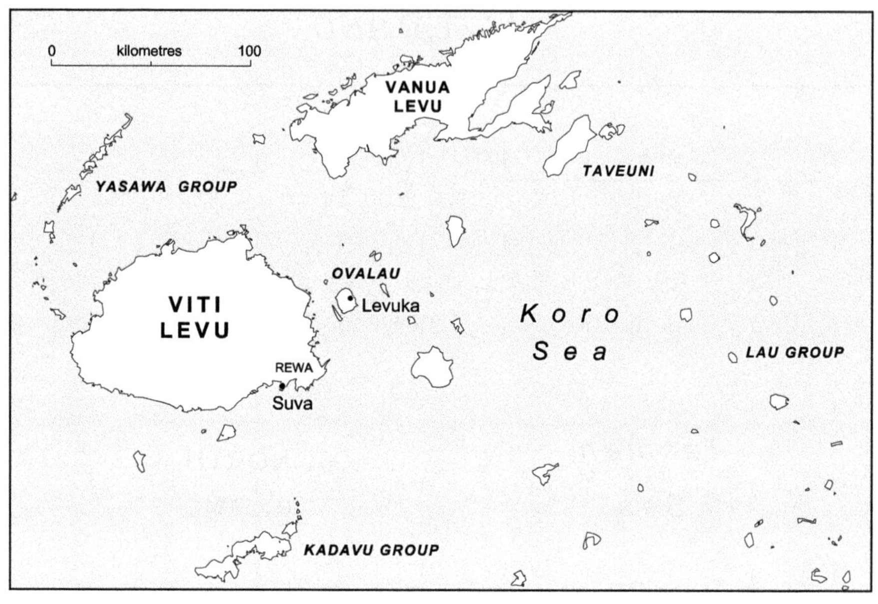

GENERAL EDITOR'S INTRODUCTION

One of the commitments of the 'Studies in Imperialism' series is to a 'de-centred' imperial history, that is, a modern approach which sees the relations of imperialism as constituting something far beyond a set of radiating connections between the metropole and the so-called periphery. This was an image that was regularly perpetuated in the world maps of trade and steamship lines common in the nineteenth and twentieth centuries. It symbolised the manner in which empire was a global terrain at which writers and cartographers looked from the vantage point of the so-called 'Mother Country'. But the establishment of colonial rule created something much more complex than this, with 'sub-imperialisms' being set up in various parts of the world, with intercolonial relationships establishing complex webs of economic, social and cultural networks. As Frances Steel demonstrates in this timely book, this was never more true than in the area of steamship histories, not least in the Pacific.

There are a number of new perspectives established in this focus upon New Zealand and Oceania. First, steamship lines are no longer seen as capitalist organisations that connected the centre of European empires to their colonial outposts. Second, the emphasis shifts from the prime concerns of past histories which have examined the Atlantic and Caribbean worlds, as well as steamer connections with Africa, the Middle East, the Indian subcontinent, Australia, South-East Asia and the Far East. Third, earlier works, both popular and academic, have tended to look at the large companies, the high-profile shipping lines which constituted (in the words of the title of an earlier book in the series) the 'flagships of imperialism'. Finally, past studies have invariably privileged ships over people, economics over social and cultural relations.

As I have myself written in the past, there has long been a need for studies of the apparently smaller – and no less significant – enterprises of the empire of steam.

The Straits Steamship Company, the Irrawaddy Flotilla Company, Burns Philp of Sydney, steamers on the African lakes, and many others are as deserving of research as Cunard, P&O, Union-Castle and British India. The Union Steam Ship Company of New Zealand comes into the same category. These companies with a lower profile (at least in Europe) had a powerful impact upon the coastal, riverine, lakeshore and archipelagic areas in which they operated. They were equally significant in bringing the transformations of the imperial relationship to bear upon indigenous peoples and their multiplicit relationships with Europeans and the British world. Moreover, each ship was itself an imperial microcosm, carrying within itself evidence of new building techniques, of steam technologies, of human class and racial hierarchies, of social and culinary conventions, of working relationships, of the variable mobility of peoples, and of the cargoes which were representative of each regional economic system. Among the passengers and crew of each vessel were to be found varied examples of dominant and subordinate peoples, travelling and working in a wide variety of guises within colonial systems. Moreover, steamships imposed themselves upon indigenous nautical traditions which had transferred peoples and goods along coasts, between islands, around lakes, even across continents (like the Indian Ocean dhow or the Chinese junk). But they seldom achieved a sudden or easy victory. Such older methods survived and coexisted, performing parallel, related or different functions which colonial rule never quite succeeded in eliminating. These rich textures are more than adequately surveyed in this fascinating work.

It is a special pleasure and privilege for me to introduce this book since it is a field that has intrigued me since childhood, even although I have contributed comparatively little to its study. An upbringing near the docks in a great imperial port (Glasgow) provided me with a fascination with steamships, their operations and the people who worked and travelled in them at a time when quaysides were readily accessible, even to schoolchildren, and health and safety regulations were unknown. Glasgow was proud of its ships, shipbuilders and seafarers, although it is true that, as Frances Steel observes, the local press invariably privileged ships over people in its pictures and stories. From the 1950s onwards and over many decades, I have been fortunate enough to travel back and forth by sea to Africa, North America, South and South-East Asia. As an adventurous young academic I travelled on steamers on African lakes. Later, I developed an acquaintanceship with the operations of the British India Line, a high-profile company founded in India, particularly with its vessels which connected Bombay (Mumbai) to the Persian or Arabian Gulf and eastern India to Singapore. This gave me a long-standing interest in the hermetic world of the ship, which continued to reveal its social and racial hierarchies into the post-colonial world. On the BI I found Indian, Goanese, Chinese and other crew member all performing what I have described as 'invented traditions of ethnic specialisms', a phenomenon that was also evident in other parts of the world. Visits to Australia and New Zealand, not least to their maritime museums, introduced me to the companies, people and trades centred upon those territories and the network of routes that fanned out in the Pacific and Indian Oceans. It is for all these reasons, as well as the quality of the research, the writing, and its many people-centred insights that it gives me pleasure to introduce this book into the MUP 'Studies in Imperialism' series. It should secure an audience well outside its specific hemisphere, for the insights and methodology encapsulated here are readily applicable elsewhere.

John M. MacKenzie

Introduction

A building of particular note stands at the intersection of Dunedin's Water and Cumberland streets. Unlike other well-preserved examples of the city's rich architectural heritage, upgraded for new offices or converted into inner-city apartments, it is now largely unoccupied. Broken windows and grime-streaked paintwork speak of years of neglect (figure 1). This building was constructed in the early 1880s, a time of unparalleled growth and prosperity in Dunedin as the city capitalised on the rush to Central Otago following the discovery of gold in 1861. The handsome solidity of the original structure embodies the certainty and progressive vision of the city's political and business leaders (figure 2). It was from these premises, centrally located in the railway, harbour and exchange precinct, the city's former commercial and transport hub, that the Union Steam Ship Company of New Zealand (USSCo.) commanded a vast network of steamers, port branches and maritime labour in the late nineteenth and early twentieth centuries. Today this building stands as a rather tired remnant of what was one of the largest and most important maritime enterprises in the history of the South Pacific.

The company was established in 1875 by a young entrepreneur, James Mills. As a teenager Mills went to work for the local whaler and shipowner Johnny Jones in Waikouaiti, a small coastal settlement just north of Dunedin. Jones soon put Mills in charge of his Dunedin Harbour Steam Company. On Jones's death in 1869, Mills, then aged twenty-two, was appointed leading trustee of his estate. Over the next few years Mills gradually achieved a prominent position in the local shipping industry and in 1874 he travelled to Britain seeking financial backing to expand his Dunedin-based shipping operations into the long-distance coastal trades. By chance he met a prominent Scottish shipbuilder, Peter Denny, managing director of William Denny and Brothers at Dumbarton. Mills's ambitious vision impressed

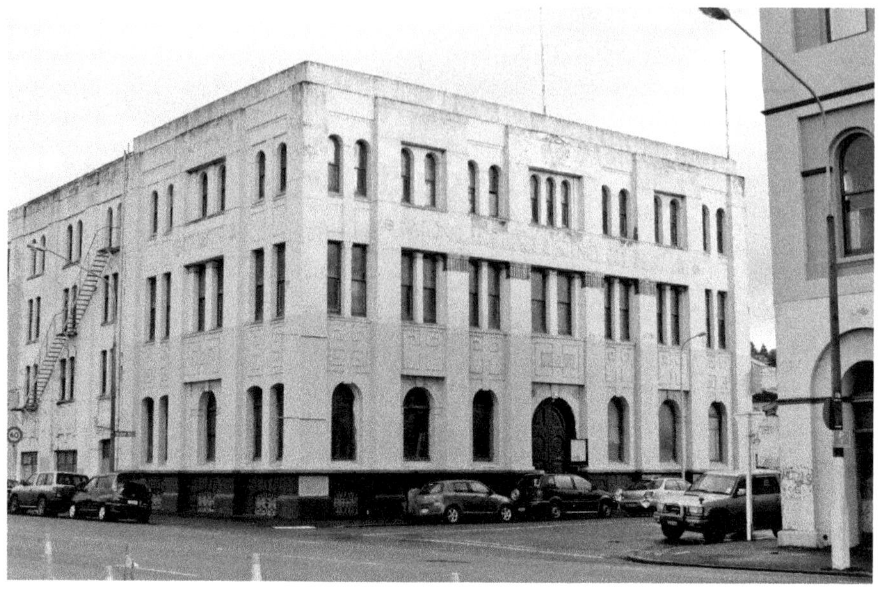

1   Former USSCo. building, Water St, Dunedin, 2010

Denny, who offered to build the first two vessels and took shares in them himself. Through a series of amalgamations and takeovers, the company went on to play a dominant role in the New Zealand coastal, trans-Tasman, Tasmanian and Pacific Island shipping routes. Vessels steamed to North America on the transpacific mail routes and also traded to South-East Asia, India and Europe. On the eve of the First World War the company commanded a fleet of seventy-five steamers. This tentacular stranglehold over regional maritime transport services soon earned it the disparaging title 'The Southern Octopus'.[1]

As with the former head office, now shorn of its original rooftop finery and extensive façade, the historical record of the company's influence is not prominently etched on the land and seascapes of the Pacific. Steamers did not survive beyond their years of active service. Company histories catalogue their often untimely and violent demise: ships were wrecked, grounded, broken up, scuttled, burnt out, dismantled or laid up.[2] You can still find them preserved in perfect miniature, for some of the original builders' models are encased in glass cabinets in the maritime gallery at the Otago Museum. As a child I remember being captivated instead by the huge fin whale skeleton, which stretched nearly the length of the hall, and the diving suit with the plaster dummy man trapped inside, forever staring blankly out of the bulbous copper helmet. These were two mysterious and slightly eerie

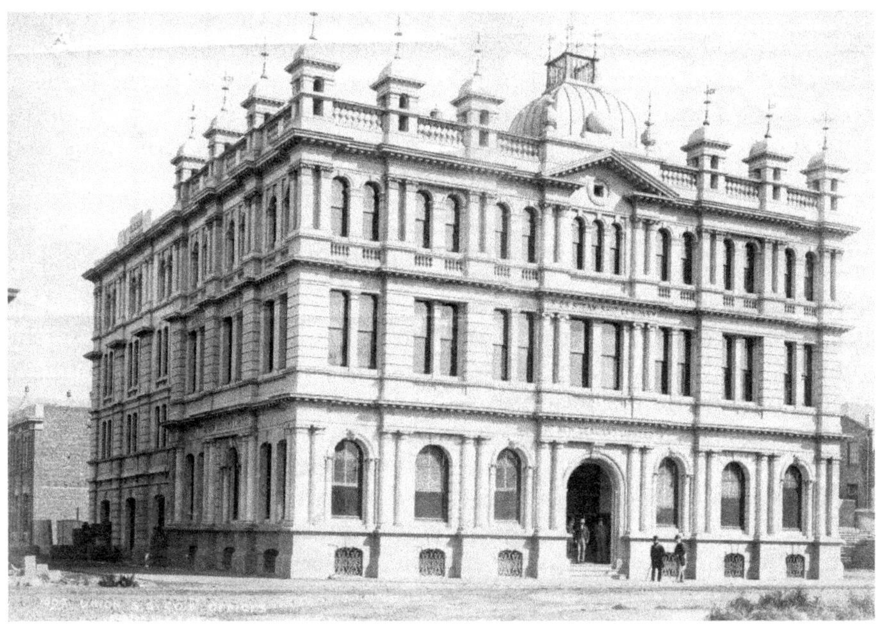

2 USSCo. building, Water St, Dunedin, 1880s

relics of the oceanic world beneath, rather than the more mundane history of industrial activity across its surface.

The physical demise of maritime architecture ashore and afloat catalogues a gradual reorientation away from the ocean and towards the land as a source of collective wealth and identity. Today most people have limited first-hand knowledge of ships and few have experienced lengthy coastal or ocean journeys on anything like a routine basis. Working ports are typically rather uninviting industrial spaces with towering cranes, rows of shipping containers and storage sheds fenced off from the public. Once proximate to the wharf, road and bridge construction and a strip of oversized commercial premises have gradually partitioned the Water Street site from the city's harbour basin. The writing of history has itself reinforced this landwards orientation, for terracentric narratives of imperial expansion, colonialism and nation-building have predominated at the expense of maritime themes. In a region like the Pacific, a vast ocean basin in which many small islands are scattered, studies of the nature and significance of seaborne connections, particularly those networks forged between the white settler colonies of New Zealand and Australia with their closest island neighbours in the western Pacific, are underdeveloped.

Oceania under Steam revisits a period when the sea and the ships that traversed it occupied a more immediate and pervasive presence in everyday life. Throughout I use the historical example of the USSCo. to connect a series of sea-focused stories in colonial history. In doing so, I seek to integrate shipping in the broader cultural structures that have shaped the history of empire and Oceania.

Writing empire and steam

The final decades of the nineteenth century marked a revolution in deep-ocean transport. Steam had been in use in shipping early in the century. In their initial phases of development steamships promised much, but the construction of safe and efficient ships suited to long ocean passages was fraught with difficulty. More efficient propulsion mechanisms, notably the screw propeller in the 1840s, the triple-expansion engine in the 1870s, and the steam turbine at the end of the century, eventually produced more power from every ton of coal, making steam a more reliable and cost-effective technology. Furthermore, the introduction in the 1880s of steel as a structural material opened up new design possibilities. Steel reduced a hull's weight, enhanced its stability and allowed the construction of higher and larger decks. Enthusiasm for larger, faster and more technically ambitious ships gained momentum. All the leading shipowners were ordering steamers of a size 'which some years ago would never have been dreamt of', remarked the *Glasgow Herald* in 1881. They were engaged in that 'peaceful rivalry in the production of big ships'.[3]

An established literature has examined this new era of industrial innovation. Steamers, together with railways, medicines, weapons and the telegraph cable, came to embody the key values of progressive Europe: complexity, power, precision, discipline and the mastery of time and space. As the self-styled 'titans of technology', Victorian Britons regarded these industrial products as potent evidence of superiority and power, fashioning what Michael Adas has labelled 'ideologies of western dominance'.[4] These 'tools of empire' fostered a stronger, more confident articulation of industrial achievement with national strength and imperial influence.[5] The historian J. R. Seeley's *The Expansion of England* (1883), which sold 80,000 copies in one year, presented an influential commentary on the power of the scientific inventions of steam and electricity in collapsing space and drawing together a Greater Britain.[6] Imperial powers began to extend, consolidate and exploit their overseas territories in ways not previously possible. The marriage of new technical innovations and imperial expansion laid the foundations, as Daniel Headrick put it, 'for a new global civilisation based on Western technology'.[7]

Professional communities of shipping firms, shipbuilders, engineers, bankers, merchants and coal suppliers in Liverpool, Glasgow and Newcastle – what Robert Kubicek has called the 'techno-financial commercial ship nexus' – were powerful agents of the new imperialism of the late nineteenth century. Their activities were as crucial to Britain's rise to global dominance as the London-based gentlemanly capitalists.[8] Shipping networks were increasingly influential in all spheres of metropolitan life, from trade and politics to culture and religion. Shipbuilding projects, exhibitions, travel guidebooks and histories such as *The Steamship Conquest of the World* communicated the imperial power of steam to metropolitan audiences. The underlying message, as John MacKenzie concludes, was that British shipping was the strongest in the world and should be supported.[9]

To date, most studies of the ascendancy of steam and the rise of the 'big ships' have been motivated by questions about the explanatory power of technology in an age of global empire. They have turned to technological innovations to understand better the timing and progress of imperial expansion and empowerment. My starting point in this book is different. Rather than conceiving of imperialism as an abstract system in order to talk in general terms about the 'impacts' and 'outcomes' of steam, I locate transport technologies and systems in the contexts of their everyday use. The pioneering work on technology and empire directed us to the globalising power of modern communication and transport systems, yet the older language of the 'penetrating, conquering, exploiting' force of steam is now less satisfactory.[10] It suggests an inherent inevitability, a friction-free imposition of total control over passive receiving societies at the edges of empire. It works to smooth out and compress what were always messy, contested and open-ended processes.

The broader political and economic investments in new transport systems remains an important line of enquiry, but in *Oceania under steam* I also open up an historical analysis of steamships and empire to the more complex and layered histories of transnational and transcolonial activities, lives and identities. I unpack the human stories at the heart of this technical subject, examining the ways in which technologies did not have stable meanings that were neatly defined by the elite. They were transformed and found meaning in specific colonial settings as they were used (or not) by a range of people, often to pursue quite different agendas from those envisaged by their creators.[11]

In this respect, developments in transport history more broadly conceived demonstrate the possibilities opened up by cultural approaches to shipping and the sea. Scholars in the evolving area of the 'history of transport turned history of mobility' are working to integrate questions

of production and use to examine more closely the ways people consumed and experienced transport in the past. A greater emphasis on
the 'techno-cultural' act of transport use, on the cultures of mobility
(and immobility), can enrich analyses of the tools of the scientific,
political and commercial elite to tell us more about the ways transport
systems and technologies have shaped society and, equally, about the
social shaping of transport technologies.[12]

Adapting key concepts from automobility history, Colin Divall,
a railway or 'railing' historian, argues for understanding railing 'as
a bundle of three socio-technical dimensions that constitute one
another: rail-subjects, rail-objects, and rail-scapes, all of them defined
through their physical-functional and symbolic-expressive relations
one to the other'. This means bringing together workers, passengers,
traders and companies (subjects), with the things that produced their
mobility, such as vehicles, tracks, stations, operating rules, laws and
social conventions (objects), as well as the spaces and temporalities
within which railing occurred (scapes). Such a synthesis advances
railway history as 'mobility history'.[13] This integrated approach also
promises much for histories of maritime transport and empire.

To see the less linear and hierarchical histories of steamshipping also requires a reframing of imperial space. Earlier accounts
have tended to privilege the 'big ships, big waters and big trades', as
MacKenzie puts it. The gaze is fixed on the shipbuilding heartlands
in Europe and on the shipping lines that radiate out from main northern hemisphere ports. Histories of the 'smaller ships', 'smaller trades'
or 'smaller waters', the 'local agents of a decentred imperialism not
always directly linked to the distant metropolis', are less well developed.[14] By shifting the angle of enquiry away from a metropole-centred
study of Britain's rise to global maritime dominance and focusing more
closely on the 'peripheral' sites of empire at the other end of the line,
we may see better the ways in which steamships were localised by
colonial nationalists, everyday workers and indigenous communities.

The oceanic 'flavour' of a newer, decentred imperial history which
follows the exchanges that moved horizontally between different colonies, rather than the more traditional focus on the vertical metropole-
colony axis, is not as pronounced as it might be. This book places more
emphasis on the maritime spaces 'in between' – the infrastructure of
shipping routes and steamships – and those people who worked and
lived in between. In this respect *Oceania under steam* can be read as
a literal engagement with Tony Ballantyne's call to develop 'a more
mobile approach to the imperial past'.[15] There are important exceptions, seen for example in Jonathan Hyslop's engagement with the
overlapping webs of the 'steamship empire' in the Indian Ocean world,

but, as he and others recognise, historical work which engages in any extended way with the maritime world is much richer for the age of sail than it is for the age of steam.[16]

Oceania under steam

Scholarship of empire and the sea in the Pacific would tend to confirm these trends. There is a long tradition of work on European exploratory voyages and the nature and consequence of encounters between intruders and indigenous inhabitants on shipboard and shore. The Cook voyages in particular (1768–79) are an enduring source of scholarly and popular fascination.[17] The intensive and short-lived maritime trading networks, as privately funded ships came in search of South Sea cargoes to trade in Asia and Europe from the early nineteenth century, have also received attention, as have transcolonial indentured labour mobilities in the latter half of the century.[18] With scholarship on the late nineteenth century being less maritime or ocean-centred in focus, the historiography of steam is underdeveloped.

There are a number of comprehensive business histories of the main regional shipping companies, including the USSCo., the Sydney-based Burns Philp and Company and the Matson Line of San Francisco.[19] Other contributions from economic history have broadly surveyed 'the story of steam navigation' as ships criss-crossed the ocean basin, linking North America to 'the Far East and the Antipodes'.[20] More popular works catalogue the careers of 'glamour ships', effectively accounts of ships without people.[21] Collectively this work is constrained by some of the limitations discussed earlier: there is less attention to the cultural contexts in which these operations and actors are situated, and in which transport technologies find meaning in their everyday use. Except for the historical 'flash-points' of maritime strikes or shipwrecks, they tell us little about the everyday routines of work in a shipping empire. This book shifts the analysis away from narrower, nationally focused, technical and economic studies of ships, society and the sea.

With particular reference to the British settler societies in the western Pacific, histories of transport and empire have emphasised the vertical lines of connection with the imperial metropole, that ongoing project to blunt the 'tyranny of distance' as charted in Geoffrey Blainey's 1966 classic of the same name.[22] James Belich has described the 'tightening' of vertical links between New Zealand and Britain that developed in the 1880s with improved communication systems. His metaphor for these networks are 'the giant meat ships' of the Shaw, Savill and Albion line: 'Carrying meat and talent out, machines and books back, and mailbags both ways, they were the corpuscles of a bilateral system'.[23] The Pacific is framed here as somehow irrelevant or a vast impediment to connections with the British homeland. For Belich, the Pacific becomes, as he argues, 'a mere space' between New Zealand and Britain; 'to a large extent, to say that New Zealand was in the Pacific was merely a geographical expression'.[24] This echoes Blainey who also perceives that, as Australia and New Zealand were so closely linked to Britain, 'their geographical position near the end of Asia's tail and near the islands of Oceania seemed irrelevant'.[25]

Shipping routes to Britain were the vital arteries that sustained these far-flung Pacific outposts and invested their physical and cultural location with meaning. At the same time, New Zealand ports were also busy with ships pursuing more localised itineraries, forging and maintaining links between settlements on either side of the Tasman Sea and into the Pacific. These places were often more accessible than those we would now define as being located in shared national space.[26] Fiji, for example, was five days' steaming from Auckland, about the same time it took to travel the length of New Zealand by train and steamer, while Australia's eastern seaboard was closer to ports in New Zealand than it was to settlements in other parts of the continent. While the cargoes of USSCo. steamers do not reveal the wealth of economic, political and cultural capital shipped by the giant meat ships, this circulation suggests much about the ways pasts are shared on a number of scales. These smaller ships and smaller trades illustrate the fuller complexity of the historical relationships between these colonies and the waters that surrounded them.

Regional connections forged between the colonies of New Zealand and Australia and the island Pacific from the second half of the nineteenth century have not entirely escaped historical attention. An older literature canvassed the political and economic aspirations, predominantly of the political and commercial elite, for sub-imperial influence. In these narratives terrestrial boundaries remain coherent, reinscribed rather than refigured, as the maritime traffic that brought these sites together is not fully historicised. So, for example, Angus Ross could argue that his *New Zealand Aspirations in the Pacific in the Nineteenth Century* 'emphasises the New Zealand end of the story, which in this book, has been treated as an aspect of New Zealand rather than of Pacific island history'.[27] This scholarly separation of island space has created, in Kerry Howe's words, 'two historiographic worlds': New Zealand and Pacific history (and we can also include Australia here to effect a tripartite division) have developed along separate trajectories.[28]

Over the last decade, a number of studies have placed New Zealand and 'other Pacific Islands' in a single interpretative frame, whether through the circulation of colonial ideas about race, as in Damon Salesa's work on the shifting status of mixed-race individuals in New Zealand and its Samoan territory in the early twentieth century, or in Ballantyne's account of Aryanism and the intellectual webs of empire.[29] Other studies have tracked more material exchanges, as in Katerina Teaiwa's evocative historical ethnography of the aggressive decades of phosphate mining on Ocean Island (Banaba), where the island was literally stripped bare and shipped out to fertilise the grasslands revolution in New Zealand and Australia.[30] Collectively, such studies go some way to recover the 'Pacificness' of New Zealand history, and to unsettle the nation-centred framing of the historical discipline itself.

There is more scope to examine the ways in which transport operations were vital to the formation and maintenance of regional colonial history. Historical geographer Gordon Winder has recently argued that shedding a 'landlubber's gaze' for a 'seafarer's gaze' might 'lend a viewpoint, scale and character' to New Zealand's historical geographic imagination long missing. Using Auckland in 1908 as a focal point, he describes that city as a 'floating world' of vessels, crews and cargo to emphasise the importance of the interlocked scale of local, regional and global maritime networks in its history.[31] I adopt a more multi-sited (-sighted) gaze and use the steamship both as a site and a symbol to write New Zealand into Pacific exchanges in new ways.

As the USSCo.'s operations were not contained by national boundaries, this book moves beyond a single national historiography. 'Oceania' in the book's title signifies this. Coined by French geographers in 1804, Oceania originally referred to the East Indies (Borneo, modern Indonesia, Timor-Leste, Singapore, the Philippines), New Holland (Australia), Van Diemen's Land (Tasmania), New Zealand and the 'South Sea Islands' as they were collectively known. Maritime South-East Asia soon dropped out of popular usage. For the white settler colonies in New Zealand and Australia, 'Australasia', a place-marker which came to distinguish British colonial territory in the western Pacific, tended to circumvent this broader regional designation.[32] Oceania has found new purchase in post-colonial framings of the Pacific. In a seminal article, Epeli Hau'ofa rejected the entrenched marginalisation of 'islands in a far sea', an isolated, resource-poor, dependent and marginal world made up of tiny parcels of land. He emphasised the long-standing processes of maritime connectivity and exchange between island societies, drawing continuities between Islanders' ancient navigational practices and their present-day transnational mobilities, now by air routes, to the larger states on the ocean's rim. He understood the sea as an expansive, active, connecting place and a material and symbolic resource. Privileging both water and land equally as sites of history, he argued Oceania is 'Our Sea of Islands'.[33]

Hau'ofa wrote to counter the contemporary belittlement of outsider academics, aid donors, diplomats and the like, rather than explicitly to forge an ocean basin historiography. His framing emphasised the ways in which indigenous people connected with each other, rather than the relationships between Islanders and newcomers to the region. Yet I draw inspiration from this vision, as have so many other historians in the Pacific. This reconfiguration of maritime space and its historical significance encourages us to think differently about regional connectivities and interrelationships, as well as the asymmetries of power that both support and are produced by them.

This book does not attempt a history of the whole ocean basin, nor does it disregard the wider paradigm of the global sea. It uses Oceania more as an organising concept, one infused with a maritime sensibility, to demonstrate the ways in which local, national and imperial identities were shaped as much by transoceanic networks as by land-based affiliations. As Fernand Braudel referred to the Mediterranean as 'a complex of seas' and Sugata Bose to the 'hundred horizons' of Indian Ocean history, so too does R. G. Ward remind us that 'there are many "Oceanias", and its parts may have several versions'.[34] The particular version emphasised in this book is a regional sea in the British Pacific, one mapped out by Union Company shipping, as depicted in the 1910 chart of routes (figure 3). This chart was designed to be read alongside the company's monthly pocket guidebook, which listed timetables and other information regarding steamer movements.

Maritime transport was always more dynamic and uneven than rigid lines, carefully calculated distances and timetabled arrivals and departures can represent. Patterns of regional contact and integration varied greatly. The USSCo.'s tentacular grip did not immediately extend inland beyond port sites and coastal settlements. Whole communities had little to do with maritime industry. Shipping operations were cyclical and steamers touched briefly at island ports only once or twice a month. But shipping installed a particular rhythm to colonial life. Steamer days were concentrated periods of activity in ports, giving the embodied, material expression to transcolonial interdependencies.

Newer histories attuned to the variegated webs of empire have unsettled a core/periphery model by repositioning the imperial metropole as just one node, albeit a significant and powerful one, within a more complex and integrative network of imperial relations.[35] This study of a Pacific 'shipscape' focuses on the lateral connections between regional ports, but it does not neglect the metropole. The USSCo. was fostered by British capital, its ships designed and built in Scotland

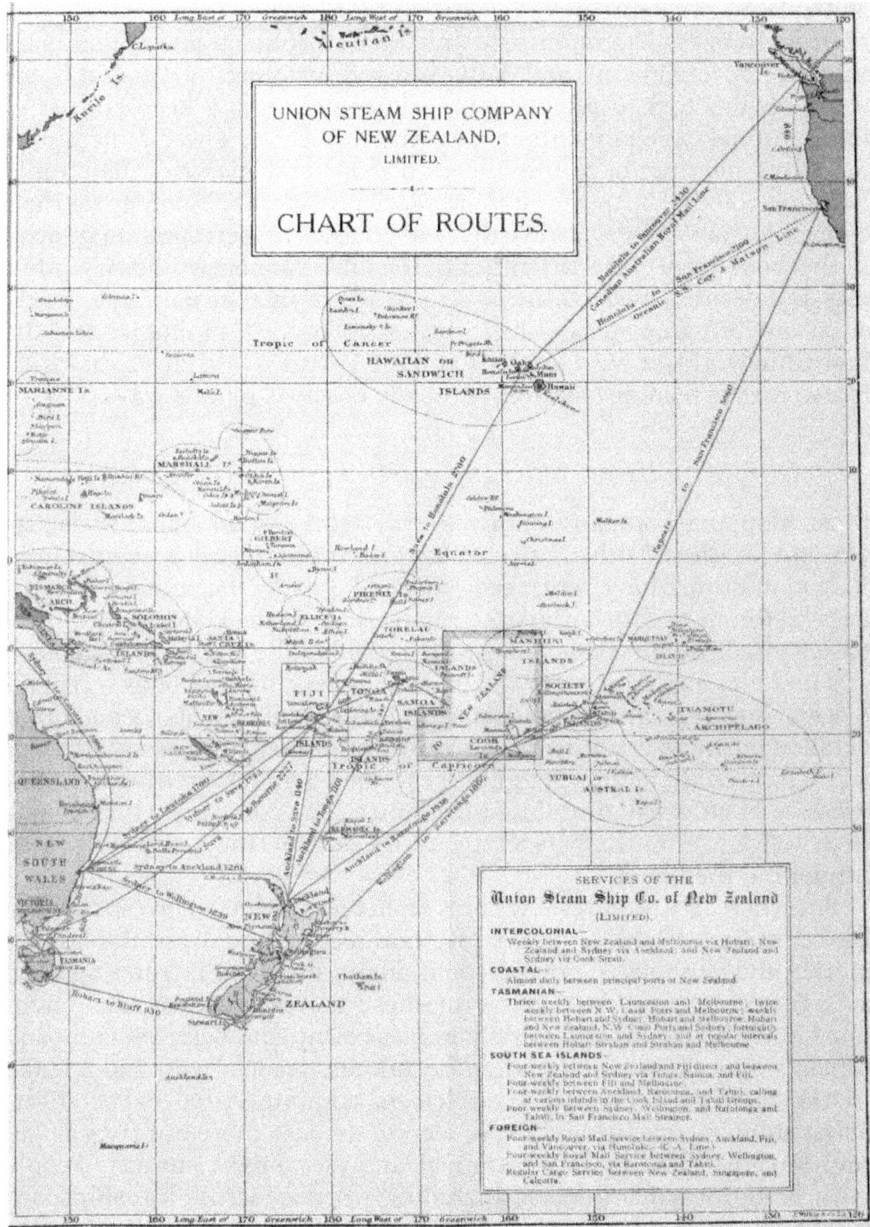

3   Union Company Chart of Routes, 1910

and crewed predominantly by British-born sailors in its early years. Metropolitan leaders monitored and advised colonial governments on shipping developments and Mills himself appointed a London-based board of directors to relay shipping information and keep abreast of international developments in the shipping sector. These professional networks and lines of communication shaped the histories that unfold here, yet colonial outposts also embraced transport technology for their own ends, sometimes in ways that ran counter to metropolitan desires. In this book I pay closer attention to the different configurations, interests and desires invested in the rise of steam in southern seas. To do so means bringing areas of historical scholarship – of empire and the maritime world, of New Zealand and the Pacific – into closer dialogue. It also means reading shipping company archives in new ways.

Shipping lives: working with a company archive

Most shipping company archives still tend to 'lie like fossils', as Crosbie Smith and other cultural historians of the ocean steamship in Victorian Britain have remarked, 'touched only by the occasional business historian or ship enthusiast'.[36] The scale of the USSCo. enterprise has ensured the survival of company records. The archive is extensive and includes annual reports and balance sheets, minute books, general ledgers, registers of shareholders, ship plans, staff rule books and other detailed business documents. The most prominent voices are those of well-connected, middle-class European men bent on securing the profitability of an expanding shipping empire. The company's history has been written from the perspective of these men, the company's most influential members.

But there are archives within archives. Various correspondence files contain less official, more informal records and detail the human stories and the messy interpersonal affairs involved in running such a large-scale operation. Letters in these correspondence files circulated between senior and middle management, and between company officials and various political and economic leaders who had a stake in the USSCo.'s success. Such letters communicated expectations about shipping operations. These records are also more multivocal and multilayered than earlier historical analyses might suggest. People with little formal influence, including workers across the shipboard hierarchy, their relatives and members of the travelling public, also wrote letters to company managers. These archival fragments from the 'bottom up' offer fleeting glimpses of the broader range of people who directly participated in this new world of transport and trade, or were increasingly reliant on or affected by it.

Their letters archive a myriad of concerns, complaints and requests, with the company head Mills petitioned as an employer and a man of more general civic influence. As one friend put it, tongue-in-cheek:

> Still another favour, but please don't curse me, and remember how large a portion of the world gravitates around you! I have a brother, a nice white man, coming out to New Zealand via Australia . . . do you mind 'issuing orders' to secure him a good cabin and if possible one to himself. . . . All your good deeds you must remember count towards that extra fine niche they are preparing for you next door to Nicodemus, or some other swell.[37]

One of the first pieces of correspondence I read detailed a passenger's complaint about an alleged drunken assault by a steamship captain on the passenger's wife during a voyage between Levuka and Suva in Fiji in 1884.[38] Further reading revealed more of the often troubling encounters that occurred as the company extended its services beyond the New Zealand coastal trades. Such letters encouraged me to think past the technical shell of steamships and the economics of industry to the workers and passengers that set these histories in motion. That said, I do not disregard the institutional context. Earlier histories that detailed maritime politics and policy, or the workings of managerial capitalism, particularly Gavin McLean's detailed and lively account of the company's first decades, have been key sources for this study. It is, however, my intention here to broaden the frame of reference and bring questions about gender, race, space and colonialism to our understanding of transport's historical significance.

Questions remain, though, about what cannot be accessed in this archive. What are its exclusions and silences? Written documentation produced by ordinary working men and women is thin and fragmentary. Seafarers are doubly challenging as working-class subjects, for their everyday maritime mobilities compound the limitations of fleeting documentary evidence. To recover indigenous engagement in this world of transport and trade also means confronting similar limitations. Islanders only appear in the archive when their work is necessary for the USSCo.'s operations. We cannot access the full complexity of their lives which continued out of reach of the archival gaze; they appear here only as labourers. They are also more anonymous than white workers. Very few wrote letters to company managers and in managerial correspondence indigenous sailors and wharf labourers are typically referred to only as 'natives' rather than named as individuals. At times this makes it difficult to determine whether the 'natives' in question were indigenous to New Zealand or other Pacific Islands, or in fact non-white labour indentured from other parts of the empire, particularly India, to work in the Pacific.

The routine references to the arrival and departure of vessels in regional ports attest to a world of activity about which there is only limited textual evidence. Nevertheless, there are occasional letters penned by workers to their superiors, usually to communicate problems, and by reading them alongside a range of other sources, including seafaring memoirs, newspaper articles, seamen's union records and photographs, it is possible to build up a picture of the maritime world in which such men and women laboured and to recreate some individual experiences. Shipping was the subject of a series of official enquiries, conferences and legislative measures in the late nineteenth and early twentieth centuries and maritime workers were often at the heart of these debates. Drawing on conference proceedings, reports from commissions of enquiry and select committees, parliamentary debates and other official records provides further insights into the social visibility of maritime workers in national and imperial life.

Emphasising the multifaceted circuitries of empire, newer imperial history has entailed a critique of the organisation of official archives and the ways historians have traditionally approached them. A reliance on state-produced archives has worked, as Ballantyne argues, 'to reinscribe the boundaries of colonial states and, in effect, has tended to remove particular colonial states from the larger imperial systems within which they operated'. Yet all the while the archives of empire are 'imprinted by and record' transnational mobilities and cross-cultural exchanges.[39] The shipping company archive readily lends itself to this sort of transcolonial and transnational research. USSCo. records are multi-sited in provenance and filed according to port branches across New Zealand, the eastern half of Australia, and various islands in the Pacific. They bear the imprint of routine boundary crossings and demonstrate how business, as Miles Ogborn has noted with respect to the East India Company, was 'locally situated' in particular places and 'widely dispersed', conducted 'in place and in the relationships between places'.[40] As such these records require us to bring diverse spaces into a single interpretative frame, from the small-scale confines of the ship, to the wider political and economic 'territorialisation' of the imperial sea.

Head office in Dunedin necessarily occupied a prominent position, the site from which most of the important decisions were made and communicated. Yet these decisions always rested on widely dispersed lines of communication. Not slavishly bound to their desks, senior officials were frequently on the move, overseeing shipbuilding operations in Britain, inspecting steamers and branches throughout the Pacific and meeting with political and economic leaders across the empire. Their mobilities attest to the fragility and frustrations of the business letter as a technology of communication. Writing could not always master the distances between port branches. There was power bound up in 'being there', of coeval, embodied communication.

Correspondence networks were uneven, both in terms of the types of voices we are able to access as well as the comparative richness of records for particular places. Of the islands included in the company's shipping empire, Fiji figures most prominently. A branch line to Levuka was introduced in 1881, the first route that extended beyond the New Zealand coastal and trans-Tasman trades. This confirmed Fiji's developing status as a central hub in the western Pacific and its membership of the 'colonial sisterhood' of British Australasia. Smaller Pacific ports were not accorded an equivalent branch status, and staff on board ship, rather than agents stationed ashore, handled most of the company's business concerns. As a result, daily affairs and developments in the Fijian ports of Levuka and Suva can be pieced together with more ease than those in other island communities. The archives of the colonial state also complement company records, as the USSCo.'s presence, and hence the wider regional and imperial networks which shaped Fiji's colonial development, is well documented in Fiji's official archive. The labour demands of industrial shipping, as well as the new opportunities for travel to regional ports and beyond, created new paper trails and connected archives (with information often literally shipped by the steamer) as colonial leaders attempted to mediate influences deemed unsettling for indigenous subjects.

While remaining attentive to the inherently uneven and partial nature of the evidence that has survived, this book displays an archival richness, placing primary material in the foreground of each chapter. It aims to create livelier, peopled accounts of this industrial subject, and to connect the lives of 'small' people to the bigger concerns of interregional relations in the colonial Pacific and the broader imperial world in the age of steam.

The structure of the book

This book tracks the beginnings of routine steamship operations in the 1870s and the consolidation of regional trading relations in the Pacific, through to the years immediately preceding the outbreak of the First World War. The period spanning five decades, the 'high point' of coal-fired ships, allows for a focused analysis of the cross-cutting stories of steam. Towards the end point of this study, the international shipping industry underwent a series of changes. The USSCo. secured a merger with the British Peninsular and Oriental Steam Navigation Company (P&O) in 1917 and was absorbed within the vast empire of the shipping magnate Lord Inchcape. The company continued to operate out of New Zealand, management remaining with a local board of directors. Head office relocated from Dunedin to the capital Wellington in 1922.

Drawing on aspects of the company's pre-war history, before these broad imperial realignments, the book adopts a tripartite thematic structure: Afloat, Aboard and Abroad. Each part engages with the period in question from a particular angle of enquiry, beginning with the political and symbolic investment in transport routes and steamers, moving to the working cultures on board ship, and ending with an extended analysis of the industry's historical significance in one island locale. As a whole, the analysis is framed against the broader backdrop of assertive colonial nationalism and intensified British imperialism in the age of steam.

Part I establishes the context of steam in the Pacific. The first chapter charts the rise of the USSCo. and its extension into the island and transpacific trades. It examines the ways in which political leaders in New Zealand and Australia recruited maritime transport operations to support their regional agendas and the tensions that ensued. The commercial interests of the steamer company did not always respect the borders of the emergent nation-state, nor did the overarching imperial investment in free trade. The focus of chapter 2 lies with the ship and its cultural and symbolic power. It examines the enormous investment in steamers and the development of an elite culture of comfort and safety at sea. These vehicles told particular stories about a modernising nation and a transnational world of travel and trade, stories that can be explored through the choice of names and fitting-out policies, which invested each new addition to the company fleet with meaning.

Part II, Aboard, moves towards a consideration of the working cultures on board steamers. Together these three chapters animate the ship as a space of history, recovering a range of human stories of seafaring and the power dynamics across class, gender and race. Chapter 3 accounts for both continuity and change in crew culture heralded by the transition from sail to steam and the rise of managerial capitalism in the late nineteenth century. There were ongoing tensions between enclosure – the ship as a floating world with its own temporal and spatial order – and connectivity, the ship tied to shore through relations with management, social reformers and family. Chapter 4 revisits working cultures aboard ship more explicitly through the lens of race. The imperial maritime labour market was racially diverse, yet the steamers trading from the 'white men's' countries of New Zealand and Australia were to be white men's ships. This was a highly politicised development. Related debates overshadowed a number of imperial conferences and maritime-focused enquiries over these decades, further demonstrating the relationality of the world afloat and ashore. For all this talk about men – and the industry was an inherently masculine one – women did work at sea and did travel by ship. Chapter 5 explores what their presence as stewardesses and passengers did for notions of space and order on board. Women had routinely to negotiate limited employment opportunities, unfavourable gendered stereotypes and, in some cases, the unwelcome attentions of male crew.

Part III addresses the island trades of the USSCo. and explores the common history of the societies and individuals linked by maritime activity in the late nineteenth and early twentieth centuries. It recovers the histories of a range of workers in a Pacific context, taking Fiji as an extended case study for the reasons outlined earlier. Narratives of steam's easy triumph can be unsettled by drawing on the firsthand accounts of those working and living at the 'coal face' of a new world of transport and trade. Chapter 6 looks specifically at the white workers on steamers and in port branches, cataloguing the trials they faced in conducting shipping operations at a tropical distance from New Zealand. Chapter 7 serves as a micro-history of Suva's early years as the Fijian capital, and its growing character as a multiracial littoral world. It examines the challenges different people faced, whether as dock workers, indigenous leaders in outlying villages or travellers arriving from other islands, as regional steamer services drew the port into new webs of connection and exchange. The final chapter emphasises Islander engagement with this industry as sailors and passengers, as well as the ways in which colonial officials attempted to mediate and restrict their mobilities in the age of steam.

What emerges across all eight chapters is an extended engagement with the multifaceted meanings invested in steam technology – meanings made by imperial officials, company management and commercial elites, as well as seamen, firemen, stewardesses, wharf labourers and passengers – for what they reveal about the fuller complexity of maritime relationships and experiences in the Pacific world. This book is intended as a contribution to a newer maritime history, one infused by cultural and post-colonial perspectives. Creating a more multivocal history of steam has also meant crafting a more spatially complex history. Dunedin necessarily occupies a prominent position in the chapters that follow, being the initial location of the USSCo. head office, the place where much of the correspondence analysed was despatched and received, and the site today of the company's early records. Yet the shipping archive reveals a complex framed by port branches with steamers moving inbetween. This book mirrors that spatiality by shifting the analysis offshore to the colonial world of Oceania under steam.

[17]

Notes

1 For a business history of the company see Gavin McLean, *The Southern Octopus: The Rise of a Shipping Empire* (Wellington: New Zealand Ship and Marine Society and Wellington Harbour Board Maritime Museum, 1990).

2 Ian J. Farquhar, *Union Fleet, 1875–1975* (Wellington: New Zealand Ship and Marine Society, 2nd rev. edn, 1976).

3 'The race for big ships', *Glasgow Herald* (5 March 1881), reprinted in *Fiji Times* (28 May 1881). For an important discussion of the early development of steamers as 'highly unstable and contingent' industrial products, see Ben Marsden and Crosbie Smith, *Engineering Empires: A Cultural History of Technology in Nineteenth-Century Britain* (Houndmills: Palgrave Macmillan, 2005), 88–128.

4 Michael Adas, *Machines as the Measure of Men: Science, Technology, and Ideologies of Western Dominance* (Ithaca: Cornell University Press, 1989).

5 Daniel R. Headrick, *The Tools of Empire: Technology and European Imperialism in the Nineteenth Century* (New York: Oxford University Press, 1981).

6 J. R. Seeley, *The Expansion of England: Two Courses of Lectures* (London: Macmillan, 1883); Daniel Deudney, 'Greater Britain or greater synthesis? Seeley, Mackinder and Wells on Britain in the global industrial era', *Review of International Studies*, 27 (2001), 187–208.

7 Headrick, *The Tools of Empire*, 177.

8 Robert Kubicek, 'The proliferation and diffusion of steamship technology and the beginnings of "new imperialism"', in David Killingray, Margarette Lincoln and Nigel Rigby (eds), *Maritime Empires: British Imperial Maritime Trade in the Nineteenth Century* (Woodbridge, Suffolk: The Boydell Press, 2004), 107.

9 John M. MacKenzie, 'Lakes, rivers and oceans: technology, ethnicity and the shipping of empire in the late nineteenth century', in Killingray, Lincoln and Rigby (eds), *Maritime Empires*, 113–18.

10 Headrick, *The Tools of Empire*, 206.

11 These arguments have also been made by Robert Kubicek, 'British expansion, empire, and technological change', in Andrew Porter (ed.), *The Oxford History of the British Empire*, vol. 3 (Oxford: Oxford University Press, 1999), 247–69. For more general reflections on the historiography of technology and empire, see David Arnold, 'Europe, technology and colonialism in the 20th century', *History and Technology*, 21:1 (2005), 85–106.

12 Gijs Mom, Colin Divall and Peter Lyth, 'Towards a paradigm shift? A decade of transport and mobility history', in Gijs Mom, Gordon Pirie and Laurent Tissot (eds), *Mobility in History: The State of the Art in the History of Transport, Traffic and Mobility* (Neuchâtel: Alphil, 2009), 19. And see Colin Divall and George Revill, 'Cultures of transport: representation, practice and technology', *Journal of Transport History*, 26:1 (2005), 99–111.

13 Mom, Divall and Lyth, 'Towards a paradigm shift?', 31–2.

14 MacKenzie, 'Lakes, rivers and oceans', 125.

15 Tony Ballantyne, *Orientalism and Race: Aryanism in the British Empire* (Basingstoke and New York: Palgrave Macmillan, 2002), 14.

16 Jonathan Hyslop, 'Steamship empire: Asian, African and British sailors in the merchant marine, c.1880–1945', *Journal of Asian and African Studies*, 44:1 (2009), 49–67.

17 This literature is too vast to survey here, but for a recent work which challenges earlier models of 'first contact', see Margaret Jolly, Serge Tcherkézoff and Darrell Tryon (eds), *Oceanic Encounters: Exchange, Desire, Violence* (Canberra: ANU E-Press, 2009).

18 Including H. E. Maude, *Of Islands and Men: Studies in Pacific History* (Melbourne: Oxford University Press, 1968); Dorothy Shineberg, *They Came for Sandalwood: A Study of the Sandalwood Trade in the South-West Pacific, 1830–1865* (Melbourne: Melbourne University Press, 1967); Tracey Banivanua-Mar, *Violence and Colonial Dialogue: The Australian-Pacific Indentured Labor Trade* (Honolulu: University of Hawai'i Press, 2007).

19 McLean, *The Southern Octopus*; Ken Buckley and Kris Klugman, *The History of Burns Philp: The Australian Company in the South Pacific* (Sydney: Burns Philp & Co., 1981); William Worden, *Cargoes: Matson's First Century in the Pacific* (Honolulu: University of Hawai'i Press, 1981).

20 E. Mowbry Tate, *Transpacific Steam: The Story of Steam Navigation from the Pacific Coast of North America to the Far East and the Antipodes, 1867–1941* (New York: Cornwall Books, 1986). Earlier studies include: William Lawson, *Steam in the Southern Pacific: The Story of Merchant Steam Navigation in the Australasian Coastal and Intercolonial Trades, and on the Ocean Lines of the Southern Pacific* (Wellington: Gordon & Gotch, 1909); Lawson, *Pacific Steamers* (Glasgow: Brown, Son & Ferguson, 1927).

21 For 'shipspotting' narratives, see N. H. Brewer, *A Century of Style: Great Ships of the Union Line, 1875–1976* (Wellington: A. H. & A. W. Reed, 1982); Jack Churchouse, *Glamour Ships of the Union Steam Ship Company NZ Ltd* (Wellington: Millwood Press, 1981).

22 Geoffrey Blainey, *The Tyranny of Distance: How Distance Shaped Australia's History* (South Melbourne: Macmillan, 1975); Frank Broeze, 'Distance tamed: steam navigation to Australia and New Zealand from its beginnings to the outbreak of the Great War', *Journal of Transport History*, 10:1 (1989), 1–21.

23 James Belich, *Paradise Reforged: A History of the New Zealanders from the 1880s to the Year 2000* (Honolulu: University of Hawai'i Press, 2001), 86.

24 *Ibid.*, 237. See also, Keith Sinclair (ed.), *Distance Looks Our Way: The Effects of Remoteness on New Zealand* (Auckland: University of Auckland, 1961).

25 Blainey, *The Tyranny of Distance*, 200.

26 A similar point has been made by Damon Salesa, 'New Zealand's Pacific', in Giselle Byrnes (ed.), *The New Oxford History of New Zealand* (Melbourne: Oxford University Press, 2009), 150.

27 Angus Ross, *New Zealand Aspirations in the Pacific in the Nineteenth Century* (Oxford: Clarendon Press, 1964), x. For the Australian context see Roger C. Thompson, *Australian Imperialism in the Pacific: The Expansionist Era, 1820–1920* (Carlton: Melbourne University Press, 1980); John Young, *Adventurous Spirits: Australian Migrant Society in Pre-Cession Fiji* (St Lucia: University of Queensland Press, 1984). See Salesa's arguments for reconceptualising New Zealand as an 'empire state': 'New Zealand's Pacific', esp. 149–51, 155, 172.

28 K. R. Howe, 'Two worlds?' *New Zealand Journal of History*, 37:1 (2003), 50.

29 Damon T. Salesa, 'Half-castes between the Wars: colonial categories in New Zealand and Samoa', *New Zealand Journal of History*, 34:1 (2000), 98–116; Ballantyne, *Orientalism and Race*.

30 Katerina Martina Teaiwa, 'Our sea of phosphate: the diaspora of Ocean Island', in Graham Harvey and Charles D. Thompson Jr (eds), *Indigenous Diasporas and Dislocations: Unsettling Western Fixations* (London: Ashgate, 2005), 169–91.

31 Gordon M. Winder, 'Seafarer's gaze: Queen Street business and Auckland's archipelago, 1908', *New Zealand Geographer*, 62 (2006), 51, 62.

32 Bronwen Douglas, 'Foreign bodies in Oceania', in Douglas and Chris Ballard (eds), *Foreign Bodies: Oceania and the Science of Race, 1750–1940* (Canberra: ANU E-Press, 2008), 5–13. For 'Australasia': Donald Denoon, 'Re-membering Australasia: a repressed memory', *Australian Historical Studies*, 34:122 (2003), 290–304.

33 Epeli Hau'ofa, 'Our sea of islands', *Contemporary Pacific*, 6:1 (1994), 148–61. It must of course be noted that this Sea of Islands does not faithfully engage the histories of Islanders who structured their lives around communal land tenure, agriculture, overland trading networks and 'grounded' attachment to place, and who may have never even seen the sea: a point made by Margaret Jolly, 'On the edge? Deserts, oceans, islands', *Contemporary Pacific*, 13:2 (2001), 423.

34 Fernand Braudel, *The Mediterranean and the Mediterranean World in the Age of Philip II*, trans. Siân Reynolds, vol. 1 (London: Collins, 1972–73 [1966]), 17; Sugata Bose, *A Hundred Horizons: The Indian Ocean in the Age of Global Empire* (Cambridge, Mass.: Harvard University Press, 2006); R. G. Ward, *Widening*

Worlds, Shrinking Worlds? The Reshaping of Oceania (Canberra: Centre for the Contemporary Pacific, Pacific Distinguished Lecture 1999, ANU, 1999), 3.

35 For an overview of these developments, see Alan Lester, 'Imperial circuits and networks: geographies of the British empire', *History Compass*, 4:1 (2006), 124–41. For the 'web' model of empire, see Ballantyne, *Orientalism and Race*, esp. 13–17.

36 Crosbie Smith, Ian Higginston and Phillip Wolstenholme, '"Imitations of God's own works": making trustworthy the ocean steamship', *History of Science*, 41:134 (2003), 380.

37 Hocken Collections (HC), USSCo. Records, AG-292-005-001/048, Craddock to Mills, 25 February 1899.

38 *Ibid.*, AG-292-005-001/002, Ford to Mills, 1 December 1884 and 24 December 1884.

39 Tony Ballantyne, 'Mr. Peal's archive: mobility and exchange in histories of empire', in Antoinette Burton (ed.), *Archive Stories: Facts, Fictions and the Writing of History* (Durham N C: Duke University Press, 2005), 106, 104.

40 Miles Ogborn, *Indian Ink: Script and Print in the Making of the English East India Company* (Chicago: Chicago University Press, 2007), xi, 21.

PART I

Afloat

CHAPTER ONE

Steam's 'magic touch': routes, rivalries and regionalism in the Pacific

In 1895, New Zealand settler Edward Reeves boarded a USSCo. steamer for a month-long excursion around islands in the western Pacific. The following year he took another trip, this time on a route further east. His travels convinced him of the dawning of a new era in regional relations. The fact that the USSCo. even bothered to offer a service to the Cook Islands, 'an insignificant little protectorate fifty-three miles in circumference', a distance of seven days' steaming, is perhaps, he argued, 'one of the most remarkable evidences of New Zealand maritime enterprise'. He concluded that it 'shows that the little "Britain of the South" is a worthy child of Britannia and Father Neptune, and alive to the destiny of her geographical position as mistress of the South Pacific'.[1]

Over the course of the nineteenth and early twentieth centuries, political and economic leaders enthusiastically predicted a great maritime destiny for this island nation. Rather than being grafted onto earlier indigenous traditions of regional seaborne circulation and exchange, this destiny was typically regarded as an appropriate mirror of British imperial power. By commanding the surrounding seas New Zealand would prosper as the Britain of the South, a regional centre of governance, trade and cultural influence. The rhetorical highpoint of this vision broadly coincided with the rise and consolidation of the USSCo. The company's successful expansion into the Pacific appeared to offer further proof of New Zealand's fitness and natural suitability for regional leadership.

While expectations of maritime transport mingled with expectations of future economic, political and social order, the commercial imperatives that underpinned the USSCo.'s operations were not always in harmony with the ambitions of political leaders in the Pacific. Furthermore, the growing confidence of colonial states in controlling and extending their own maritime interests in the Pacific often conflicted with the imperial embrace of friction-free transoceanic trade. Exploring the relationship between maritime transport and the politics of nation-building, colonialism and sub-imperialism in the south-west Pacific through the example of the island trades of the USSCo. can shed light on the ways in which the promise and potential of steam transport was both imagined and constrained in the late nineteenth and early twentieth centuries.

The island trade routes

By the time of Reeves's travels at the end of the nineteenth century, a number of routes, introduced by the USSCo., the Sydney-based Burns Philp and Company and the Australasian Steam Navigation Company (ASNCo.), connected the Australasian colonies and the island Pacific. The company model gradually produced more concentrated, bureaucratic and professional shipping operations in the second half of the nineteenth century, replacing private syndicates and single-ship ventures. Corporate growth in shipping, as Gordon Boyce outlines, depended on the development of private channels of communication (familial, commercial and political) which businessmen used to attract capital, vital trade-related intelligence and cargo. The segmented nature of the industry meant that tramp (unscheduled steamer) and liner trades required different channels of specialised knowledge. These networks were supported by organisational structures that facilitated the various transactions and the delegation of control.[2]

The Australasian colonies were particularly interested in trade to Fiji. This island group was favourably located in the western Pacific, positioned directly along the transpacific 'highway' between Sydney and North America. It was also regarded as a gateway into the eastern Pacific, for, as the *Otago Daily Times* declared in 1870, 'whoever rules at Fiji will command the trade of the South Pacific'.[3] Following the decline of the Victorian and Otago gold rushes and the outbreak of war in northern New Zealand, many recent immigrants regarded Fiji as a site of investment and on-migration in the late 1860s. The island group seemed well suited to fill a void in the cotton industry after the outbreak of civil war in America disrupted cotton production there. In 1868 members of the Melbourne Polynesia Company, envisaged as the 'East India Company of the Pacific', arrived in Fiji to explore possibilities for investment in plantations. The first regular schooner service between Auckland and Levuka began the following year and schooner traffic and the number of Australasian migrants to Fiji gradually increased.[4]

New Zealand colonists frequently asserted they were in the best position to secure exclusive economic and political relations with Fiji. New Zealand had a 'natural affinity' with Fiji: it was closer to the islands than Australia was, and the prevailing winds afforded 'greater facilities of intercourse', as the New Zealand Governor noted to the Secretary of State for the Colonies in 1873. Others argued that New Zealand needed tropical territory to provide some form of 'balance', for Australia already had enough of its own. The naturalness of this complementary pairing was likened to the relationship between the West Indies and Great Britain.[5]

The ports of Auckland and Sydney were particular rivals in the competition for Pacific trade. Located at the northern end of New Zealand and boasting a large and safe harbour, Auckland was favourably positioned as a regional hub. It was, as one colonial booster put it, 'geographically en rapport' with Fiji.[6] In the early 1870s, eighteen Auckland shipping agents were engaged in the export trade to Fiji, shipping processed food, drapery, general merchandise, agricultural implements and supplies, building supplies, liquor and timber. Cotton seed, hides, copra (dried coconut flesh used in the industrial manufacture of soap and margarine), oil, corn, fruit, maize and peanuts made up a typical return cargo.[7] Yet Sydney always dominated this trade. As a trans-shipment port for British exports to Fiji, Sydney enjoyed significantly cheaper rates on freight from Britain and could offer commodities at lower prices than Auckland. Moreover, the city worked its tropical island trade in conjunction with Queensland, and with the establishment of a Lever Brothers soap factory it could manufacture copra on-site. The port's favourable regional placement was also enthusiastically espoused in the local press. As Bernhard Wise, a Sydney lawyer and, later, federal politician, concluded in 1884, 'Sydney is by its position the emporium of the island trade'.[8]

Even from mid-century, steam's promise in the Pacific appealed to local settlers. In his 1857 book promoting migration to New Zealand, recent colonist Charles Hursthouse envisaged that the many Polynesian islands 'slumbering in their summer seas' needed 'only the magic touch of steam to open new worlds to our commerce'.[9] The first regular island steamer services began in the early 1870s. The ASNCo. launched its timetabled Sydney–Fiji run in 1874, the same year Britain formally annexed Fiji, the service having started on an irregular footing in 1870. Coleman Phillips, a youthful Auckland law clerk, published numerous opinion pieces about a New Zealand empire in the Pacific. He encouraged Auckland merchants to challenge Sydney's dominance in the Fiji trade and secure a £3,000 steamer subsidy offered by the Fiji Government. Local businessmen invested £10,000 in a steamer. The

Auckland Packet Steam Company's *Star of the South* shortened the journey between Auckland and Levuka from eight days to five. Phillips was a passenger on the inaugural trip in 1873, landing 200 sheep and 30 cattle in Levuka, 'practically the first consignment of New Zealand livestock sent to a foreign market'.[10]

The Fiji press echoed the rhetorical investment in steam. While population was the 'first necessity' for all young colonies, the *Fiji Times* noted in 1877 that this meant little unless means of intercolonial communication were also established. Steam services between colonies would be 'one of the first elements of [Fiji's] prosperity'.[11] Settlers had faith that these ships impressed upon indigenous communities and imperial rivals alike the power and influence they could command across the seas. Steam was embraced as a technology of rule, a disciplining force to quell any threat of indigenous resistance to the British presence. As the *Fiji Times* celebrated in 1877, 'the very consciousness impressed by the fact that a few days will suffice for bringing to the assistance of any person aggrieved or outraged, the power of British interference, is of itself quite sufficient to ensure respect in the native mind'. Furthermore steamers represented a 'degree of vested interest in the commerce of the islands'. This would 'render any idea of occupation by another Power a contingency very remote if not altogether improbable'.[12] Steamers buffered British settler interests in the islands, the physical and symbolic expression of pervasive and dependable imperial networks.

A ship was only one link in a maritime trading system. Improvements in port construction and handling facilities were also required if steamers were to bring all of their imagined benefits to traders and shippers. This was especially so for people living in outlying islands who relied on trans-shipment services from the main steamer ports. Such improvements could not, it seemed, accommodate indigenous participation in its current form. If Levuka were to remain a port of entry for larger and larger ships, the *Fiji Times* asserted, 'it would be deplorable to have to land luggage through the surf, and to carry ladies and gentlemen ashore on the oily backs of natives covered with steaming perspiration in the hot sun'.[13] In 1877 the newspaper lamented the fact that discharging cargo from the Sydney steamer at Levuka took as long as the seven-day passage between the two ports. Trams for the carriage of goods were suggested, as this would eliminate dependence on native labourers who carried packages from ship to shore 'at the rate of one per hour'.[14] With lighterage done by boats and a small punt, consignees' good suffered, for cargo was 'tossed about on the beach'. When trade was conducted solely by sailing vessels people were accustomed to ships lying in the harbour for weeks, but steam demanded a new industrial consciousness. Timetabled services required a quick despatch, and large steamships needed more permanent and extensive wharf accommodation.[15]

In 1881 the *Fiji Times* denounced the Auckland–Fiji route, operated at this point by the Auckland Steam Ship Company's *Southern Cross*. Where schooners had happily accommodated shippers of all sizes, the largest traders now monopolised steamer freight space and shut out all smaller merchants: 'The man whose timber or merchandise has been left behind in Auckland join[s] complaint with the man whose goods are shut out in Levuka, while the voices of both are drowned in the wail of him whose deck cargo has been swept overboard or entirely spoiled through what he asserts to be the overloading of the vessel.' This steamer was too small and the Auckland market was too limited. It was feared this further diverted shipping profits away from New Zealand towards Sydney. People were also discouraged from travelling to the 'natural sanatorium' of New Zealand during the tropical summer, as the passage by steamer was so uncomfortable.[16]

At this point the USSCo. entered the fray. In 1877, two years after its establishment, the company had secured a contract for the carriage of mails and passengers between New Caledonia and Sydney. They soon passed on this service to the ASNCo. after it proved unprofitable. James Mills was uneasy about re-entering the island trades, but in 1881 he purchased the *Southern Cross* and took over the operation of the Auckland–Fiji run. This takeover marked a change in attitude and more services followed. In 1882 the company gained rights over the Melbourne–Fiji trade from James McEwan and Company and by the end of the decade had a strong foothold in the Sydney–Fiji trade. This service was initially conducted Melbourne–Sydney–New Hebrides–Fiji, supported by a subsidy from the Victorian Government, a response to a request from missionaries active in Melanesia. In 1889 the USSCo. introduced two monthly round-trips between Auckland to Sydney via Tonga, Samoa and Fiji to complement the Auckland–Fiji direct service.[17]

The company's reach soon stretched into the eastern Pacific. In the 1890s Auckland traders to Rarotonga and Tahiti frequently petitioned the USSCo. to run in competition with the local trading firm Donald and Edenborough. They alleged the firm refused to ship goods that might interfere with its own business interests in the islands. The trade should be in independent hands, Mills informed the New Zealand Prime Minister, Richard Seddon, for interested parties 'would feel that their business would not necessarily be known to their rivals, with the result that enterprise would be stimulated'.[18] The USSCo. soon acquired the goodwill of Donald and Edenborough along with their steamer. It also successfully contracted for inter-island services

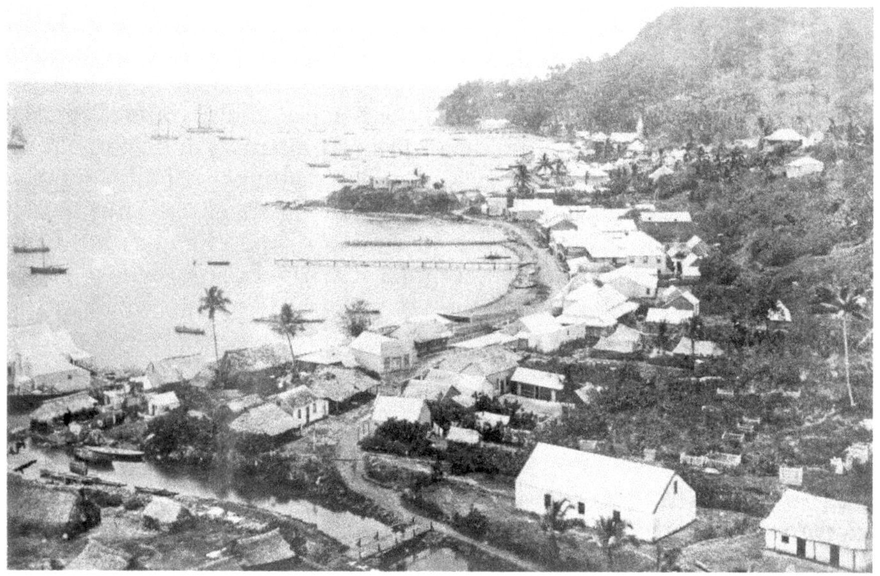

4 View of Levuka, c.1875

around Tahiti and the Marquesas. By the turn of the twentieth century, seven company vessels traded to the islands each month. The USSCo. stationed a branch manager in Suva and a branch sub-manager in Rarotonga, and appointed trading companies as agents in Papeete and Apia. The pursers of each ship acted as agents in Tonga.

Pacific ports were enrolled at different levels and in differing degrees into these new shipping networks. As transport geographers point out, time and space collapse differentially on the introduction of new modes of transport. Steamers tended to privilege the larger transport hubs; as these drew closer together through faster transit times, smaller centres became relatively more peripheral.[19] Developments in Fiji illustrate this point. On the small island of Ovalau, Levuka was the pre-colonial European centre and first colonial capital. After British annexation in 1874, colonial officials planned to relocate the capital to Suva on the south-east coast of the largest island, Viti Levu. Mountainous terrain hemmed in the township of Levuka along a narrow beach strip (as depicted in figure 4), and poor drainage, limited water supply and the landholding dominance of the Wesleyan Church precluded hinterland expansion and port development. Moreover, it was principally the protection extended by the chief of the region, Tui Levuka, which had initially attracted Europeans to the region, rather than any advantages it may have possessed as a maritime centre.[20]

After the relocation of the capital in 1882, Levuka continued to enjoy calls from colonial steamers. The USSCo. initially appointed a Levuka resident as agent and, like other mercantile establishments, operated agencies out of both Suva and Levuka. In the following years Levuka residents were concerned the port was declining as a hub of maritime commerce and feared it would be closed as a port of entry. Steamer calls gradually dropped away as Suva grew and cargoes to and from Levuka diminished.[21] The USSCo. closed its offices there in 1888, although a shipping agent remained. Shippers and traders in Levuka voiced their frustrations about limited transport services, for they incurred many extra costs getting their goods to and from Suva each month. In 1909 the USSCo. eventually abandoned the Levuka call by the direct Auckland steamer altogether, as cargo seldom amounted to more than fifty tons per trip. Traders' requests to resume calling a year later were 'largely owing to sentiment', argued the Suva branch manager, for 'the Levuka people didn't like to feel that the port was going back'.[22] The 'one stock grievance', as noted at a commission of inquiry into Fiji shipping in 1914, was the irregularity of the USSCo.'s services to that port.[23]

Steam quickly came to define the locational advantage or disadvantage of ports in the western Pacific. In 1889 Fiji agent Alex Duncan proposed to modify the island round-trip route from Auckland, placing Tonga rather than Fiji as first and last call. Fiji's colonial government objected. It believed steamer routes should reinforce rather than undermine Suva's position as the 'centre of British trade and influence' in the western Pacific. Under Duncan's proposal Fiji would be 'relegated to a third place' after Tonga and Samoa and thereby 'practically prohibited' from opening up mercantile connections with these islands.[24]

In 1914 the USSCo. abandoned the round-trip service that placed Tonga in a direct relationship with Auckland. Auckland traders were concerned that island trade would be diverted to Sydney as a result. Making investigations, the Department of Industries and Commerce asked the USSCo. to indicate how different islands were connected to New Zealand, 'that is length of time involved from the date of loading produce until its arrival in the Dominion'.[25] Tongan officials were upset that they would effectively be placed at a greater distance from New Zealand. In the new arrangement, after a steamer called at Tonga it would then proceed to Samoa and Fiji before returning to Auckland, meaning Tonga was now some twenty days' steaming from Auckland. The USSCo. argued that the Tongan fruit trade was unreliable and that the country's chief export was copra, the bulk of which was sent to Britain and Europe, not New Zealand. The company would still make arrangements to connect Tonga with Auckland on a six-day schedule when cargo allowed. Moreover, if banana production in Tonga improved, they could ship it to Sydney instead by the company's other regional service, rather than glut the Auckland market with fruit.[26]

Other frictions attended the introduction of steam, highlighting the spaces or gaps in USSCo. networks. Local traders did not necessarily divert all their freight to the steamers and continued to value schooner services, especially where they offered cheaper rates on general freight when a quick despatch was not so crucial for non-perishable goods. In the early 1890s the USSCo. was frustrated that Tongan shippers had lobbied hard for a steamer, but would only use it to ship fruit to New Zealand and Australia, rather than all cargo. The Auckland manager felt 'somewhat sore' and 'should like to retaliate on them', as he confided to Mills, for the USSCo. could not afford to lose any cargo.[27] Schooners and cutters were always much cheaper to construct and operate and were better able to negotiate reef passages and shallow lagoons. This practicality ensured their continuing importance in inter-island trades well into the twentieth century.[28]

Other shippers were unhappy with regional disparities in freight rates. The carriage of deadweight freight between Sydney and London, for example, was cheaper than between Sydney and Suva. It cost three times as much to ship cargo such as bran between Auckland and Suva as it did between Bluff and Auckland, even though the intercolonial distance was slightly shorter, a sore point for traders in Fiji reliant on the USSCo. services.[29] So while steam may have eliminated the environmental challenges of wind and waves to a greater extent, although they were certainly never overcome, other frictions remained. Distance was measured in cost in money as well as cost in time.

Transpacific routes

In addition to these more circumscribed trade routes, the USSCo. was a key player in the long-distance mail routes. Governments were quick to recognise the value of steam for the improved carriage of the 'cream end' of the freight market, including first-class passengers, mails, urgent packages, other essential goods and perishables. They began to offer shipping companies financial assistance in order to secure direct benefit from these services.[30] Subsidies were generally granted in return for a stipulated number of voyages each year. Suitable vessels were to leave specific ports at stated intervals regardless of the amount of cargo or numbers of passengers on offer. Although state intervention contradicted the doctrines of laissez-faire, governments deemed these policies necessary to safeguard national and imperial interests and security.[31] Merchant vessels could be requisitioned in times of war, for steamships, as the *Otago Witness* put it, 'shall be bridges in times of peace and floating batteries in the hour of danger'.[32] Official assistance alone did not secure the profitability of the mail lines and shipping companies were heavily reliant on passenger and freight revenue.

Optimistic appraisals of steam's transformative power in the long-distance trades were commonplace in the colonial press. Commentators drew on the example of steam in the northern hemisphere to map out a progressive future in southern seas. In 1842 the *Sydney Herald* remarked on the ways 'the magical power of steam had lately caused the broad Atlantic to shrink to a third of its primitive dimensions'. The newspaper anticipated a comparative reduction for the nine-month voyage between London and Sydney.[33] Maritime transport was celebrated as being even more transformative than rail, for seaborne networks were not limited by the extent of a fixed-track network. Even by the middle of the century some settlers had grown impatient with such predictions; as an 1851 editorial in the *Nelson Examiner* put it: 'shall we recapitulate for the twentieth time the advantage which Steam communication would bestow upon us?'[34]

Rivalry between local ports and colonies did much to determine the progression of steamer services between Australia and Britain. New South Wales favoured a northern route through the Torres Strait and down the east coast, while Australia's southern colonies naturally preferred a southern route via the Cape of Good Hope. Admiral John Lort Stokes, who had spent many years surveying Australian and New Zealand waters, sought to debunk exaggerated claims about the navigational challenges of the Torres Strait and celebrated this route via Singapore as being more scenic, interesting and safe, avoiding the 'continual roll, with nothing but sea! sea! sea!' on the Indian Ocean passage. Another advantage was a terminal point at Sydney rather than Melbourne, with Sydney's superior harbour facilities and proximity to New Zealand and Polynesia. This route, he believed, would also encourage closer European settlement in the north of the continent.[35]

A number of British mail lines on the important imperial trunk routes were established during the 1830s and 1840s. The P&O linked Britain with India from 1842, with an extension to China introduced in 1845. A further extension to Australia was initiated in 1852, terminating in Sydney via Albany in Western Australia and Melbourne. While initially beset by problems associated with the long distances and lack of remunerative freight as well as the shipping demands of the Crimean War, P&O held a monopoly over imperial mail routes to Australasia until the mid-1870s. The company's 'flagships of imperialism' did not immediately take over the deep-ocean routes from sailing ships. The latter continued to carry second- and third-class passengers and all imports and exports.[36]

The Australian ports of Adelaide, Brisbane and Hobart were dissatisfied with their omission from this mail route, while Sydney was unhappy receiving the mails after Melbourne. In New Zealand, Auckland and Wellington were hooked up to these services through branch connections across the Tasman Sea. This added a week to the delivery and despatch of colonial mails. Leaders in New Zealand began exploring the possibility of faster services to and from London and looked to direct inclusion on lines across the Pacific via San Francisco or Vancouver. This also appealed to New South Wales as a way to ensure Sydney would receive the mails before other Australian ports.[37]

Several costly attempts to instigate a regular San Francisco route failed in the 1860s and 1870s. In October 1875, the American Pacific Mail Steamship Company secured a ten-year contract with the New South Wales and New Zealand governments for the Sydney–London service via San Francisco. This initially amounted to an annual subsidy of £100,000. This service also called at Galoa Harbour in Kadavu, a southern island in the Fiji group, which was also mooted as a replacement capital for Levuka. After the contract expired in 1885, the USSCo. took over this service in conjunction with the American Oceanic Steam Ship Company, managed by J. D. Spreckels, a financier and eldest son of a Hawaiian sugar magnate, Claus Spreckels. The USSCo. recognised that participation in the mail lines furthered a number of interests over and above improved regional and global communications. Trade and tourism both stood to benefit from the addition of regular connections across the Pacific to North America.

Auckland and Wellington competed for inclusion on these routes. The *New Zealand Herald* welcomed the USSCo.'s involvement in the Frisco route, declaring it would contribute to Auckland's status 'as a leading, if not the principal, centre of traffic and commerce in the Pacific'.[38] Wellington proponents believed their port was better placed, for nowhere else 'can a large steamer be more readily and expeditiously handled, loaded, and discharged'. Wellington was developing as New Zealand's key steamer port in the interprovincial and intercolonial trades, and was 'only on the threshold of her splendid future as the great mercantile and maritime centre of New Zealand'.[39] Similar claims had been made on the introduction of a new colonial mail arrangement in 1864. Four steamers were to leave Wellington each week to deliver mail to both ends of the country, demonstrating that the port 'has rapidly been acquiring for itself the character of being the natural centre for steam'.[40] On the occasion of the transpacific line, however, the USSCo. selected Auckland over Wellington (the route to

San Francisco also included calls at Apia and Honolulu). Dunedin, the location of the USSCo. head office, was not considered New Zealand's maritime hub. The city's main deep-water port at Port Chalmers, halfway along the harbour entrance to the city, was ill equipped to accommodate large vessels. Dunedin was connected to the deep-ocean routes by local coastal branch services.[41]

The San Francisco service was a challenging venture. The first ships put on the route were not built specifically for transoceanic trading. They were too slow and small and had to carry more fuel, which took up valuable space otherwise reserved for mails and freight. Moreover, Spreckels proved a dishonest and reckless business partner, and relations between Union and Oceanic were never smooth.[42] In any case, the USSCo. withdrew following the annexation of Hawai'i in 1898 and its incorporation as a territory of the United States in 1900. Under American law only local companies could conduct shipping between domestic ports. These restrictions extended to include Honolulu as an American coastal port. Now denied access to the most remunerative section of transpacific trade, as well as a sizeable state subsidy only available to American companies, the USSCo. had no option but to pull out of the mail line altogether. Company officials were irritated by the fact that there were no restrictions placed on foreign companies for the Auckland and Sydney leg, effectively the 'British' section of the route.[43]

In order to counter negative sentiment directed at his company in the local press, Spreckels pointed out that the USSCo. had seriously explored the possibility of either registering or constructing its steamers in the United States in order to continue running in the trade: 'so you can see how willing the USSCo. were to waive the "all-red" sentiment provided there was an advantage in doing so for themselves'.[44] Over the following years Spreckels confronted ongoing problems with poorly constructed steamers, incompetent crew, corruption and a freeze on state subsidies. He withdrew from the route in 1907.[45]

The USSCo. eventually re-entered the Sydney–San Francisco service in 1909, steaming from Wellington via Rarotonga and Tahiti. Dissatisfied with its status as a port of trans-shipment from Auckland in the local trade to Rarotonga, Wellington agitated for a direct service from its port. Trans-shipment frequently entailed over-handling, delays, pillage and expense: major problems where perishable fruit cargoes were concerned. The USSCo. met these demands but delayed its announcement until after local elections, for any connection from Wellington, as managing director Charles Holdsworth reflected, 'would be badly received by the Auckland people'.[46] The company extended the service to Tahiti in order to connect with Spreckels's San Francisco–Tahiti line, thereby renewing indirect links between New Zealand and the USA. The New Zealand Government granted an annual £25,000 subsidy to extend the service to San Francisco direct the following year. In 1911 the itinerary also included Sydney. This route provided a twenty-four-day mail service from Wellington to San Francisco and a thirty-five-day service to London (five days by train to New York and six and a half days by steamer to London), a gain of a few days over the Suez route. It also promised to boost American tourist numbers in the Pacific by capitalising on the recent promotional work of the New Zealand Tourism Department in North America. So, again, the mail route realised a triple objective of improved communications, extension of trade and tourism development. Known as the Union Royal Mail Line, this service continued until 1936 when competition with the heavily subsidised American Matson Line forced it off the route.[47]

The Canadian Australian Line (CA Line) configured another shifting web of regional port relations. Sydney-based James Huddart initiated this route in 1893. He took up the offer of a ten-year, £25,000 annual subsidy from the Canadian Government designed to promote trade with the Australasian colonies. The 'all-red' route, which carried mails between British territory exclusively on British-owned ships, connected Sydney, Brisbane, Honolulu, Victoria and Vancouver. A call at Wellington replaced Brisbane, but New Zealand opted out when the Brisbane call was later renewed. The service was now 'rendered absolutely useless' as a mail route. Touching at Brisbane first on the inwards voyage from Vancouver and last on the outwards, it would not provide New Zealand with an improved mail service, for it took seven days to make the trans-Tasman round trip via Wellington.[48]

After Huddart's company went into liquidation in 1898, the USSCo. acquired a controlling interest in the line in 1901. It placed Suva on the route on a permanent basis from 1902 (the steamers had previously called there intermittently until Fiji's Governor withdrew an annual subsidy), but the lack of a direct call at New Zealand was still contentious. Under the existing arrangement, New Zealand was connected to the CA Line by the USSCo. branch connection between Auckland and Suva. While the outward mails reached England in the same time as mails from Brisbane, the inward mails were held up at Suva until the departure of the first New Zealand-bound steamer, which entailed a delay of ten days.[49] Replacing Brisbane with a local port would secure a faster mail service to and from London (thirty-one days, in contrast to an average thirty-seven via Suez) and stimulate trade with Canada in meat, butter and cheese.

Queensland opposed any change, fearing the loss of the associated trade and prestige, but the alteration in favour of Auckland was finally achieved in 1911. By this time the USSCo. was the sole proprietor of the line. New Zealand contributed £20,000, Fiji £5,000, which represented a large increase as a result of USSCo. pressure, and Canada £37,000.[50] The name of the route was altered slightly to the Canadian Australasian Line to better reflect the inclusion of New Zealand. Australia pulled out of contract renegotiations, opposed to the 1904 preferential trade agreement between New Zealand and Canada. Although the Australian Government no longer contributed subsidies, Sydney remained the terminal port as the USSCo. sought to forestall Spreckels's renewed bid for the transpacific trade. The route Sydney–Auckland–Suva–Honolulu–Victoria–Vancouver remained in operation until 1953.

By the beginning of the First World War, the USSCo. held a monopoly over both transpacific mail routes. It had also built up a lucrative transpacific cargo trade alongside. Neither service displaced the Suez route. The New Zealand Government paid subsidies for all three separate routes (from 1882, the New Zealand Shipping Company and the British Shaw, Savill and Albion Company shared a direct mail contract between New Zealand and London via Suez). Some believed it made sense to merge the subsidies and support only one route that could provide a much faster mail service. A realistic subsidy for a desired twenty-one-day service to London would amount to at least £100,000. The Prime Minister, Joseph Ward, rejected this proposal, given that the three separate services met different cargo and passenger purposes.[51] The land bridge across North America with its two trans-shipment ports meant that the transpacific routes were not competitive in the transport of migrants and general freight. But they were marketed as 'the quickest, most picturesque and most instructive' way to travel between Great Britain and the Australasian colonies.[52] The USSCo., as Holdsworth reflected in 1914, looked upon the North American trade 'as our own province'.[53]

Steam and the sub-imperial push

The extension of steamer services and the construction of new ships were frequently seized upon as an index of national development and maturation. As the *New Zealand Official Year Book* remarked in 1893, the USSCo.'s history 'is a reflex, to a great extent, of the later history of the colony – as the one has grown, the other has expanded'.[54] Newspaper reports of each new addition to the company's fleet made particular reference to tonnage, effectively a shorthand for the progress of the colony. On the occasion of the arrival of a new intercolonial steamer in 1905, for example, the company's history was said to 'read

like a romance'. The total tonnage of the USSCo. fleet at its foundation in 1875 was 4,000 tons; thirty years later it had grown to 112,000
tons. The *Evening Post* remarked that the company had the progressive
qualities 'usually ascribed to the colony as a whole'.[55] More than this,
there was also an official impression that 'New Zealand and the Union
Company are bound together by common ties of mutual support', as a
state official had to 'respectfully remind' Mills on noting that he was
not directing all of the company's cable traffic through the state-owned
Pacific Cable in the first years of the twentieth century.[56]

Political interest in a sub-imperial agenda in the Pacific preceded the
establishment and growth of the USSCo. Governor from 1845–53, Sir
George Grey was the first leader to champion New Zealand's regional
involvement. Prime Minister Julius Vogel followed suit in the 1870s,
pushing for commercial and political engagement. The vision of New
Zealand's unique island destiny gained heightened political impetus as
the Australasian colonies began to debate a federated future from the
1880s. The first federal conferences and confederations included representatives from both New Zealand and Fiji. Fiji pulled out because,
as Governor Charles Mitchell reported to the Colonial Office in 1887,
'from a financial point of view he could consent to nothing that would
involve any expenditure and from a social standpoint he would chiefly
represent a race that has nothing in common with the Anglo-Saxon
communities of Australasia'.[57] New Zealand also opted out of the
federal compact, fearing, as Angus Ross suggests, that its own expansionist agenda in the Pacific would be sacrificed for 'purely Australian
needs'. Frustrated by the restrictions and limitations of Crown rule,
some of Fiji's white residents approached both Victoria and New South
Wales in the 1880s about the possibility of formal incorporation. Little
headway was made with either, and there were also two unsuccessful movements for the formal federation of Fiji and New Zealand in
1883–85 and 1900–2.[58]

Prime Minister Seddon was a prominent figure in these debates at
the turn of the century. He took an island tour in 1900 on the government steamer *Tutanekai*, ostensibly to recuperate after a spell
of ill health, yet this trip was also usefully timed to promote New
Zealand's regional aspirations to various island communities. Hoping
to undercut the dominance in the Pacific of Sydney and, by extension,
the newly federated Australia, Seddon targeted maritime transport
operations to give practical expression to these aspirations. In a public
speech at Suva he signalled his intention to 'shorten the distance
between Fiji and New Zealand' and reduce prohibitive freight and
passage rates. He also believed that the connection between Tonga and
Auckland was 'not what it ought to be'. He desired the addition of a

call at Tonga on the Auckland–Fiji direct service. While he had nothing against the USSCo., for 'it has done great things' for New Zealand, it had to meet the colony's aspirations 'otherwise the company must lose as well as the colony'.[59]

Public rhetoric, which extolled the success of the USSCo., could not disguise an undercurrent of suspicion and distaste directed towards large companies and big business. Mills knew quite well that the Seddon Government 'certainly does not like us'.[60] Company management opposed Seddon's suggested island trade alterations along with the broader implication that the USSCo. somehow simply operated to satisfy political agendas. Seddon's sub-imperial vision sat awkwardly alongside the spatial realities of regional shipping, which functioned through a decentred port complex. After Seddon's visit, the Fiji branch manager, Duncan, opined that in all of his propositions 'the desire is to cut Sydney as far as possible out of the trades'. The USSCo. needed free access to all ports in Australia and New Zealand and any rigid territorialisation of the surrounding seas in the attempt to divert regional traffic away from Sydney was short-sighted.[61] In any case, as the *Sydney Daily Telegraph* had remarked many years earlier, since the company had extended its 'steam girdle' across the Tasman and around a portion of Australia's eastern coastline, it could no longer be regarded exclusively as a New Zealand company: 'It is much, and more, Australasian.'[62]

Seddon's opponents also recognised the part transport played in refiguring regional relationships. New Zealand assumed the administration of the Cook Islands and Niue from Great Britain in 1901. *The Australasian* queried whether Australia was threatened with a rival power, that of 'Greater New Zealand'. As many islands were already on the USSCo.'s itinerary, Seddon might utilise these networks to alter free trade in the region and subject Australian goods to customs charges.[63] Burns Philp and Company, which had extensive Pacific interests in plantations, trade stores and shipping, maintained that if there were any serious question of Fijian annexation in 1900, the colony 'with which they are in closest relationship', that being New South Wales, should be involved.[64]

Agitation for the formal union of New Zealand and Fiji was ultimately unacceptable to the Colonial Office. Fiji was already part of the British Empire and New Zealand, in a subordinate relationship to Britain, did not wield sufficient power to take an independent stance in the region. But sub-imperial agitation was also unrealistic because it artificially restricted the broader regional connections between the colonies on Australia's eastern seaboard and Fiji. Island commerce developed from the efforts of traders in both the Australian and New

Zealand colonies and could not be redirected into one narrow channel, nor could a national vision undercut the shifting investment patterns and interest in the trade at the level of the colonial port. New South Wales sent petitions to the Colonial Office protesting against Seddon's moves, citing the extensive investment of Australian firms in the island group. Yet as Roger Thompson observes, this desire to arrest New Zealand's ambitions in Fiji was limited to Sydney interests. The editorial columns of Melbourne and Brisbane newspapers were comparatively quiet on these issues.[65] These uneven investments in the possibilities of island empire were, as Damon Salesa concludes, more like 'domestic colonies of imperial interest'.[66]

The long-distance mail routes were also particular targets of colonial leaders. As such they brought the political question of speed into greater focus. In attendance at international conferences to discuss shipping matters, Mills was regularly frustrated by talk by the prime ministers of New Zealand and Australia of the desirability of eighteen-knot services across the Pacific. Such services were simply not commercially viable. The annual operational costs of a fifteen-knot ship were estimated at £215,000, while those of a seventeen-knot ship sky-rocketed to £319,000. Mills was concerned that such whimsical suggestions hindered discussions about practical improvements to regional shipping operations.[67] When rumours of a New Zealand extension to a new mail service between Adelaide and Brindisi began to circulate in 1906, one USSCo. representative opined that 'politicians were generally at sea when dealing with shipping matters'.[68]

As steamer operations exercised regional port rivalries for political and economic influence, there were also concurrent tensions about the relationship between colonial maritime developments and over-arching imperial concerns. Alive to the importance of mastery along their own coastlines and surrounding seas, New Zealand and Australia both drafted legislation to require visiting British and foreign ships to conform to local regulations while trading in local waters. Section 10 of the New Zealand Shipping and Seamen's Act 1896 stipulated the payment of local wages to crew working on ships trading along the New Zealand coast. Imperial shipping interests were initially alarmed that this applied to all ships in New Zealand waters, whatever their trading intentions. In doing so it contradicted the British Merchant Shipping Act 1894 which upheld free trade. The section was amended to apply only to those ships engaged in the New Zealand coastal trade. In turn, the Australian Navigation and Shipping Bill introduced in 1904 aimed to reserve the Australian coastal trade for vessels registered in Australia. No British or foreign ship without a special licence could carry passengers between Commonwealth ports. Ships that received any form of subsidy from a foreign state would not receive a licence. By ensuring crews would be paid the federal wage rate while trading in Australia, this bill was designed to eliminate the lower-paid non-white crew on many foreign ships.[69]

Imperial officials and British shipowners were wary of increasing colonial confidence in maritime affairs. The repeal of the British Navigation Acts in 1849 freed the merchant marine from a restrictive and complex mesh of laws, which had limited the carriage of British trade to British ships for almost two centuries. The gradual abolition of duties on imports from the 1850s further encouraged the extension of free trade, although shipping was not freed entirely from state interference.[70] By the turn of the twentieth century, Britain carried over fifty per cent of international trade (although this was in gradual decline from a peak of sixty per cent in 1890), and controlled over ninety per cent of imperial traffic.[71]

Vessels were deployed in two main ways. Liners traded along set routes at set times. Tramps operated on more flexible itineraries in order to secure as much cargo as possible. They needed to be able to go anywhere and accept all employment on offer to avoid voyages in ballast. Uniformity in international maritime law was crucial. A vessel could not be transformed at every port of call to meet the prevailing manning, accommodation and victualling requirements and wage scales without great inconvenience, delay and expense. If Australia or New Zealand imposed local conditions on foreign vessels, foreign powers might retaliate and restrict British vessels from trading in their waters. Foreign powers were also unlikely to distinguish between restrictive shipping legislation in colonial ports and in Britain itself. With entrances and clearances of foreign vessels being much more numerous at British than Australasian ports, Britain would bear the brunt of foreign retaliation. From this perspective, moderation from self-governing colonies in maritime affairs was imperative.[72]

The merchant shipping legislation conference held in London directly before the 1907 Colonial Conference brought together representatives from Britain, Australia and New Zealand to address questions of maritime jurisdiction, with the draft Australian legislation of particular concern. The meaning and interpretation of coastal trades came up for debate. Following the standard definition, a vessel was coasting when it took on board cargo or passengers in any port in a colony and carried, landed and discharged them at another port in the same colony. The Australian Attorney General, William Morris Hughes, took the definition of coastal trading one step further. He proposed that the Pacific trades should be reclassified as Australian coastal rather than foreign. In extending their three-mile territorial waters, Australia would thereby monopolise the island trades and exclude foreign ships, particularly German vessels, which traded more cheaply. German companies paid crew significantly lower wages than their Australian counterparts and also had reduced provisioning costs. As such they stood to profit more from these trades, endangering Sydney's long-standing investment in the Pacific.

The New Zealand Prime Minister, Sir Joseph Ward, was more cautious. He believed that the adherence of foreign ships to local regulations when in New Zealand's coastal waters went far enough. Foreign vessels had 'a perfect right equally with ourselves' to the sea traffic across the Pacific, for this ocean was not Australasia's exclusive maritime territory. He feared any restrictions would draw the hostile attention of more powerful maritime nations. New Zealand would object if another nation imposed restrictive new conditions on its ships, so, he argued, it would be prudent to avoid setting such a precedent. Yet Hughes maintained that 'the Islands of the Pacific ought to be (if they are not) our exclusive monopoly so far as trading is concerned'. He believed that everybody should be on the same footing in such a competitive trade and, because it 'was practically a coastal trade', it should be Australian conditions that applied. Also in attendance, Mills pointed out that it had in any case become 'the custom of the country' to maintain the same regulations regarding wages, holidays and other matters on vessels trading between New Zealand and Australia and from these countries into the Pacific.[73]

The Colonial Office strongly opposed Hughes's suggestion. As Bertram Cox stressed, 'you cannot regard as coasting every ship that competes with yours'. The President of the Board of Trade, David Lloyd George, suggested that 'the real meaning' of the resolution was 'an attempt to impose Australian suzerainty over the Islands of the Pacific'. Australian delegates maintained it was simply an attempt to clarify the meaning and extent of coastal trading. This issue was left unresolved. The Board of Trade was uncomfortable with the conference discussing such questions, for it 'is not shipping legislation; it is a great Imperial question'. Hughes retorted that 'it is not shipping legislation by you but it is shipping legislation by us, and the objection to shipping legislation by us is that it might involve you'.[74]

At the opening of the Colonial Conference that followed, the First Lord of the Admiralty appealed to the delegates, reminding them that 'there is, after all, only one sea that laps around all our shores. The sea is the link that joins us together. It was the reason of your upspringing. It is our first defence. It is the origin of our great commerce. It is the outlet and inlet of our exports and imports . . . There is one sea, there is one Empire, there is one Navy.'[75] The loud demands of colonial states unsettled this investment in the sea as a space of imperial unity, an expression of British patriotism through nautical metaphors. At the conference the Australian Prime Minister, Alfred Deakin, complained that Britain 'mishandled' and neglected imperial affairs in the Pacific, and both Australia and New Zealand, who knew the region more intimately, suffered as a result. British officials strongly refuted his accusations, although the visit of Sir Charles Lucas to Australia, New Zealand and Fiji in 1909, the first visit of a senior Colonial Office official, was motivated by Deakin's criticisms.[76]

Lucas acknowledged the historical legacy of imperial distance in fostering feelings of 'inequality and subordination' in the New Zealand and Australian colonies. Yet he was particularly impressed by the scale of USSCo. operations. The fact of the company's existence 'at almost the furthest possible point from the great centres of European and American commerce' was rather remarkable. It demonstrated to him that colonial citizens could 'retain in full measure the creative power of the British race'.[77] He went on to reflect that the scientific inventions of steam and electricity had done much to 'fill out' each separate colony and to improve relations between them, echoing Seeley's influential commentary in *The Expansion of England* in 1883.[78] Yet Lucas stressed that the 'rise of the south' and 'the growth of the southern peoples' was still 'retarded' by their distance 'from the more thickly populated parts of the world'. Imperial administration in the Pacific could not be run 'on the cheap' and further integration would require more steamers and telegraphs.[79]

These tools of empire, while harnessed to dissolve negative talk of 'Downing Street' in the self-governing Dominions, also empowered New Zealand and Australia in their own regional sea and reduced dependence on Britain. In 1910 New Zealand drafted the Shipping and Seamen's Amendment Bill, a reaction to the announcement that P&O was extending its Britain–Australia service to New Zealand. The company's liners normally spent three weeks at Sydney between voyages and the management decided to relieve this unremunerative lull by extending the itinerary to Auckland. New Zealand's draft legislation extended the meaning of coasting, so that ships trading between New Zealand and either Australia or the Cook Islands would follow local manning and wage rates, in good part a reaction to the fact P&O carried cheap 'coloured' labour. The Minister of Labour and Marine, John Millar, argued that 'we have as much right to say that the sea from here to Australia shall be controlled by our law as Australia has to say that the sea between Tasmania and her coasts shall be controlled by her law'. P&O believed the USSCo. had engineered this legislation and declared they would register company ships in Melbourne rather than Britain to circumvent any new restrictions.

The legislation was submitted to the Imperial Government for final approval, but the Secretary of State for the Colonies opposed it on the grounds that it went beyond New Zealand's legislative power. Trading between New Zealand and the Cook Islands could be deemed coasting; trading between New Zealand and Australia could not. From an imperial point of view, as one London journal pointed out, to penalise a company's intercolonial and coasting branches was effectively to penalise its imperial functions: 'It should not be possible for any member of the Empire to legislate antagonistically to Imperial interests, however carefully it cares for, and is to be supported in caring for, its own.'[80]

This legislation and the Australian Navigation Bill were both the subject of further debate at the 1911 Imperial Conference. Delegates heard more strident demands for colonial autonomy in maritime affairs. Ward put forward a resolution that the self-governing Dominions had now reached a stage of development 'when they should be entrusted with wider legislative powers in respect to British and foreign shipping'. This was rejected as too wide and vague a proposition. It was agreed, however, that the Imperial Government would no longer enact shipping and navigation legislation that applied automatically to the self-governing Dominions.[81] Running at a heavy loss, P&O withdrew from trans-Tasman trading in 1913. The Australian Navigation Bill received the royal assent in 1912, but its coastal trading provisions did not become operative until 1921 at the request of the Imperial Government, itself under pressure from shipping interests led by the P&O and British Orient.[82]

Shipping and the spatial politics of the sea

Maritime history, as Glen O'Hara reflects, is 'synthesised with, and allied to, a sense of state formation', and at the same time overlaps and collides national cultures.[83] The extension of steamer routes into the Pacific did not anticipate the extension of formal political relations between New Zealand and other islands, but the USSCo.'s regional expansion occurred at a time when the larger colonies of white settlement were developing and asserting a sense of national character and regional awareness. As the Pacific Ocean became more heavily utilised, this encouraged claims of exclusive use. Colonial nationalists in Australasia attempted to harness maritime transport to pursue an independent path in the western Pacific. Imperialism, moulded as it was by powerful British shipping interests, ultimately moderated the maritime ambitions of the self-governing Dominions. And while political leaders had a growing fascination with high speed, ever-expansive services and a clearer demarcation of national interests over regional waterways, faster ships were prohibitively expensive to build and routes were circumscribed by a range of commercial considerations.

The tensions between British and Australasian maritime policy and the conflict between the USSCo. management and colonial nationalists demonstrated that, even in this new era of regimented industrial shipping, with timetables, contracts and subsidies, the sea remained an open-ended space of debate and negotiation. Steamer routes were highly politicised relationships in a contested colonial world.

Notes

1   Edward Reeves, *Brown Men and Women; or, the South Sea Islands in 1895 and 1896* (London: Swan, Sonnenschein & Co., 1898), 200.
2   Gordon Boyce, *Information, Mediation and Institutional Development: The Rise of Large-Scale Enterprise in British Shipping, 1870–1919* (Manchester: Manchester University Press, 1995).
3   *Otago Daily Times* (24 June 1870). For Fiji's pre-cession history see R. A. Derrick, *A History of Fiji* (Suva: Fiji Government Press, 1946).
4   John Young, 'Sailing to Levuka: the cultural significance of the island schooners in the late 19th century', *Journal of Pacific History*, 28:1 (1993), 38–40. Young frames Fiji as an 'Australian frontier' in *Adventurous Spirits*.
5   James Fergusson to the Earl of Kimberley, 22 October 1873, *Appendices to the Journals of the House of Representatives (AJHR)*, A-3 (Wellington: Govt. Printer, 1874), 16; Frederick J. Moss, *A Planter's Experience in Fiji: Being a Concise Account of the Country, Its Present Condition, and Its Prospects as a Field for Emigration* (Auckland: Jones and Tombs, 1870), 63. This parallel was also made with respect to Victoria and Fiji, see Nicholas Thomas and Richard Eves, *Bad Colonists: The South Seas Letters of Vernon Lee Walker & Louis Becke* (Durham, NC: Duke University Press, 1999), 36.
6   'Memoranda by Mr Sterndale on some of the South Sea Islands', *AJHR*, A-3b (Wellington: Govt. Printer, 1874), 1.
7   R. J. Munro, 'Otago Interest and Intercourse with Fiji, 1870–73' (MA dissertation, University of Otago, 1967), 26, 34.
8   Bernhard Wise, letter to the editor, *Sydney Morning Herald* (31 December 1884), 7.
9   Charles Hursthouse, *New Zealand, or Zealandia, The Britain of the South* (London: Edward Sanford, 2nd edn, 1861), 52, 279.
10 Alexander Turnbull Library (ATL), Coleman Phillips Papers, MSY-4803, Scrapbook, *New Zealand Herald*, n.d., and qMS 1643, Life history to 1924.
11 *Fiji Times* (2 May 1877).
12 *Fiji Times* (3 November 1877).
13 *Fiji Times* (24 October 1874).
14 *Fiji Times* (30 June and 8 September 1877); Young, 'Sailing to Levuka', 51–2. For more general reflections on these points see Jason Gilliland, 'Muddy shore to modern port: redimensioning the Montreal waterfront time-space', *Canadian Geographer*, 48:4 (2004), 448–72.
15 *Fiji Times* (1 November 1873).
16 *Fiji Times* (2 and 20 July 1881).
17 Bruce Knapman, *Fiji's Economic History, 1874–1939: Studies of Capitalist Colonial Development* (Canberra: The Australian National University National Centre for Development Studies, 1987), 65–83.
18 HC, USSCo. Records, AG-292-005-004/060, Mills to Seddon, 16 January 1896.

19 Richard D. Knowles, 'Transport shaping space: differential collapse in time-space', *Journal of Transport Geography*, 14 (2006), 423.

20 National Archives of Fiji (NAF), Colonial Secretary's Office (CSO), 76.138, F. E. Pratt, Commanding officer of Royal Engineers, 25 January 1876; CSO, 77.942, Petitioners in favour of removal, 11 April 1877.

21 NAF, CSO, 87.2559, Levuka Warden to Colonial Secretary, 10 October 1887.

22 HC, USSCo. Records, AG-292-005-001/093, McLennan to Holdsworth, 2 February 1909; AG-292-005-001/096, McLennan to Holdsworth, 11 October 1910.

23 *Report of the Commission Appointed for the Purpose of Inquiring Into and Reporting Upon the Shipping Conditions and Facilities of the Colony, Having Reference More Especially to the Carriage of Passengers, General Cargo, Fruit and other Produce – Council Paper No. 111 (Fiji Shipping Commission)* (Suva: Legislative Council, 1914), 187.

24 NAF, CSO, 89.640, Colonial Secretary to Duncan, 20 March 1889.

25 HC, USSCo. Records, AG-292-004-004/018, Holdsworth to Allen, 13 February 1914; AG-292-005-001/113, Pope to Holdsworth, 15 August 1914.

26 'Island steamer service: dissatisfaction in Tonga', *Evening Post* (29 January 1914), 2.

27 HC, USSCo. Records, AG-292-005-001/027, Henderson to Mills, 19 August 1892.

28 Young, 'Sailing to Levuka'.

29 Ward, *Widening Worlds, Shrinking Worlds?*, 22; *Fiji Shipping Commission*, vi. Bluff to Auckland was 1167 miles while Auckland to Suva was 1140 miles. The USSCo. shipped bran at 14s. 6d. per ton within New Zealand, yet it cost 45s. per ton to ship to Suva.

30 Frank Broeze, 'Private enterprise and public policy: merchant shipping in Australia and New Zealand, 1788–1992', *Australian Economic History Review*, 32:2 (1992), 14.

31 Kubicek, 'British expansion, empire, and technological change', 257.

32 'Shall New Zealand have steam?', *Otago Witness* (5 March 1853), 4.

33 'Australian steam navigation', *Sydney Herald* (12 February 1842), 2.

34 *Nelson Examiner* (4 October 1851), 126.

35 J. Lort Stokes, 'On steam communication with the southern colonies (Australia and the Cape of Good Hope)', *Journal of the Royal Geographical Society of London*, 26 (1856), 183–8.

36 For a detailed analysis of development of mail routes between Britain and Australasia, see Broeze, 'Distance tamed, 1–21. For a history of P&O see Freda Harcourt, *Flagships of Imperialism: The P&O Company and the Politics of Empire from its Origins to 1867* (Manchester: Manchester University Press, 2006). Queensland established a direct link to London through the Torres Strait in 1880 under the British India Company.

37 Broeze, 'Distance tamed', 7–8.

38 *New Zealand Herald* (13 August 1885).

39 *New Zealand Times* (24 September 1886).

40 'New Zealand, Wellington, as a steam port', *Journal of the Society of Arts*, 12 (29 April 1864), 379. For more on Wellington's dependence on shipping and its status as a colonial entrepôt see Rollo Arnold, *New Zealand's Burning: The Settlers' World in the Mid 1880s* (Wellington: Victoria University Press, 1994), 199–208.

41 The port's 'coming of age' was celebrated a couple of decades later in 1908 when the RMS *Athenic*, a large liner of the Shaw, Savill and Albion Company, berthed in Port Chalmers. Local businessmen celebrated the fact that this event enabled the city to 'score one on the northern ports'. See 'The port of Otago', *Otago Witness* (28 October 1908), 16.

42 See McLean, *The Southern Octopus*, 70–81.

43 HC, Cameron Family Papers, MS 1046, Box 14, Cameron to Chamberlain, 6 February 1906.

44 'The Frisco mail service', *Evening Post* (23 November 1901), 2.

45 For a general overview, see J. H. Hamilton, 'The all-red route, 1853–1953: a history of the trans-Pacific mail service between British Columbia, Australia and

New Zealand', *British Columbia Historical Quarterly*, 20 (January–April 1956), 1–126.

46   HC, USSCo. Records, AG-292-004-004/010, Holdsworth to directors, 30 September 1908.

47   McLean, *The Southern Octopus*, 67–81; Hamilton, 'The all-red route', 113–14. See also, Kosmas Tsokhas, 'Cartels, imperial relations and Australian shipping policy in the Asia-Pacific region, 1914–1939', *Journal of Contemporary Asia*, 27:3 (1997), 363–7.

48   'The ocean mail services', *Otago Witness* (2 March 1899), 12; Sir Joseph Ward, 'Vancouver mail service', in *NZPD*, vol. 156 (Wellington, 1911), 22.

49   HC, USSCo. Records, AG-292-005-001/093, 10 April 1909.

50   *Ibid.*, AG-292-004-004/010, memo re Vancouver mail contract, 17 May 1910; AG-292-005-001/097, Mills to Minister of Trade and Commerce, Ottawa, 5 June 1911.

51   See *NZPD*, vol. 126 (Wellington: Government Printer, 1911), 22–34.

52   HC, USSCo. Records, AG-292-005-004/096, brochure for the A&A Line (n.d.).

53   20 March 1914, cited in McLean, T*he Southern Octopus*, 140. See also *ibid.*, 127–40. It should be noted that New Zealand ownership of the USSCo. ended in 1917 when P&O bought the company. It remained under local management.

54   *New Zealand Official Year Book* (Wellington: Government Printer, 1893), 332.

55   'The new turbine steamer', *Evening Post* (22 November 1905), 8.

56   HC, USSCo. Records, AG-292-005-001/101, J. A. Talbot to Mills, 20 May 1909.

57   NAF, CSO, Despatches from the Governor of Fiji to the Secretary of State, vol. 7, despatch no. 141, 4 November 1887.

58   Ross, *New Zealand Aspirations in the Pacific*, 157–60, 271–8.

59   Edward Tregear, *The Right Hon. R. J. Seddon's (the Premier of New Zealand) Visit to Tonga, Fiji, Savage Islands, and the Cook Islands* (Wellington: Government Printer, 1900), 423.

60   HC, Cameron Family Papers, MS 1046, Box 8, Mills to Cameron, 25 May 1898.

61   HC, USSCo. Records, AG-292-005-001/052, Duncan to Mills, 4 October 1900; AG-292-005-004/104, Henderson to Mills, 17 September 1900.

62   *Sydney Daily Telegraph* (20 May 1882).

63   *The Australasian* (6 October 1900).

64   HC, USSCo. Records, AG-292-003-001/014, minutes of meetings of Directors, 12 July 1900.

65   Thompson, *Australian Imperialism in the Pacific*, 165. Debates for and against formal federation between New Zealand and Fiji also rested on comparisons of the nature of initial white settlement, forms of colonial governmentalities, indigenous–settler relations, constructions of whiteness, indigeneity and the environment.

66   Salesa, 'New Zealand's Pacific', 154.

67   McLean, *The Southern Octopus*, 131; HC, Cameron Family Papers, MS 1046, Box 9, Mills to Cameron, 18 August 1903.

68   'Surprise in local shipping circles', *Otago Witness* (18 July 1906), 29.

69   In a New Zealand Court of Appeal decision in 1906 Chief Justice Sir Robert Stout ruled that a ship registered in New Zealand remained under New Zealand law even when trading beyond territorial waters. This contradicted imperial law which held that colonial courts could only enforce imperial law, not colonial law, on ships trading beyond territorial waters. Locally owned and registered colonial vessels were captured within a higher jurisdiction. See Keith A. Berriedale, 'Merchant shipping legislation in the colonies', *Journal for the Society for Comparative Legislation*, 9:2 (1908), 202–22.

70   Sarah Palmer, *Politics, Shipping and the Repeal of the Navigation Laws* (Manchester: Manchester University Press, 1990).

71   For more on Britain's rise to global maritime dominance, see Boyce, *Information, Mediation and Institutional Development*, 13–25.

72   Imperial Conference, 1911, 'Minutes of proceedings', *AJHR*, A-4 (Wellington: Government Printer, 1911), 415. See also 'Appendix A: Memorandum submitted to the conference by the representatives of British shipowners', *Merchant Shipping*

Legislation Report of a Conference between Representatives of the United Kingdom, the Commonwealth of Australia, and New Zealand, 26th March–2nd April, 1907 (Sydney: Government Printer, 1907), 169–70.

73   *Merchant Shipping Legislation*, 73, 82.

74   *Ibid.*, 65, 82–5.

75   Lord Tweedmouth in *Colonial Conference 1907: Minutes of Proceedings* (London: HMSO, 1907, Cd. 3523), 129.

76   *Colonial Conference 1907*, 548–9. And see Marilyn Lake, '"The brightness of eyes and quiet assurance which seem to say American": Alfred Deakin's identification with Republican manhood', *Australian Historical Studies*, 38:129 (2007), 44. Lake has recently explored Deakin's ambivalence towards Britain and his identification with republican modes of political authority. In response to his hostile reception at the Colonial Conference, Deakin, who evidently suffered a nervous breakdown as a result, invited the United States naval fleet to extend its Pacific tour to include Australia, 'a provocative gesture of political independence': Lake, '"The brightness of eyes. . .'", 47.

77   Charles Lucas, *Dominions No. 1: Note on a Visit to Australia, New Zealand, and Fiji, in 1909*, Cd. 5100 (London: HMSO, Colonial Office series, 1910), 7.

78   Seeley, *The Expansion of England*, 64, 75. And see Deudney, 'Greater Britain or greater synthesis?', 187–208.

79   Lucas, *Note on a Visit*, 4, 5.

80   'Ships and the sea. Imperial shipping. Australasia taken to task', *Evening Post* (22 April 1911), 12.

81   M. L. McConnell, 'Cabotage and the colonial corset: the great Australian bind', *Maritime Law Association of Australia and New Zealand Journal*, 5 (1988), 3–18.

82   For the position of Burns Philp in relation to the Navigation Act in its Pacific trades, see Buckley and Klugman, *The History of Burns Philp*, 235–41.

83   Glen O'Hara, '"The sea is swinging into view": modern British maritime history in a globalised world', *English Historical Review*, 124:510 (2009), 1134.

CHAPTER TWO

The liner: cultures of maritime technology

> Every addition to the service, that links Australia and her sister
> Dominions of such a standard, is a valuable asset to the Empire . . . She
> is a 'thing of beauty' from bulkhead to bulkhead, without and within,
> equipped with every safeguard to withstand the moods of ocean and
> ride triumphantly through storm or sunshine, the emblem of a Nation's
> prosperity, a demonstration of man's latest achievement in scientific
> enterprise, and a living link in the bonds of Empire.
>
> *Shoalhaven News* (31 May 1913)

A passenger liner was one of the defining images of modernity.
The RMS *Niagara* (figure 5) was one of the largest, fastest and best-
appointed liners in operation outside of the transatlantic trades in the
early twentieth century. Constructed for the USSCo. by Clyde shipbuilders John Brown and Company, the ship entered service on the
Canadian Australasian Line, which linked Sydney with Vancouver,
in 1913. At 13,500 tons the vessel represented the 'high point' of the
USSCo.'s pre-war shipbuilding and initiated a 'new epoch' in New
Zealand's transoceanic trade.[1] As celebrated by the *Shoalhaven News*
on its inaugural arrival in southern ports, the ship brimmed with
technological and cultural significance. It had accommodation for 281
first-, 223 second- and 191 third-class passengers and was complete
with a system of wireless telegraphy, electric elevators, darkrooms
for developing photographs, a children's saloon, a music room and
a recreation room: 'practically everything required for the comfort
or amusement of passengers'.[2] It was also the first coal steamer to
have a British Board of Trade certificate to burn oil. This triumphant
account of enterprise and technological innovation also placed careful
emphasis on safety and security.

Steamships were not just the focus of private companies, but prominent objects of national and imperial pride and concern. The growing
fleet of USSCo. ships became iconic expressions of New Zealand's

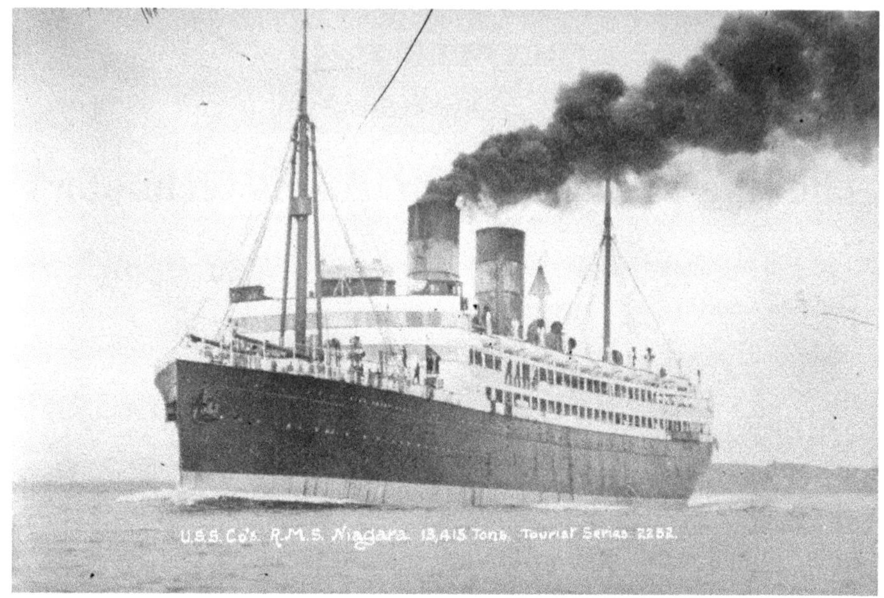

5   RMS *Niagara*

maturing identity as a modern maritime power in the South Pacific. Connecting British ports within and across this ocean basin, they were also the physical and symbolic expression of imperial kinship. Navigating these various and at times competing loyalties, shipowners hoped to foster amongst the travelling public a strong sense of identification with their vessels, particularly through interior design and choice of names.

Fashioning spaces to arrive at 'perfection'

Vessels in the USSCo.'s fleet never rivalled the largest transatlantic liners in speed, size or interior opulence. The *Niagara* was completely dwarfed by the world's biggest ship in 1913, the German-built, 52,117-ton *Imperator*, 'the colossus of the Atlantic'. Enormous and elaborate ships were prohibitively expensive to build and difficult to run at a profit. James Mills prioritised sensibly designed, economical ships more in keeping with the practical concerns of transporting cargo and comparatively small numbers of passengers within and across the Pacific. But the company could boast many innovations in ship design. The *Rotomahana* (1879) was the first ship in the world built of mild steel, while the *Manapouri* (1882) was the first fitted throughout with incandescent electric lighting. The *Loongana* (1904) was the first deep-sea turbine steamer built by any company while, as noted, the *Niagara* (1913) was the first ship registered with the Board of Trade to burn oil as well as coal. USSCo. officials valued such innovations as a way to popularise the company 'not only in the eyes of Australians but also in the eyes of the world'.[3]

From the time of its establishment the USSCo. worked very closely with the shipbuilders William Denny and Brothers of Dumbarton (Denny's). Mills's standards were exacting. Over time Denny's gained a good appreciation of the specific requirements and features for ships in the southern hemisphere trades. The USSCo. stationed a superintending engineer, John Darling, in Glasgow to oversee building operations on the Clyde. A strong personal and professional relationship of trust developed and the USSCo. had little reason or desire to offer building projects to other shipyards. Yet when Peter Denny, Mills's original collaborator, died in 1895, the close working relationship was strained. Denny's grew increasingly dissatisfied with the USSCo.'s practice of buying near-new freighters for its general cargo trades rather than placing construction orders with the shipyard. A series of technical problems with new steamers created further rifts and in 1897 Darling committed suicide, after battling depression and anxiety, apparently fearful that Mills blamed him for these troubles and would dismiss him. His replacement was Angus Cameron, who held the position of marine superintendent until 1906. From the turn of the century the USSCo. tended to place orders on an individual basis with different shipyards. This was a strategy common to most large shipping companies. Combined with large corporate structures and shipping conferences or rings – a rate-fixing agreement between main competitors in a trade – such practices countered the disruptions of fluctuating and declining rates which made the timing of new building projects problematic.[4]

As operations expanded in the 1890s, Mills recognised the importance of entering impressive steamers, particularly on the prestigious mail routes connecting Australian, New Zealand and North American ports, in order to maintain a leading position and remain competitive. A bad name stuck to a boat, Mills noted, and this underscored the importance 'of a new ship being strong in every respect'. Vessels constructed for the company, as Cameron relayed to Darling in 1896, 'should look smart – we must keep our prestage [*sic*] up for style and speed in all the passenger boats'.[5]

A standardised, international appeal to the wealthy classes developed alongside the connection between national pride and technological innovation. The interiors of liners mirrored the most fashionable styles on land, as ocean-going architecture emerged in the era of late Victorian grand-hotel formality. The idea of the grand hotel was itself comparatively new as the rise of industrial transport on land and sea enabled more people than ever before to travel and lodge abroad. The use of steel in ship construction provided the foundation for balustrade staircases, high ceilings, large public rooms and private suites. Also with extravagant, opulent fittings, each new steamer was likely to be described as a 'floating luxury hotel' or 'floating palace'.[6]

There were two passenger classes: saloon class, which accommodated first- and second-class passengers, and steerage, or third class as it was generally known from the late nineteenth century. Separate entrances, public rooms and deck spaces were designed to keep these classes separate. First class was located in the preferred midship area, while third was found in the forward or aft areas, the less comfortable parts of the ship which were affected more by rough weather at sea. On-board facilities improved as companies competed for passengers. First-class public spaces, including de luxe cabins, saloons, libraries and smoking and music rooms, were styled with Louis XVI and other revival themes, fitted out with dark, polished wood panelling and ornate cream plaster work. Smoking rooms, which were exclusively male spaces, were typically darker, with lighter surroundings favoured for women's areas. Plush upholstery, antique furniture, rugs, ornate carvings, paintings, mirrors and lamps contributed to the overall effect of classically inspired grand-hotel hospitality. These 'floating anthologies of period styles', as John Brinnen puts it, stood as embodiments of past cultural greatness and emblematic achievements of a progressive modern era.[7]

The USSCo. took special note of favourable public comments about its vessels. The impressions of a British war correspondent, Archibald Forbes, were reproduced in a travel guide to New Zealand published by the company in 1888. 'I have not yet seen an Atlantic liner whose state-room accommodation is equal in completeness, prettiness, and comfort to that which the Australasian voyager will find on some of the best of the Union Company of New Zealand's steamers – the *Wairarapa*, for instance, or the *Manapouri*', he reflected. 'Spring mattresses, electric lights, smart and sedulous attendance, perfect cleanliness of linen, airiness, and ample daylight these latter afforded.'[8] Figure 6 juxtaposes the functional, mechanical exterior of the *Wairarapa* with the opulent, cosy interiors of the ladies' boudoir, social hall, smoking room and saloon.

Although the USSCo. provided 'wonderfully comfortable' and 'gorgeously decorated' public rooms, the services of the 'gilder and the sign painter' would not win travellers over, opined an editorial in the

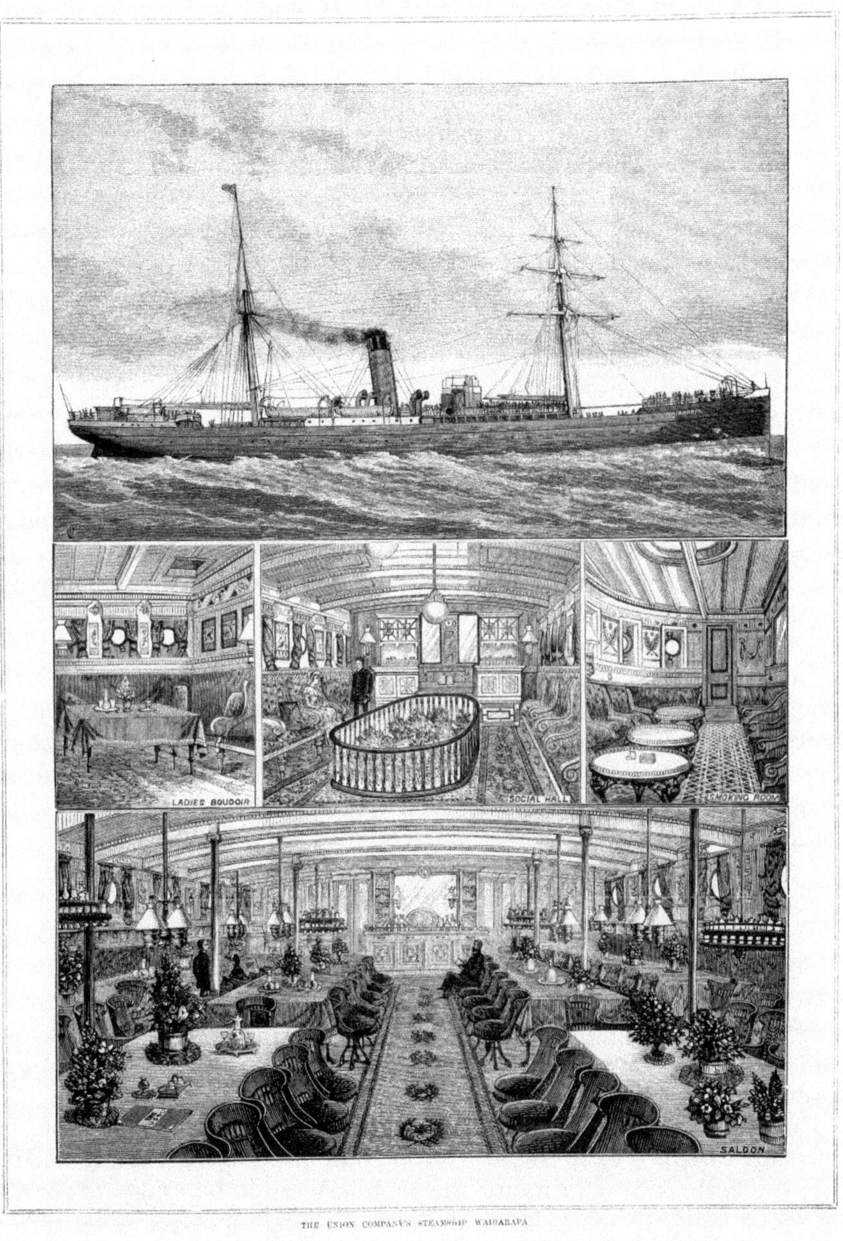

6   The Union Company's steamship *Wairarapa*

Evening Post in 1883. With four people to a cabin, sleeping quarters were crowded and poorly ventilated. Correspondence on the topic was also 'teeming' in the English press at the time, indicating the pervasive challenge of interior design. The newspaper recognised that cost prohibited the provision of single-berth cabins, and in any case more spacious berths would never eliminate other discomforts such as the roll of the sea, the groaning of the screw or the smell of hot grease and oil. Yet the question of accommodation remained one of 'the greatest drawbacks to the comfort of marine travelling'.[9]

These concerns were compounded in the island trades. Company vessels quickly proved unsatisfactory for tropical conditions. The berths were too small and poorly ventilated, which caused crew and passengers discomfort. The holds were unsuitable for the carriage of fresh produce, while deck space for livestock was limited. The USSCo. began building vessels especially suited for its routes into the Pacific. The *Taviuni*, the *Ovalau* and the *Upolu* were built between 1890 and 1891, but the latter two failed to perform and were sold in the early twentieth century. The *Navua* (1904), the *Atua* (1906) and the *Tofua* (1908) followed. More apparatus was fitted for passenger comfort and convenience to streamline services across intercolonial and island trades, including electric fans and printing presses, and a bugler replaced the dinner gong.[10] Yet design difficulties continued: the provision of more roomy accommodation interfered with hatch space, ventilation proved inadequate, and toilet placement ignited debates. Increased wardrobe space for passengers, who required more clothes on longer tropical voyages, as well as more promenade space, also complicated construction.[11]

Company officials evaluated every new ship in great detail for performance, functionality and comfort. They took special note of the finer details of shipboard operations during their own travels. Mills often made reference to the impressions and suggestions of his wife, who could provide valuable first-hand assessments of the amenities provided for women. Each new shipbuilding project presented an opportunity to improve on design and appearance so that 'we shall no doubt some day arrive at perfection'.[12]

Correspondence relating to the specifications for new mail steamers illustrates Mills's exacting attention to detail. He instructed Darling that the bathroom mirrors for the *Moana* were to be long and narrow 'so that a lady can see to her waist'. Smaller mirrors were to be adjustable, for Mills's wife complained of 'the difficulty for women who have to hold their heads to one side when brushing their hair'. Crockery and cutlery, floor tiles and curtains were all finished to precise specifications. Bills of fare on tables should be printed, he directed, rather than handwritten. Handwritten menus on local steamers now appeared 'slovenly' compared to printed ones on the larger ships. By the turn of the century Mills felt it was time that 'all our decent steamers' had their own printing presses. He was also concerned, having recently visited the transpacific steamer the *Monowai* for afternoon tea, that 'the first thing which caught my eye when I sat alongside the Captain today was a second-class dessert spoon'. He hoped such carelessness was not common to all the smart steamers.[13] Even the sound of a steam whistle could be improved. The latest mail steamer sounded 'quite mean' at San Francisco, and Mills insisted that all whistles should be 'the best quality and from America'.[14]

The quality of furnishings from the upholstery department at Denny's was a growing source of annoyance. Mills criticised their workmanship as 'very poor', complaining that 'the cushions are unsatisfactory: they are flabby and have not sufficient hair'. He hoped to update interior fittings and furnishings, but also found fault with Cameron, for his 'great idea is to have something durable, and [he] looks upon red Utrecht velvet . . . as the acme of perfection'. Cameron chose walnut dado for the finishing of the saloon and music room of one new steamer, which Mills thought far too sombre, while 'the upper part is the old story of satin wood and ornamental cabinet work'. He complained to Denny's for 'not breaking away from the beaten path and giving us something new', but they insisted that Cameron, who was seventy years old by this time, would not listen to their suggestions. Mills noted he had to give 'the poor old man several bad half hours'.[15] Mills especially desired 'something novel' in the saloon and music rooms 'as they come most under the eye of the public, and it should be our aim to attract the interest of passengers in this respect, and give them something to talk about'.[16] He admired German marine architecture; Germans were 'miles ahead of British builders'. More than once he instructed Cameron to travel by a German vessel to learn more about construction, equipment and workmanship: 'there are a thousand things to be learned from them with regard to detail'.[17]

In 1905 Mills proposed panels of Maori carving for the music room, saloon and smoking room of new ferry steamers. He consulted with Augustus Hamilton, director of the Colonial Museum in Wellington. Hamilton, a biologist and ethnologist, had spent twenty years writing *Maori Art: The Workmanship of the Maori Race of New Zealand*. He was strongly influenced by the British Arts and Crafts Movement. This movement valued ornament, not as 'mere' decoration, but as the appropriate and 'natural' application of art. Hamilton believed Maori art could play an important role in 'every-day colonial life', lending itself to a 'national characteristic'.[18]

Mills did not want an entire scheme of Maori carving, 'as it would be too sombre and difficult to keep clean', and suggested a series of carved panels to be done 'as far as possible without fault'.[19] He had the renowned mixed-race carver Jacob Heberley in mind, yet Heberley died in 1906 before the project commenced. The USSCo. placed notices in local newspapers requesting expressions of interest. Several men responded, one being the nephew and protégé of the late carver. Others were Europeans who either lived near Maori settlements and had observed the techniques, or had studied carvings in other places and copied designs.[20] The project was eventually abandoned because of the costs and logistics involved. Hamilton was preoccupied with overseeing the construction of the model Maori *pa* (fortified village) at the New Zealand International Exhibition to be held in Christchurch over the summer of 1906–7. Mills hoped instead to settle for one or two carving specimens, which would be fitted after the arrival of the steamer in New Zealand. He also introduced New Zealand woods for interior panelling as another way of giving new vessels a 'local character'.[21]

From the late nineteenth century, the image of sea travel was slowly transformed from one of discomfort, disease and danger to one of comfort, safety, health and pleasure. The shipboard recreation of land-based comforts cushioned passengers from both the raw oceanic elements and the interior industrial experience. In diverting attention from the surrounding technological situation through wood panelling, upholstery and paintings, shipbuilders imparted a sense of security and reassurance based on the familiar; the gaze turned inwards to the interiors of buildings passengers had temporarily left behind. They could forget they were ever at sea. In this respect steamships transcended their immediate functional purpose. Arthur Davis, creator of the Ritz hotels in London and Paris, also designed the interiors of ocean liners with his French colleague, architect Charles Mewès. When Davis asked the directors of one transatlantic company in 1907, 'why don't you make a ship look like a ship?', they replied that 'the people who use these ships are not pirates; they do not dance hornpipes; they are mostly seasick American ladies, and the one thing they want to forget when they are on the vessel is that they are on a ship at all'.[22] Over time a greater variety of public spaces was introduced so passengers could find more ways to pass the time at sea. An early twentieth-century transatlantic steamer might have included a Turkish bath, a squash court, a gymnasium, an exclusive restaurant and an indoor swimming pool, as well as the traditional smoking and music rooms, library and saloon.

Some commentators, and Joseph Conrad was perhaps the most eloquent opponent, lamented the barriers steamships placed between people and the sea. 'The sea of today', Conrad argued in *An Outcast of the Islands* in 1896, 'is a used-up drudge, wrinkled and defaced by the churned-up wakes of brutal propellers, robbed of the enslaving charm of its vastness, stripped of its beauty, of its mystery and its promise'.[23] Hulks of metal belching black smoke were a rude intrusion into the graceful white-winged world of sail. Alfred St Johnston travelled on an island schooner in the Pacific in the 1870s. He mused: 'I cannot think how people who have both wealth of time and money can travel by noisy, dirty steamers, which by their very din and commotion frighten from them every wonder of the deep, when they could, if they would, *sail* over the great sea and watch it in all the beauty of its calm and the grandeur of its storm.' From the hurricane deck of a crowded steamer the sea lost all charm. Really to know it 'one must live with it; float on it when becalmed, hot, glassy, and clear; or career and bound over it before a gale, when dull-coloured but living, at the wayward will of the winds and of itself. Tear through it with the monotonous "thud-thud" and even pace of time-regulated steamers, and one can never know the ocean.'[24]

Extensive public relations campaigns heralded the launching of larger and larger steamships. Posters, travel guidebooks, exhibitions and shipboard tours recruited popular confidence in steamers, celebrated ocean travel and marshalled support for the large-scale technological projects of the modern industrial nation.[25] Bernhard Rieger probes some of the uncertainty and disquiet about efficacy and safety that mingled with the awe and fascination. Most people had little access to shipbuilding yards and no real sense of the circumstances of liner construction. These massive machines appeared to come from 'nowhere', imparting a sense of temporal rupture to the modern age. To emphasise scale, company advertisements often depicted enormous steamers superimposed over parts of cities, or placed the largest steamers alongside buildings such as skyscrapers and St Peter's Basilica. This helped locate superliners in a longer history of human innovation and ingenuity, and made them less intimidating and more coherent.[26]

The USSCo. enthusiastically seized any opportunity to make a favourable public impression. When the New Zealand Shipping Company's transpacific mail liner, the *Aorangi*, arrived in Sydney in 1897, the company 'made a great display and gave a grand dinner and talked big things about what they were going to do now they had such a magnificent boat as the *Aorangi* on the Vancouver Route'. In response, Mills travelled to Sydney to await the arrival of their own vessel, the *Moana*, on the San Francisco run. As Cameron enthused, 'we ought to go one better, as the saying is, and take the wind clean out of the *Aorangi*'s sails'.[27] A couple of years later Mills enthused that the *Moana* was in excellent order and the captain related that 'it is quite remarkable to what extent the Honolulu people hang back for the *Moana*', even though rival boats left immediately ahead of theirs.[28]

The USSCo. began to place impressive new vessels in the local colonial trades to build up a rapport with the travelling public on both sides of the Tasman. The arrival of the *Loongana*, built for the Melbourne–Tasmania trade in 1904, attracted widespread interest along Australia's eastern seaboard. The USSCo. hosted a luncheon on board for sixty guests and opened the ship to public inspection, charging a small fee in order, Mills reported, 'to keep out the rougher class'. Over 800 prominent men including federal and state politicians, leading businessmen and professionals were also invited on a harbour excursion, the first of its kind hosted by a shipping company. Six hundred men accepted and Mills delighted in the fact that 'it was said on all sides that the gathering was the most representative one that had ever taken place in Melbourne under any circumstances'.[29]

There was long-standing resentment in parts of New Zealand that the company's best boats were placed in the intercolonial trades, which left some ports with the oldest, least efficient and most uncomfortable ships. A Greymouth resident wrote to Mills complaining of the 'shabby' treatment doled out to South Islanders on the west coast, the company sending them old, slow boats with poor passenger accommodation. This was 'disgusting everyone who is compelled to use your ships' and he implored Mills to 'consult the passenger trade which hitherto you have treated as a mere nuisance and subordinated entirely to cargo'.[30] Mills recognised that if the *Loongana* were a success, they would have to enter a ship of similar quality on the ferry service between Lyttelton and Wellington. In 1905 a new vessel, the *Maheno*, was designed to be superior even to the *Loongana*. Cameron felt sure that the introduction of such a vessel would demonstrate that 'the Union Co. is always well to the front in providing for the travelling public'.[31] On its completion, it was recommended that the ship visit Auckland 'so as to show herself off there, as the people there are very jealous of the other ports having the best boats running'. The vessel was described as 'simply a floating palace . . . there has never been anything like her seen in these waters'.[32] The *Maheno* completed the Sydney–Wellington run in an efficient time of seventy hours. The speed was worth celebrating, but it was regrettable that passengers could not spend longer enjoying their novel shipboard surroundings, which included moveable settees in the music room, removing some of the former stiffness of stationary seats, along with the 'cosy corners screened from view, exquisite writing desks, easy chairs, electric heaters'.[33]

These amenities prioritised elite consumption and engaged social fantasies of material luxury and cosmopolitanism. Ornamental opulence did not find its way down to steerage. Berths and amenities for this class of travel showed more of the functional and mechanical parts of the ship. The discomfort and privations travellers experienced on the earliest steamers remained routine, but gradual improvements were made, including the replacement of large open dormitories with cabins.

In the early twentieth century, commentators on occasion projected the evolution of the steamship from floating hotel to floating apartment block or city. As the *Western Pacific Herald* reported, 'if the liner is to be truly marine-metropolitan, the steerage tenement will have to develop with the saloon apartments'.[34] The Cunard Line's *Lusitania* was described by one journalist as 'a floating town', although the article went on to state that 'everything has been designed to look as little like a ship and as much like the Carlton and Ritz as possible', indicating that only elite shipboard spaces were of interest.[35] Urban space in the late nineteenth and early twentieth centuries often figured as an unsettling and contested site of social and political ferment. For this reason Rieger suggests that the 'steamship as city' was a rarer metaphor than the 'floating palace', for the latter more readily restrained concerns among elite travellers about the heterosocial realities of steamer confines and the unwelcome spectre of social tension across and within the separate areas of the ship.[36]

Shipboard spaces for crew seldom figured in the public descriptions of new ocean liners. While the furnaces, cylinders, reciprocating engines and other mechanisms were often described for their technical wonder, it was unusual to read of the living and working conditions of the men who built and operated these vessels, or to see crew members in the photographs and posters of ships which instead emphasised mechanical size and scale.[37] This deflected attention from less than salutary labour conditions on board, particularly in the hot, dark, dangerous confines of the stokehold, a space that ignited debates about the racial suitability of certain men for such work, as I discuss in more detail in following chapters.

Naming ships

Christening ships remains an important maritime tradition, a ritual that bestows a sense of individuality to each vessel. A ship's individuality is of a different quality to that of other modes of mass transport. Trains and aeroplanes are usually best remembered by technological monikers or specific flight or route numbers. 'A ship *is* her name,' concludes

James Hamilton-Paterson, 'right to the bottom and beyond, connoting a moment of history as much as a vague locus on the seabed'.[38]

The symbolic power of ship names can be charted across a range of maritime epochs. French and British ships that entered Pacific waters during the eighteenth century were exemplars of European scientific enterprise. James Cook's lavishly funded voyages took place on vessels whose names referenced their heavy material and cultural freight: *Endeavour*, *Resolution*, *Adventure* and *Discovery*. The ships of the French explorer La Pérouse were named after scientific instruments: *L'Astrolabe* (the astrolabe) and *La Boussole* (the magnetic compass), while Nicolas Baudin's ships were known by names of scientists, *Le Géographe* (the geographer) and *Le Naturaliste* (the naturalist). These vessels did not simply transport Enlightenment scientists to the South Seas, but were scientific instruments in their own right.[39]

Cunard's *Mauretania* and *Lusitania* recalled Roman provinces, connecting 'the ancient empire with its modern British counterpart'.[40] The Royal Navy's naming policy shifted from classical gods to counties and cities in England, Scotland, Wales and Ireland in the early twentieth century, reflecting its unionist concern to link local, regional and national loyalties. Names also referenced the imperial significance of warships and symbolised the familial links between metropole (*Sovereign*) and colonies (*Good Hope*, *Dominion*, *Commonwealth* and *New Zealand*). When New Zealand commissioned a battle-cruiser in 1910, the *Zealandia* was coined to rename a ship called *New Zealand* and release that name for the new vessel. The Admiralty had declined *Maori*, suggested by the New Zealand High Commissioner and the Governor General, as it 'was not prepared to name a warship after an aboriginal people'.[41] Reasons for this are unclear and perhaps reflected a reluctance to vaunt the martial qualities of indigenous subjects; however from its inception the USSCo. chose Maori names for its steamers.

One director initially suggested the *City of Dunedin* and the *City of Auckland* for the first two ships, yet Mills did not like long names as they were awkward to write.[42] Other shipping companies already monopolised Maori names of rivers and mountains so USSCo. ships were named after lakes, the first two being the *Hawea* and the *Taupo*: 'They are, I think, pretty, soft names, and appropriate', Mills reflected.[43] The policy broadened at the turn of the century, with cargo vessels given names beginning with 'K' or 'W', and passenger vessels' names beginning with 'M'. This process was somewhat arbitrary, with words simply chosen if not yet appropriated for other ships in accordance with Board of Trade regulations. In general, names did not typically refer to the seascape or the literal space of the ship, but were emblematic of New Zealand and reinforced the steamship as a national icon.

Company directors consulted dictionaries and public men with knowledge of Maori language and culture when deciding on new names. F. W. Riemenschnieder, a former native interpreter in the House of Representatives who took an ongoing interest in USSCo. affairs, supplied a list of steamer names and their translations for a public pamphlet printed in 1901. Letters from members of the public with suggestions and newspaper commentary about the meanings and pronunciations of various words attests to a level of public interest in this naming policy.[44] On two occasions Mills requested that Richard Seddon choose names for new steamers that were destined for his West Coast home electorate. There was an occasional attempt to consult with Maori to ascertain the meanings of words, although this seemed to be more of an afterthought than standard practice. Before cabling one name to the Board of Trade, Charles Holdsworth instructed the company secretary, Thomas Whitson, to 'ascertain from [a] Maori scholar say Dr Pomare [prominent politician and health reformer] if the word is a Maori one'.[45]

In 1908 directors proposed renaming their cadet-training ship the *Dartford* as *Aotearoa*. Whitson regarded this name as too long and preferred instead a word that was 'short, euphonious, and appropriate'.[46] 'Euphonious', an adjective frequently used in this context, suggests that favoured words sounded good and were not challenging for non-indigenous speakers to pronounce. Steamer names might be 'strange to look at', an editorial in the company's short-lived literary magazine the *Red Funnel* reflected, but they 'are easy to pronounce, and sound sweetly to the ear when the accent falls on the right place'.[47]

The as yet unnamed *Niagara* was the second of two company vessels built in 1912. The first was destined as the sister ship of the *Maori* on the domestic inter-island route between Lyttelton and Wellington. Mills suggested *Pakeha* (white man), *Rangatira* (man of high rank) or *Wahine* (woman) as possible names.[48] Holdsworth agreed with *Pakeha*, and informed Mills that 'indeed, the public have already settled that her name is to be "Pakehi"!' The Board of Trade, however, declined this choice as it was already in use by another shipping company. Another suggestion was *Ruakawa*, but finding a reliable definition for the word proved difficult. Holdsworth 'turned up the authorities' but could not find anything. A similar word, *Raukawa*, appeared in one history as the name for Cook Strait, 'but we could not get confirmation of this'. Further research indicated the word had another meaning of 'an odoriferous shrub'.[49] Whitson suggested *Maronui*, which he translated as 'the wife of an absent Maori'. As the two ships would rarely be in port together it seemed an appropriate choice.[50] Management eventually chose *Wahine* for the new ferry.

As maritime trades expanded across the Tasman Sea and into the Pacific, the choice of steamer names broadened to embrace this sense of transnational and regional connectivity. Ships were sometimes given Australian Aboriginal names, while a new series of vessels built especially for the tropical trades were named after islands in the Pacific. The company sought advice on Aboriginal words for steamers in the intercolonial trades from Professor Baldwin Spencer, 'who is the greatest authority here on native words in Australia', and also consulted Joseph Milligan's 1890 vocabulary on Tasmanian dialects. *Ponrabbel*, a native name for the Tamar River, was 'not by any means appropriate' for a new steamer, unlike *Loongana* 'meaning swift. It sounds very softly and would, I think, suit for the new turbine,' noted the Tasmanian manager in 1903. Following the purchase of a vessel named the *Port Kingston*, one manager suggested it be renamed *Ringarooma*, 'this being an Australian name might propitiate the Commonwealth people'.[51]

Steamers to Fiji were christened after islands in that group: *Taviuni* (a misspelling of Taveuni) and *Ovalau*. The *Navua* (1904), *Atua* (1906) and *Tofua* (1908) followed. Both the Governor of German Samoa, Dr Wilhelm Solf ('admittedly the best Samoan scholar not excepting the chiefs'), and a Wesleyan missionary were concerned that *Atua*, meaning ancestral spirits as well as the Christian God, was as inappropriate a ship's name as 'God' or 'The Almighty' would be in the eyes of native English speakers. Mills regretted the choice, but by the time their concerns were raised it was too late to reverse the decision.[52]

Management chose a Maori name, *Makura*, for the first vessel designed exclusively for the Canadian Australian Line in 1908, for this appeared to be the closest Maori equivalent to 'All Red'. The word was an appropriate suggestion of 'loyalty and kinship between the United Kingdom and the oversea[s] colonies'.[53] On Australia's withdrawal from contract renegotiations in 1911, the USSCo. decided to acknowledge its partnership with Canada by choosing a Canadian name for the new transpacific liner. Maori names now seemed too parochial and less reflective of the company's globalising interests: as Holdsworth commented, 'I have realised lately that there is a drawback in the company making too much of our New Zealand connection.'[54] Adopting names from other places established the company's legitimacy in new trades, enhancing the recognition and popularity of its steamers amongst a cosmopolitan travelling public. The elision of 'New Zealand' from the company's title, shortened to the 'Union Company' or the 'Union Line', also reflected such sentiments.[55] As the *Red Funnel* put it, 'in its nomenclature the Company has a graceful way of paying a compliment to the places with which its steamers trade'.[56]

The company's Vancouver manager, J. C. Irons, approached Pauline Johnson, 'a learned Indian Chieftainess', for indigenous Canadian words that might suit the new transpacific steamer. Mills deemed her suggestions, which included *Ojistoh* and *Karahkontye*, 'out of the question'. They were difficult to spell and pronounce and were 'so little in harmony with the softer New Zealand names'. Irons noted that all the easily pronounced indigenous words were currently taken by other companies. He coined some names, including *Canaustral*, and attempted to make a word by combining the first letters of the names of company directors, 'but there are too many R's at my disposal'.[57]

While Maori words spoke too overtly of New Zealand, words drawn from other places were filtered through the same criteria: they had to be easily pronounced and sound agreeable to native English speakers. Other suggestions included *Calgary*, *Ottawa*, *Sicamous*, *Rimouski* and *Winnipeg*. Mills believed *Calgary* could be translated as 'a patch of scrub'. Geographical irrelevancy and denotative ambiguity precluded the choice of *Rimouski*: 'the place is so far east and . . . it seems to suggest a Polish Jew rather than Canada'. Mills proposed *Sicamous* for the new steamer even though it was 'rather suggestive of a bad time at sea'. This choice received bad press at head office (corrupted as 'sick-a-mess'), with an even worse reception predicted from the travelling public. Moreover, Irons commented that the word was 'not thought of much locally'. After finally deciding to revert to a Maori choice, the Melbourne-based Canadian Trade Commissioner suggested a few words that he believed immediately spoke of Canada. One of these, *Niagara* ('thunderer of the waters'), appealed to Mills. As an iconic landmark, the Niagara Falls was symbolic of the power and grandeur of the new steamer.[58]

In discussing names for a sister ship a few years later, Mills preferred an Australian name, but Australia's participation in the mail contract was still uncertain. Finding a 'pleasant sounding' word was also likely to cause problems, especially as *Canberra* was already taken. Mills then proposed a New Zealand name, *Aotearoa*, 'a fine and representative name', although it was also difficult to pronounce and 'I dare say the public would shorten it into "A-te-roa"'. He thought the abbreviation might work: 'I dare say there would be some criticism for a while about our mutilating the native name of the Dominion, but this would soon be forgotten.' Mills also sought a Maori word for the Sutherland Falls, the highest waterfall in New Zealand, and consulted Dr Pomare, who in turn consulted some 'old Natives'.[59] Yet before it entered service for the company, the ship was requisitioned in the First World War as the *Avenger*. Had it survived the war, it was to be renamed the *Aorangi* ('cloud piercer', the highest mountain in New Zealand), a fitting complement to the *Niagara* as an iconic natural landmark.[60]

Maoriland at sea

Scholars have concluded that 'the prominence of indigenous reference' in the emergence of a national consciousness in New Zealand from the late nineteenth century has been 'unique'.[61] The years between the 1880s and the First World War marked a kind of ongoing 'identity crisis' in New Zealand. *Pakeha*, the white settlers of predominantly British heritage, appeared collectively to pause and take stock, looking back on decades of rapid and tumultuous change, back to 'Old New Zealand', and towards the future of the modernising nation. The number of native-born settlers now exceeded immigrants. They increasingly sought ways to bridge their inheritance from Britain with the influences of a new home. 'Having achieved material sufficiency,' Jane Stafford and Mark Williams suggest, 'the country was looking to accumulate cultural capital'.[62]

Writers, composers and promoters frequently referred to New Zealand as 'Maoriland' at this time, not in the sense that the country properly belonged to Maori – that it was literally Maori land – but, rather, that it was a land inhabited by settlers who were now comfortable enough to self-identify as 'New Zealanders', borrowing from those they had supplanted. Maori were physically displaced as the settler population grew and encroached ever further on to their territory. Many commentators were also convinced that the indigenous population was under threat of extinction. In the face of physical marginalisation and imagined disappearance, *Pakeha* simultaneously recalled Maori through words, images and symbols, reinventing 'timeless' indigenous traditions on the site of their loss. By invoking the primitive, *Pakeha* manufactured for themselves a past and in turn a more secure, if sentimentalised, attachment to place. Paradoxically, this localised nostalgia was also forward-looking; it expressed a desire for change, progress and modernity.[63]

The decorative features of Maoriland included an enthusiasm for indigenous nomenclature and material culture. Names for some natural features and settlements were introduced from Britain, but Maori words were also recognised and preserved, if unevenly, in local usage, creating a layered and multivocal landscape.[64] A trend also emerged to christen European homes and significant public buildings with indigenous names. Some settlers extended this borrowing or appropriation to their domestic interiors, decorating rooms with

Maori curios or carving designs on mantelpieces, door frames, posts and pieces of furniture.[65]

This borrowing drew on the conventions of romanticism, but as Stafford and Williams note, were also 'filtered through colonial ethnology to give it an air of authenticity and of ownership'.[66] Ethnologist James Herries Beattie denounced the *Pakeha* practice of bestowing 'fictitious' Maori names on parts of the country, particularly where genuine indigenous names were displaced by words 'concocted in a modern office with the aid of a Maori dictionary'. He was less averse to coining native names for houses and farms, for the two practices 'are very different. One is public, and the other private. One goes on a map where people think it is a genuine Maori place-name, the other is on a private property and the supposition is that it was an individual selection and privately given'.[67] Similar sentiments were expressed in parliamentary debates over the Designation of Districts Bill, introduced in 1894 to resolve inconsistent names for towns and settlements throughout the colony. Some members complained about the 'vulgar vanity' of naming places in honour of local officials, while others felt it would be better to introduce historical English names 'which would remind the people they were part of a great empire'. The Member for Northern Maori, Hone Heke, objected to the manufacture of indigenous names. *Monowai*, a lake name and the name of a transpacific mail steamer, was, he pointed out, a mixture of Latin and Maori.[68]

One can understand the naming and fitting out of ships within this broader colonial practice of deploying idealised symbols of indigeneity in white settler nation-building. Unlike homes and other domestic buildings, the USSCo. steamers were public spaces. They made and were a part of colonial territory. The choice of Maori names and panelling in native wood expressed something of local development and aspirations, transforming or localising the more generic industrial products of Scottish ship yards.

Company officials were concerned with authenticity and accuracy. This demonstrated a certain respect for Maori culture and heritage, linking an idealised and romanticised indigenous past to a technologically progressive future. But this was always a highly selective process, and commercial imperatives informed and filtered these choices. The USSCo. wanted to project the 'right' image, one that would appeal to the travelling public and kindle a sense of popular attachment to and identification with its steamer fleet; hence an emphasis on short, pronounceable, euphonious and appropriate Maori names. This also made verbal and written business correspondence more efficient. In the Australian context, as Paul Carter argues, privileging euphonious or 'nice-sounding' words emptied them of contextual meaning.

They became little more than 'a record of environmental sounds'. There are echoes of this in Canada too, where the enthusiasm of Euro-Canadian settlers for indigenous nomenclature in the late nineteenth century related more to the 'musicality of polysyllabic words', than to the indigenous meanings and histories.[69] The USSCo. archival trail revealed that the selection of steamer names was often a tentative, confusing endeavour. Ambiguous definitions were unsettling, particularly when provided by European authorities, and highlighted a measure of uncertainty about New Zealand's bicultural landscape.

When viewed from the deck of a USSCo. mail liner plying across the Pacific, this embrace or co-option of an imagined native world must be understood as a way not only to place British settlers on New Zealand soil, but also to articulate New Zealand's place in a regional and globalising setting. My earlier account of port rivalries illustrated that any collective national interests in maritime networking easily fragmented into narrower, local loyalties. And, at particular times, more expansive concerns overshadowed national ones. Holdsworth's disquiet about an overt identification between the company's ships and the nation demonstrates that these vessels were not only the vectors but also the objects of transoceanic exchange. Steamers were shared by a transnational travelling public. As USSCo. operations expanded in the first decades of the twentieth century, the broadening naming policy charts the modifications deemed necessary to locate these prestige items in the entangled trajectories of nascent nationalism, transnational community and imperial kinship.

Notes

1 McLean, *Southern Octopus*, 136; *Auckland Star* (8 May 1913), cited in Keith Gordon, *Deep Water Gold: The Story of R.M.S. Niagara: The Quest for New Zealand's Greatest Shipwreck Treasure* (Whangarei: SeaROV Technologies, 2005), 40.

2 *Vancouver News Advertiser* (28 May 1913) cited in Hamilton, 'The all-red route', 76.

3 HC, Cameron Family Papers, MS 1046, Box 13, Cameron to Strang, 4 August 1904.

4 McLean, *The Southern Octopus*, 150–4; Kubicek, 'The proliferation and diffusion of steamship technology', 106–7.

5 HC, Cameron Family Papers, MS 1046, Box 19, Mills to Cameron, 24 August 1896; Box 16, Cameron to Darling, 1 September 1896.

6 Philip Dawson, *The Liner: Retrospective and Renaissance* (London: Conway, 2005), 10, 52–3.

7 John Malcolm Brinnen, 'The decoration of ocean liners: rules and exceptions', *The Journal of Decorative and Propaganda Arts*, 15, Transportation theme issue (1990), 42; Lorraine Coons and Alexander Varias, *Tourist Third Cabin: Steamship Travel in the Interwar Years* (New York: Palgrave Macmillan, 2003), 172.

8 Insert on back cover of *New Zealand, the Wonderland of the World* (Dunedin: USSCo., 1888).

9 'Steamship accommodation', *Evening Post* (14 April 1883), 2.

10 *Western Pacific Herald* (2 September 1904).

11 HC, USSCo. Records, AG-292-005-001/069, Mills to Holdsworth, 1 September 1903; AG-292-005-001/085, Mills to shipbuilder, 9 October 1907 and Mills to Holdsworth, 22 May 1907.
12 HC, Cameron Family Papers, MS 1046, Box 9, Mills to Cameron, 31 October 1904.
13 HC, USSCo. Records, AG-292-005-001/046, Mills to Holdsworth, 15 June 1899.
14 HC, Cameron Family Papers, MS 1046, Box 7, Mills to Darling, 5 September 1896 and Box 19, Mills to Cameron, 24 August 1896.
15 HC, USSCo. Records, AG-292-005-001/069, Mills to Holdsworth, 11 September 1903.
16 *Ibid.*, Mills to Cameron, 22 February 1904.
17 HC, Cameron Family Papers, MS 1046, Box 9, Mills to Cameron, 31 October 1904.
18 Hamilton, cited in Anna K. C. Petersen, 'The European use of Maori art in New Zealand homes, c.1890–1914', in Barbara Brookes (ed.), *At Home in New Zealand: Houses, History and People* (Wellington: Bridget William Books, 2000), 64.
19 Wellington City Council Archives (WCCA), USSCo. Records, Box 157, Hamilton to Mills, 16 March 1906; HC, USSCo. Records, AG-292-005-001/079, Mills to Holdsworth, 16 April 1906.
20 WCCA, USSCo. Records, AF080, various letters, August 1906.
21 HC, USSCo. Records, AG-292-005-001/081, Mills to Holdsworth, 14 August 1906.
22 Cited in Richard Prior (ed.), *Ocean Liners: The Golden Years* (London: Tiger Books International, 1993), 14.
23 Joseph Conrad, *An Outcast of the Islands* (Oxford: Oxford University Press, rev. edn, 2002 [1896]), 14.
24 Alfred St Johnston, *Camping Among Cannibals* (London: Macmillan and Co., 1883), 8.
25 Bernhard Rieger, *Technology and the Culture of Modernity in Britain and Germany, 1890–1945* (Cambridge: Cambridge University Press, 2005), 162–3.
26 *Ibid.*, 34, 43.
27 HC, Cameron Family Papers, MS 1046, Box 6, Cameron to Strang, 12 May 1897.
28 HC, USSCo. Records, AG-292-005-001/046, Mills to Holdsworth, 5 July 1899.
29 HC, Cameron Family Papers, MS 1046, Box 9, Mills to Board of Directors, 24 October 1904.
30 *Ibid.*, Box 18, R. S. Hawkins to Mills, 1 April 1903.
31 *Ibid.*, Box 9, Mills to Cameron, 19 September 1904; Box 13, Cameron to Irvine, 21 January 1905, Cameron to Sleigh, 11 February 1905.
32 *Ibid.*, Box 11, D. M. Craig, superintending engineer (Sydney), to Mills, 13 November 1905.
33 *Red Funnel*, 1:6 (January 1906), 552.
34 *Western Pacific Herald* (9 July 1907).
35 *Western Pacific Herald* (3 September 1907).
36 Rieger, *Technology and the Culture of Modernity*, 164.
37 *Ibid.*, 173.
38 James Hamilton-Paterson, *Seven Tenths: The Sea and its Thresholds* (London: Hutchinson, 1992), 260.
39 Richard Sorrenson, 'The ship as a scientific instrument in the eighteenth century', *Orisis*, 2nd Series: Science in the Field, 11 (1996), 221–2, 227.
40 Stephen Fox, *The Ocean Railway: Isambard Kingdom Brunel, Samuel Cunard and the Revolutionary World of the Great Atlantic Steamships* (London: Harper Perennial, 2003), 402.
41 Jan Rüger, 'Nation, empire and navy: identity politics in the United Kingdom, 1887–1914', *Past and Present*, 185 (2004), 170–1, 175.
42 Cited in Gavin McLean, 'Naming the "Niagara"', *New Zealand Marine News*, 36:2 (1986), 47.
43 HC, USSCo. Records, AG-292-004-001/002, Mills to Denny, 29 October 1874.
44 For example, 'Names of vessels', *Grey River Argus* (15 November 1883), 2; '"Manipori" or "Manapouri"', *Grey River Argus* (16 October 1891), 4; 'Names of the Union Co.'s steamers', *Otago Witness* (2 October 1907), 81.
45 HC, USSCo. Records, AG-292-004-004/010, Holdsworth telegram, 6 February 1909.

46 *Ibid.*, AG-292-005-001/086, Whitson to Holdsworth, 30 October 1908.

47 'A modest beginning', *Red Funnel*, 1:1 (August 1905), 89.

48 HC, USSCo., AG-292-005-001/097, Mills to Holdsworth, 29 September 1911.

49 *Ibid.*, AG-292-004-003/002, Holdsworth to Mills, 18 March and 2 April 1912; AG-292-004-003/003, 7 May 1912.

50 WCCA, USSCo. Records, AF080:9:12, Whitson to Holdsworth, 2 May 1912.

51 HC, USSCo. Records, AG-292-005-003/015, David Mills to Whitson, 9 September 1904; WCCA, USSCo. Records, AF080:9:12, Henderson to Whitson, 31 August 1903; HC, USSCo. Records, AG-292-005-001/103, Strang to Holdsworth, 22 August 1911.

52 WCCA, USSCo. Records, AF080:9:12, Irvine to Whitson, 9 March 1905 and Mills to Whitson, 6 March 1906.

53 'New steamers for the Union Company', *Otago Witness* (8 January 1908), 66.

54 HC, USSCo. Records, AG-292-005-004/137, Holdsworth to Mills, 19 December 1911.

55 Appointed manager for Tasmania after the company bought out local opposition in 1891, Holdsworth respected local sensibilities in repainting the Hobart office with 'Union Line of Steamers', rather than 'Union Steam Ship Company of New Zealand'. See Holdsworth to Mills, 22 April 1892, cited in McLean, *The Southern Octopus*, 55.

56 'A modest beginning', *Red Funnel*, 1:1 (August 1905), 89.

57 Johnson, a performer and writer of English and Mohawk heritage, is remembered for her commitment to connecting indigenous pasts to an inclusive national future in Canada. For a biography, see Veronica Strong-Boag and Carole Gerson, *Paddling Her Own Canoe: The Times and Texts of E. Pauline Johnson (Tekahionwake)* (Toronto: University of Toronto Press, 2000), 186; also HC, USSCo. Records, AG-292-005-001/098, Mills to Holdsworth, 16 February 1912; AG-292-005-004/114, Irons to Mills, 27 January 1912.

58 Commentary on these suggestions can be found in McLean, 'Naming the "Niagara"', 49; HC, USSCo. Records, AG-292-005-001/103, Aiken to Holdsworth, 19 June 1912; AG-292-005-004/114, Irons to Holdsworth, 11 June 1912; AG-292-005-004/124, Ross to Holdsworth, 6 August 1912.

59 HC, USSCo. Records, AG-292-005-004/141, Mills to Holdsworth, 6 May 1914; WCCA, USSCo. Records, AF080:9:12, 10, 11, 13 and 31 July 1914.

60 HC, USSCo. Records, AG-292-005-004/139, Holdsworth to Directors, 1 July 1915.

61 Nicholas Thomas, *Possessions: Indigenous Art / Colonial Culture* (London: Thames and Hudson, 1999), 106. See also Margaret Werry, 'Tourism, Ethnicity and the Performance of New Zealand Nationalism, 1889–1914' (PhD dissertation, Northwestern University, 2001).

62 Jane Stafford and Mark Williams, *Maoriland: New Zealand Literature 1872–1914* (Wellington: Victoria University Press, 2006), 18.

63 *Ibid.*, 11.

64 Giselle Byrnes, '"A dead sheet covered with meaningless words?" Place names and the cultural colonisation of Tauranga', *New Zealand Journal of History*, 36: 1 (2002), 18–19, 27; Hong-Key Yoon, *Maori Mind, Maori Land: Essays on the Cultural Geography of the Maori People from an Outsider's Perspective* (Berne: Lang, 1986). See also Peter Gibbons, 'Cultural colonisation and national identity', *New Zealand Journal of History*, 36:1 (2002), 5–17.

65 Petersen, 'The European use of Maori art', 57–72.

66 Stafford and Williams, *Maoriland*, 11.

67 HC, James Herries Beattie, Notebook entitled 'Maori ethnology. Nondescript Maori topics', PC-0189, 'Fictitious Maori placenames' [n.d.] and 'Picking Maori names for houses and farms' [n.d.].

68 'What's in a name?', *Timaru Herald* (17 September 1894), 4.

69 Paul Carter, 'Travelling blind: a sound geography', *Meanjin*, 51:2 (1992), 440; Strong-Boag and Gerson, *Paddling Her Own Canoe*, 186.

PART II

Aboard

CHAPTER THREE

Crew culture: maritime men in an iron world

On 1 April 1885 Annie Young walked down to the wharf at Circular Quay in Sydney to await the arrival of the USSCo. steamer *Rotomahana*. On board was her lover, William Colquhoun, the first officer of this intercolonial vessel. Young had given birth to their first child in Auckland the previous year, but had since moved to Sydney in order, as she put it, 'to hide my shame'. Colquhoun had promised to marry her when he 'could afford to do so', but 'now he can he wont do so'. On this occasion she went to meet him because of his promise of £10 'to keep her altogether away from him'.

The ship docked on time and, after the passengers had disembarked and the general rush subsided, Colquhoun approached her, but he had also 'fetched a donkey in the shape of a gentleman called the ship's doctor' to join him in confronting her. Colquhoun had questioned the child's parentage before, the baby having been born six weeks earlier than expected. This time he invoked the spectre of interracial mixture to challenge paternity. After looking at the child, the doctor declared it did not resemble Colquhoun very much, and could not, in fact, be his for its 'curling brown hair and brown eyes' marked the child as a 'half caste'.

Young was incensed. A week later she penned a letter to James Mills. 'I hope you will excuse me for addressing you', she began, 'but I think it write [*sic*] to let you know what sort of men you have in your employment. There is one . . . and he is not fit to be a road sweeper for he is no man.' After outlining her situation, she insisted: 'don't think that I want you to ask any favours for me and my babe far from it only that I said I would show him up he is so mean'. Moreover, 'that gentle-man that goes by the name of doctor . . . I think he had no write [*sic*] to interfere in what did not concern him'.[1]

Mary Blair's problems were different. A widow in Wellington, she was increasingly anxious about the welfare of her large family during the early months of 1892. After her husband's death, her eldest son David became her mainstay, giving her 'all his earnings to educate and bring up the others'. For the last three and a half years he had worked as an engineer in various company steamers. But, at the age of twenty-seven, she was worried he was stagnating. Technology changed, it seemed, with every new vessel that arrived at local ports from the Scottish ship yards. After talking to engineers and others, she feared he was losing his best years and gaining no experience in the new steamers with their more modern machinery. Feeling 'so grieved to see him no further on after so many years of hard work', she summoned courage to share her concerns with Mills. Like other parents who wrote seeking assistance, she hoped he would put in a word and 'help David on'. Mills acted promptly. Within a fortnight David was promoted. In writing her thanks, Blair noted that 'it adds to the many favours and obligations I already owe the Union Company & gratefully remember'.[2]

These letters reveal two very different gendered relationships between the world of the ship and the world ashore. Young's situation sets up an uneasy and tenuous connection between the two, whereas Blair confidently articulates their mutual dependence. Her son's wages find life in a wider familial context; this is their proper destination. Young had to fight for access to such resources. In her experience the steamship company harboured an irresponsible man, segregated from his domestic obligations on shore. Her complaint reveals less admirable aspects of crew culture on board, with men standing in solidarity, guarding each other against encroachments and interference in their seafaring life. This incident aligns with deep-rooted perceptions of the seafaring profession as one of masculine independence, adventure and freedom, an escape from women and family.

In the age of steam the legacies of an earlier maritime age shaped the gendered nature of workplace relations afloat and domestic relations ashore, yet the rise of large shipping companies and managerial capitalism also forged new expectations about their interdependence. Adopting a double vision here, I explore the internal complexity of the world afloat, examining the changes steam wrought to shipboard organisation, leadership and discipline. Stepping back from these micro-geographies to view the ship from shore reveals some of the broader changes in the relationship between humanity and the sea in a modern era of nation- and empire-building.

'A curious machine': the way of a ship

Work at sea traditionally entailed a division of labour, a regimented labour process, continuous shiftwork organised through a watch system, close supervision and harsh discipline. The rise of capitalism introduced a more rigid division of labour, a reduction in tasks for each division, increased specialisation and closer supervision. This shift took hold before the dominance of industrial technology, but increasing mechanisation infused the labour process with more order, regularity and intensity. Where wind was once liberating, the advent of steam kept the ship always at work.[3]

Three departments staffed steamships: officers and seamen on deck; engineers, firemen, coal-trimmers and greasers in the engine-room or stokehold; stewards, stewardesses and cooks in the providore or catering department. Each department had its own strict hierarchies. The chief officer (first mate), chief engineer and chief steward wielded control over their respective crew, while the captain (master) had primary responsibility for the entire management of the ship. Many crew members were now engaged in jobs not traditionally found on sailing ships such as stoking fires and engineering. As an example of crew size, the USSCo.'s 1727-ton *Rotomahana* typically carried a crew of sixty. Along with the master, three mates, the chief engineer and three engineers, there were fourteen able-bodied seamen (ABs), one boy, a carpenter, lamp-trimmer, purser and clerk, six firemen, eight trimmers, nine stewards, one stewardess, two saloon waiters, five cooks, one pantryman and a butcher.

The transition from sail to steam modified the ship as a labour site and the nature of workplace culture. As noted in chapter 1, shipowning gradually became a specialised field of business and large steamship enterprises produced more formal and bureaucratic operations. Mills's early career was typical: having first acquired experience in another firm, he then entered the local trades on a small scale and experienced incremental growth, built up through an expanding network of interpersonal ties and a solid public profile.[4] In the USSCo., he created a centralised, tiered management structure; by 1905 his chain of command embraced twenty-seven branches and sub-branches throughout New Zealand, Australia and the Pacific. As New Zealand's largest private-sector employer, he employed 2,200 men afloat and 460 ashore (not including wharf labour), with an annual wage bill of £600,000.[5] The Dunedin head office sat at the pinnacle of this shipping empire, supported by both a local and a London-based Board of Directors, with Mills firmly convinced that 'the more power in the hands of the manager . . . the better'.[6]

Mills implemented strict and uniform codes of conduct across all of the company's operations and demanded unwavering loyalty to 'the Service'. The first was his 1878 *Instructions to Masters*. This code soon expanded, setting out detailed instructions to all crew. It was known colloquially as the 'Red Book'. These regulations replaced customary knowledge and labour relations on board ship and narrowed officers' discretionary powers. The establishment of New Zealand's Marine Department in 1877, the rise of trade unions from the 1880s (which were relatively weak and fragmented until the early twentieth century), and the introduction of the state-controlled industrial arbitration system at the beginning of 1895, ensured that pay, food, accommodation, hours of work and other related employment conditions were now negotiated by the shipping company, the unions and the state, rather than by captain and crew.

Following British enquiries into safety at sea and the quality of seafarers in the 1830s and 1840s, alongside the repeal of the Navigation Acts in 1849, new laws were implemented in the form of the Mercantile Marine Act 1850 and the Merchant Shipping Act 1854. This legislation, along with later amendments, provided for the certification of masters, mates and engineers, the surveying of ships, and minimum victualling and accommodation standards. The Merchant Shipping Act 1869 granted colonial legislatures the right to establish their own crew certification procedures and the power to regulate their own coasting trades. New Zealand's first domestic Shipping and Seamen's Act 1877 defined the legal responsibilities of employers and employees and outlined penalties for breaches. Acts of 1894 and 1896 set out manning schedules for steamers trading in New Zealand waters. Crew numbers were regulated according to each vessel's horse power or tonnage and all men were paid the colony's ruling rate of wages. Manning schedules were the only instances where colonial maritime legislation diverged from the imperial standard. As such they were proudly regarded as progressive local provisions.[7]

The size, type and trade of each vessel dictated the manning requirements, status and influence of different crew. The USSCo. fleet was organised into three classes: intercolonial and transpacific passenger steamers, coastal passenger steamers, and cargo steamers, with each class further subdivided. Senior crew commanded the highest wages on the first-class steamers, while the lowest wages were reserved for coastal tramp steamers under 200 tons register. By the early twentieth century, masters earned between £21 and £34 per month, depending on steamer classification, chief officers £15–17, and so on down the ranks to ABs who earned £7. Chief engineers earned slightly less than masters, firemen received £9 and trimmers £7. Pursers received between £8 and £16. Masters who served twelve months without an accident were paid a performance bonus of one month's salary. They also received monthly bonuses after long service at the maximum pay.[8] Officers were promoted on the basis of seniority, yet at all times 'ability, zeal, good conduct, and abstinence' weighed with management in making such decisions.[9]

Under steam, the master was transformed from a semi-entrepreneur to a salaried company employee, but he alone was still directly responsible for the ship, the work of its crew and the safety of its passengers. The sanctity of his authority was fundamental to the social and moral economy of the ship.[10] Management could not entrust the running of steamers to less than competent masters, for the efficiency, safety and popularity of vessels rested on their leadership. The master performed a fundamental civic role, working for the state and the travelling public, as well as the shipping company. No commander could afford to be unpopular. One USSCo. captain, Walter Manning, noted in his popular account of crew dynamics, *Below and Above the Water-Line*, that 'personal peculiarities, laxity in manners or conduct, roughness in speech and innumerable small defects in character will disqualify him for command in some classes of vessels'.[11]

Mills's close attention to the finer details of ship design extended to the men in his employ. In 1908 he complained of the bearing of the captain of the *Maheno*, a luxury intercolonial liner: 'It makes me sad to see a man like Neville in command of so fine a ship. He is a bit of a swine, and it makes one feel quite sick to see him gouging his teeth and to hear him making a noise with his mouth when eating. When he laughs too, he seems to bring up so much phlegm that he nearly chokes.'[12] The best men tended to take shore positions and this invariably caused management 'a good deal of disappointment'. Many younger masters, Holdsworth lamented, 'do not seem to possess the qualities we want for commanders of big passenger ships'.[13]

The captain delegated routine contact with deck crew to the chief officer. The 'Red Book' outlined expectations regarding their interactions with subordinates:

> It should be a point with Officers to bear themselves temperately towards their men. All orders should be given firmly and clearly, and implicit obedience exacted, but bullying or harassing of men should be avoided. Competent Officers should never require to have recourse to such practices to make their authority respected, and it must be clearly understood that while the legitimate authority of Officers will be strictly upheld, intemperate language or conduct on their part will meet with disapproval and censure.[14]

Bearing, accent and respectability, rather than threats, abuse or brute force, underpinned the ideal of gentlemanly managerial expertise, an oceanic example of the shift to highly refined and internalised forms of discipline in the industrial age.[15]

Cooperative sociability was necessary for the work of the whole ship, with emphasis placed on efficiency and systems. Men who stayed aloof or caused friction were invariably viewed with suspicion. While management could happily sketch out the most desirable shipboard organisation, they had to count on suitable men, for as Holdsworth put it, 'so often the personal equation governs the whole question'.[16] Negotiating interpersonal relations on board was often a delicate endeavour. As one ship's master wrote to Mills on hearing that his chief steward might be transferred, a 'ship's company is a curious machine and what may have been a success in one vessel may be a failure under other circumstances'. He believed things were working well and it would only take one man to make things miserable.[17]

The company avoided fostering individuality on board ship. When reviewing pay scales for pursers, whose main duties related to receiving, measuring and delivering cargo in port, Holdsworth rejected a suggestion to rank men on the basis of their personal abilities, rather than the trade in which they worked, for it would be 'difficult to avoid invidious distinction'.[18] In this respect steamers were little different from sailing ships where, as Greg Dening has concluded, any concept of the personal or any notion of exclusivity was highly problematic on board the ship as a totalising institution.[19]

Sailors signed legally binding and enforceable articles, or fixed-term employment contracts. These lasted either for the duration of a particular voyage or for a term of six months, the latter generally the case for the USSCo.'s intercolonial and island trades. Seamen's articles embodied an agreement between the master of a vessel and the crew who signed their consent individually. The articles defined the duration of the agreement and the wages and provisions to which crew were entitled. Before signing New Zealand articles as an AB, men required proof (in the form of discharge certificates) of four years' sea-going experience. An amendment in 1909 reduced this period to three years. References were essential for employment. In testimonials attached to ABs' applications, key attributes repeated time and again included that they were attentive, strictly sober, painstaking, reliable, capable, competent, trustworthy and steady.[20] While the USSCo. allowed either party to walk away from the contractual relationship after giving twenty-four hours' notice, punishment was also embedded in the contract. Seafarers faced imprisonment for walking off the job before their articles expired, lost any wages earned on other ships after deserting, and were expected to pay the difference between their own wage and that of a more expensive replacement. In New Zealand the maximum sentence for desertion was reduced from three months to one month in 1903, and in 1909 imprisonment was abolished for those who signed on under New Zealand articles.[21] Capitalist relations of production were increasingly contractual and impersonal, yet the more traditional personal and familial relations and forms of social authority persisted into the early twentieth century, as evidenced by the number of letters from employees or their families in USSCo. archives requesting favourable individual treatment.

Deck-hand labour was reduced and redefined under steam. With complex sail-handling no longer central, deck work now consisted mainly of cleaning, chipping, painting and driving winches – simple, menial and repetitive tasks. The law classed seamen as skilled, given the required three-to-four-year term to reach the status of an AB, yet Mills, along with many others, regarded seamen as unskilled labour.[22] Briefly defined, skill related to knowledge, training and discretion. Discretion referred to the judgement, wisdom and control an individual exercised over the labour process. In an industrial age, discretion and control were increasingly separated from manual labour and concentrated among the most senior crew, as was the conception of a task from its execution. Skill was tied to the mastery of machines and to the authority and power this knowledge afforded. In this way it was possible to regard steamer work as initiating a process of de-skilling for deck crew. Yet seamen still needed a sound knowledge of nautical terms and the various parts and functions of the ship, as well as the ability to work complicated cargo machinery. This level of control and responsibility was not unskilled and as David M. Williams remarks, although 'old-fashioned' seamanship was in decline as a result of these technical changes, 'skill of a very different order was very much in evidence'.[23]

The rise of steam appeared to sound a slow death knell for the science and art of seamanship. 'Old salts' frequently denounced steamer labour as 'half landsmen', or as having 'given up the sea'.[24] Master mariner W. E. Dexter recalled the contempt sailors held for steamship crew whom they regarded as 'renegades':

> They had deserted their first love for the 'flesh-pots'; they had lost their sense of beauty and were content to sail in a 'kettle-bottomed coffee-pot'; they were effete and effeminate, lacking in resource; and in port they were the cynosure of all sailing-ship men, who watched their every movement for mistakes. We heard of the three watches for the officers, four hours on and eight hours off, steam-heated cabins, many-course dinners, and classed steamship men as not fit for a sailor's notice.[25]

In a similar vein, one commentator in the *United States Gazette* in 1877 asserted that 'steam may not have quite emasculated seamanship, but it has made rapid strides in such direction'. Seamanship was a science under sail, 'whatever it may now be'.[26] Sailing men looked upon steamer work as 'drudgery', noted Manning or, as maritime author Frank Bullen put it, seamen were a kind of 'male housemaid'. Such weary, monotonous deck service 'offers no attraction to the hardy manly spirits who naturally turn to the sea', attested Lord Brassey.[27]

There was often a tendency to romanticise and construct a heroic mythology around the dying age of sail. The sea was framed as a site of boldness and virility, the sailor an icon of a tough and hardy masculinity. This gained particular currency in maritime history with the publication of Frederick William Wallace's *Wooden Ships and Iron Men* in 1924.[28] The respective merits of sail- as compared to steam-trained officers were much debated in maritime forums around the turn of the twentieth century. Yet, as one article in the *Nautical Magazine* emphasised in 1911, masters generally found steam-trained men of better quality: 'they are more active owing no doubt to the hurry scurry of steamer life . . . the days of sailing ships are gone never to return'.[29] Williams has examined the long-running debate about the quality, skill and supply of maritime labour in Britain, which spanned some six decades from the mid-nineteenth century. He notes that much of the anxiety was ill founded and generally stemmed from an 'inability to come to terms with a new maritime environment in which labour was both more diffuse and more specialised'.[30]

With the reliance on coal and machinery for power, rather than wind and the white wings of sail, the engine-room was a new space afloat, with a new class of supervisory and manual labour. The engineer was responsible for the routine work connected with boilers and engines. He had to monitor the oil, water, steam and vacuum, and supervise the firemen's work. The occupational and social status of the engineer overlapped. He was drawn, in Manning's words, 'mainly from the middle or higher working classes, intelligent, well-educated, frequently well-read, a skilled mechanic, and often a scientist on his own speciality'. Chief engineers had the 'peculiar demeanour' apparent in all with 'power and mastery over men and things'. Through their seriousness and dignity 'they may be regarded as fitting characters to sustain the human part in the twentieth century epic of "Tools and the Man".'[31]

As the USSCo.'s shipbuilding projects expanded in the early twentieth century, it received many more applications for work from engineers than it had positions. Holdsworth reflected that there seemed to have been 'a great over-production of the young engineer during the last seven to ten years and I do not think I should be exaggerating to say that we have hundreds of applications from young men anxious to go afloat'.[32]

While the captain held supreme authority, 'perfect understanding' with the chief engineer was crucial to the efficient working of the ship. A newspaper cutting slipped into an 1895 edition of the 'Red Book' cautioned that steamers operating with divided responsibility on board, where captain and chief engineer were played off against one another, 'are little hells'.[33] Captains were sensitive to perceived slights. In the early twentieth century there was a shortage of suitably qualified masters on some steamers. The appointment of less qualified men on a lower wage than the chief engineers was unavoidable. This pay disparity was a source of ill feeling among masters who could normally be assured of earning the highest wage on board any steamer.[34]

Other workers below deck included trimmers, who shovelled coal from bunker to furnace and cleaned out the ashes, firemen who stoked the fires, and greasers who lubricated the hot, moving machinery, a task colloquially referred to as 'feeling her over'. An experienced and efficient fireman knew to cast coals evenly across the grates, and to read the way in which they burned and where clinkers, the stony residues of burnt coal, formed. He periodically raked out the cinders and clinkers, stirring up a draught to keep the fires burning cleanly. Inferior coal burned badly, making this task particularly laborious. In rough seas, firemen battled to stay upright as the ship rolled and pitched. This violent motion also threatened to dislodge the towering, grimy walls of coal in the bunkers. During long ocean crossings the 'coal face' rapidly receded and trimmers had to venture ever further back into the dark, cavernous holds to barrow a full load of coal to the firemen. Bunkers were poorly ventilated, the air laden with coal and ash dust. There were only limited attempts to mechanise the delivery of coal from bunker to furnace.[35]

Stokehold crew altered the hierarchy of work and the wage structure afloat. Over the sixty years between 1870 and 1930, the number of deck crew employed on vessels in New Zealand hovered at about 3,000, whereas stokehold crew increased from 200 to 1,000 in the 1890s, and doubled to 2,000 in the decade after 1910.[36] Given their difficult work conditions, firemen enjoyed longer breaks between shifts than deck crew (eight rather than four hours off between each four-hour shift), higher wages, faster promotion and often better food. On certain steamers they were entitled to the remains of the saloon passengers' fare, known as the 'black pot'.[37] Toiling away in the ship's dark, dirty depths, these men were the unseen workers of the steam age. Passengers may have on occasion toured the engine-room and observed the firemen, yet the trimmers were seldom acknowledged. As one worker penned: 'We are not for show or story. We are not for trippers' eyes. We are just the trimmers working in a bit o' Hell's

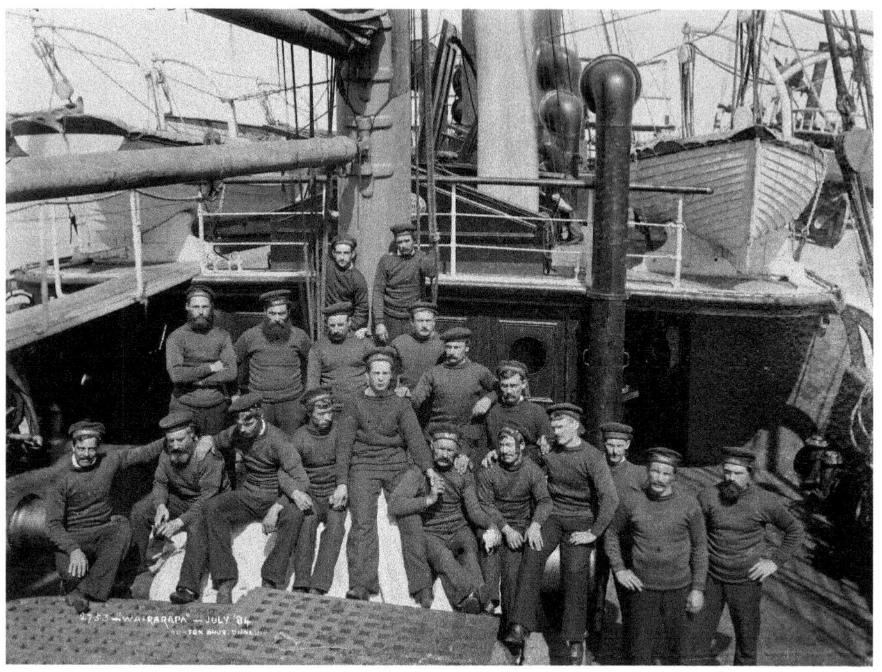

7   *Wairarapa*, July 1884

disguise.'[38] Where Bullen reproduced this hierarchy in his book on the mercantile marine, opening with 'the rise of the master' and closing with a description of the firemen and trimmers, Manning reversed it, devoting his opening chapter to these marginalised and invisible workers.[39]

The deck and the engine departments were entirely separate workplaces and their respective crew seldom interacted, as encapsulated by the saying 'oil and water do not mix'. These divisions were further marked by a racial hierarchy in crewing, as I discuss in the following chapter. USSCo. management aimed to foster good feeling throughout the service and issued a circular to staff setting out that 'all departments should feel that it is to their interest to work together harmoniously for the general good'. The photograph of the *Wairarapa* crew (figure 7), taken by Dunedin photographer Alfred Burton before a cruise though the South Pacific in 1884, communicates something of shipboard camaraderie in the steam age. There is an easy intimacy between the men, an air of relaxed companionship.

In the wake of the 1890 maritime strike, the USSCo. introduced a number of measures to blunt the power of unionisation. In order that all men received 'fair pay for fair work', in 1891 the deck and engine departments were each instructed to appoint one spokesman who could bring any concerns before the captain or chief engineer. This spokesman would be rotated every month, so all crew had the chance to fill the role. Nobody else was entitled to make representations on behalf of crew.[40] Mills also used blacklists to exclude strikers from future employment and introduced a Mutual Benefit Society (disparaged by unionists as the 'Deaf and Dumb Society'), which sailors were expected to join. The membership fees were designed to undermine trade unions, for few men could afford to pay subscriptions to both.[41]

Space, hierarchy and reform

The ship's system of internal boundaries gave spatial expression to the division of labour and the construction of social hierarchies on board. Vessels designed in the nineteenth century generally followed the traditional layout of sailing ships. The forecastle was traditionally reserved for the quarters of seamen and firemen, with the space divided between them by a lengthwise bulkhead, as illustrated by the plan of the *Rotomahana* (figure 8). It was the most uncomfortable part of the ship, as the bow sustained the worst impact of the ship's pitching and rolling. Newer steamers tended to enforce the complete separation of the quarters of seamen and firemen, located at opposite ends of the ship. In twentieth-century steamship design, a large raised deck structure amidships was increasingly used for all accommodation. This decreased the physical separation between officers and crew, and the latter often felt their new proximity afforded superiors more opportunity for close and constant supervision.[42]

Ships were also designed to ensure a clear separation of crew and passengers and to make crew quarters and activities as inconspicuous as possible. Saloon dining with passengers was restricted to the captain, chief and second officers, chief engineer and purser. In reviewing the plans for one steamer in 1904, Mills suggested that the crew be berthed forward, not only because the space at the front of the ship was less valuable, but also because of objections to having them aft where they tended to mix freely with the second- and third-class passengers. He was also concerned to avoid 'untidiness' in port. He insisted the working department should be on the starboard side in all new ships, so that when alongside the wharf, cooks and scullerymen could no longer shove their heads out the ports for all to see, and firemen and 'other idlers' could not hang over the rails in full view of the general public about the wharf.[43]

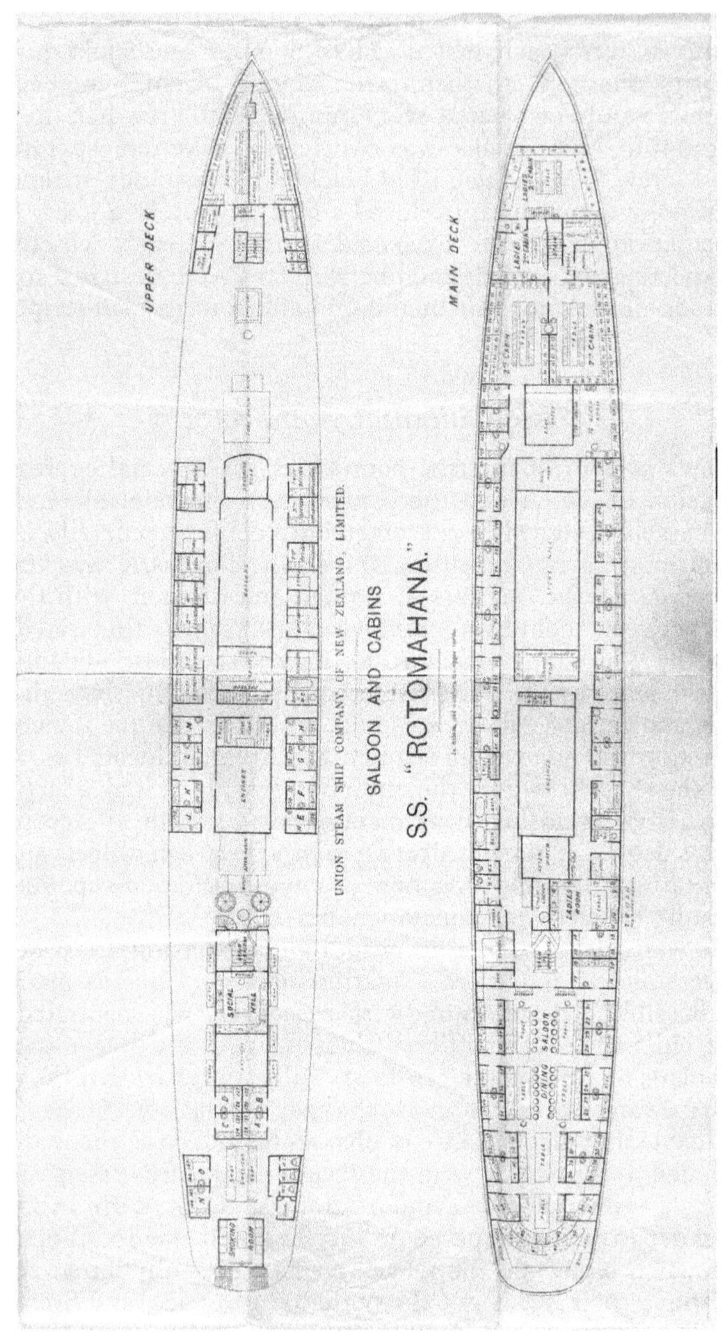

8 Plan of the *Rotomahana*

The specification booklet for the *Navua*, a steamer built for the island trades in 1904, details the spatial dimension of crew hierarchy and division. The captain's cabin was situated on the boat deck, 'painted with four coats of best white lead paint, finished flat, and picked out in gold'. It was furnished in hardwood with tapestry curtains, carpet, a sofa 'stuffed with best curled hair', a wardrobe, writing desk, reading chair, bookcase and safe. The officers' and engineers' cabins were fitted out less luxuriously, but with similar facilities. The firemen's quarters were located on the main deck and supplied with iron bunks and basic fittings, including chairs and fold-out tables. Seamen's quarters were located on the awning deck forward, and furnished in a similar fashion. Iron bunks were deemed an improvement, for this helped prevent vermin which lodged in the seams of wooden bunks. Toilets were attached to the cabins of the captain, officers and engineers. Facilities for firemen and seamen were located under the forecastle deck at the front of the ship.[44]

The sailor's isolation from family and domestic comforts was not in itself fundamental to the working of the ship, but a side effect of its main function to transport cargo and people between colonial ports. With the rise of seamen's unions on both sides of the Tasman in the late nineteenth century, there were more strident protests about the inadequate compensation sailors received for sacrificing domestic ties and intellectual communion ashore to work at sea. Where the USSCo. went to a lot of effort to improve passenger comforts on board new vessels, shipboard conditions for crew demonstrated no marked improvement, as William Belcher, a vocal official of the Federated Seamen's Union of New Zealand (FSU), put it:

> The seaman is compelled to live in miserable and contracted quarters often devoid of light, ventilation and other conveniences necessary to civilization. He has no messroom or facilities for taking his meals. He has to eat, sleep, contract all manner of diseases, and sometimes die in the same miserable hovel, and into the bargain is, in bad weather, literally washed right out of his quarters.[45]

Conditions on board should be 'made more homely' so as to encourage men to stay on board when in port, rather than to frequent public houses and brothels. The passenger was merely 'a bird of passage', but the ship was a sailor's home.[46]

After visiting ships in Wellington Harbour in 1906, the Member of Parliament for Lyttelton, George Laurenson, believed the accommodation provided for sailors was getting worse. Damp, dark, cramped quarters were 'primitive', 'unhealthy' and 'evil'. On inspecting fifty-three steamers, he discovered that only one provided baths, and of the seventy-two berths inspected, less than half were fitted with tables for the crew to eat off. He sought improvements in the space and facilities allocated for workers afloat.[47]

The size of crew quarters affected company profitability as berths were carved out of the space available for cargo and passengers. In early 1907 the Minister for Marine and former FSU secretary, John Millar, advocated that the minimum space for men's quarters should be 120 cubic feet (currently 72 cubic feet), in line with recent provisions made in Britain.[48] This did not become law in New Zealand until 1909 and did not alter the specifications on ships already in service. There was a similar emphasis on the urgent need for improved space, ventilation and light in ship accommodation at the Australian Royal Commission on the Navigation Bill in 1906. Commissioners stressed that the steamship did not compare favourably with even the worst quarters available to workers ashore. As a result, the sailor 'cannot help being both envious and dejected at the contrast'.[49]

Captains, officers and engineers began to form their own professional associations, which paralleled the rise of the seamen's unions. They acted together to demand changes to ship facilities and workplace conditions and, as Mills noted, 'there is a tendency to be more exacting to details'. A general shortage of toilets and baths on company vessels caused particular trouble, leaving officers to use the same facilities provided for saloon passengers. More facilities for crew were provided on new steamers.[50] Toilets were often sites of conflict over shipboard status. The 1907 design proposals for the *Atua* did not include separate toilets for the master. Captain Rutter, sent to Scotland to bring the new vessel back to New Zealand, made a 'great fuss'. He threatened to write to Mills with his complaints, but as Mills reflected to Holdsworth:

> Fortunately for himself he has not done so. I should have told him straight that if it did not suit him we could get someone else to take the ship out. It seems to me rather an impertinence on his part, and only emphasises what I have been told before, that captains when they come here [to Scotland] to look after vessels show more concern about the gratification of personal fads than about the general welfare of their vessel.[51]

Spatial expressions of the personal and the privileges of shipboard status had clear limits, for they could undermine or disturb the necessary work at hand. The company was not in the business of cultivating individual vanities and from a managerial perspective crew of all rank were ultimately interchangeable.

Shipboard confinement affected both mental and physical wellbeing. During his steamer inspections, Laurenson observed that the stokehold temperature in one steamer rose from 90 to 123 degrees, with the result that 'man after man was collapsing'.[52] Others high-lighted the hazardous conditions firemen and trimmers faced in their daily work. There were not five firemen aged over fifty in Auckland, asserted a union official in the Arbitration Court in 1902, for 'the nature of their employment kills them . . . they all die a premature death. I have seen on the New Zealand coast, and it is a frequent occurrence in the Island trade that firemen come on deck, exhausted, gasping for breath, fall on the deck, and leave the marks of the sweat oozing out of their bodies.'[53] On the USSCo.'s *Arawata*, a steamer occasionally called into the island trades, nearly fifty firemen were discharged within four months in 1899, noted the Auckland manager, 'as they cannot stand the heat in stoke hole'.[54]

This was an empire-wide concern. Firemen committed suicide at a startling rate, declared Joseph Havelock Wilson, president of the National Sailors' and Firemen's Union (NSFU) at the 1907 shipping legislation conference.[55] Every month on British ships 'probably' fifteen to twenty men died; 'they come up from the stokehole and jump right overboard . . . I say that is due to excessive work'. The Board of Trade representative tabled an official return, which recorded an average sixty suicides a year, much less than Havelock Wilson's estimates. Nevertheless, the suicide rate on board ships (480 to every million) was almost double the on-shore rate (250 to every million).[56] One shipping representative giving evidence at a Board of Trade com-mittee of enquiry into the mercantile marine in 1902 believed a 'kind of heat insanity' drove stokehold hands to take their own lives.[57]

Safety at sea improved from the late nineteenth century through steam technology, navigation equipment, more detailed and accurate charts, lighthouses, union agitation and shipping laws which enforced such measures as load limits. In 1896 the death rate for seamen in the imperial merchant marine was one in sixty under sail; on steamers it was one in 180. Yet the worst maritime disasters in New Zealand occurred between 1880 and 1910, and all involved USSCo. vessels.[58] Most fatalities at sea were due to drowning, but the ship itself remained a hazardous space. Steamers removed the dangers of falling on deck or into the sea while working aloft, but cargo, machinery and rough weather all caused workplace accidents. Some of the injuries reported to the Marine Department in the year ending 31 March 1908 on board USSCo. vessels indicate the daily dangers faced by all crew. One fatality resulted from routine deck work. The chief steward of the Calcutta trader, the *Aparima*, sustained fatal injuries after he was knocked overboard by a sling and fell into a lighter, 'sustaining such severe injuries that he died almost immediately'. In April 1907 Mary Jones, a stewardess on board the *Te Anau*, injured her head and leg when she fell through an open hatchway. A fireman named Thomas Brown on the island steamer *Manapouri* injured his stomach: 'Whilst vessel was rolling heavily, Brown slipped from one side to the other of the stokehold, sustaining injury which caused haemorrhage of the stomach.' H. Vernon, an AB on the *Waikare*, injured his shin when going off watch, falling against some timber on deck. Early in 1908 a trimmer on board the *Maori* burnt his knees after kneeling in carbolic acid. Some injuries resulted from fights. One trimmer on the *Maori* was knocked down and broke a leg 'whilst fighting in the forecastle with others of the crew'.[59]

Through the company's written instructions and regulations and the clear demarcation of boundaries on board, ships are materialised as spaces operating under rigid, hierarchical and uniform power structures. Yet, in everyday practice shipboard relations were more fluid and contested than this. Ships were complex sites of competing priorities and messy interpersonal relations. Sailors both gave and withheld their consent to their superiors. Incidents of fighting, as recording in the injury tally, reveal informal hierarchies and power struggles at work, and it is likely that such cases more often than not went unreported and were resolved internally. Widespread alcohol abuse also highlights the difficulties company management faced in maintaining a seamless, top-down operational model of shipboard authority.

Dealing with drink, domesticating the sea

The USSCo. archives are studded with concerns about alcohol abuse. As Gavin McLean has concluded, alcoholism troubled the USSCo. 'more than socialism until well into the 1900s. Drink was a curse it never overcame'.[60] Any disorder associated with drinking did not completely disable the company's operations, but it is the case that the prominence of issues surrounding alcohol offers a window onto the world of the ship and some of its workers that we might not otherwise gain. It is also an important indication of the limits of the power of employers to discipline their workforce.

Mills's first circular to masters in 1878 immediately referenced concerns about drinking. He informed them that 'you will be good enough to advise promptly any instance of drunkenness on the part of any of your Officers, and such offender will be instantly dismissed'. Officers would only receive preferential treatment for promotion if a 'total abstainer'.[61] Captains and officers could access alcohol at sea, but there were no longer daily rum or ale rations for all crew as had once been the norm on longer journeys under sail. When stokehold hands requested rum rations to ease the burden of firing boilers on long tropical passages, management flatly refused.[62] The monthly pay scale for masters included a wine allowance, renamed a 'petty expenses' allowance in 1895, which was only to be used to defray necessary hospitality costs. No expenditure for liquors was recognised unless under 'exceptional circumstances'. Masters were expected to exercise a wise discretion and 'wine money will not be allowed when Masters are ashore on leave or during any period their ships may be laid up'.[63] Stewards were instructed not to serve alcohol to officers in their cabins, except in cases of illness, and to enter all transactions in a book, rather than receive cash, with the accounts settled by the purser at the end of each month and forwarded promptly to the Stores Department in Dunedin.[64]

Mills relied on his branch managers and visiting inspectors to make careful observations of daily affairs in each port. In 1898 Mills suspected widespread alcohol abuse in the Tasmanian trades and hoped Holdsworth would 'get some satisfactory information as regards "ye habits and customs" of the officers'. One captain 'denies everything' and 'states that he has had nothing but claret across his lips', nor ever seen any of his officers and engineers the worse for drink. Mills was 'perfectly convinced he is lying'.[65] One captain working the east coast of the North Island was frequently the worse for drink and this appeared 'to have been more commonly known throughout the service than it has to management'. Mills resolved that 'we must deal with him in order to set an example'. The isolated and strenuous nature of the work in the coastal trade was discussed as a contributing factor.[66] In one of the more extreme cases, the captain of the company's Calcutta steamer was confined to his cabin for most of the passage to India and back again. On examination of the books, it appeared that he had consumed a bottle of whisky every second day, and on some occasions a bottle a day. He had also bought a case of whisky at Calcutta and another in Singapore.[67]

Management was generally quick to dismiss men who transgressed, even when their work was in other respects sound. In 1905, for example, a captain in the Tasmanian trades began drinking heavily again after a previous caution when he had taken a temperance pledge. The marine superintendent was sorry to see him go 'as he was a man who kept his ship in splendid order and was always up to time in the different ports'.[68] Nevertheless, by 1907 Holdsworth informed Mills that 'we are having quite an epidemic of trouble with some of the masters and officials'. He could not understand 'why men should fail in the point of sobriety, particularly in view of their clear knowledge of how the Company views it', but supposed that across a fleet of sixty ships 'there must be a proportion who will fall before a too common temptation'. Mills concurred, noting this issue was 'very vexing'. He felt that the marine superintendent was not strict enough and that men did not fully appreciate the company policy of promotional preference for abstainers.[69] Cases of alcohol abuse also demonstrate the extent to which the multi-sited, mobile world of the steamship empire posed particular challenges for managerial surveillance and regulation.

These troubles were prevalent among both senior and junior crew. One AB on his second trip on a coastal steamer got drunk 'and bit Captain Adams on the nose'.[70] A seaman was placed on the ineligible list after being found with a bottle of spirits in his cabin, apparently with the intention of retailing it for his own advantage. The same year a purser, Rupert Isaac, was dismissed after being charged by police for not paying for drinks at a bar in port. On a previous occasion ashore he was robbed of the ship's money. One manager concluded that he was 'shifty cunning lazy and unreliable generally'.[71] In 1899 the Auckland branch manager noted the trouble they invariably had on island steamers 'with firemen being drunk, or failing to join'.[72] A couple of years later the Wellington branch manager deplored that the fireman of one steamer *utilised the recess as a urinal*! Two of the firemen are disgustingly drunk and the ship is detained – How can men be such *beasts?*'[73] There are many more instances scattered throughout company records. Where Manning was proud to note that a 'wave of sobriety' had swept through the industry from the late nineteenth century, USSCo. management could not share this confident conviction.[74]

The testimony of British shipowners and captains at maritime committees of enquiry attest to the widespread concerns about declining standards of discipline in the imperial mercantile marine. When questioned on their recruitment practices, many maritime leaders repeatedly denounced the character of the British sailor. He was a drunkard, unreliable, ill-disciplined and troublesome. Some put his decline down to the expansion of legislation that curtailed masters' disciplinary powers, the growth of militant unionism from the 1880s, and their combined impact on power relations afloat. Crew were now more likely to assert their rights and challenge the master's authority. Logging misbehaviour was no deterrent, asserted one experienced shipmaster. It would be better to 'put the malcontents in irons for a few hours', for 'Jack was always a better man under severe discipline'.[75]

Some believed steam technology degraded the seafarer, for it allowed a different class of man to go to sea. Higher pay, better food, shorter voyages and less trying duties attracted the best sailors from sail into the regular passenger liners, but the majority served on tramp steamers where voyages could last for months. Christopher Gardner, former HM Consul at Amoy, asserted that 'a great many who serve in tramps are rather the wastrels – men who get kicked out of liners for misconduct, or the men who could not get into a liner'.[76] The poorest of these worked in the stokehold, a space not invested with any seafaring traditions. Many commentators framed firemen, as 'strangers' to the sea, as a new and highly visible factor in labour recalcitrancy. They were untrained, drawn straight from factories and other onshore professions 'where they have been independent and undisciplined', asserted one superintendent, 'and on board ships they are just as bad'.[77] The maritime historian Alston Kennerley records a working-class hierarchy, for it appears that firemen were recruited from the poorest districts in Britain.[78]

Errant behaviour was also more visible on steamers. Departure times were fixed in a way they had not previously been and so tardiness in boarding a ship was more disruptive. And steamers were in port more often, with 'go ashore' behaviour more freely indulged.[79] When faced with growing foreign competition, shipboard insobriety and insubordination were severe commercial liabilities. Such apparent failings amongst the British working class were used to justify the replacement of white stokehold hands and seamen with 'tractable' foreign and 'coloured' colonial labour. Returning to Williams's analysis, however, it is also clear that many of these complaints were related to the adjustments everyone had to make in a changing maritime work environment, and while many shipowners and political leaders were quick to vocalise their concerns, they were slower to take action that might improve the situation for common seafarers, such as raising wages and reforming shipboard conditions.[80]

Yet others proposed a scale of white decline, with colonial firemen 'of a far better class' than their British counterparts. The English fireman was 'the dregs of humanity', asserted one captain, whereas firemen on the Australian coast were better behaved as they enjoyed higher wages.[81] Manning also attested that drunken disorder was more marked amongst firemen on English ships, for 'the colonial fireman is of a higher type and the average colonial lad of a self-assertive character'.[82] The secretary of the Australasian Institute for Marine Engineers requested that the USSCo. exert stricter control over drunken firemen, including imposing heavier fines, and give engineers authority to dismiss men without providing a return passage. 'Many respectable young Colonials' were attracted to the work as it paid well, yet 'they have been brought up decently and after making one trip they leave disgusted with the life in the forecastle', serving alongside drunk British firemen.[83] In response to the earlier complaint about the 'beastly' behaviour of steamer crew, the seamen's union suggested this was the company's fault for employing men from overseas.[84]

Well into the twentieth century the USSCo. relied predominantly on British-born seamen as steamer crew. The company occasionally conducted crew surveys. One 1899 survey recorded that of the 179 masters and officers in the service, 175 were British-born and the rest were foreigners. Among the 160 engineers, there was only one foreigner, with the rest recorded as New Zealanders or Scottish, English, Australian, Irish and Tasmanian. Of the 433 deck crew, sixty-one were foreigners, while only sixteen foreigners served among the 427 firemen and greasers. In response to these figures, the *New Zealand Times* confidently declared, 'no British-owned shipping company in the world has so few foreigners in its service'.[85] Five years later the proportion of foreign to British-born crew above and below deck remained about the same (around fourteen per cent and four per cent respectively).[86] Those classed as foreign rather than British or colonial-born were predominantly from Scandinavian countries, with a few from Northern and Eastern Europe.

The Marine Department published details of convictions of seafarers between 1908 and 1919. Desertion and absence without leave accounted for nearly two-thirds of the 1,000 cases. Drunk and disorderly behaviour accounted for only three per cent, but it seems likely that alcohol abuse underpinned a good percentage of convictions for failing to return to ships.[87] For many crew, particularly those in the stokehold, resort to drink was one way simply to cope with difficult working conditions. Drinking was one of the few avenues of release open to them. It was also an effective way to exercise some control over their superiors. Alcohol consumption may have played a prominent role in constructions and assertions of masculine working-class identity as it did in other labour contexts, yet the USSCo. archives indicate that drinking was also a solitary practice, particularly in the case of captains and senior crew, and often a response to loneliness and social isolation and the unrelenting pressures of shipboard management.

From the mid-nineteenth century, seafarers assumed a potent social visibility as objects of pity and subjects of reform. Many official commissions and committees of enquiry, as well as learned societies and pressure groups, addressed questions of shipping safety and loss of life at sea; the general comfort and well-being of sailors; methods of wage payment; manning requirements; the racial composition of crew; and the prevalence of desertion and other offences against shipboard discipline.[88] Evangelical and temperance reformers demonstrated a particular interest in the welfare of seafarers when ashore. Various charitable and voluntary societies were active on the wharves from the 1820s. The Missions to Seamen, founded in Bristol in 1855 under the auspices of the Anglican Church, sought to 'girdle the ports of the world with links of brotherly kindness', as the superintendent of the missions, Reverend G. F. Wilson, put it on a visit to New Zealand in 1907.[89] They provided an alternative shelter for those without families or friends in port. Members offered accommodation, food, reading material and entertainment on their premises, delivered sermons and lectures, and distributed religious tracts. In New Zealand such work usually began with committed individuals visiting men at the wharf, as was the case in Dunedin in the early 1860s. Over time, sailors' homes and rests were established.[90]

Branches of the Women's Christian Temperance Union and the Gospel Temperance Union were also active amongst seafarers. Members of the former set up a sailors' rest in Dunedin in 1887, providing reading material, food and comfortable surroundings where men could relax and write letters. Hundreds of letters were sent from their premises and, like other maritime missions and institutes, they received many letters from wives and mothers writing in the hope they might know the whereabouts of missing men.[91] The Otago Branch of the Missions to Seamen welcomed donations of reading material and scraps of carpet for firemen to use in handling hot slices. Sailors valued their premises as a quiet place to read and write, the missionaries assured their donors, 'as may be seen when we consider that they have to come a quarter of an hour's walk from the wharf and past many attractions'.[92]

The Wellington Missions to Seamen was established in 1898 and in the first six years the mission moved premises twenty-five times. A new building was completed in 1904 after the widow of a local captain donated £7,000 towards its construction. At the official opening, dignitaries attested to the improved tone of the wharves since the mission was established. One official wondered how it was that firemen 'had taken to putting on stand-up collars and black coats to go off the wharf in, and had forgotten, on coming back, to knock down the quartermaster on duty'.[93] The annual report of 1906 recorded 1,500 ship visits and 22,757 attendances at church services; 485 men signed the pledge of total abstinence, 7,300 letters were written at the premises, and they received 2,235 letters from sailors.[94]

The USSCo. made regular donations to these charitable institutions, although it apparently did not believe its men made extensive use of the services. In writing thanks for a contribution, one mission representative noted that USSCo. men made frequent use of his branch. The previous month, for example, a 'notable case of our being able to help one of your men occurred'. This man could not get into hospital and looked to the mission for assistance. As it was a case of syphilis he 'did not apply through your recognised channels'. The missionary went on:

> At most of our Social gatherings some of your men like to come & feel greatful [*sic*] for an evening spent with us and that must mean their being free for one night at least from a Public House and some waste of money apart from the elevating influence of a talk with our men who being all working men with one or two exceptions can enter into their feelings well.[95]

The USSCo.'s rapid growth was frequently lauded as an index of national progress and maturation, yet such praise did not extend as readily to the crew who were responsible for the everyday work of the ships. There was growing public commentary about the declining appeal of the sea as a professional calling to young colonial men. Attempts were made to intervene in order to challenge worn stereotypes about working life at sea. 'Week by week' in 1907, the *New Zealand Herald* probed the possible reasons for this state of affairs. These included 'impatience of discipline or restraint' among youth. Another 'most potent cause' was 'that the old-time glamour of the sea is worn threadbare by modern methods of communication'. With the rise of steam the sea appeared to have lost its romance. The modern maritime experience was now a dingy, noisy, dirty affair. The tramp steamer had 'no time for leisure or romance about her'. Importantly, too, the popular representation of men who took to the sea was less than favourable. Writers continued to frame such men 'as of necessity a combination of knave, fool, and brute in the first place, and secondly, a habitual drunkard from choice'. These ideas should be interrogated, for 'on the whole, the seaman compares not unfavourably with any other working class man in intellect, honesty and sobriety'.[96]

Manning wrote his book on the merchant marine as a way of enlightening the general public about the realities of shipboard life. As noted, he gave prominence to stokehold crew. Given the nature of their work, he reflected, 'it is hardly reasonable to expect beatified saints to emerge from a stokehold'. Yet these were men of 'sterling qualities' and were they of a higher station in life they would be 'conspicuous as heroes or philanthropists'. When the 'personal and social limitations of this class of men are considered, the wonder is, not that they are so bad, but that they are so good'.[97] Union officials were also prominent in challenging popular stereotypes. There was much praise for maritime workers in the time of danger, 'then we have a lot of sentimental gush about "boys of the bulldog breed" and the courage of the men becomes a household theme', yet this did not extend to the everyday representation of men who were more often criticised for errant behaviour ashore.

Seamen and firemen 'are not angels any more than newspaper scribes, and the former class is not the only class that commits lapses during holidays'.[98] There was also the occasional direct intervention from steamer crew. Whenever a fireman did anything wrong, journalists depicted him as a social 'outcast', deplored one fireman, whereas if an officer gets drunk 'he is treated as a fellow citizen who has temporarily lapsed'. As a result, stokehold workers held the press in an odious light.[99] As the USSCo. archives record as much despair over the failings of masters and officers as they do over those of firemen, the 'public face' of company alcohol abuse was indeed distorted.

Rearticulating the domestic image of the seafaring profession was not confined to the colonial maritime world or the merchant marine. Valerie Burton has examined official investigations into the consumption habits of male workers in the imperial metropole, and suggests British seafarers probably attracted undue attention given their established status as popular heroes with bachelor freedoms. In the steam age, sailors began to forge more regular and stable connections to family, mixed more often with non-seafarers and had the opportunity to compare their labour conditions more directly with workers ashore. As a result, she argues, they challenged the stereotype of the wayward, drunk, irresponsible seafarer and opposed increased state regulation of wage disbursements to families. They regarded family provision as their patriarchal right, not to be usurped by their employers to legitimise the hegemony of the ruling class.[100] Mary Conway has also traced the way in which images of naval manhood were transformed between the Georgian and Edwardian eras. Dominant images of Royal Navy seafarers shifted from an easy dichotomy between the hero afloat and the deviant ashore, to a domesticated vision of maritime manhood tied to the respectable roles of dutiful husband and father.[101]

A colonial crew culture?

Throughout the nineteenth century, the homosocial, communal work organisation and customs of maritime workers influenced other crew-like working groups in the Australasian colonies, including agricultural and timber workers, gold miners and shearers. At least half the men trading out to the colonies, as one maritime author put it in 1903, 'may be said to have had a dual profession, sailoring and sheep-shearing'.[102] Maritime labour networks and immigration networks overlapped. The historian James Belich reflects that this 'crew culture' was more about 'betweenness' than any overriding attachment to place. There was a sense that crews 'were *in* New Zealand', he argues, 'but not *of* it'. And their itinerancy meant they were easily written out of local history, 'even when they began it, as was very often the case'.[103] But as questions of labour assumed a prominent place in national politics on both sides of the Tasman in the late nineteenth century, and as the status and welfare of seafarers ashore and afloat became a cause of concern and a target for reform, 'it was rather as though wandering crews had been captured and forced to work under a new system, much more controlled and stationary than the old'. This broader pitch for an increasingly integrated, respectable and harmonious society Belich labels the 'Great Tightening'.[104]

New pressures were brought to bear upon maritime workers with the increased emphasis on speed, efficiency, accountability, professionalism and profits. The legend of the archetypal seafarer was worked upon, improved and adapted to the conditions of modern labour. The ship's iron world was mirrored by the 'iron world' ashore. The civilising processes of an industrialising society idealised the family and stable employment as sites of true manhood. Colquhoun, after abandoning his lover and child, was 'not fit to be a man'. It relieved some of Young's anger and disappointment just to inform Mills of the fact. What Mills made of Colquhoun is undocumented. When the USSCo. itself appeared to fail on this score by overlooking Blair's advancement, his mother petitioned successfully for this recognition and secured his promotion.

Yet Colquhoun's desire to lead an itinerant life, free of ties to family and domestic responsibilities, was facilitated by working on the steamers that plied between New Zealand and Australian ports. It is difficult to know how many more men in the USSCo.'s employ lived as he did, given that the company archives contain very limited information about the broader social world of maritime workers. In electoral rolls, too, such as those examined by Neill Atkinson, many men list boarding houses and ships as their home address, with little being known about their marital and family status.[105] The USSCo.'s crew surveys sometimes included questions on marital status. One survey in 1902, which excluded captains, engineers, stewards and pursers, found that of 896 men, 212 men – or twenty-four per cent – were married. This contrasts with British figures, first collected in 1891, which showed that forty-six per cent of men were married or once married.[106] The nature of the social and domestic connections individual men forged with particular colonial ports, their own self-fashioning as merchant sailors in settler societies, and the practices and patterns of USSCo. recruitment all warrant further investigation.

Records also suggest that seafarers remained quite mobile in their employment, moving between different ships, between colonies, and between the colonial setting and the imperial metropole. Moreover, men also frequently moved between ship and shore work. The number of requests to crew new steamers out to the colonies suggests a lingering overlap between maritime labour and immigration networks. In the early twentieth century, there were an estimated 27,000 desertions from British ships each year. The desertion of seamen and firemen in Australasian ports was high, for wages were higher on local ships and in land-based industry. It was common for vessels 'to lose half a dozen men in a New Zealand port'.[107] These figures remind us that individual experiences easily diverged from broader social trends and expectations; there was no typical sailor and no typical way of bridging life at sea with life ashore.

Notes

1   All preceding quotations are from HC, USSCo. Records, AG-292-005-001/010, Young to Mills, 8 April 1885.
2   *Ibid.*, AG-292-005-001/030, Blair to Mills, 27 April and 14 May 1892.
3   Marcus Rediker, *Between the Devil and the Deep Blue Sea: Merchant Seamen, Pirates and the Anglo-American Maritime World, 1700–1750* (Cambridge: Cambridge University Press, 1987), 113–14. See also Rediker, 'The common seaman in the histories of capitalism and the working class', *International Journal of Maritime History*, 1:2 (1989), 339–42.
4   For more on the pattern of shipowning in Britain, see Boyce, *Information, Mediation and Institutional Development.*
5   *Cyclopedia of New Zealand: Otago and Southland Provincial Districts*, vol. 4 (Dunedin: The Cyclopedia Company, 1905), 402.
6   Mills, cited in McLean, *The Southern Octopus*, 43.
7   For example, *New Zealand Times* (3 December 1901).
8   *Fiji Times* (8 October 1890) and WCCA, USSCo. Records. I was unable to confirm wages for chief and second engineers in company archives, but their pay scale was suggested by Ian Farquhar (personal comment, 8 November 2007).
9   USSCo., *General Instructions for Captains and Officers in the Service of the Union Steam Ship Company of New Zealand* (Dunedin: USSCo., 1895), 5–6; McLean, *The Southern Octopus*, 44.
10   McLean, *The Southern Octopus*, 106; 'The shipmaster's position', *Nautical Magazine*, 74:10 (October 1905), 903.
11   'Seafarer' [Walter Manning], *Below and above the Water-Line* (Christchurch: Whitcombe and Tombs Limited [1908]), 118–19.
12   HC, USSCo. Records, AG-292-005-001/086, Mills to Holdsworth, 3 April 1908.
13   *Ibid.*, AG-292-005-004/137, Holdsworth to Mills, 19 December 1911.
14   USSCo., *General Instructions*, 33–4.
15   As also documented by Eric W. Sager, *Seafaring Labour: The Merchant Marine of Atlantic Canada, 1820–1914* (Kingston, Ont.: McGill–Queen's University Press, 1989), 264. Greg Dening discusses the concerns for 'scientific management' held by some naval officials in the late eighteenth century, who believed shipboard violence was counterproductive. See especially *Mr Bligh's Bad Language: Passion, Power and Theatre on the Bounty* (Cambridge: Cambridge University Press, 1992), 142–56. For general commentary about these shifts in disciplinary mores, see Michel Foucault, *Discipline and Punish: The Birth of the Prison*, trans. Alan Sheridan (New York: Vintage Books, 1979).
16   HC, USSCo. Records, AG-292-005-004/137, Holdsworth to Mills, 18 June 1912.
17   *Ibid.*, AG-292-005-001/024, James Grey to Mills, 26 December 1891.

18 *Ibid.*, AG-292-004-004/001, Holdsworth, Memo, 8 October 1898.
19 Dening, *Mr Bligh's Bad Language*, 81–3. The concept of total institution derives from Erving Goffman, *Asylums: Essays on the Social Situation of Mental Patients and Other Inmates* (Harmondsworth, Middlesex: Penguin, 1968).
20 See WCCA, USSCo. Records, Masters' and Officers' Personal Files.
21 Neill Atkinson, *Crew Culture: New Zealand Seafarers Under Sail and Steam* (Wellington: Te Papa Press, 2001), 95–6; Sager, *Seafaring Labour*, 103; HC, Cameron Family Papers, MS-1046, Box 13, Cameron to C.H. Cooper, 5 July 1904.
22 ATL, FSU Records, MSY-1030, Industrial and General, 3 June 1899; Atkinson, *Crew Culture*, 14.
23 Sager, *Seafaring Labour*, 8–9, 261; David M. Williams, 'The quality, skill and supply of maritime labour: causes of concern in Britain, 1850–1914', in Lars U. Scholl (ed.), *Merchants and Mariners: Selected Maritime Writings of David M. Williams* (St John's, Newfoundland: International Maritime Economic History Association, 2000), 282.
24 Atkinson, *Crew Culture*, 22.
25 W. E. Dexter, *Rope-Yarns, Marline-Spikes and Tar* (London: William Hodge and Company, 1938), 10.
26 *United States Gazette*, n.d., reprinted in *Fiji Times* (17 October 1877).
27 Manning, *Below and Above the Water-Line*, 58. For Bullen and Brassey see *Report of the Committee Appointed by the Board of Trade to Inquire into the Mercantile Marine: II – Minutes of Evidence* (London: 1903, Cd 1608), 618, 279.
28 Valerie Burton, '"Whoring, drinking sailors": reflections on masculinity from the labour history of nineteenth-century British shipping', in Margaret Walsh (ed.), *Working out Gender: Perspectives from Labour History* (Aldershot: Ashgate, 1999), 95. See also the introduction to Margaret S. Creighton and Lisa Norling (eds), *Iron Men, Wooden Women: Gender and Seafaring in the Atlantic World, 1700–1920* (Baltimore: Johns Hopkins University Press, 1996), vii, x.
29 As recorded in HC, USSCo. Records, AG-292-005-001/097, Mills to Holdsworth, 22 September 1911.
30 Williams, 'Quality, skill and supply', 278.
31 Manning, *Below and Above the Water-Line*, 9, 23.
32 HC, Cameron Family Papers, MS-1046, Box 11, Holdsworth to Williams, 1 August 1905.
33 USSCo., *General Instructions*, 10. Misc. newspaper cutting, n.d., enclosed in HC copy of *General Instructions*.
34 WCCA, USSCo. Records, AF080:1:7, Strang to Holdsworth, 26 November 1902.
35 Alston Kennerley, 'Stoking the boilers: firemen and trimmers in British merchant ships, 1850–1950', *International Journal of Maritime History*, 20:1 (June 2008), 194.
36 Atkinson, *Crew Culture*, 16. See relevant years of the *New Zealand Census* for more details on these statistics.
37 Frank T. Bullen, *Men of the Merchant Service, Being the Polity of the Mercantile Marine for 'Longshore Readers* (London: Smith, Elder & Co., 1900), 322.
38 Anonymous, 'Trimmers', from the *Bulletin* (Sydney), n.d., cited in Atkinson, *Crew Culture*, 19.
39 Bullen, *Men of the Merchant Service*, and Manning, *Below and Above the Water-Line*.
40 HC, Cameron Family Papers, MS-1046, Box 25, USSCo. Regulations (1 January 1891).
41 McLean, *The Southern Octopus*, 114–19.
42 Atkinson, *Crew Culture*, 32.
43 HC, Cameron Family Papers, MS-1046, Box 9, Mills to Cameron, 23 April and 18 July 1904.
44 WCCA, USSCo. Records, B97/6, David J. Dunlop & Co., 'Specifications of a Twin-screw Steamship for the USSCo. of NZ Limited', 10 November 1904.
45 William Belcher, *Dunedin Evening Star*, n.d. [September 1907], enclosed in HC, USSCo. Records, AG-292-005-001/096, Smith to Holdsworth, 10 January 1911.

46 'Ships and sailors: bettering the condition of the men: Australian navigation commission', *Evening Post* (20 March 1906), 6.

47 George Laurenson, 20 October 1906, *NZPD*, vol. 138 (Wellington: Government Printer, 1906), 724–6.

48 *New Zealand Herald* (3 January 1907).

49 *Report of the Royal Commission on the Navigation Bill* ([Melbourne]: Government Printer, 1906), xii.

50 HC, Cameron Family Papers, MS-1046, Box 9, Mills to Cameron, 18 July 1904.

51 HC, USSCo. Records, AG-292-005-001/085, Mills to Holdsworth, 22 May 1907.

52 George Laurenson, 20 October 1906, *NZPD*, vol. 138 (Wellington: Government Printer, 1906), 724–5.

53 ATL, FSU Records, MSY-0131, Industrial and General (1901–9); *New Zealand Times* (29 January 1902).

54 HC, USSCo. Records, AG-292-005-001/012, Thomas Henderson to Mills, 2 February 1899.

55 Formed in 1887, it was known as the National Amalgamated Sailors' and Firemen's Union until 1895.

56 *Merchant Shipping Legislation: Report of a Conference between Representatives of the United Kingdom, the Commonwealth of Australia, and New Zealand, 26th March–2nd April, 1907* (Sydney: 1907), 88–9, 92.

57 *Mercantile Marine: II – Minutes of Evidence*, 28. See also commentary in Kennerley, 'Stoking the boilers', 217–19.

58 Sager, *Seafaring Labour*, 308, footnote 6; Atkinson, *Crew Culture*, 51.

59 *AJHR*, H-15 (Wellington: Government Printer, 1908), 38–43.

60 Gavin McLean, *Captain's Log: New Zealand's Maritime History* (Auckland: Hodder Moa Beckett Publishers Ltd, 2001), 120; McLean, *The Southern Octopus*, 99.

61 WCCA, USSCo. Records, Box 335, 'Instructions to Masters', 25 November 1878.

62 ATL, FSU Records, MS-Papers-0650-006, Executive Council Correspondence to and from USSCo., Kennedy to Young, 25 August 1911.

63 HC, Cameron Family Papers, MS-1046, Box 25, Circular to Masters, 1 April 1886.

64 USSCo., *General Instructions*, 29.

65 HC, USSCo. Records, AG-292-005-001/046, Mills to Holdsworth, 4 November 1898.

66 *Ibid.*, Mills to Holdsworth, 12 September 1899.

67 HC, Cameron Family Papers, MS-1046, Box 9, Strang to Cameron, 29 September 1903. And see the 'Report of enquiry into insobriety of Capt. Courbarron while on trip to Calcutta', HC, USSCo. Records, AG-292-005-004/107.

68 HC, Cameron Family Papers, MS-1046, Box 11, Strang to Cameron, 13 November 1905.

69 HC, USSCo. Records, AG-292-004-004/009, Holdsworth to Mills, 5 July 1907; AG-292-005-001/085, Mills to Holdsworth, 16 August 1907.

70 HC, Cameron Family Papers, MS-1046, Box 4, Strang to Cameron, 3 March 1892.

71 HC, USSCo. Records, AG-292-005-001/046, Aiken to Mills, 30 December 1899.

72 *Ibid.*, AG-292-005-001/045, Henderson to Mills, 6 April 1899.

73 ATL, FSU Records, MS-Papers-0650-006, Correspondence to and from USSCo. (1902–20), Kennedy to Young, 5 September 1903 (emphasis in original).

74 Manning, *Below and Above the Water-Line*, 50.

75 *Report on the Supply of British Seamen, the Number of Foreigners Serving on Board British Merchant Ships, and the Reasons Given for Their Employment, and on Crimping and Other Matters Bearing on Those Subjects* (London: Eyre and Spottiswood 1886, C-4709), 9.

76 *Mercantile Marine: II – Minutes of Evidence*, 693.

77 *Ibid*, 10.

78 Kennerley, 'Stoking the boilers', 214.

79 *Report on the Supply of British Seamen*, 3–16; *Mercantile Marine: II – Minutes of Evidence*, 98.

80 Williams, 'Quality, skill and supply', 288–90.

81 *Royal Commission on the Navigation Bill*, 394.
82 Manning, *Below and Above the Water-Line*, 15.
83 HC, USSCo. Records, AG-292-005-004/124, 23 November 1911.
84 ATL, FSU Records, MS-Papers-0650-006, Correspondence to and from USSCo. (1902–20), Young to Kennedy, 9 September 1903.
85 ATL, Roth Papers, 94-106-43/06, *New Zealand Times* (26 July 1899).
86 *Ibid.*, 94-106-43/07, misc. newspaper cutting (5 February 1906). In 1902 there were 470 British and ninety-three foreign seamen on deck, and 477 British firemen and twenty-nine foreigners in the engine-room. Two years later British numbers had increased slightly, to 480 on deck and 512 in the engine department. The number of foreigners had dropped to sixty-three and twenty-three respectively.
87 McLean, *Captain's Log*, 120.
88 For an important discussion on the growing attention to the mercantile marine, see David M. Williams, 'Mid-Victorian attitudes to seamen and maritime reform: the Society for Improving the Condition of Merchant Seamen, 1867', in *Merchants and Mariners*, 229–52.
89 'Girdling the ports of the world: the missions to seamen', *Evening Post* (5 February 1907), 7.
90 'Seamen's mission', *Otago Witness* (13 February 1869), 17.
91 J. A. Torrence, 'Public institutions', in Alex Bathgate (ed.), *Picturesque Dunedin, or Dunedin and its Neighbourhood in 1890* (Dunedin: Mills, Dick & Co., 1890), 237 and 'Dunedin Sailors' Rest', *Otago Witness* (13 November 1907), p. 89.
92 HC, Third Annual Report of the Otago Branch of the Missions to Seamen (September 1911–August 1912), 3–4.
93 'Wellington Sailors' Mission', *Star* (26 August 1904), p. 3.
94 'Missions to seamen: eighth annual report', *Evening Post* (13 July 1906), p. 2.
95 HC, USSCo. Records, AG-292-005-004/135, Mission to Seamen to Holdsworth, 7 August 1910.
96 *New Zealand Herald* (1 June 1907).
97 Manning, *Below and Above the Water-Line*, 4, 8.
98 University of Auckland Library Special Collection, FSU Auckland Branch Records, D8, Box 1, *Auckland Star* (6 January 1913).
99 ATL, FSU Records, MS-Papers-0650-097A, Shipping clippings, unknown newspaper [*New Zealand Times*?] (7 January 1913).
100 Valerie Burton, 'The myth of bachelor Jack: masculinity, patriarchy and seafaring labour', in Colin Howell and Richard J. Twomey (eds), *Jack Tar in History: Essays in the History of Maritime Life and Labour* (New Brunswick: Acadiensis Press, 1991), 180–1, 193–7; Burton, '"Whoring, drinking sailors". . .', 89–90. See also Williams, 'Mid-Victorian attitudes to seamen'.
101 Mary Conway, *From Jack Tar to Union Jack: Representing Naval Manhood in the British Empire, 1870–1918* (Manchester: Manchester University Press, 2009).
102 Charles Protheroe, *Life in the Mercantile Marine* (London: John Lane, 1903), 106.
103 James Belich, *Making Peoples: A History of the New Zealanders: From Polynesian Settlement to the End of the Nineteenth Century* (Honolulu: University of Hawai'i Press, 1996), 431–6.
104 Belich, *Paradise Reforged*, 145.
105 Neill Atkinson, 'Auckland Seamen and Their Union, 1880–1922' (MA dissertation, University of Auckland, 1990), 42. Colquhoun, in fact, went on to lead a distinguished career in the Victorian colonial navy. After serving in the Boer War, he was Naval Commandant at Brisbane until his death in 1908 at the age of forty-nine. He was survived by his wife Emmie and three children. See 'Death of Captain Colquhoun: a distinguished naval officer', *Advertiser* (Adelaide) (19 August 1908), 10.
106 HC, USSCo. Records, AG-292-005-003/016, Whitson to Mills, 10 March 1902; Burton, 'The myth of Bachelor Jack', 187, footnote 27.
107 Atkinson, *Crew Culture*, 111.

CHAPTER FOUR

Labour, race and empire: debating the 'lascar question'

Lying at the bottom of the English Channel at Anvil Point, a few miles off the Dorset coast, the USSCo.'s *Aparima* forms part of an eerie underwater fleet, berthed in broken pieces amongst other wartime wrecks. A keen recreational diver from Hampshire, Dave Wendes, explored these wrecks throughout the 1980s. As diving conditions deteriorated in the winter months, he took to researching the history of the ships. In 1987 he wrote a letter of thanks to the director of the New Zealand Maritime Museum for photographs and information on the *Aparima*, recording what he knew of the wreck from his six or seven dives: 'the teak decking has gone except from some left on the stern, the gun lies on the sea bed just south of the wreck, all the super-structure has long since collapsed, littering the midships area. The bow has broken off and points almost vertically to the sky. . . . That aside . . . the general consensus among us divers is that she is the finest wreck around here.'[1]

Diving company websites record more recent exploits forty metres below. One site contains photographs of exuberant, fresh-faced divers enjoying wine and food on board their chartered boat after complet-ing dives to different wrecks earlier that day. These photographs are juxtaposed with grainy, black and white archival images of the ships in active service.[2] Another site added the *Aparima* to its wreck list in December 2006. It informs prospective divers of the ship's original specifications and its present location on the seabed. And it briefly records how the *Aparima* met its fate: 'Torpedoed by the German submarine UB-40. The explosion took place at 00.50 a.m. without warning, the vessel sinking in five minutes, giving the crew no time to launch the boats. A total of 26 European and 30 native crew members were lost.'[3]

This attack occurred in the early morning of 19 November 1917. Eighteen of the twenty-six Europeans killed were New Zealand and

Australian cadets. They were not in active war service, but serving maritime apprenticeships. The native crew members were Indian seamen, known as lascars, who signed articles with the company a year earlier in Calcutta to work on board as firemen, coal-trimmers, stewards and cooks.

In its regular peacetime service, the *Aparima* served as a cadet-training ship in the USSCo. merchant trade. The ship was initially requisitioned in the First World War as a troop carrier. Deemed too slow for this service, it was loaded with produce from New Zealand and sent to London in 1917. Four days before the submarine attack, the Imperial Government assumed control of the vessel and sent it on the ill-fated mission around the English coast en route to New York. Twelve cadets and thirty-one lascars survived the German attack.[4]

The *Aparima* was the only steamer in the USSCo. fleet manned with a non-white crew. In the imperial mercantile marine, by contrast, Indian and other 'coloured' colonial labourers were routinely employed from the late nineteenth century. In Australasia, political leaders and seamen's union officials opposed this multiracial recruitment practice, both for their own vessels – and the *Aparima* was a periodic target – and for foreign ships trading in local waters. Maritime labour policies were also hotly debated at imperial conferences and other official forums and the question of lascar recruitment came to represent a clear point of rupture between British and Australasian leaders.

These politicised debates offer a fresh oceanic perspective to complement traditionally terracentric narratives of the intersections between race, labour and nation-building. Questions of maritime labour were entangled with the immigration and land-based labour policies of the 'white men's countries' of New Zealand and Australia. In this respect the maritime setting was significant not only as a space of transit and arrival, depositing successive waves of migrants on these shores, but also as a working environment fundamental to the development and prosperity of the British settler societies in the south.

The maritime dimensions of White Australasia

Indian sailors were some of the earliest recorded Asian people in New Zealand, arriving from the late eighteenth century on board East India Company vessels. One lascar deserted ship in 1810 and settled amongst Ngapuhi Maori in the Bay of Islands. Others were incorporated into Kai Tahu communities in the south.[5] In Australia, too, some of the first Indian immigrants were shipwrecked seafarers or those left behind by their masters.[6] The reminiscences of Louisa Worsfold, born in 1872 in the Bay of Islands, are particularly instructive. Her childhood memories include being carried along the beach in the arms of 'George Calcutta': 'It always seems queer to me, that the first brown face I remember should not be Maori, as one might suppose, but of a Punjabi – an Indian boy who was left in Russell many years earlier.' She also mentioned other Asian seafarers – a lascar, a Malay and an Arab – who lived in Russell for a time.[7] Before engaging more closely with the history of Indian seafarers in Australasia, white settler agitation directed towards Chinese labourers over the course of the nineteenth and early twentieth centuries is worth briefly exploring, as in many ways it anticipated the response to lascar crews on steamers trading in and to the region at the turn of the century.

Chinese men arrived in large numbers to mine for gold, first in Victoria in the 1850s and then in Central Otago from the 1860s. They were met with widespread and persistent hostility. From the perspective of their white co-residents, the basic premise was that the Chinese were unable to assimilate into the prevailing cultural and social norms of these nascent British settler communities.[8] Agitation against the Chinese spread from land-based to maritime industry. The first major Australasian maritime dispute erupted in Sydney when the ASNCo., having tried out Chinese sailors in its Pacific Island trades, moved to introduce them on steamers in the Australian coastal trades in 1878. In the ensuing protests, white sailors initially sought a legislative solution in the form of the wholesale exclusion of Chinese from the colony. When this did not succeed, they pursued an immediate and narrower industrial solution, striking to exclude Chinese from the steamers. They mobilised widespread financial and moral support, and after thirteen weeks claimed victory, with the ASNCo. forced dramatically to reduce Chinese crews. Within three years the company had terminated Chinese recruitment altogether.[9] It was in the context of this strike that the FSU was established. The Victorian president of the Australian Seamen's Union, George Sangster, visited New Zealand in 1880 and used the spectre of cheap Chinese labour to encourage the formation of a union across the Tasman.[10]

A cartoon (figure 9) by William Blomfield neatly encapsulates popular racial prejudice towards the Chinese. In 1892 the USSCo. dispensed with its European grower and contracted a Chinese market gardener to supply steamers with fresh produce. The European grower had failed to serve the company to a consistent standard despite repeated warnings and the company turned to the Chinese supplier, even though he was more expensive.[11] The cartoon, drawn in response to this development, deploys an array of race, class and gender stereotypes. The Chinese grower supplies cheaper goods than the European, even though this was not the case. Bent over and subservient, the

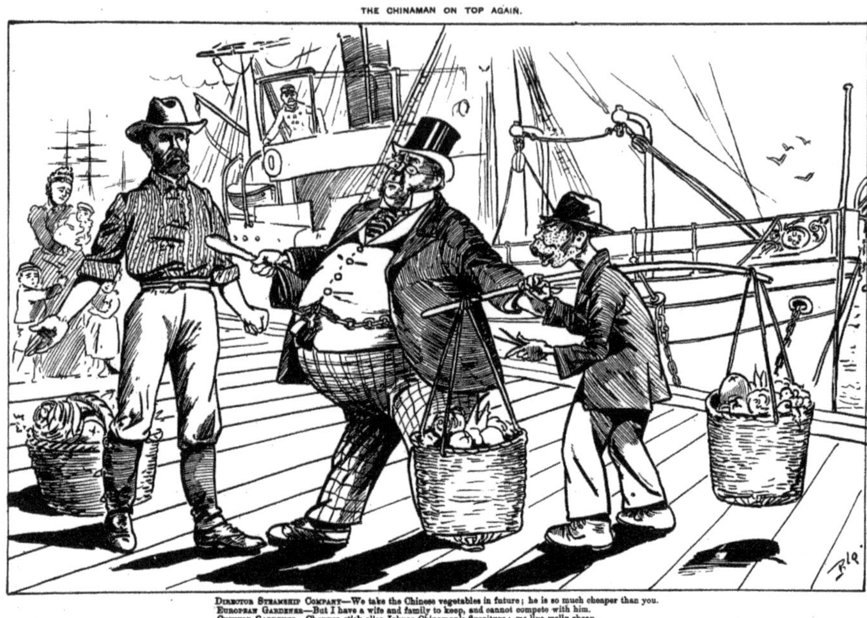

9   'The Chinaman on top again', *New Zealand Observer* (6 August 1892)

'Chinaman' declares his only furniture is a pair of chopsticks. He can live more economically than the white producer who has his family to support in tow. The young, white settler family and the male bread-winner are fetishised. The European grower is trim, muscular, tall and morally upright. He represents the proper, honest, moral exercise of social power. His clothing has a rural look. The bowyangs, or cloth over-boots, worn to prevent trousers dragging and to aid freedom of movement, served as a code for manual workers.[12] The obese company director lords it over the wharf. The 'Fat Man Capitalist', the enemy of 'the People', was a famous villain during this period. His monopolistic desires stand in opposition to the values of the idealised Australasian male worker. He is seen as callous and lacking compassion. In league with the 'Chinaman' villain, he threatens material well-being and the gender and racial order. In the background the steamer captain laments the likely replacement of his white crew with a 'measly' Chinese one, portraying a sense of the inevitable march of monopoly.[13]

The cartoon represents the inherent tensions between a globalised, cosmopolitan capital, embodied by the steamship company direc-tor and his overriding commercial imperatives, and a more humble, localised capital, tied to the land and to community through the figure of the white grower and his family. Colonial liberalism informed this tension. Broadly conceived, the liberal ethos embraced a balance of power between labour and capital. From this platform, 'greedy commercial dictators', those Fat Man Capitalists, who preferred to hire cheap labour, were as repugnant as the (racially inferior) workers they exploited.[14]

While the 1878 strike ended the use of Chinese as domestic crew in Australia, agitation continued against foreign and British-owned steamers trading in Australasian waters with 'coloured' and foreign crew. Companies targeted in the 1880s included the Pacific Mail Steamship Company, the North German Lloyd Steamship Company and the P&O.[15] In 1888 the Sydney Maritime Council, established as a maritime trades organisation incorporating sailors, wharf labourers and coal miners, targeted J. D. Spreckels's Oceanic Steam Ship Company, which operated the San Francisco to Sydney mail service in conjunction with the USSCo. The Maritime Council demanded Spreckels pay off his Chinese firemen and put in their place local union men at higher wages. He refused, and when cautioned by the USSCo. he insisted he would use the labour 'that suits me best'. White crew were scarce in San Francisco. If he signed on men at Sydney for the round trip they were likely to desert, attracted by the high wages in the American port. It was not a question of cost, he argued, for the Chinese were better firemen and more obedient: 'I would even prefer them were the cost greater.' He simply objected to 'being dictated to by men who have no interest in my steamers'.[16] It 'surprises us here', he added, to see how companies in the Australasian colonies yielded so easily to labour demands. He maintained that shipping companies should wield more clout.[17] Spreckels's new contract with the New South Wales Government in 1889 stipulated that only white crew were to be employed on the steamers carrying the colonial mails. Yet four months later he could only procure five or six white men willing to fire steamers through the tropics.[18]

This labour agitation broadened from the industrial front into a full-scale political movement. During the gold rushes, some colonies had introduced legislative measures against the Chinese. In 1881 most Australasian colonies, including New Zealand, imposed a poll tax of £10 on Chinese immigrants and limited the number of Chinese immigrants a ship could carry through tonnage restrictions (one person for every ten tons of cargo). Over time these laws were made more stringent. New Zealand raised its tonnage restrictions to one Chinese person to every 200 tons and increased the poll tax to £100 in 1894. Anti-Chinese sentiment was always more than crude racism or a reaction to job competition; it was intimately connected to state practices. The colonial state deployed race to control labour and economic relations. In *State Experiments in Australia and New Zealand*, published in 1902, William Pember Reeves, a Fabian Socialist and New Zealand's first Minister of Labour (1892–6), argued that New Zealand's progressive nature was not only ensured by the exclusion of Asiatics, but that its very future as a national community was also protected.[19]

New Zealand's Asiatic Restriction Bill of 1896 (a revised version of a defeated 1895 bill) was designed to restrict immigration on the grounds of race. It targeted Japanese as well as Chinese, while the second draft excluded reference to British Indians in the recognition of their shared imperial citizenship.[20] This legislation did not receive the imperial assent. Britain looked to safeguard its commercial and military ties with Japan under the Anglo-Japanese treaty of 1894, and objected to any overt colonial discrimination towards 'Asiatics'. The Secretary of State for the Colonies, Joseph Chamberlain, explicitly stated this imperial principle at the 1897 Conference of Colonial Premiers. He urged delegates not to exclude immigrants solely on the basis of race or colour so as to avoid offending the monarch, vast portions of the British Empire and non-white nations in the international community. Chamberlain advised colonial prime ministers to word restrictions with reference to the 'character' of the immigrant instead. An immigrant was undesirable, not because of colour, but 'because he is dirty, or he is immoral, or he is a pauper'. Tests which made no explicit reference to race, such as Natal's dictation test (the 'Natal formula'), were more acceptable. They effectively did the same job by enforcing tests in languages non-white immigrants were unlikely to know.[21]

New Zealand's Immigration Restriction Act 1899 stipulated that prohibited immigrants (those not of British or Irish parentage) must fill out an application form in 'any European language'.[22] In Australia similar restrictions were enshrined in the Immigration Restriction Act of 1901, one of the first substantive pieces of legislation, along with the Pacific Island Labourers Act and the Post and Telegraph Act (also of 1901), passed by the national Government after Federation. Through the legislative framework of White Australia (the popular, rather than official, label for these policies), non-Europeans were effectively excluded from the new nation. This was a grounded project of border control, but it also extended offshore to embrace ships. Legislation addressed the racial character of immigration and settlement as well as the racial composition of ships' crew, a highly mobile set of workers who may have only touched Australian coasts intermittently. Non-white workers were excluded from ships and settlements to bolster and protect the position of white workers. While the relationship between the state and the indigenous populations diverged significantly in Australia and New Zealand, dominant attitudes towards the undesirability of non-white immigration were the same and in this respect we can speak of a White Australasia, a trans-Tasman or intercolonial story about the racial politics of the maritime world.[23]

Over 10,000 Pacific Islanders resided in Queensland in 1901, some of the 62,000 Melanesians who had been indentured for three-year terms to work on sugar plantations since 1863. They were not embraced as settlers, but rejected as temporary, expendable labourers. Under the Pacific Island Labourers Act, men and women could only enter Australia under licence as indentured servants until 31 March 1904. The Act served as an instrument of mass deportation from the end of 1906, with over 7,500 returned to islands in Melanesia by 1908.[24] The expulsion of Islander labour whitened the Australian plantation labour force, yet exemptions were made for the maritime industries in northern Australia. Pacific Islanders were allowed continued access to crew the ships. This was due in good part to labour shortages in the bêche-de-mer and pearl shell fishing industries. Few white Australians were willing to work in these industries and, in any case, diving work was officially deemed too dangerous for whites. These were multi-racial enterprises, with Japanese, Papuan, Melanesian, Torres Strait Islander and Aboriginal labourers working within a racially segregated labour market, each group subject to specific restrictive and protective legislation. Following Federation, workers in the pearl shell industry could only enter Australia under a contract of indenture, normally for three years. The employer deposited a bond with the Queensland Government to ensure that indentured labourers did not penetrate the mainland labour market.[25] As Kay Saunders suggests, these industries functioned at the boundary between mainland Australia, Asia and the Pacific: 'the periphery was thus demarcated as a transitional zone between progressive white Australia, where trade unionism flourished, and repressive coloured Australia, where indentured servitude continued'.[26]

Throughout the 1890s, intercolonial postal and telegraph conferences made recommendations to the Imperial Government to enforce white labour on steamers operating under colonial mail contracts. This culminated in the preferential white-labour clause in the Commonwealth of Australia's Post and Telegraph Act 1901. Section 15 prohibited 'coloured' labour on board steamers operating under a Commonwealth mail contract. There were no exemptions in this labour clause, for mail steamers were more prestigious vessels than ships in the northern tropical trades. This was a controversial move. The Bengal Chamber of Commerce objected that it was a retrograde piece of legislation, which imperilled the livelihoods of the 70,000 Indian seamen and firemen employed on mail liners.[27] There were also protesting sections of the Australian community, including the Chamber of Commerce, the Dairymen's Association, the Royal Agricultural Society and the Master Builders' Association. They met collectively with the Prime Minister to demand the repeal of the clause, concerned it would damage imperial relations. They also stressed the inherent difficulty in relying on 'the waifs and strays of white humanity' to stoke the steamers.[28]

The inauguration of White Australia ushered in new state-sanctioned narratives about the relationship between space, race and labour. Racial ideology supporting beliefs that tropical plantations and steamer stokeholds were not suitable places for white labour had to shift to accommodate fully White Australia. Suddenly white men were required to work in positions in the sugar industry previously deemed 'nigger work'; sugar production methods were transformed and production costs increased.[29] A level of anxiety persisted regarding work conditions in the hot, dark, dust-laden confines of steamer stokeholds. In 1906, a royal commission into the feasibility of a Commonwealth-owned mail service to Great Britain debated this issue. The Chairman of the British Orient Steam Navigation Company, Kenneth Anderson, argued that it was not simply a matter of heat, but voyage length. White men were generally reluctant to sign on for the four-month round trip from Britain to Australia, preferring shorter absences from their families. Shipping merchant William Scott Fell maintained that the endurance of the white stoker was poor in the tropics 'because he is out of his element'. The North German Lloyd Steamship Company was only able to employ white stokers to Australia as it did not run that route on a regular basis and men did not mind working it occasionally. German law stipulated that their constant employment was not beneficial for health reasons, so the company had to rotate them or risk penalties.[30] Despite these concerns, the Australian commissioners concluded that any future contract for an ocean mail service should maintain a white stokehold crew. They anticipated no difficulty in supplying boats with white firemen 'of a satisfactory and reliable class'. They maintained that it was the combination of poor ventilation in the stokehold and low wages, rather than inherent racial traits, which had previously discouraged white men in this work.[31]

Agitation also extended to the cable-repairing steamer, *Iris*, which was jointly owned by the British, Canadian, Australian, New Zealand and Fiji governments and managed by the Pacific Cable Board. It employed Chinese firemen and stewards. Over the course of 1904, Australasian seamen's unions and trades councils made many deputations to their political leaders to have the men removed.[32] They received a sympathetic hearing and in 1906 mixed-race men from Norfolk Island (Anglo-Tahitian descendants from the *Bounty* mutineers who had relocated from Pitcairn Island in 1856) were engaged as replacements. Yet again, however, the discrimination against non-white labour attracted vocal opponents. An article in the *New Zealand Observer* opined that 'if it is "inadvisable" to employ Chinese on the cable ships, is it not also "inadvisable" to employ them as washerwomen and gardeners and cooks and cabinet-makers ashore?' It queried why the New Zealand Prime Minister Richard Seddon 'wants to do on sea what he either cannot do or does not admit the propriety of doing on land?' Moreover, the 'briny deep belongs to the Empire that Richard is so fond of celebrating, and the Empire entertains no prejudices against Chinese or any other alien race whatsoever'. This was deemed a 'silly protest' and unworthy of support.[33]

Shipping companies also began complaining about the 'harassing' effect of Australia's Immigration Restriction Act where cases of shipwreck were concerned. British law, which made no reference to race, stated that distressed sailors must be landed from a wrecked vessel. The Australian law prohibited the landing of aliens. When the USSCo. rescued some Indians from a wrecked vessel in Fiji in 1910, it attempted to take them to Australia, but was sent away. One Indian escaped and the company was liable for a £100 fine.[34]

Manning the mercantile marine: the 'lascar question'

Until the repeal of the British Navigation Acts in 1849, the imperial mercantile marine was effectively closed to foreign ships and foreign seafarers. After various legislative restrictions were removed, the proportion of foreign sailors serving on board sailing ships and steamships increased from four per cent in the early 1850s to fourteen per cent by 1884.[35] Most were of European descent; seventy per cent were Scandinavian and German. Given that their overall participation was small and most were generally employed on deep sea, rather than home and coasting trades, a royal commission into shipping safety in the late 1880s advised against legal interference in their employment.[36]

Alongside the growing participation of foreign sailors, men were engaged on special work contracts known as Asiatic articles of agreement. They were referred to as lascars, a word derived from the Persian *lashkar*, meaning an army or a camp. From the late seventeenth century, Indian seafarers had been engaged on European-registered vessels trading in Eastern seas, particularly vessels operating under the British East India Company charter. Under the terms of the Merchant

Shipping Act 1823 (the Lascar Act), Indian sailors were not freely entitled to serve on merchant vessels trading internationally, but after the repeal of the Navigation Acts they were generally acknowledged to be British, and shipowners began to engage them in increasing numbers. Malays, East Africans, Arabs and other non-Europeans who were often hired at ports in India were also designated 'lascars'. Defining the term's parameters was a source of contestation well into the twentieth century.[37]

There are no reliable statistics regarding Indian participation in the British mercantile marine before 1891. In 1896, lascars made up about fifteen per cent of crew serving on all British steam and sailing vessels and this participation ratio remained steady into the early twentieth century. On steamers engaged in foreign trades, Indians made up about a quarter of all sailors, but as Jonathan Hyslop notes, such figures should be approached with caution given the complexity of maritime recruitment.[38]

Men were hired cheaply in India, at rates one-third to one-fifth of those enjoyed by white and black sailors in the nominally free European labour market. Provisioning costs were also about one-quarter to one-fifth of those stipulated for British seafarers. Indians also had less living space on board ship, worked longer hours and were exempt from state and union-sanctioned protection including overtime, accident compensation and pensions. An Indian recruitment agent (*ghat serang*) and a boatswain or petty officer (*serang*) mediated the engagement and labour processes in ports and on ships. Lascars served as stokehold hands, sailors and stewards. Men were recruited in an atmosphere of inter-company rivalry at the main ports of Calcutta and Bombay and, as shipping companies disliked 'mixed crew', each steamer department was made up of men from different regions on the sub-continent. Ravi Ahuja has outlined the spatial and social dynamics of the recruitment networks, which spanned from village to port to steamship, and the ways in which these layered transactions further diminished the power of individual seamen in the global labour market.[39]

The high spatial mobility of Indian sailors, who typically travelled far from their inland home districts to engage on foreign ships, did not translate into occupational mobility. As Ahuja stresses, there was an enduring stability to the racialised segmentation of the maritime labour market.[40] Moreover, under Asiatic articles overseas discharges were prohibited; lascars were only to be signed on and off in Indian ports to prevent them settling in Britain. This did not prevent small communities of Asian seafarers doing so, a source of tension leading to social unrest in the early twentieth century. This was directed more at Arab, Malay and Maltese communities, however, with no more than

8,000 Indian sailors estimated to have settled in Britain before the 1950s.[41]

Lascars reputedly possessed virtues that white working-class Britons increasingly appeared to lack: sobriety, discipline, self-control and obedience. One manager of the Orient-Pacific Line related to a Mercantile Marine Committee, appointed to enquire into the racial composition of imperial shipping, that ongoing troubles with white firemen in the 1890s led to increased coal consumption, the late delivery of mails and bargaining over steamer speeds: 'we had disgraceful scenes; we had to take men on board by force, handcuffed together, and so on; we could not go on with it any longer, and we decided to carry Lascars'. He maintained that they 'are cleanly, orderly, docile; they are like children. You must not drive them, but lead them.'[42] Again, as Ahuja has discussed, rather than some inherent racial trait, the 'docility' of Indian sailors indicated that imperial labour controls were effective. Indians worked longer hours than white seafarers and were expected to be at the disposal of the shipmaster at any time, thereby curtailing opportunities to 'let loose' onshore and cause disruption on returning to the ship.[43]

As contracts to commit workers to specific labour sites for finite periods of time, articles of agreement resembled the terms of indenture under which many Indians, Chinese and Pacific Islanders laboured on imperial plantations. Terms of indenture typically entailed five years of plantation work, with workers entitled to a free return passage after another five years of industrious residence. These contracts encoded the same imperial demands for tractable, cheap and continuous labour. Plantation labourers ('coolies') had little control over their own person or their time. The threat and reality of violence overshadowed their term of indenture and there were extensive restrictions on movement and discharge. The coolie was not simply a person working for wages, but a worker requiring discipline.[44]

The status of free or time-expired Indians was particularly problematic; Europeans struggled to extend to them the privileges of full and equal British citizenship, a situation paralleled across colonial sites. In Fiji, for example, 60,000 Indian men and women were indentured there between 1879 and 1920. Forty per cent returned to India after their terms of indenture expired. While Fiji's first Governor, Sir Arthur Gordon, regarded the permanent settlement of time-expired Indians in Fiji in a positive light, indigenous Fijians and white residents for the most part did not.[45]

In Fiji, Indian workers did not self-identify as coolies, but as *girmitiyas*, named after their labour contract, the *girmit* (agreement). For them the indenture system was based on deception and exploitation; it was an entire social existence, one not confined simply to contract and labour as the label 'coolie' implied.[46] British colonial officials routinely disregarded recruits' diverse caste and social positions, treating them uniformly as people of the lowest rank. Recruits were confronted with caste pollution at recruiting depots and especially on board ships where people of differing backgrounds were expected to live close together, mix food, and cross the *Kala Pani* (black water), or the deep ocean, a space associated with danger and the unknown.[47]

Following reports of abuse, Fiji's plantations were monitored 'with excruciating exactitude', as John Kelly discusses, with statistics gathered on work rates, absences, wages, birth, death and crime rates, education and return passages.[48] By contrast, the recruitment processes of lascars in port and the labour conditions on board ship were not; little official knowledge was produced regarding the 'lascar experience' in the late nineteenth and early twentieth centuries. Shipowners wielded significant power in imperial Britain and colonial India and, as G. Balachandran discusses, they 'resisted inquiries that, while deepening the state's knowledge about Indian crews, might increase the danger of substantive regulation'.[49] Moreover, the *ghat serangs*, as Conrad Dixon notes, maintained a stranglehold over recruitment and effectively blocked attempts at labour reform.[50]

Preference for lascars was also based on the belief that certain racial groups were naturally suited to tropical regions and to certain types of strenuous, menial, hot work, while others were not. The perceived natural ability of lascars to tolerate tropical and stokehold heat did not make them deserving of equal pay; combined with their infantile status, this was in itself understood as a sign of inferiority.[51] While Indian seafarers were hired for their racial attributes and not skill, their supposed physical inferiority translated into efficient stoking. As the Liverpool superintendent of the mercantile marine noted, they could stand the heat and fired the furnaces steadily which maintained an even steam pressure, whereas white stokers were inclined to shovel a large load of coal and then come up to deck for fresh air, which resulted in loss of pressure.[52]

As colonial labour sites, ships were more contested than plantations (although plantations in Australia's tropical north were unique in this respect). Seamen's unions sought to uphold the autonomy of white shipboard labour. Joseph Havelock Wilson opposed the increasing presence of Indian sailors in the mercantile fleet and recognised that introducing equal pay and conditions would reduce their numbers. In the 1890s he agitated on an issue that came to be known as 'lascars' spaces', demanding the same bunk space on ships for Indians and white Britons. While the British courts ruled that the Board of Trade could enforce British law on British ships in British waters, Indian laws were followed in waters to the east and south of Suez where most British steamers manned by lascars traded.[53]

When the NSFU repeatedly denounced lascar deckhands as 'mere coolies' and, therefore, unused to the sea, shipowners maintained that they were hereditary sailors, members of a 'natural seafaring race'. Driven off the Indian coasting trade by the British in the nineteenth century, they were now forced to seek employment on British steamers in foreign trades; this opportunity should not be denied them.[54] In highlighting maritime 'prowess', shipowners constructed affinities across lines of difference, for the British took pride in their own maritime heritage. But again this appeal to natural aptitude, rather than skill, justified paying lower wages.[55]

This language of racialised capacity for work also aligned with older languages of military recruitment on the Indian sub-continent. In its unanimous report in 1903, the Mercantile Marine Committee defended lascar employment. Stokers who 'belonged to the northern and warlike races' impressed the committee 'with their manly character'.[56] This martial-race discourse emerged in its most coherent form in the 1880s. As Heather Streets and David Omissi discuss, it was based on a historical memory of loyalty to the British in the 1857 mutiny. The rebel *sepoys* (soldiers) were principally from the Bengal Army, a division made up of high-caste men from Awadh in the north-east. In uprising against colonial authority they were redefined as effeminate, weak, feeble, easily incited to passion and disloyal – completely unfit for military service. From the early 1880s, military recruitment shifted steadily northwards towards the Punjab and Nepal, and away from the southern states of Madras, Bombay and Hindustan. The supposed 'martial races', particularly Sikhs and Gurkhas, were valued for their distance from 'fanatical' caste ritual and their particular masculine qualities: inherent loyalty, honour and devotion, in addition to racial hardness.[57]

Soldiers were essential participants in the imperial project, but were also potentially dangerous and their activities were closely scrutinised.[58] In their seafaring capacity lascars were not deemed a threat and the imperial gaze never lingered very long on merchant vessels, another reason, Balachandran suggests, for the lack of detailed documentation about lascars.[59] Yet as mercantile ships were likely to be requisitioned in times of war and the mercantile marine recruited for fighting forces, questions of loyalty and strength were paramount. In this respect the wholesale denunciation of British sailors as outlined in chapter 3 had its limits. As one enquiry into loss of life at sea concluded: 'British seamen even when inclined to be unruly in ordinary times, have, in times of emergency and danger, courage, coolness . . .

and resources, which are not to be found equally in their more submissive mates from abroad'.[60] This created a tenuous position for Indian sailors: the traits that made them superior, favoured for their 'submissive' nature, also made them inferior, derided for lack of courage and tenacity under fire. Only British sailors excelled in the hour of crisis.[61]

Shipowners manipulated and conflated race and gender stereotypes to legitimate the shipboard division of labour and to bolster their own power and prestige. White and 'coloured' labourers were both denounced in different ways as 'less than men' – the former to justify being replaced, and the latter to justify being paid considerably less for the same work. Ultimately, white working-class insubordination and lascar docility were both unmanly.[62] The voices of these Indian seafarers were seldom heard. Few working-class men left behind their own accounts and most would have been illiterate. Only with the formation of Indian seamen's unions in the 1920s did different stories emerge to challenge publicly these dominant racialised narratives.[63] Yet, as historians of the Indian Ocean have recently emphasised, even *without* rich documentary evidence, tracing the actual circuitries of Indian men across ship and shore can free us from narrower 'victimological' readings of the 'lascar experience'. These mobilities demonstrate the extent to which men circumvented imperial power hierarchies and made their own meanings of labour opportunities in the 'steamship empire'.[64]

Australasian debates

In putting imperial and Australasian maritime trade in the same frame, late nineteenth-century metropolitan debates were replayed in intra-imperial forums in the early twentieth century. Many of the same justifications used both to support and oppose the presence of foreign and 'coloured' colonial labour on board British ships were aired again at imperial conferences. But the debate was also refashioned as steamships were scrutinised not only as labour sites, but also more intently as symbolic and material spaces of seaborne connection and exchange. Questions of shipboard labour, a ship's movements and the places to which a ship could legitimately trade were inseparable. The wholesale celebration of the 'conquest of distance' is again tempered in this context. Steamships were recast as threatening spaces of unwelcome proximity and a potent cause of disaffection between the Australasian colonies and Britain.

By the time of the 1907 conference on merchant shipping legislation, British shipping industry representatives were clear on the position of lascars in the imperial mercantile marine: they were there to stay.

New Zealand FSU representative, William Belcher, was in attendance at the conference. A strident opponent of non-white labour, Belcher had previously lauded the pre-eminent suitability of white stokehold hands. He framed the stokehold not as a place of debility and degeneration, but as a proving ground for masculine and racial strength, the pinnacle of true maritime manhood. He opposed claims that while New Zealand boys desired a life at sea, they had limited opportunities to enter this profession, for 'so far as I am aware, the New Zealand youngster shows no keen desire to go to sea, except where he can fill a man's place & receive a man's wages, i.e. in the stokehold or engine-room. Going through the various grades on deck is most distasteful to him & he rarely attempts anything in this direction'.[65]

Belcher proposed a resolution: 'That this conference is opposed to the employment of Lascars, Coolies, Chinamen, or persons of any other alien race on any vessels owned, registered, or chartered to trade in the Commonwealth or New Zealand.' He targeted local vessels that traded beyond territorial waters to the East with Asiatic labour, including the USSCo.'s *Aparima*, as well as other British and foreign ships that traded intermittently in Australasian waters. In repeating the familiar contention that Chinese and Indians were ultimately unreliable crew, he raised the moral stakes: these men were unable to engage in social intercourse with the people of Australia and New Zealand. Only white crew would ensure racial purity and bolster White Australia and 'its less formal counterpart in New Zealand'.[66]

Also in attendance, USSCo. head James Mills supported confining the New Zealand coasting trade to 'our own countrymen', for 'there is no stronger supporter of white labour than myself'. While he reflected that 'I do not like to say so – it does not do to publish these things far and wide', he declared that in the USSCo.'s limited experience the conduct of lascars was 'not only exemplary, but compares more than favourably with the conduct of white crews under similar conditions'.[67] Mills impressed at this conference and it was reported that Havelock Wilson found it difficult to know if he were a shipowner or a seamen's representative, given his 'Imperial and unbiased view of what was good for the shipping world'.[68]

The use of 'coloured' labour on board USSCo. steamers had initially been floated as a way of countering trade union agitation and wage bargaining, or at least blunting its impact on commercial productivity.[69] The *Aparima* was built in 1902 and management made enquiries about the possibility of lascar recruitment from Asiatic Homes in London before the ship was completed. London-based management noted that this would be difficult as a full complement was hard to procure at once and Mills would do better to make direct enquiries in Calcutta.[70]

Indians were tried out in the ship throughout 1903. Belcher related a complaint that the noise and smells coming from Indian crew were offensive to Europeans. He requested that their galley be moved, as in its present location it was too close to the white quarters and 'the continuous noise of the natives combined with the fumes arising from the cooking is well nigh intolerable'. As the Indian men slept at the aft end of the ship, at the opposite end from the whites, he suggested moving the galley there. 'This would keep the two races separate & obviate the inconvenience & unpleasantness to which the European crew have apparently been subjected.' The acting marine superintendent judged such alterations 'highly inconvenient', but 'as a compromise' the lascars would be paid off when the ship returned to Calcutta.[71]

A formal substitution, with Indian sailors replacing white (but retaining senior European crew), occurred in 1904 following Captain McDonald's insistence regarding efficiency in tropical trades. The firing work of Indian men was more economical and their maintenance work on the vessel in port saved the company even more money. Mills was especially sensitive to unwelcome attention from journalists and politicians and initially delayed crew replacement in Calcutta as the steamer was scheduled to return to New Zealand when Parliament was sitting. If done later in the year, Mills noted in private correspondence, 'it may be forgotten before next session'. A local director also expressed concerns about the likely reaction of 'White Australian people' and the potential withdrawal of official subsidies for the company's trans-pacific routes, yet such fears were not realised.[72] By January of the following year, the captain reported favourably on the results, indicating annual savings of £3,000.[73]

As there are few archival clues about individual Indian men, it is difficult to know much about their ethnic backgrounds or seafaring careers, or whether it was common for men to sign on articles with the USSCo. more than once. The photographs (figures 10 and 11) were taken by the company secretary, Thomas Whitson, on a voyage on the *Aparima* from New Zealand to London in 1911. As the visual archive of common sailors is so limited, these photographs are particularly interesting. While Whitson recorded the names of senior European crew on the reverse of two other photographs taken at the same time, these men were simply labelled 'members of *Aparima*'s crew'.[74]

Like Belcher, Australia's chief delegate at the 1907 conference, Sir William Lyne, was by necessity forced to counter claims that white men and stokeholds did not mix. He pointed out that British naval vessels employed whites in the tropics and when steaming at higher speeds. Belcher's resolution should be carried, he concluded, for 'it certainly does express the sentiment of Australia'. Yet Australian federal

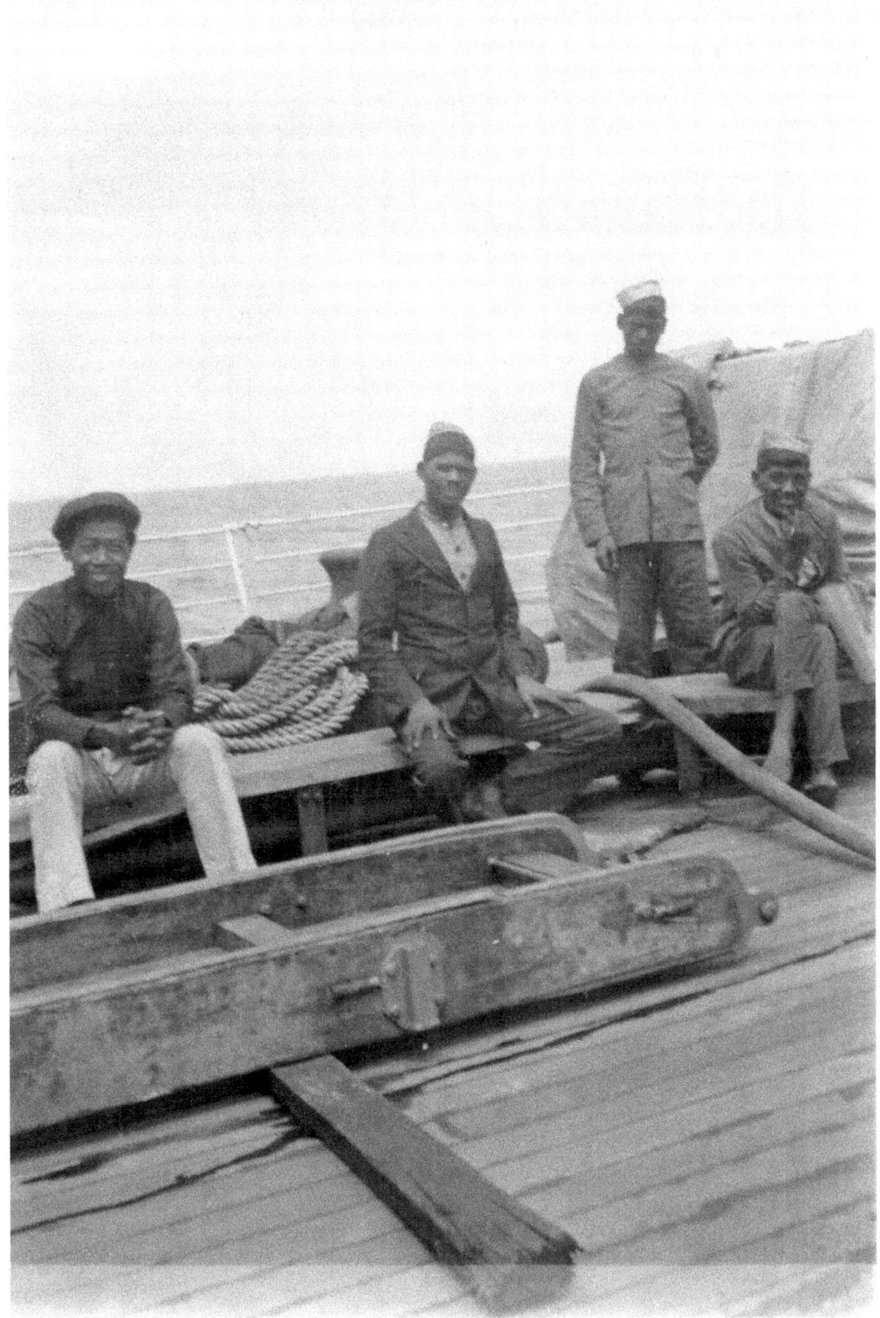

10   Members of *Aparima*'s crew, 1911

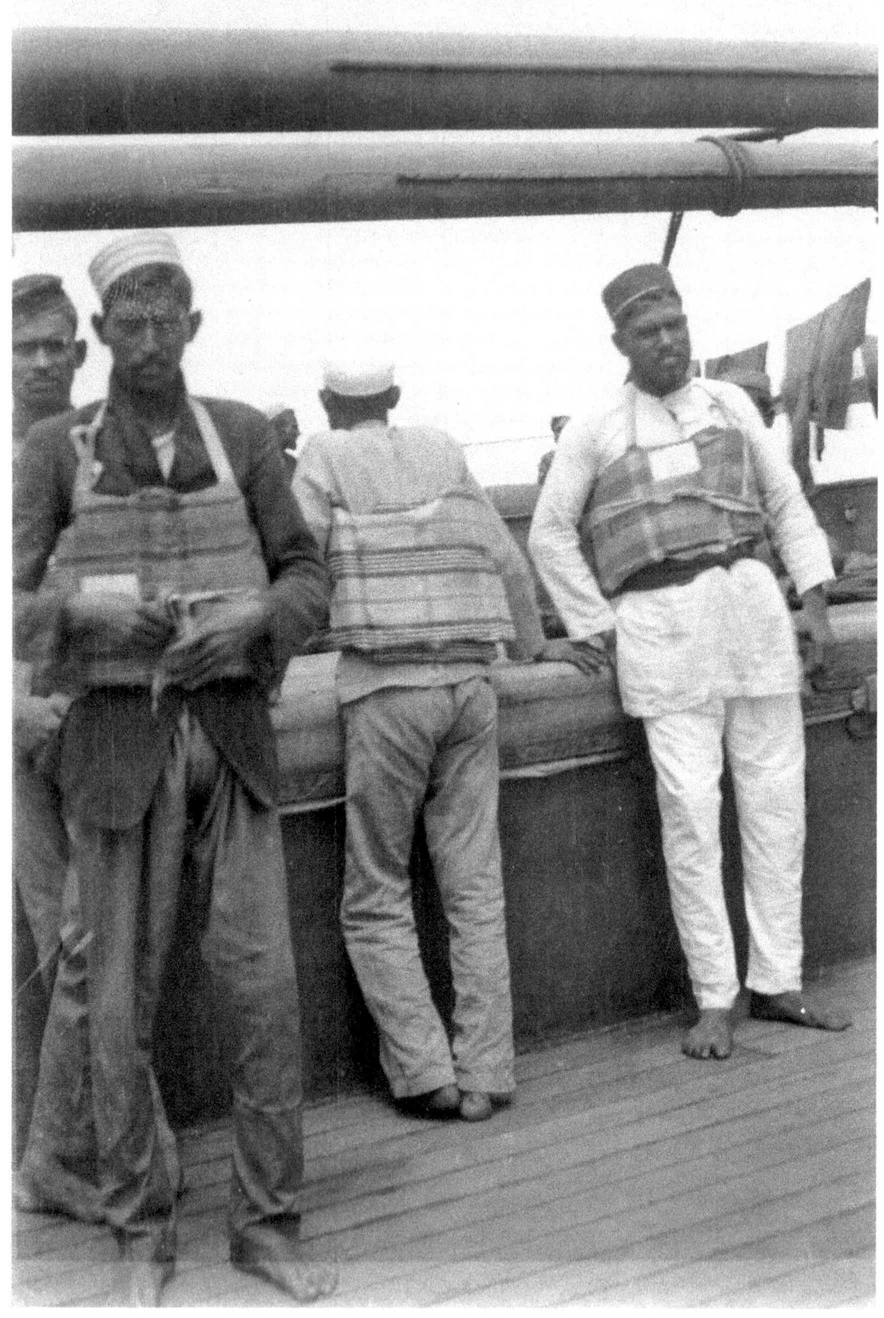

11 Members of *Aparima*'s crew, 1911

representative Dugald Thomson regretted that as the wording stood 'there is a very inconvenient and undesirable reflection on British subjects'.[75] British delegates were naturally opposed to denying Indian men employment opportunities in the imperial mercantile marine for the reasons outlined above: they were 'natural' seafarers, they had been squeezed out of their local trades, and they were loyal British subjects. It was not in the imperial interest to offend or insult India.[76]

British delegates linked steamer-manning to colonial immigration policies. Explicitly to exclude steamer labour on the basis of colour would compromise an important imperial principle. 'Coloured' maritime labour was already effectively excluded in Australasia on grounds that made no specific reference to race, including local manning, dietary, accommodation and wage scales.[77] Belcher saw the futility in pursuing his resolution when the British delegates refused to adopt it. The self-governing Dominions ultimately accepted they could not control British ships leaving British waters before coming into Australasian waters. Yet the conference confirmed the autonomy Australia and New Zealand already enjoyed over domestic maritime law and, as the *New Zealand Herald* concluded, it 'will pave the way to legislation that will guarantee Australia as a white man's country by sea and land'.[78]

The *Aparima* was scheduled for a number of Auckland–Fiji trips in the months after the conference (the ship occasionally made voyages between India and Fiji direct). Although the island trades were not coastal trades, the USSCo. operated them as if they were, with white crew paid the local rate of wages and entitled to the same work conditions. The seamen's union and the local press pressured the USSCo. into replacing the lascar crew with white sailors.[79] Mills wrote to Charles Holdsworth with his misgivings and hoped the issue would be resolved before Belcher and the New Zealand Prime Minister, Joseph Ward, returned from the maritime conference 'as the former will undoubtedly make a fuss about it and we cannot well defend it'. He instructed Holdsworth to remove the Indian crew members to laid-up vessels and put on a temporary white crew. White crew were subsequently employed to Fiji on the condition the seamen's union did not raise the issue publicly. While the local journalists were 'very anxious' to know the state of affairs, the Auckland manager reported that they were 'all put off with evasive replies'.[80]

When the P&O entered the intercolonial steamer trade in 1909, as discussed in chapter 1, Belcher 'waged the war' against the company's lascar crews 'as strenuously as possible'.[81] The USSCo. did not welcome competition from the P&O's large vessels, notwithstanding the more expensive saloon rates charged, and gave covert support to the propaganda campaign.[82] This agitation coincided with a period of mounting dissatisfaction with the Liberals and the state arbitration system. Dominated by the coal and waterside workers' union, the revolutionary Federation of Labour (Red Feds), established in 1908, rejected the arbitration system in favour of collective bargaining and direct action. There was a growing number of strikes in defiance of the arbitration laws. The FSU played no part in labour unrest between 1908 and 1913, committed instead to political reforms. Its expectation of securing improvements through more moderate means was raised by the appointment of John Millar, former secretary of the FSU, as Minister of Labour and Marine in Ward's Government in 1906. This campaign against 'coloured' labour distanced the FSU from industrial militancy in New Zealand and fostered stronger connections with Australian seafarers rather than New Zealand workers, thereby privileging transnational occupational ties over local working-class solidarity.[83]

While the huge ocean leviathans of companies such as P&O looked impressive alongside local wharves, these vessels, Belcher insisted, symbolised a danger to national life: 'They may fly the British flag, but the instincts of their owners are decidedly Oriental, and there is no place on such vessels for the democratic and white-skinned Australasian who desires to earn a crust under decent and humane conditions at sea.' Again, this was not a narrow industrial dispute confined to firemen, seamen or shipowners: 'If the aliens were objectionable on land they were objectionable at sea also.'[84] Belcher argued that economic considerations lay at the heart of this issue, yet at other times he insisted he would still object to Indian sailors if they were paid the same wages as white men: 'We do not want to see a person in the country who is not fit to marry our daughters. That is what it amounts to. We do not want to see them permanently here.' He hailed the 1878 Sydney strike against the Chinese, where 'the men and women of the country rose as one and routed them out of the ships'.[85] In another union pamphlet, Belcher printed a full version of one letter published in edited form in the *Otago Daily Times*. The omitted sections made frequent reference to the 'pet niggers' of the P&O, demonstrating the ease with which these questions could slip into racial hysteria and vitriol.[86]

Seafarers were periodically issued with circulars containing such statements as: 'A warning to persons intending a sea voyage. Be wise! Do not risk your life on any ship that carries a Lascar crew. Patronise those ships whose patriotic owners employ crews of your own countrymen.' The pamphlet went on to list cases in which Indian and Chinese crew were not amenable to discipline and emphasised that

The Lascar Question.

AN APPEAL TO PATRIOTISM.

Is Our Mercantile Marine to be Sacrificed to Imperialism?

The Dominion Must Maintain Its Own Ships.

National Assistance Required to Maintain Our Rights.

12 Federated Seamen's Union pamphlet, September 1910

'Every one of these acts of cowardice happened recently, and shows that the Lascar is not to be relied on in times of stress. "Take heed", travellers, it may be your turn tomorrow.'[87] The header from one union flyer (figure 12) demonstrates how the question of race was recruited to frame imperialism as overbearing and smothering of national self-interest. In the flyer Belcher went on to attack the 'huge impalpable mass of Imperialism, which seems to overshadow our local statesmen'. Australasian immigration policies had not impaired imperial stability to date, Belcher maintained, so broader imperial concerns should not overshadow shipping questions. He used the example of Canada, where the imperial assent was no longer required for domestic shipping legislation. This refusal to accept imperial 'interference' in local affairs 'has in no way weakened the bonds of Empire, nor has it interfered with the loyalty of Canada to the Flag'.[88]

Union agitation prompted the introduction of the Shipping and Seamen's Amendment Bill in 1910. It extended the meaning of New Zealand coasting trades, but it also imposed a stamp duty on steamers manned by Asiatic crews unless they were paid the New Zealand rate of wages. Millar emphasised that as New Zealand had used the poll tax to restrict Asiatic workers from landing onshore in the late nineteenth century, so too should such restrictions extend to ships to prevent unfair competition.[89] Member for Southern Maori, Tame Parata, queried whether the Bill would have force in the Cook Islands, now under New Zealand administration. Ward replied that the Bill would not affect the native races of New Zealand. He did not wish to 'introduce the question of colour as against any other country', but the Government 'had to look after its own people'.[90] When submitted to the Imperial Government for final approval, the Secretary of State for the Colonies opposed it on the grounds it went beyond New Zealand's legislative power. It was also objectionable in discriminating against vessels carrying British Indian subjects or subjects of friendly or allied powers.[91]

In good part as a response to the recent New Zealand legislation, which was still held over awaiting the royal assent, the India Office submitted a memorandum to the 1911 Imperial Conference stating that India's significance was widely misunderstood. It outlined the position of Indians in the self-governing colonies under three areas: the entry of new immigrants, the status and condition of Indians who had been allowed to enter, and the employment of Indians on ships in colonial waters. While the India Office accepted that the founding of white men's countries was absolutely incompatible with the idea that every British subject was free to move unrestricted throughout the British Empire, certain policies had put Asiatic British subjects on the same footing as alien Asiatics, such as Chinese and Japanese. It reiterated that immigration should only be restricted upon a criterion other than colour or race. Acknowledging that Indian immigration was of less significance for Australia and New Zealand than for Natal and Canada, it focused instead on Australasian shipping legislation, noting the disagreeable aspects of New Zealand's recent legislation and the controversy caused by the Commonwealth's Post and Telegraph Act.[92]

A London journal also opined at the time that, as a new country, Australia had the right to forbid the immigration and settlement of 'coloured' people, 'but it is stepping beyond that right when a colonial government forbids a British ship employing coloured labour, even when that labour is subject to the British crown, to enter its ports or to have the privileges of ordinary traders'. Australians 'cannot stand for a moment before the Imperial argument, and they cannot stand before the practical argument of use and wont'. It urged the conference to accord such shipping questions 'more rational and businesslike treatment'.[93]

Little was resolved at the conference, and in the years directly preceding the outbreak of the First World War the 'Indian problem' remained in the public eye and the *Aparima* remained a periodic target. The USSCo. employed the vessel as a cadet-training ship from 1912 to replace the sailing ship *Dartford*. The steamer was refitted to accommodate forty-eight cadets. While there were some concerns about maintaining a racially mixed crew, Holdsworth noting that 'we have frequently had difficulty with junior officers and engineers who have come from ships manned by coolies', the ship's captain insisted that lascars saved money by chipping, painting and cleaning the vessel in port, work which would otherwise be done by shore labour at great expense.[94] The lascar deck crew were removed, but stewards and stokehold hands were maintained. As to their mixing with the cadets, 'they are kept entirely separate, the boys working one end and the men the other and I find it works much better than I had hoped for as the boys are on their mettle and don't like to think they are being beaten by a crowd of "black fellows"', reported Captain McDonald in 1913.[95]

With steamers in short supply upon the outbreak of war, the *Aparima* was initially employed in the New Zealand coastal trade. The FSU demanded that the USSCo. follow regulations and pay all crew, including lascars, the rates prevailing on the coast. Increasing wages for the native crew was 'extremely undesirable', asserted the captain, as 'it would unsettle them and they would not understand the reason why the increase was given'. The USSCo. was prepared to pay the white crew more, but as the cadets did the bulk of cargo work, it felt that the steamer should be considered exempt from local regulations.[96] The 'lascar menace' lurked again in press reports of a firemen's strike on the domestic inter-island steamer, the *Maori*, in 1915. Amid confused accounts of reasons for the strike, the *New Zealand Truth* reported that the 'real cause' was the men's dissatisfaction with the continued presence of lascar stokehold crew in the *Aparima*.[97]

The wartime loss of the *Aparima* in 1917 mobilised a range of responses towards the Indian sailors. One newspaper reported that they all showed 'exemplary conduct', stressing their collective orderly, calm behaviour on board the ship before it sank.[98] Captain Gerald Doorly escaped to a lifeboat and watched the ship sink two minutes after he abandoned it. He then followed 'the maddening cries of frenzied men struggling in the water'. He rescued a few, but his attempts were hampered 'by the number of Natives on [the boat] who appeared to be absolutely terror stricken and incapable of movement'. The boat filled with water. He singled out two men for praise, 'the Cassub (Deck Storekeeper) Hassanuoolla, and the Saloon Topass, Moni Lall', for working hard at bailing out the boat, 'the only two Natives who were of any assistance in our dire predicament'.[99]

One cadet wrote to his brother of floating on a hatch, repelling any Indian boarders, until he reached a crowded upturned boat. He avoided swimming towards it until he had ascertained that they were white crew, as he and other cadets had fought with the Indian firemen in the days before the sinking.[100] A surviving engineer, Maurice Mayo, relayed the final hours to his mother. Along with the second mate and a cadet, he was the only white crew member in his lifeboat. Both the cadet and mate eventually 'went mad' and fell back into the sea, and of the twenty Indian seamen with him, only six remained after six hours, 'the poor devils were dying like flies their cries were pitiful'.[101]

Doorly later fictionalised the *Aparima*'s loss in one chapter of his novel *The Handmaiden of the Navy* (1919). He concluded, 'be it said to the everlasting honour and pluck of our gallant merchant seamen that, nothing daunted, they promptly shipped away to the sea again loyally to complete their "bit" for the cause of freedom and justice'. He implicitly praised white sailors here, yet in reality it was only the lascar crew that 'promptly shipped away' again. The surviving white crew received a first-class passage out to New Zealand, whereas most of the surviving lascar stokehold hands signed on to work a Hall Line steamer in Liverpool one month after the attack.[102]

White men's ships, white men's shores

The redefinition of shipboard work, skill and status in the age of steam was clearly racialised and politicised. The 'lascar question', as it came to be known, preoccupied maritime officials and workers from the mid-nineteenth century as Britain relaxed legislation providing for the preferential recruitment of British sailors on board British ships. Shipowners and politicians deployed racial stereotypes to enforce the division of shipboard labour, although the national seamen's union under Havelock Wilson contested these policies from the 1890s. In Australia and New Zealand, political and labour leaders used arguments about racial proclivities to drive lascars out of their local industries and opposed the presence of vessels trading in territorial waters without white crew. As the largest imperial employer of lascar labour, P&O looked at the issue from 'a very broad point of view', and regarded the increasing employment of lascars as 'a safeguard to our Indian Empire'. This attitude did not translate seamlessly to the Australasian colonies. P&O met opposition from the state and the seamen's union, as well as the USSCo.[103] The transnational commercial imperatives of large steamer companies and the nation-centred platform of seamen's unions were united at times, yet diverged at others. For while the USSCo. deferred to the prevailing political climate in its local operations, it held firm on its lascar recruitment policy in trades to Asia, stressing, as other companies did, the protection this afforded white men from poor work conditions, and endorsing the comparative efficiency and loyalty of Indian crew.

The triangular debates amongst Australia, New Zealand and Britain demonstrated the ways in which different strategic interests in different imperial centres affected respective attitudes towards the racial limits of exclusion and inclusion. Maritime labour concerns were enmeshed in broader debates about colonial autonomy over maritime boundaries and immigration policies. Australia and New Zealand fostered visions of nationhood that pathologised and excluded certain individuals who had the rights of imperial citizenship. These modern states strove to regulate mobility by passing acts that restricted immigration, and delimited sovereign maritime space and the terms of passage in and out of territorial waters. Such measures ultimately produced tensions and fissures within a multiracial empire, an empire united by 'one sea'.

Notes

1 WCCA, USSCo. Records, Box 13 'Aparima', Dave Wendes to Jack Churchouse (New Zealand Maritime Museum), 12 January 1987.
2 http://www.jadiving.co.uk/gallery/displayimage.php?album=search&cat=0 &pos=7 (accessed 27 April 2007).
3 http://www.ukdiving.co.uk/wrecks/wreck.php?id=27 (accessed 27 April 2007).
4 Over 3,000 Indian sailors were killed in the First World War: G. Balachandran, 'Circulation through seafaring: Indian seamen, 1890–1945', in Claude Markovits, Jacques Pouchepadass and Sanjay Subrahmanyam (eds), *Society and Circulation: Mobile People and Itinerant Cultures in South Asia, 1750–1950* (Delhi: Permanent Black, 2003), 101.
5 Anne Salmond, *Between Worlds: Early Exchanges between Maori and Europeans 1773–1815* (Honolulu: University of Hawai'i Press, 1997), 234–5, 289–90, 312, 491–2; Tony Ballantyne, 'Teaching Maori about Asia: print culture and community identity in nineteenth-century New Zealand', in Henry Johnson and Brian Moloughney (eds), *Asia in the Making of New Zealand* (Auckland: Auckland University Press, 2006), 18.
6 Frank Broeze, *Island Nation: A History of Australians and the Sea* (St Leonards: Allen & Unwin, 1998), 197–8; Heather Goodall, Develeena Ghosh and Lindi R. Todd, 'Jumping ship – skirting empire: Indians, Aborigines and Australians across the Indian Ocean', *Transforming Cultures eJournal*, 3:1 (2008), 50–1, 57–65.
7 ATL, qMS 2294, Louisa Worsfold, 'Social history of Russell' (1946).
8 Brian Moloughney and John Stenhouse, '"Drug-besotten, sin-begotten fiends of filth": New Zealanders and the Oriental other, 1850–1920', *New Zealand Journal of History*, 33:1 (1999), 43–64; Ann Curthoys, 'Conflict and consensus', in Ann Curthoys and Andrew Markus (eds), *Who Are Our Enemies? Racism and the Australian Working Class* (Neutral Bay, NSW: Hale and Iremonger, 1978), 51–8.
9 Curthoys, 'Conflict and consensus', 52–8.
10 Brian Fitzpatrick and Rowan J. Cahill, *The Seamen's Union of Australia, 1872–1972: A History* (Sydney: Seamen's Union of Australia, 1981), 9.
11 HC, USSCo. Records, AG-292-005-001/027, Henderson to Mills, 4 and 8 August 1892.
12 Marian Quartly, 'Making working-class heroes: labor cartoonists and the Australian worker, 1903–16', *Labour History*, 89 (2005), 163.
13 Nick Dyrenfurth and Marian Quartly, 'Fat man v. "the people": labour intellectuals and the making of oppositional identities, 1890–1901', *Labour History*, 92 (2007), 46.
14 Curthoys, 'Conflict and consensus', 54.
15 Raymond Markey, 'Race and organised labor in Australia, 1850–1901', *The Historian*, 58:2 (1996), 348–9; *Report from the Royal Commission on Ocean Shipping Service* (Melbourne: Government Printer, 1906), 210.
16 HC, USSCo. Records, AG-292-005-001/016, Spreckels to Mills, 7 March, 30 June and 23 August 1888.
17 *Ibid.*, Spreckels to Mills, 22 September 1888.

18 *Ibid.*, AG-292-005-001/019, Spreckels to Mills, 27 July 1889. American legislation also troubled Spreckels's operations. The passage of the Chinese Exclusion Act in September 1888 prohibited the Chinese from landing at San Francisco after they had left that port. White labour was in reality no easier to procure and Chinese crews continued to serve on transpacific steamers until the passage of the Seamen's Act in 1915 which stipulated that seventy-five per cent of crew must be able to understand English. The use of sign language and pidgin English was acceptable and some Chinese crew were retained.

19 William Pember Reeves, *State Experiments in Australia and New Zealand*, 2 vols (London: Richards, 1902), see vol. 2, chapter 4, 'The exclusion of aliens and undesirables'. See also Tony Ballantyne, 'Writing out Asia: race, colonialism and Chinese migration in New Zealand history', in Charles Ferrall, Paul Millar and Keren Smith (eds), *East by South: China in the Australasian Imagination* (Wellington: Victoria University Press, 2005), 95–7. For a discussion of the increasing control of the modern colonial state over intra-imperial mobility and immigration in the early twentieth century, and the ways in which this entailed the 'yoking together of "nation" and "state" on the terrain of race', see Radhika Viyas Mongia, 'Race, nationality, mobility: a history of the passport', in Antoinette Burton (ed.), *After the Imperial Turn: Thinking with and through the Nation* (Durham, NC: Duke University Press, 2003), 196–214. Quotation is from 210.

20 Sekhar Bandyopadhyay, 'A history of small numbers: Indians in New Zealand, c.1890–1930', *New Zealand Journal of History*, 43:2 (2009), 155.

21 Chamberlain's comments reprinted in 'Imperial conference, 1911 – Minutes of proceedings', *AJHR*, A-4 (Wellington: Government Printer, 1911), 272–3. The Natal test was itself modelled on literacy tests enacted by America's southern states to disenfranchise black voters, see Marilyn Lake, 'From Mississippi to Melbourne via Natal: the invention of the literacy test as a technology of exclusion', in Ann Curthoys and Lake (eds), *Connected Worlds: History in Transnational Perspective* (Canberra: ANU E-Press, 2005), 210–29.

22 From 1907 each prospective Chinese immigrant was expected to read out a hundred randomly chosen English words to a customs official: P. S. O'Connor, 'Keeping New Zealand white, 1908–1920', *New Zealand Journal of History*, 2:1 (1968), 44.

23 James Bennett, *'Rats and Revolutionaries': The Labour Movement in Australia and New Zealand, 1890–1940* (Dunedin: University of Otago Press, 2004), 41–56.

24 Clive Moore, *Kanaka: A History of Melanesian Mackay* (Port Moresby: University of Papua New Guinea, 1985); Raymond Evans, Kay Saunders and Kathryn Cronin, *Exclusion, Exploitation and Extermination: Race Relations in Colonial Queensland* (Sydney: Australia and New Zealand Book Co., 1975). The estimated figure of 62,000 includes those recruits who returned for a second or third period of indenture. For details on exemptions from compulsory deportation see Moore, *Kanaka*, 274–85.

25 Regina Ganter, *The Pearl-Shellers of Torres Strait: Resource Use, Development and Decline 1860s–1960s* (Carlton, Vic.: Melbourne University Press, 1994), 14–60, 107.

26 Kay Saunders, '"A new race, bred of the soil and sun": conceptualising race and labour, 1890–1914', in Mark Hearn and Greg Patmore (eds), *Working the Nation: Working Life and Federation, 1890–1914* (Annandale, NSW: Pluto Press, 2001), 91.

27 'Asiatic labour in Australia', *Evening Post* (4 January 1902), 5.

28 'Coloured labour on mail steamers', *Advertiser* (Adelaide) (4 August 1903), 5.

29 Saunders, "A new race", 78, 92.

30 *Report from the Royal Commission on Ocean Shipping Service* (Melbourne: Government Printer, 1906), 68, 108, 210.

31 *Ibid.*, xv. The federal contract for this service with the Orient Steam Navigation Company (1907–10) enforced the preference for white firemen.

32 See correspondence in University of Auckland Library Special Collection, FSU Auckland Branch, 91/3, Box 2.

33 'A silly protest', *New Zealand Observer* (17 December 1904), 3.
34 'A grievance: shipping companies complain', *Evening Post* (30 June 1910).
35 *Report on the Supply of British Seamen*, 5.
36 British Parliamentary Papers, *Shipping Safety: Loss of Life at Sea, 1887–1889*, vol. 9 (reprinted Shannon: Irish University Press, 1970), 39. 'Home trade' referred to traffic between Britain and the continent of Europe between the River Elbe and Brest. Men from the United States, Austria, Russia, Holland, Greece, Italy, Spain and Portugal also routinely signed on as crew on British ships.
37 Laura Tabili, *'We Ask for British Justice': Workers and Racial Difference in Late Imperial Britain* (Ithaca and London: Cornell University Press, 1994), 46; Balachandran, 'Circulation through seafaring', 101.
38 *Return of the Number, Ages, Ratings, and Nationalities of the Seamen Employed on the 25th Day of March 1896*, C-8579 (1897); 'Papers laid before the Imperial Conference, 1911', *AJHR*, A-4A (Wellington: Government Printer, 1911), 293; Hyslop, 'Steamship empire, 56.
39 Ravi Ahuja, 'Networks of subordination – networks of the subordinated: the ordered spaces of South Asian maritime labour in an age of imperialism (c. 1890–1947)', in Ashwini Tambe and Harald Fischer-Tine (eds), *The Limits of British Colonial Control in South Asia: Spaces of Disorder in the Indian Ocean Region* (London: Routledge, 2009), 22–33. For more on the history of lascar engagement on British ships, see Conrad Dixon, 'Lascars: the forgotten seamen', in Rosemary Ommer and Gerald Panting (eds), *Working Men who Got Wet: Proceedings of the Fourth Conference of the Atlantic Shipping Project* (Newfoundland: Memorial University of Newfoundland, 1980), 265–77.
40 Ravi Ahuja, 'Mobility and containment: the voyages of South Asian seamen, c.1900–1960', *International Review of Social History*, 51: Suppliment S14 (2006), 112–20.
41 See special issue 'Ethnic labour and British imperial trade: a history of ethnic seafarers in the UK', *Immigrants and Minorities*, 13:2-3 (1994); Tabili, *'We Ask for British Justice'*, chapters 3 and 4.
42 *Mercantile Marine: II – Minutes of Evidence*, 543, 546.
43 Ahuja, 'Mobility and containment', 116–17.
44 For more on indentured labour see Hugh Tinker, *A New System of Slavery: The Export of Indian Labour Overseas 1830–1920* (London: Oxford University Press, 1974).
45 John D. Kelly, *A Politics of Virtue: Hinduism, Sexuality, and Countercolonial Discourse in Fiji* (Chicago: University of Chicago Press, 1991), 66, 70, 75–85.
46 Kelly, *A Politics of Virtue*, 26–31. See also Brij V. Lal, *Girmitiyas: The Origins of the Fiji Indians* (Canberra: Journal of Pacific History, 1983) and Lal (ed.), *Crossing the Kala Pani: A Documentary History of Indian Indenture in Fiji* (Canberra: Australian National University, 1998).
47 This transoceanic experience is now recovered as essential to the emergence of an identity politics of 'coolitude', a politics which celebrates hybridity, decentring and connectedness. Sea routes were pathways to new identities – the ship and the voyage itself, rather than an essentialised Mother India, were key points of departure. This is seen most notably in the work of the Mauritian poet Khal Torabully: see Veronique Bragard, 'Transoceanic echoes: coolitude and the work of Mauritian poet Khal Torabully', *International Journal of Francophone Studies*, 8:2 (2005), 219–33.
48 Kelly, *A Politics of Virtue*, 30.
49 G. Balachandran, 'South Asian seafarers and their worlds, c. 1870–1930s', in Jerry H. Bentley, Renate Bridenthal and Kären Wigen (eds), *Seascapes: Maritime Histories, Littoral Cultures and Trans-Oceanic Exchanges* (Honolulu: University of Hawai'i Press, 2007), 190.
50 Dixon, 'Lascars: the forgotten seamen', 272–3.
51 Laura Tabili, '"A maritime race": masculinity and the racial division of labour in British merchant ships, 1900–1939', in *Iron Men, Wooden Women*, 184.

52 *Mercantile Marine: II – Minutes of Evidence*, 21.
53 G. Balachandran, 'Conflicts in the international maritime labour market: British and Indian seamen, employers, and the state, 1890–1939', *The Indian Economic and Social History Review*, 39:1 (2002), 91–2.
54 Mercantile Marine Committee, *Report of the Committee Appointed by the Board of Trade to Inquire into the Mercantile Marine: I – Report*, Cd 1607 (London: HMSO, 1903), vi.
55 Tabili, '"A maritime race". . .', 185.
56 *Mercantile Marine: II – Minutes of Evidence*, vi, paras 14–15.
57 Heather Streets, *Martial Races: The Military, Race and Masculinity in British Imperial Culture, 1857–1914* (Manchester: Manchester University Press, 2004), 11–12. See also David E. Omissi, *The Sepoy and the Raj: The Indian Army, 1860–1940* (Basingstoke: Palgrave Macmillan, 1994).
58 Omissi, *The Sepoy and the Raj*, xviii.
59 Balachandran, 'Circulation through seafaring', 103.
60 *Shipping Safety*, 297. See also evidence submitted at *Mercantile Marine: II – Minutes of Evidence*, 27.
61 Tabili, '"A maritime race". . .', 186–7.
62 Tabili, *'We Ask for British Justice'*, 53.
63 Balachandran, 'South Asian seafarers', 190.
64 Hyslop, 'Steamship Empire', 51. See also Goodall, Ghosh and Todd, 'Jumping ship–skirting empire'. Thanks to Tony Ballantyne for pressing this point.
65 ATL, FSU Records, MS-Papers-0650-004, Executive Council – General correspondence (1896–1902), Belcher to Jones, 13 August 1896.
66 *Merchant Shipping Legislation: Report of a Conference between Representatives of the United Kingdom, the Commonwealth of Australia, and New Zealand, 26th March–2nd April, 1907* (Sydney: Government Printer, 1907), 100, 108–9.
67 *Ibid.*, 109.
68 'Sir Joseph Ward's speech', *Otago Witness* (15 May 1907), 18.
69 HC, USSCo. Records, AG-292-005-001/003, W. Macandrew to Mills, 1 January 1885.
70 HC, Cameron Family Papers, MS 1046, Box 9, C. H. Cooper to Cameron, 6 December 1901 and 10 March 1902.
71 HC, USSCo. Records, AG-292-005-001/071, Belcher to Holdsworth, 16 September 1903 and Strang to Holdsworth, 26 September 1903.
72 *Ibid.*, AG-292-005-001/069, Mills to Holdsworth, 4 June 1904; AG-292-005-001/073, McLean to Mills, 12 September 1904.
73 *Ibid.*, AG-292-003-001/019, minutes of meeting of directors, 19 January 1905.
74 *Ibid.*, AG-292-005-001/101, Whitson to Holdsworth, 11 May 1911.
75 *Merchant Shipping Legislation*, 109–10.
76 *Ibid.*, 115.
77 *Ibid.*, 115.
78 *New Zealand Herald* (2 May 1907).
79 UASC, FSU, Auckland Branch Records, 91/3, Box 2, Young to Kneen, 19 July 1907.
80 HC, USSCo. Records, AG-292-005-001/085, Mills to Holdsworth, 31 May 1907; AG-292-003-001/021, minutes of meeting of directors, 1 August 1907; AG-292-005-001/082, Irvine to Holdsworth, 5 August 1907.
81 UASC, FSU, Auckland Branch Records, D-8, Box 1 – Correspondence General, 1900–13, Belcher to Kneen, 9 May 1910; 91/3, Box 2, Belcher to Kneen, 26 August 1910.
82 McLean, *The Southern Octopus*, 174–5.
83 The different political complexion of the three branches also worked against a united approach. The conservative branches in Auckland and Dunedin were strongholds of Liberal influence, while the Wellington branch under Tom Young was more militant. Under his leadership, the FSU officially parted from the Liberals and transferred political loyalty to the independent and socialist New Zealand Labour Party. Young assumed the presidency of the newly formed United

Federation of Labour (UFL) in 1913, a body initiated by the Red Feds in order to seek more unity with the moderates they had previously condemned. The Dunedin and Auckland branches of the FSU refused to affiliate with the UFL. In 1913 the building wave of industrial unrest culminated in a massive strike, paralysing ports, mines and urban industry for sixty-five days. The FSU entered the strike rather belatedly. After the Massey Government suppressed the strike, the Red Feds entered politics and dominated the leadership of the new Labour Party in 1916. With Young firmly in control of the FSU, the policy of separatism came to an end; seamen increasingly perceived themselves as working-class. See Neill Atkinson, 'Against the tide: the Auckland Seamen's Union 1880–1914', in Pat Walsh (ed.), *Trade Unions, Work and Society: The Centenary of the Arbitration System* (Palmerston North: The Dunmore Press Ltd, 1994), 69–90; Atkinson, 'Auckland Seamen and their Union'.

84 ATL, Roth Papers, 94-106-43/07, Belcher, Seamen's Union circular, 16 August and 28 September 1910.

85 Dominions Royal Commission, *Royal Commission on the Natural Resources, Trade, and Legislation of Certain Portions of His Majesty's Dominions Minutes of evidence taken in New Zealand in 1913*, Cd 7170 (London: HMSO, 1913), 227.

86 ATL, Roth Papers, 94-106-43/07, Seamen's Union pamphlet, 29 October 1910.

87 HC, Pamphlets collection, Seamen's Union pamphlet, vol. 50, no. 13 (1911) (emphasis in original).

88 ATL, Roth Papers, 94-106-43/07, Seamen's Union pamphlet, 8 September 1910.

89 15 November 1910, *NZPD*, vol. 153 (Wellington: Government Printer, 1910), 702.

90 27 October 1910, *NZPD*, vol. 153, 115. I discuss the participation of Maori and Pacific Islanders in more detail in Part III.

91 13 January 1911, *AJHR*, A-2 (Wellington: Government Printer, 1911), 67–8.

92 'Papers laid before Imperial Conference, 1911: position of British Indians in the Dominions', *AJHR*, A-4A (Wellington: Government Printer, 1911), 272–9. It also noted the debate over the Commonwealth's Customs Tariff Bill 1906, which proposed to levy preferential duties in favour of British goods imported in British ships manned by white labour. Following discussions at the Colonial Conference 1907 this bill did not come into operation.

93 'Imperial shipping: Australasia taken to task', *Evening Post* (22 April 1911), 12.

94 HC, USSCo. Records, AG-292-004-003/002, Holdsworth to Mills, 22 December 1911; AG-292-005-001/098, Mills to Holdsworth, 2 January 1912 and Small to Mills, 6 February 1912.

95 WCCA, USSCo. Records, Box 13 'Aparima', McDonald to Strang, 7 March 1913.

96 National Archives New Zealand (ANZ), Marine Department Records, M-1-17/11/5, Kennedy to Minister Marine, 16 September 1914.

97 'The *Maori*'s malcontents', *New Zealand Truth* (6 February 1915), 5.

98 ATL, MS-Papers-0687, Captain Gerald Doorly, Selections from scrapbooks, misc. cutting.

99 WCCA, USSCo. Records, Box 13 'Aparima', 20 November 1917.

100 *Ibid.*, 29 November 1917.

101 ATL, MS-Papers-5742, Maurice Mayo to his mother, 29 November 1917.

102 Gerald Doorly, *The Handmaiden of the Navy* (London: Williams and Norgate, 1919), 144: WCCA, USSCo. Records, Box 13 'Aparima', Doorly to Mills, 5 January 1918.

103 Edward Trelawney, *Report of the Royal Commission on the Navigation Bill* (Melbourne: Government Printer, 1906), 265.

CHAPTER FIVE

Guardians and troublemakers: confining women at sea

A montage by prominent Port Chalmers ship photographer David Alexander de Maus (figure 13) memorialises Miss MacQuaid, Mrs McDonald and Miss Grinrod, three Union Company stewardesses. They died in the wreck of the *Wairarapa*, an intercolonial steamer that struck Great Barrier Island off the far north-east coast of New Zealand on 29 October 1894. De Maus photographed a painting of the shipwreck and superimposed portraits of each stewardess and a photograph of a monument erected to the trio. The painting by E. B. Hayward depicts a foreboding and rugged seascape. Fog closes in around the dark cliffs. The steamer is nearly completely submerged, battered against the rocks by rough seas. The rigged masts jut out in a final futile gesture, emphasising tragic human fallibility in the face of turbulent nature. In the upper half of the image the perfectly spherical head-and-shoulders portraits of the stewardesses are suspended above the wreck, suggestive of their passage to the afterlife. Frozen in formal poses and haloed by the stark studio backdrop, their collective feminine stillness and poise contrast with the unruly, violent energy of the ocean beneath.

Built in 1882 for the small fleet of luxury intercolonial steamers, the *Wairarapa*'s final voyage began twelve years later in Sydney in the early evening of Wednesday, 24 October 1894. Under the command of Captain John McIntosh, it left Circular Quay bound for Auckland's Queen Street wharf. First landfall was the Three Kings Islands off the northernmost tip of New Zealand. It reached and passed this point in the early morning of the fourth day. On its usual passage, the ship then turned south-east, and later south along the east coast towards Auckland. Yet on this occasion McIntosh did not order the ship to turn. The *Wairarapa* continued to steam to the east on a divergent course. Thick fog rolled in and soon obscured all sight of land. Pushing the steamer at its maximum speed of almost fourteen knots, McIntosh did not adjust speed for the poor conditions despite nervous suggestions

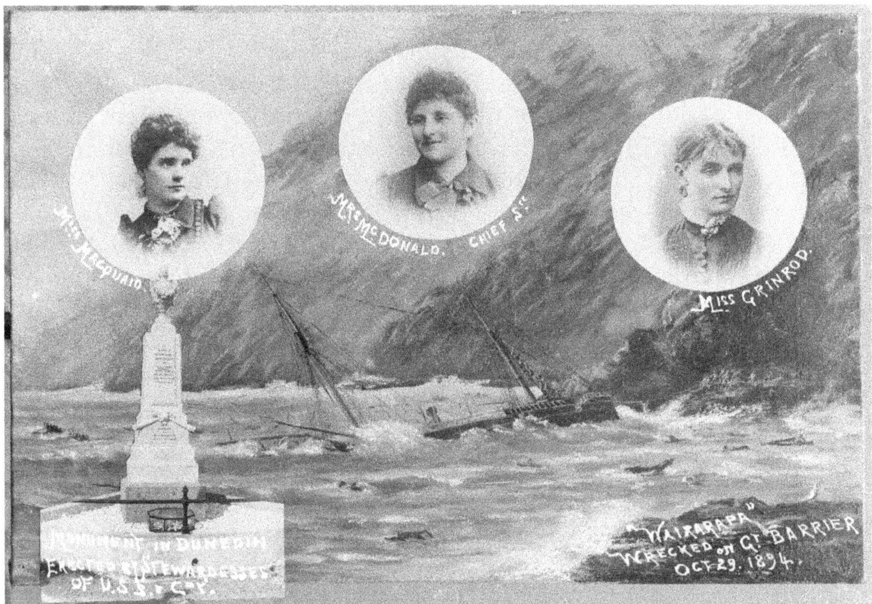

13 Photograph of a painting depicting the *Wairarapa* wreck

from senior crew. When the southerly course was eventually adopted, now many miles to the east, the *Wairarapa* was headed directly for the northern cliffs of Great Barrier Island, the largest offshore island in New Zealand, named for the shelter it provides the Hauraki Gulf from the vagaries of the Pacific Ocean. At eight minutes past midnight on Monday, 29 October 1894, the ship rammed headlong into steep cliffs near Miners Head. The vessel came to a sudden standstill in the pitch black, lodged fast on the rocks.

Awakened from their sleep, passengers scrambled to deck in their bedclothes. As they did so the ship lurched violently to port and came to rest on its side. Scores of people, livestock caged on deck and crates of cargo were flung into the rough seas. Many people could not swim and were drowned. Some were struck and killed by the horses, wreckage and heavy cargo. The passengers that managed to remain on board scrambled up the masts and clung to the rigging. Only two of the six lifeboats were launched safely and they both reached a bay about ten miles from the ship. The rest were swamped or stove in and smashed against the rocks. About three hours after the ship had struck the cliff-face, the captain threw himself from the ship's bridge and was not seen again.

Once daylight broke, two of the crew swam ashore with ropes to form a lifeline for those still clinging to the ship's rigging. Some passengers were rescued in this way. Survivors huddled on rocks for over thirty hours, their only sustenance oranges and tins of pineapple floating near the wreck. The steamer also carried four life-rafts. Three men launched one and managed to reach the settlement of local Ngati Rehua Maori at Katherine Bay further down the coast to raise the alarm. People in Auckland knew the vessel was overdue but had no idea where it was. With the only contact between New Zealand's North Island and Great Barrier Island being a weekly steamer, it was three days before Auckland learned of the *Wairarapa*'s fate. Of the 186 passengers and sixty-five crew on board, 101 passengers and twenty crew were drowned.[1]

In the days following the disaster, male crew and passengers were widely condemned. They saved themselves, it was alleged, leaving women and children to perish. In the two lifeboats lowered safely there were fifty men and only five women on board. In a report of the investigation of the wreck scene it was noted that 'one after another, the bodies of noble women have been found with children clasped to their bosoms'.[2] In his account of the disaster, R. H. Bakewell, an Auckland resident, noted that fifty-six per cent of male passengers and seventy-four per cent of male crew survived, compared with only twenty-three per cent of female passengers and no female crew. 'These figures are enough to make one ashamed of one's manhood,' he deplored.[3]

The stewardesses demonstrated 'self-denying heroism'. The chief stewardess, Charlotte McDonald, was thirty-four, a widow with four children. Her husband had been employed as a shore hand for the USSCo. at Port Chalmers. He had drowned two years earlier after falling overboard from a company vessel. She went on this voyage with a heavy heart, it was reported, as her mother was dying, 'but duty must be done'. Annie MacQuaid was twenty-seven years old and unmarried, a resident of Dunedin. Thirty-four-year-old Lizzie Grinrod was also unmarried and a resident of Melbourne.[4] The last time MacQuaid was seen she was fastening her own lifebelt to a small child. Some members of the public proposed a memorial to MacQuaid, yet her parents declined this honour, insisting she was not the only one who deserved recognition. A monument was subsequently erected to all three stewardesses at the entrance of Dunedin's Northern Cemetery in January 1896.[5]

In leaving women and children behind on the wreck, the behaviour of most of the male crew and passengers was adjudged 'selfish and unmanly' by the *New Zealand Observer*. On reaching Great Barrier Island some of the male survivors continued to behave in a 'despicable' fashion. Many women dragged alive from the sea were left partially clothed or completely naked. Fully clothed men, including a 'clerical gentleman comfortably wrapped in *two* overcoats', did not offer women items of clothing until ordered to by others.[6] In the 'Sketches suggested by scenes at the enquiry' (figure 14), such men do not fare well. In the bottom right, Percival Fenwick, the ship's purser, grudgingly removes one pair of trousers for a fellow male survivor, while two naked women huddle in the background. To the right of this, a villainous caped figure, identified as a 'brave parson', climbs to safety, stepping past others on the ropes. At the top, two Chinese survivors ('the despised Chinamen') are aiding the rescue of others, while MacQuaid saves young children. Maori were also widely praised for their rescue efforts. They 'behaved splendidly' in providing for survivors and burying many bodies. They passed over rings and other valuables to police, with each item marked to correspond to the numbered graves.[7] The New Zealand Prime Minister. Richard Seddon, sent them one ton of flour and boxes of tea, sugar and oatmeal in recognition of their assistance.[8]

Shipwrecks were routinely scripted as supreme tests of social values and cultural ideals, with people expected to follow and go beyond the call of duty. In accounts of the *Wairarapa* wreck, women stayed faithful to late nineteenth-century gender ideals. As mothers, female passengers protected their children, and as stewardesses, female crew also fulfilled their primary caregiving and service roles: they put others first. This extension of nurture and service from mothering to work on board ship was a powerful framework, which both legitimated and restricted women's professional positions in the USSCo.

Men, by contrast, transgressed and violated the gendered edict governing shipboard evacuations which decreed 'women and children first'. With the exception of a few crew, a couple of Chinese passengers and Maori onshore, they disregarded the welfare of others and exposed a blatant irresponsibility. At the enquiry that followed the disaster, the late Captain McIntosh was held solely responsible. He commanded the ship at full speed in poor visibility, made a crucial navigational error and did not respond to the legitimate concerns of officers and other crew; he was not the responsible patriarch of this ship. Sketches in newspapers suggested he was unduly hierarchical. Some men were singled out for praise. The Royal Humane Society awarded silver medals to the second engineer John Dunlop and a steward, Ben Kendall, for their 'heroic conduct' in constructing a lifeline from ship to shore. The official enquiry concluded that 'all we can say about Mr Fenwick, the purser, is that he saved himself', and 'of the crew, with few exceptions, very little can be said about them'.[9]

Other shipwrecks yielded invidious contrasts, providing 'glorious example[s] of how Britons can die'. In the loss of the HMS *Orpheus*, a warship that sank off the west coast of Auckland in 1863 with the loss

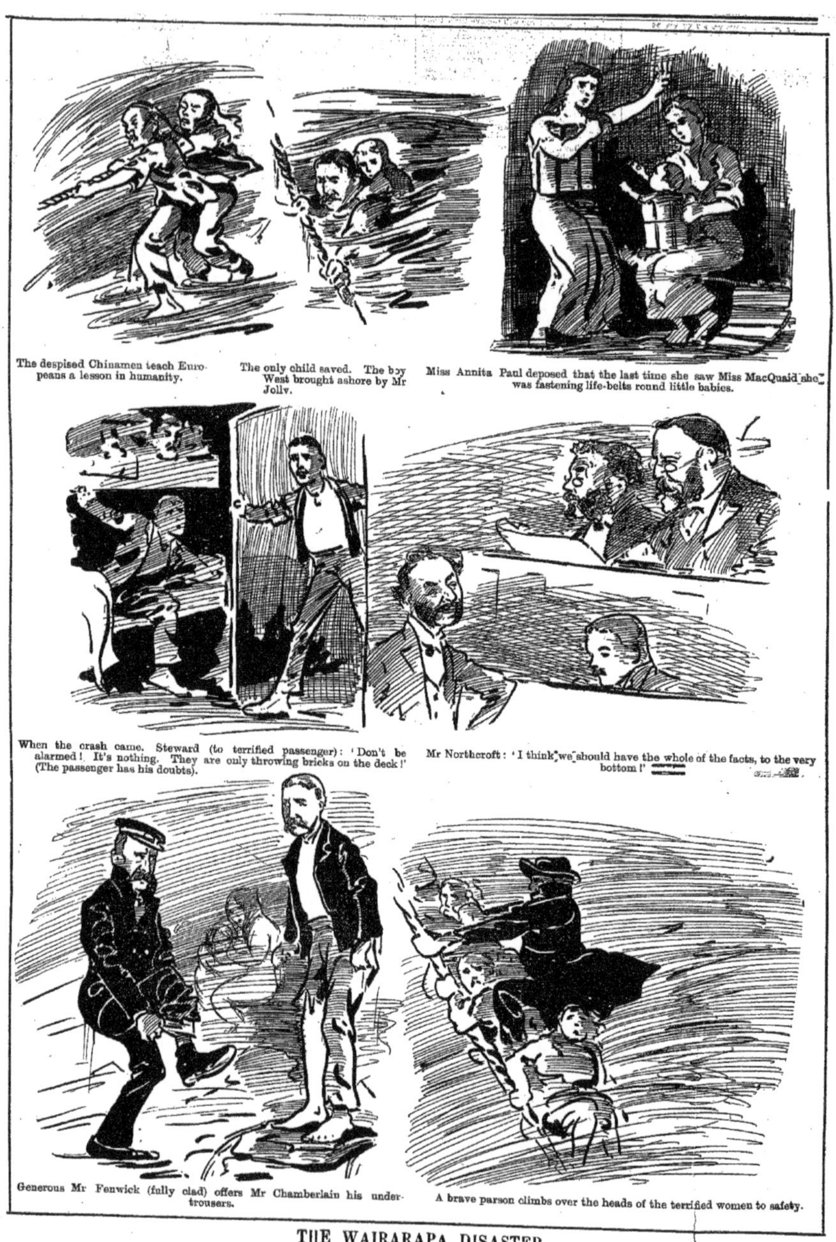

14   'The *Wairarapa* disaster: sketches suggested by scenes at the enquiry'

of 189 lives, men stood 'shoulder to shoulder' and went down with the ship. This proved that 'men of our race, placed in positions of deadly danger, have risen to the height of the situation, and *have* acted like heroes . . . the conduct of the great majority of the males among the [*Wairarapa*] crew was so despicable that I cannot trust myself to speak of it. What a contrast to that of the three stewardesses, who all died doing their duty!'[10]

Such incidents were not unprecedented in the British maritime world. Forty years earlier, in the wreck of the transatlantic steamer the *Arctic*, all women and children died, while sixty-one out of 153 crew survived, including four of the five top officers. As Stephen Fox recounts, the disaster served to 'shatter high Victorian notions of how men were supposed to respond under duress . . . it broke the social contract in alarming, revealing ways. Worse than shocking or tragic, it was shameful.'[11] Following the wreck of the London and South Western Railway's *Stella* in the English Channel five years after the *Wairarapa* incident, a number of memorials were erected to Mary Ann Rogers, a stewardess who also gave up her lifebelt to save the life of another.[12]

Viewed on its own, de Maus's montage, created sometime after the *Wairarapa* monument was erected in 1896, provides no overt commentary on the circumstances surrounding the wreck or the death of the stewardesses. Yet, when coupled with these newspaper accounts, his depiction is more obviously a memorial both to the women and the way they died.

Gendering the ship in history

As scholars began critically to explore the social and cultural dimensions of maritime history, they interpreted the ship as a site with a particular social structure, a place with its own order, rules and systems. Feminist scholars critiqued early accounts for neglecting a gender analysis in discussions of class formations afloat.[13] In his work on the Canadian merchant marine, Eric Sager reflected that the seafaring profession afforded men escape from women and family ties, yet he framed it as an escape into 'the genderless company of men', thereby conflating 'gender' with 'women' and sidestepping the construction of maritime masculinities.[14] More recently, historians have turned to address men as gendered subjects, the diverse and contested construction of masculinities afloat, and the relations between different men at sea across hierarchies of gender, race and class.

In her work on American whaling men, Margaret Creighton has examined the ship as an institution of masculine indoctrination. Men joined the ship for a number of reasons: in order to earn enough to settle ashore and attract a wife; as a way to escape home and domestic responsibilities; as an opportunity to nurture self-restraint and commit to an ascetic routine; to become closer to God; or to foster romantic male friendships. 'Seafaring', she concludes, 'spoke to men of various interests and masculine inclinations'.[15] Creighton tempers the stress others have placed on assertive, rebellious sailors and social conflicts on board, for the performance of a type of combative, muscular, hardy maritime masculinity was frequently complemented by a more 'tranquil' gendered identity, one that embraced 'feminine' domestic sensibilities.[16] In this way the sailing ship was also a heterosocial space. Women figured as symbol and image in seafaring life and shipboard ritual through shanties, yarns and sketches, in scrimshawing (the act of carving images into whales' teeth), in the figureheads on ships and in the feminised spatial language of the ship.

The feminisation of ships has a long history in the West, first referenced in the *Oxford English Dictionary* in 1375. Some suggest this was an expression of the strong sense of identification sailors felt towards their vessels: going to sea was hazardous and threw them into an intimate relationship with their ship. They frequently celebrated it for the protection, shelter and sustenance it afforded, it was understood as a strong, courageous and graceful partner.[17] Others argue that by feminising the ship and the sea, sailors worked to deflect homosexual desire by preparing men for heterosexual encounters in port.[18] For the maritime author Joseph Conrad, the sailing ship was passive, dependent and angelic, reliant for power on the combination of wind and male physical exertion. The steamer, by contrast, with 'the power she carries within herself' (the engine-room 'pulsates' and 'throbs'), was independent of nature and men. Autonomous and rebellious, she was unworthy of Conrad's affection.[19] In *The Mirror of the Sea* he lamented that working the steamship was 'less personal and a more exact calling . . . in short, less a matter of love'.[20]

Differences in seafarers' age, shipboard rank, social background and marital status also influenced these attitudes. Some men encouraged a shipboard society that excluded and condemned women and feminine virtues, while others could create a space for these attributes and for women themselves. On whaling vessels, officers were more likely than common sailors to be married. At the aft end of the ship they enjoyed homelike quarters in separate cabins and the services of personal attendants such as stewards, cabin boys and cooks. They had a degree of private space and private time on board, and many used this to mourn their separation from family, to write to wives and lovers, to gaze on their photographs and to enjoy home-cooked provisions. Moreover, about one-fifth of whaling captains sailed with their wives from the mid-nineteenth century.[21] Historians are also recovering women's fundamental contributions on board ship and in port economies, moving beyond the objectified 'wooden' images of cross-dressing pirates, port town prostitutes, and waiting, weeping wives and sweethearts onshore.[22] In all these guises, the domestic, the feminine and the women themselves were integral, not marginal, to the maritime world.

Yet in recovering such histories, many studies have simply adopted an 'additive' approach to women and maritime history. In uncritically documenting the presence of real women on board ships, women are easily reinscribed as curiosities, note Creighton and Lisa Norling, 'without questioning the gender assumptions that framed them'.[23] Similarly, Jo Stanley discerns a need for more analytical histories of the gendered structures and discourses that mediated women's and men's sea-related lives, 'to see what produced such women and how they and the stories about them produced ways of seeing sea-focused women'.[24]

A shipwreck is an extraordinary event and in many respects the *Wairarapa* disaster sits apart as an account of female participation in a traditionally masculine working environment, unique for the celebration of the stewardesses and their collective display of appropriate femininity. A discussion of the twin histories of women on board USSCo. vessels as stewardesses and as passengers, histories scholars usually address separately, can help us prise apart the often unspoken gendered attitudes and practices that shaped some women's experiences of life at sea in the age of steam.

Stewards and stewardesses

On large passenger liners the providore department was usually the largest afloat, staffed by a team of stewards, stewardesses, cooks and other kitchen staff. The chief steward wielded significant authority. Deck and engine-room crew often derided stewards as mere waiting staff, yet Walter Manning maintained that the steward of any rank, 'especially so if he is of colonial parentage . . . vividly illustrates the paradox that duties which on shore are allotted to women, and are regarded as domestic drudgery, below the dignity of men, may be performed as a means of gaining a livelihood without being in any way derogatory to manhood or inflicting any blow to self-respect'.[25] Although 'domestic drudgery' was by no means the lot of all women ashore, Manning frames the ship as a space that sanctioned particular masculine roles that could not be judged without modifying, adjusting or even subverting land-based norms. Yet the maritime author Frank Bullen believed that stewards routinely internalised the contempt of other crew and could 'never quite be rid of the feeling that they are menials', finding the tips they received from passengers 'repugnant'. This suggests that humiliation stemmed from feminised work and the commodification of such service.[26]

Stewards usually entered the providore department as 'boots', responsible for many tasks including polishing passengers' boots and acting as night watchmen in the saloon, or as messroom stewards, waiting on the master and officers and performing 'every form of domestic service which officers are entitled to'. Any sign of awkwardness, stupidity, negligence or lack of cleanliness hindered promotion to saloon class.[27] A good appearance and gentlemanly manners were mandatory for the saloon, especially on the larger liners where the quality of passenger service shaped the public assessment of the ship and the steamer company itself. One note in USSCo. personnel files listed names of stewards with short comments as to their abilities, such as 'good man'; 'suits steamer'; 'good man but no disciplinarian'; 'sober, civil, slow and sleepy'; 'good steward, sober, talks too much'; 'excitable, but on the whole good man'.[28]

From the late nineteenth century, British shipping companies increasingly engaged 'coloured' crew in large numbers as stewards, a position that *was* feminised and consequently less desirable to white crew. As Laura Tabili concludes, 'there appear to be not just similarities but mutual reinforcement among the feminisation, "racialisation", and deskilling of shipboard jobs'.[29] Goans, although Portuguese rather than British subjects, long monopolised saloon-class steward positions. A maritime official at the Victoria Docks suggested that companies favoured them (referring to them as 'half breeds' in his evidence at the 1902 Board of Trade committee of enquiry into the mercantile marine), as 'they are not so familiar with the passenger as English stewards are . . . the Goanese are very polite and obliging, and do everything they can to make things pleasant'.[30] As these men were predominantly Catholic rather than Hindu or Muslim, they could cook for anyone, free of the taboos associated with food preparation.[31]

Women were initially employed in the mid-nineteenth century to act as shipboard representatives for female emigrants, to aid them with seasickness and other intimate concerns, and to oversee the sexual division of passengers and the segregation of single women in steerage. The role of the stewardess expanded as competition between liner companies intensified toward the end of the century. Women were hired to provide more extensive and improved service to female passengers such as aiding dressing, serving meals, cleaning cabins, bathrooms and toilets, and preparing linen. Women were also hired specifically as nurses or laundresses. They did not work as cooks as they were never apprenticed as such by shipping companies. On larger liners this work was regarded as similar to hotel catering, also a male preserve at this time. In all these ways the position of the steward-ess was tied to domestic service work ashore and did not require any specialised seafaring knowledge.[32]

In the USSCo. there were limited opportunities for women to work at sea attending to female passengers. By 1906 the company employed twenty-three forecabin and fifty saloon stewardesses, about three per cent of the total shipboard workforce.[33] Sir George Grey, twice Governor of New Zealand and prominent Auckland citizen, regarded the USSCo. as a 'great educating company' for New Zealand farm girls. As stewardesses, women would be well trained for domestic life through instruction in laying tables, preparing rooms, waiting on pas-sengers and cleaning up after them.[34] More often than not, however, women were hired as stewardesses because of their prior domestic experience ashore. They were usually older than male crew and most were single or widowed. As onshore, married women were less likely to be in paid employment.[35] On the USSCo.'s intercolonial steamers, the eldest recorded stewardess was an E. Williams, aged fifty-three, while the majority of stewardesses were between the ages of twenty-six and forty-eight.[36]

Lorraine Coons and Alexander Varias suggest that in the late nineteenth and early twentieth centuries stewardesses could be cat-egorised as typical Victorian 'odd women', those women left alone to support themselves and their families for the lack of a husband, either as widows or spinsters.[37] The *Wairarapa* stewardesses broadly fit this categorisation. MacQuaid and Grinrod were both unmarried. 'Company widows' like McDonald were left destitute when their hus-bands died and had no other means of survival. The company made no general provision for widows and often hired them instead (although widows of more senior employees were sometimes awarded ongoing allowances).[38]

Union Company positions were limited and highly sought after. As was the case for stewards, an agreeable character, appearance and manner were mandatory for such opportunities. In one request, Robert Struthers put in a word for a Miss Brown. He wished to be 'straightfor-ward' with James Mills, informing him that her fiancé had abandoned her and she was pregnant, but 'notwithstanding this I can assure you that Miss Brown is anything but a fast girl, in fact the very opposite. I am sure she would make a first class stewardess if you give her the chance.'[39] Mr J. B. White wrote to Mills on behalf of his housemaid, Marion Brunning, who 'is thoroughly respectable and respectable looking – about 30 – quite reliable'.[40] The Minister for Labour, William

Pember Reeves, forwarded Mills a request from Maggie Brandon. As Brandon had noted to Pember Reeves, 'there are many applicants and there is absolutely no chance, unless great influence is brought to bear on the officials. I do not wish to take work from other women but I am anxious for work and I do not wish to ask help from any source.' She hoped to bring her girls up 'in respectability' as her husband had abandoned them.[41] Mr J. S. Menteath put in a word on behalf of 'a fine looking woman with a good figure and highly respectable'.[42] And in another communication Catherine Fraser made a request on behalf of Mrs Maureen Smith: 'I can testify to her strict integrity – she is a widow.'[43] One stewardess, Kate Higgins, was at a loss to understand her dismissal from the *Talune*. She 'tried to do the best I could and with the number of passengers and being single handed I found it very hard to show special attention to one more than another however I am dismissed'. She pleaded with the marine superintendent, Angus Cameron, to use his influence to 'get me something better as I don't like the position of forecabin stewardess'.[44] When he was in Scotland overseeing shipbuilding operations, Cameron received many letters from women as well as men hoping to work their passage out to New Zealand on the new boats.[45]

These various examples indicate the importance of an established good character and reputation. An individual's position, connections and personal history in shore-based society directly informed the company's determination of shipboard suitability. This is also reflected in the hiring practices of other companies over these decades. Promotion was also decided on the basis of an appropriately feminine and respectable appearance. One stewardess, Mrs G. H. Thompson, queried why she had been out of work for nine months as she needed to support her children and elderly mother. The manager of the Stores Department reported to Mills that she had served on five ships as steerage stewardess and 'on more than one occasion she has voluntarily resigned from her position. She is masculine in appearance and of sour aspect and quite unsuitable for saloon. She has been reported to me as encouraging passengers to complain of food etc'.[46] One stewardess, the daughter of a Melbourne USSCo. official, hoped to be promoted. Mills refused because 'an unsightly blemish on her face' meant she would be out of place in saloon class, where she would have waited on more important and wealthy passengers.[47]

The figurative presence of women on board was one thing; their physical presence was often less easy for male crew to negotiate. On British steamers, stewardesses were to spend free time in their cabins or in designated deck areas. They were not to speak to male crew or passengers except on work-related matters. They ate separately in their own cabins and were under the surveillance of a steward and the purser.[48] On USSCo. vessels, stewardess quarters were typically located near the chief steward, engineers and purser amidships, on a separate deck from ordinary seamen and stewards.[49]

Female participation in a working environment dominated by men could cause friction. As we have seen, behaviour deemed disruptive or disorderly on board the steamship as an all-male workplace generally centred on alcohol abuse, swearing, fighting, refusal to work and desertion. This could, and did, play out at all levels, from the captains to coal-trimmers. When women were added to the mix, the definition of disorder and disruption shifted – it was increasingly sexualised and framed in terms of immorality, impropriety and indiscretion. There is little written evidence of male homosexual behaviour on board USSCo. ships. As the twentieth century progressed it was the case that significant numbers of stewards on USSCo. coastal steamers self-identified as homosexual and were attracted to work at sea for the release it provided from moral prohibitions ashore.[50] While these shipboard intimacies are less visible, there are frequent references in company letters to 'inappropriate' relations between male and female crew, and between male crew and female passengers. This suggests such behaviour was more easily framed as threatening and transgressive and, therefore, more openly discussed at managerial level.

In his 1850 novel about a United States naval vessel, *White Jacket, or the World in a Man-o-War*, Herman Melville puts instances of shipboard homosexual practice down to the confines of space, rather than individual desire. He thereby displaces moral responsibility: men simply could not help themselves given the 'close cribbing and confinement . . . like pears closely packed, the crowded crew mutually decay through close contact, and every plague-spot is contagious'. It would be more threatening, Cesare Casarino suggests, to emphasise individual physical desire rather than the spatial realities of shipboard life.[51] With respect to women in the USSCo. service, by contrast, transgressive sexuality was more overtly located in their persons and their desires, rather than the restrictive confines of the ship itself.

In response to a request from one stewardess for re-employment after sick leave in 1891, the superintending steward noted that he had 'not heard anything of her, i.e. to her credit. She was carrying on with the 2nd Engineer of the vessel for some time . . . Captain Grant does not wish her back in his vessel.'[52] The following year the Stores Department reported that on ships where another stewardess, Mrs Siburn, served, 'there was always disturbance . . . and she was a great deal too fond of talking to officers and passengers'. There was some suggestion she had been sexually involved with a steward and a purser:

'She bore anything but a good reputation while with us and I was glad to get some excuse to rid us of an undesirable employee.'[53] And, in another complaint, the captain frames the stewardess, Miss White, as a distracting and domineering presence, compromising his authority through her ability to 'have her way' with male crew. By contrast, he portrays the third officer, Mr Hopkins, once conscientious and reliable, as weak-willed and incapable. Having been 'on altogether too intimate terms' for over six weeks, the captain reprimanded them, but now 'I find it is a matter of common talk in the ship that he frequently stays with her in the same hotel in Wellington.' Hopkins did not deny this when accused, as 'he seems to have become infatuated with her . . . until recently he was a very promising officer and was attentive to his duties but lately he seems to be unable to concentrate his mind on his work and is quite absent minded'. Miss White 'is able to do as she likes with him'.[54]

Stewardesses were engaged to offer comfort, moral guidance and protection to female passengers from male passengers and crew. In this way they embodied a maternal mediating position and a barrier to unlicensed sexual contact. Yet in the previous cases they are portrayed as sexually disruptive, even though older widows or spinsters were ostensibly regarded as less of a sexual threat than young women and were hired in preference to them. When stewardesses were perceived as having transgressed their limited sphere of authority on board, their sexual morality was immediately implicated. Sari Mäenpää also documents this common fear of women as a source of friction on board ship. Opportunities for promotion were limited or non-existent; stewardesses were confined to roles that posed no threat to patriarchal structures of authority.[55] As one commentator in the *Fiji Times* opined, the 'chief objection' to female captains 'is found in the fact that a female captain would flirt with handsome male passengers. The consequence would be that she would neglect her ship.'[56] And in these accounts from USSCo. records, stewardesses were easily expendable workers in the face of real or imagined disruption. These women were presumed guilty without any investigation; the testimony of their male superiors was taken at face value. In all of these cases the female crew are framed as willing agents, while the male crew, even when welcoming such contact, are regarded as distracted or duped victims. Such gendered presumptions of guilt were to persist over the following decades, as Coons's account of P&O employees between 1920 and 1950 reveals.[57]

The stewardesses of the *Wairarapa* could be honoured in photographs and monuments because they followed the predetermined script of appropriate femininity on board. Yet these were shore-based accounts of a moment of crisis at sea. Through the letters cited earlier we can garner insights into why women embraced shipboard employment, yet with all the evidence of their active service based on male-authored accounts it remains difficult to access what meanings these stewardesses made of their time afloat. Bullen suggests that the class differences between women as workers and passengers had more impact on the stewardesses' experiences than encounters with other crew. Stewardesses 'are well treated by everybody on board except their charges, but some of them can tell some queer stories of endurance at the hands of these, who owe them so much comfort'. Writing in 1900, Bullen thought it strange that 'in these days of reminiscence-writing, how carefully [stewardesses] hold their peace'.[58] Any archival traces which might detail the nature of interactions between stewardesses and female passengers on board USSCo. vessels are difficult to locate. One aside in correspondence between Cameron and his son in the days after the *Wairarapa* incident suggests that meaningful intimacies might develop between women. The latter noted that his wife was 'in a terrible state' on hearing that the stewardess who had looked after her on their recent trip to Melbourne, Charlotte McDonald, had drowned.[59]

Passengers

Manning devoted a special section to passengers in his account of the staffing structure of steamers. 'In so many ways have passengers been an impelling and corrective force', he argued, '. . . passengers must be credited as instrumental in mellowing and refining the characters and improving the manners of all seafarers, from the captain down to the deck-boy or trimmer'.[60] Although the ship was only a temporary dwelling-place for passengers, it became a more highly regulated space. The 1895 'Red Book' prohibited an officer on watch from conversing with any passengers 'beyond civilly answering any question addressed to him'.[61] On particular occasions, stewards had to defer to stewardesses, as in this rule from the 1910 'Red Book': 'Stewards shall not enter or work in a cabin where a lady is berthed, except in the case of married persons where the husband specially requests their attendance, or where their assistance is specially sought by the stewardess, who must then be present also.'[62] Some shipping companies went so far as to alter the location of crew quarters. One Liverpool shipowner noted that they moved seamen's accommodation from the traditional position in the forecastle to the after deck, following complaints from female passengers travelling to India. When walking to and fro on the ship's bridge during the day they objected to seeing crew dressing and undressing in their quarters below them.[63]

The 'Red Book' also outlined women's restricted access to parts of the ship and to certain vessels altogether. 'Ladies shall not be permitted to visit the engine room except by the permission of the Captain, and under the personal charge of the Chief Engineer'; 'With the exception of female passengers and the Stewardesses, no female shall be allowed to remain all night on board any of the Company's vessels.' The wives of officers and engineers and dependent family members were granted passages at half rates, 'but they will not be permitted to travel on board any of the ships in which such Officers or Engineers hold appointments'. Directors might grant a captain 'on not shorter intervals than once in two years, the privilege of taking his wife on a round trip free of charge . . . it must be understood that a Captain's wife does not occupy his cabin, but utilises the ordinary saloon accommodation'.[64]

The captain's wife had free access to her husband's quarters in an earlier maritime era, particularly on board whaling ships. By the late nineteenth century, the status and privileges of the captain's wife, along with those of the captain, had shifted considerably. One seafarer deplored this state of affairs in *The Nautical Magazine* in 1912. Shipping company managers were 'callous', he maintained, and 'actually think that a lady on board would be a danger to the safe navigation of the ship, and above all things, they say she interferes and causes a lot of trouble'. No man had the right to interfere with the domestic relations of another, he stressed, and only prisoners, paupers and seafarers were kept apart from their wives. There would be 'a cry of indignation throughout the land' if any shore employer attempted to control his workers in this way, 'yet the shipowner does so quite calmly without a murmur being raised'.[65] His comments echoed the concurrent debates over wage disbursements, where seafarers challenged the presumption that they were less capable and responsible than other working men and that their wages should be managed for them by their employers.

But rather than 'mellowing' and 'refining' the character of crew, some men took the opportunity to breach such codes of conduct, forcing their (generally unwelcome) attentions on female passengers. Most of these cases implicated more senior crew. Entitled to separate cabins, their status afforded them more privacy and opportunity to transgress these official gendered boundaries. In 1884, the company's branch agent in Fiji, Ernest Ford, received a letter of complaint from John McLaren, a man of East Indian descent, on behalf of his wife. She was of mixed race, her father a European trader in Levuka, her mother's background unrecorded. Mrs McLaren travelled from Levuka to Suva on a coastal steamer. Feeling seasick, she chose to sleep on deck rather than in her cabin, but alleged that the intoxicated captain,

D. McColl, approached her three times during the night. He first offered her alcohol, then grabbed her dress and demanded a kiss. Her husband alleged that 'innocent and unprotected females are too often taken advantage off [sic]' in the company's steamers. McColl denied the charge and presented statements from fellow crew that discounted the possibility of this encounter. The matter did not go further, even though management was well aware of McColl's alcohol dependency. McColl was eventually removed from his post two years later when it was reported he 'had been drinking again'.[66]

In 1889, the Fiji Government fined Captain C. Spinks £50 for supplying liquor to Elizabeth Potter, a half-caste woman, 'one of low repute', reported the next Fiji agent, Alex Duncan. Spinks asserted he supplied it for medicinal purposes only, yet he 'has no right to mix in any way with coloured passengers', Duncan declared, as 'it is degrading both to himself and to the Company . . . I have never heard of a master doing this before. We want gentlemen. Spinks has greatly disappointed me . . . even if liquor had to be given the stewardess I think should give it to female passengers when in their cabins.'[67] Spinks had 'lost his character' and, if left in the trade, 'I would suggest that he should be made to sleep on his ship and pay less attention to females ashore'. Captains of rival companies operating in Fiji 'are first class men, above suspicion, and so should ours be'.[68] In this case the colonial state intervened. Spinks's actions violated an ordinance prohibiting the supply of alcohol to 'natives', with mixed-race individuals included within its ambit. Berthed at the Suva wharf, the steamship was deemed a part of the colonial territory to which it traded, its crew now subject to a higher code of conduct than the dictates of the USSCo. 'Red Book'.

There were other incidents closer to home. On his routine shipboard inspection one morning in 1909, Captain Clift noted that his chief officer had a female passenger in his room, 'at least I only saw one'. He told him 'not to have people there especially not at that time or any other time', but that he could entertain passengers at afternoon tea in the public social space of the ship. Yet the following evening there was another female passenger in his room: 'I went down & saw for myself, so sent for him to my room, and told him that I did not allow lady passengers in officers' rooms & that it was bad for discipline of the ship, because all the others will want to do the same'.[69] The confines of the ship, the captain's surveillance and the fact that leisure and work time were never totally separable all worked to ensure that officers' cabins were not private spaces. Crew could easily learn of their colleagues' misdemeanours whatever their position in the shipboard hierarchy, and management feared that the likely disaffection would disrupt smooth operations afloat.

Another case in the same year occurred on the Auckland–Fiji run. The well-respected Captain Jordon allegedly burst into a female passenger's cabin in the early hours of the morning, pyjama-clad and drunk. He stumbled into the wrong room, mistaking it for that of another female passenger, a 'well-dressed' Mrs Johns, who had reportedly enjoyed frequent glasses of champagne during the day. There was grave concern that 'the report has been circulated widely in Fiji and on the coast of New Zealand', although an investigation ascertained there was no public scandal.[70] While Jordon escaped censure on this occasion, he had problems abstaining from alcohol and later left the service rather than submit himself for enquiry.[71] As in McColl's case, the captain's sexual disorder was coupled here with the more familiar masculine disorder of alcohol abuse. His behaviour was an affront not only to shipboard society, but also the imagined society ashore. Bullen acknowledged that there 'are drunken blackguards who make it for masters', but in reality they could not get far given the heavy responsibilities of the position. Problem crew would not go unnoticed, especially since 'every man's goings-on are known and discussed' in small coastal communities.[72] While he was speaking of the coastal trades in Britain, the same could be said of steamer trades in the Pacific. The USSCo. complex stitched communities together across shipboard and shore.

During an excursion cruise from Wellington to Picton on Boxing Day in 1909, the marine superintendent reprimanded the chief officer for bringing a female passenger into his room and offering her alcohol. He argued that he supplied liquor for medicinal purposes as she had complained of feeling ill. He may have acted in good faith, 'but at the same time the fact of his having females in his room must have been known to possibly quite a number of passengers and thus give rise to a very bad name to the ship'. The chief officer was demoted to a cargo steamer 'to show the Director's displeasure at his conduct and also be a warning to other Officers'.[73] The identity and reputation of all ships in the company's fleet derived from their respective routes, their structural qualities and their levels of comfort, but most importantly, from the service provided by various crew. Punishment was dismissal or, as in the case just mentioned, relegation to a cargo steamer where contact with passengers was eliminated.

Still, cargo steamers were not completely immune from unsanctioned boundary-crossing. In 1914 the *Aparima*'s boatswain allegedly brought a 'well-known Newcastle prostitute' onto the ship and kept her in his room in the cadets' quarters. The complainant noted that this had occurred before and one cadet wrote to his parents about the incident. 'When it came out who it was the boy was made to do a "little extra" by the Boatswain as a warning to others.'[74] The boatswain attempted to use his status to enforce a code of silence amongst the cadets. While he did not ultimately succeed, the incident sheds more light on the nature of some of the informal power relations amongst crew.

Management necessarily took a dim view of transgressive behaviour in port. As noted, the 'Red Book' prohibited the presence of women on board ship unless as employees or passengers. The company endured 'a very unfortunate scandal' in 1896 when the body of Margaret Robertson was found in Wellington Harbour 'with only her underclothes on and an officer's jacket'. Letters in the jacket identified it as belonging to Mr Phillips, the chief officer of the inter-island steamer *Penguin*. Investigations revealed he had been drinking with the woman on board the steamer the previous evening. While the verdict of death was accidental drowning, 'it did not look at all well for the officer', and Mills suspended Phillips along with the purser and steward, the latter having provided the alcohol.[75] In another incident a steward was suspended for bringing women on board the *Loongana* during Sundays when the vessel was in port at Melbourne.[76]

As feared, inappropriate behaviour did not always go unnoticed by other passengers. One Canadian passenger commented on the curtains over cabin doors that blew aside in tropical breezes, allowing seamen washing decks to look in on women in bed. He went on to note that many officers forced their presence upon female passengers, 'more particularly the second class passengers, whom they seem to regard as their particular property', highlighting here the class dimensions of feminine accessibility. He continued:

> Not only do they do this but they place their hands on the shoulders or the heads of the ladies and in some instances pat their cheeks or tip them under the chin. All this is right enough in its place, but no man likes to see another man – a stranger, I mean – go up and pat his wife's cheek and pass some familiar remark. Almost everyone likes to meet sociable officers, but not libertines; and I can refer to the doctor, 3rd and 4th officers and chief steward as nothing else; also the chief engineer (Mr Paton) should be reminded that he is expected to behave as a gentleman amongst respectable people.[77]

Male territorialism over female 'property' and class-based tensions between men were brought to the shipboard encounter.

The prestigious transpacific trades attracted wealthy passengers, and one captain made it a condition that, when mixing with passengers, all officers 'must treat all alike'. They were not to pick out any individuals, especially not 'flighty, good-looking married ladies, or actresses'. On one occasion in 1899, Mr Hodson, a new purser, paid some attention 'to a lady of this description' and went to sit with her in a dark corner during an interval in an evening dance. The captain 'as a joke and also a lesson to Hodson directed the Engineer to turn one of the electric lights on the quarter where they were sitting, and this of course caused a stir'. Hodson was quite indignant and complained to Mills, but Mills was certain Captain Carey 'had the measure of the lady' and Hodson had to fall in line with a good rule.[78]

In a more serious incident of the same year, a passenger alleged that a steward from the *Waikare* had assaulted his daughter. The family wanted to prosecute the steward but as they were leaving the country they requested the USSCo. deal with the matter instead. The employee denied the charge but was told the onus rested with him to disprove it. He was discharged from the *Waikare* before the ship embarked on an island excursion.[79]

When shore-based management travelled on company ships, they naturally paid special attention to daily operations. Male passengers were generally less respectful of their surroundings than were female passengers. In 1905, one official noted his concerns about the second-class smoking room on the intercolonial steamer *Maheno*. It was a 'fine apartment', yet 'the class of people using it . . . do not seem to appreciate the arrangements made for their comfort as they have already started to scratch matches on the polished wood'. He urged that it should be kept locked and if needed for berthing it should only be used to accommodate 'the gentler sex'.[80] Gender hierarchies were also fractured by class. Travelling with his wife a few years later, Mills complained about the state of the same vessel. The attendance of stewards was poor and toilets were frequently left in a deplorable condition, 'the litter from children and dirty women not having been tidied up and making the place offensive to decent people'. Moreover, 'I am told that for several days there have been men's boots in the ladies' bath and clothing hanging about, while this morning, although the bath was prepared for my wife and waiting for her when she went in, there were not only boots and clothes but a man's soiled shirt hanging on one of the pegs.' Mills did not wish it be seen that his wife made complaints, yet what he witnessed was 'a perfect outrage and denotes a want of discipline'.[81] One company director also complained about his fellow passengers on board the *Maunganui* in 1912: 'The upholstery and colouring are really very fine indeed – quite out of keeping I am sorry to say with the majority of passengers carried. It annoys me very much to see a man wipe his boots on the curtain or chair cover.'[82] Ships' specifications separated steerage, second and first class, and crew and passengers' quarters, yet these boundaries were difficult to police. Manning's wholesale celebration of passengers' corrective influence on shipboard society could, it seems, only ever pertain to certain people.

Transit and transgression

The easy depiction of women as sexual targets is 'one odd feature of transit', as Stanley has reflected. What might have induced people in transit to transgress?[83] As a space separate from all others, as an isolated and confined site, the shipboard location meant that social meaning was to a certain extent out of place, suspended and unsettled. Things not necessarily permissible onshore could occur at sea, or some people could at least come to believe that this was so, steaming away for a time from shore-based regimes and norms. The fleeting nature of these shipboard encounters may also have informed an individual's sense of risk-taking and the reduced likelihood of punishment.

Yet the demands of regimented shipping operations called for disciplined performances, and managers expended considerable effort to regulate, observe and report on crew behaviour. The presence of female passengers demanded the presence of female crew. As a result, the meanings attached to shipboard order, control and regimentation were increasingly sexualised. It seemed it was difficult for men of all rank to accept stewardesses as legitimate wage earners in a traditionally masculine working environment. Stewardesses were frequently framed as agents of disorder and, therefore, highly problematic co-workers. They were restricted to certain areas of the ship and were carefully scrutinised by senior crew. Stewardesses were expected to present an appropriate feminine appearance and personal history before being considered for a position. On board these credentials were always vulnerable to attack. While reports of misdemeanours involving stewardesses freely presumed their guilt, male crew were the prime transgressive subjects in cases involving female passengers, although we cannot gain much insight into passenger experiences and impressions for their histories are even more confined by male accounts. The indiscretions of male crew could also be regarded as violating the stewardesses' rightful authority to attend to female passengers, as seen in Duncan's response to the administration of alcohol to ill passengers by Spinks.

The idealised ship as a common home bonded men to the ship and to each other. Female passengers and crew, as much of this evidence attests, were feared for their power to divide men and encourage exclusive relationships antithetical to the polyandrous sociability of the all-male ship, demonstrating again Greg Dening's point that any concept of the personal or any notion of exclusivity on board was highly problematic.[84] The preoccupation with discipline and boundary-maintenance demanded the termination of established and suspected intimacies between stewardesses and crew, and between crew and passengers. If stewardesses 'had their way' with male crew they would compromise the authority of officers. If senior officers entertained female passengers in their cabins it was feared other crew would want to imitate this behaviour. Conrad's rejection of the steamship and its 'inappropriate' femininity finds parallels in these histories of female engagement on board. These problematic histories work to bolster the ship as pre-eminently a place for men, where women figured best as idea and image, rather than flesh-and-blood participants.

Notes

1   Incident recreated through newspaper reports and the report of the official enquiry into the disaster: see *New Zealand Observer* and *New Zealand Times* (November 1894 issues), *Otago Witness* (13 December 1894). See also Steve Locker-Lampson and Ian Francis, *Eight Minutes Past Midnight: The Wreck of the S.S. Wairarapa* (Wellington: Rowfant, 1981). The death toll remains a subject of conjecture, with some reports putting the total figure at 135.
2   'Fifty men and five women', *New Zealand Observer* (10 November 1894), 2.
3   R. H. Bakewell, 'Cowardice on the *Wairarapa*', *New Zealand Observer* (1 December 1894), 14.
4   'The lost', *Otago Witness* (8 November 1894), 10.
5   *Otago Witness* (23 January 1896), 14.
6   'The true story of the *Wairarapa* calamity', *New Zealand Observer* (10 November 1894), 11.
7   *Ibid.*
8   'The preliminary inquiry', *Otago Witness* (8 November 1894), 13.
9   'The *Wairarapa* disaster: finding of the court', *Otago Witness* (13 December 1894), 21.
10 Bakewell, 'Cowardice on the *Wairarapa*', 14.
11 Fox, *The Ocean Railway*, 131–2.
12 For an account of the *Stella* and Rogers see: http://www.jakesimpkin.org/ ArticlesResearch/SSStellaDisaster/tabid/62/Default.aspx and http://www.independent.co.uk/opinion/site-unseen-the-stella-memorial-southampton-1599616.html (accessed 7 September 2009).
13 For one review of Rediker's *Between the Devil and the Deep Blue Sea*, see Margaret S. Creighton, 'Review: Jack Tar fights back', *American Quarterly*, 43:1 (1991), 109; Burton, 'The myth of bachelor Jack', 182.
14 Sager, *Seafaring Labour*, 237–8.
15 Margaret S. Creighton, 'American mariners and the rites of manhood, 1830–1870', in *Jack Tar in History*, 146–8.
16 Margaret S. Creighton, 'Davy Jones' locker room: gender and the American whalemen, 1830–1870', in *Iron Men, Wooden Women*, 124.
17 Jeffrey Mellefont, 'Heirlooms and tea towels: views of ships' gender in the modern maritime museum', *Great Circle: Journal of the Australian Association for Maritime History*, 22:1 (2000), 5, 10.
18 Elizabeth DeLoughrey, *Roots and Routes: Navigating Caribbean and Pacific Island Literatures* (Honolulu: University of Hawai'i Press, 2007), 44.
19 Lillian Nayder, 'Sailing ships and steamers, angels and whores: history and gender in Conrad's maritime fiction', in *Iron Men, Wooden Women*, 193–4.
20 Quoted in C. F. Burgess, *The Fellowship of the Craft: Conrad on Ships and Seamen and the Sea* (Port Washington, NY: Kennikat Press, 1976), 76.

21 Creighton, 'Davy Jones' locker room', 132.
22 For example, Jo Stanley, *Bold in Her Breeches: Women Pirates Across the Ages* (London: Pandora, 1995); Lisa Norling, *Captain Ahab Had a Wife: New England Women and the Whalefishery, 1720–1870* (Chapel Hill: University of North Carolina Press, 2000).
23 Introduction to Creighton and Norling (eds), *Iron Men, Wooden Women*, x.
24 Jo Stanley, 'And after the cross-dressed cabin boys and whaling wives? Possible futures for women's maritime historiography', *Journal of Transport History*, 23: 1 (2002), 11, 19–20.
25 Manning, *Below and Above the Water-Line*, 27–8.
26 Bullen, *The Men of the Merchant Service*, 181–2.
27 Manning, *Below and Above the Water-Line*, 29–30.
28 HC, USSCo. Records, AG-292-005-004/054, Copies of various papers, n.d.
29 Laura Tabili, '"A maritime race". . .', 185.
30 *Mercantile Marine: II – Minutes of Evidence*, 98. Tabili notes that some companies, including the Cunard Line, did not regard lascars as suitable for the highly visible deck crews of passenger liners: Tabili, '"A maritime race". . .', 180. Goan crew were framed in this way well into the 1950s, as seen in comments from a P&O captain in 1957, reproduced in a display on cruise ships at the National Maritime Museum in Greenwich (viewed 18 July 2007).
31 M. N. Pearson, *The Indian Ocean* (New York: Routledge, 2003), 250.
32 Sari Mäenpää, 'Women below deck: gender and employment on British passenger liners, 1860–1938', *Journal of Transport History*, 25:2 (2004), 60, 64–5.
33 HC, Cameron Family Papers, MS 1046, Box 25A, April 1906.
34 HC, USSCo. Records, AG-292-005-001/027, cited by Ford to Mills, 28 February 1891.
35 Atkinson, *Crew Culture*, 21–2; Maenpaa, 'Women below deck', 68.
36 The Shipping Masters' Office of New South Wales recorded the names, nationalities and ages of all crew arriving on vessels in Sydney between 1845 and 1922. The records are searchable at: http://mariners.records.nsw.gov.au/.
37 Coons and Varias, *Tourist Third Cabin*, 108.
38 *Ibid.*
39 HC, USSCo. Records, AG-292-005-001/025, Struthers to Mills, 6 June 1889.
40 *Ibid.*, White to Mills, 3 December 1889.
41 *Ibid.*, Pember Reeves to Mills, 7 November 1892.
42 *Ibid.*, AG-292-005-001/021, J. S. Menteath to Mills, 23 September 1891.
43 *Ibid.*, AG-292-005-001/024, Fraser to Mills, 7 April 1890.
44 HC, Cameron Family Papers, MS 1046, Box 4, Higgins to Cameron, 21 February 1892.
45 *Ibid.*, Box 6, Jessie Crombie to Cameron, 3 March 1897.
46 HC, USSCo. Records, AG-292-005-001/025, 8 December 1891.
47 *Ibid.*, AG-292-005-001/021, Mills to Williams (for Millar, Inspector of Works Office), 8 January 1889.
48 Mäeenpää, 'Women below deck', 67.
49 WCCA, USSCo. Records, B99/10, plan of the *Tofua*.
50 For example, H. E. Williams, 'Homosexuality: Aspects of the problem aboard ships' (Preventive Medicine Dissertation, University of Otago, 1962).
51 Cesare Casarino, *Modernity at Sea: Melville, Marx, Conrad in Crisis* (Minneapolis: University of Minnesota Press, 2002), 37–9.
52 HC, USSCo. Records, AG-292-005-001/024, McNicol to Mills, 10 December 1891.
53 *Ibid.*, AG-292-005-001/025, Williams to Mills, 31 October 1892.
54 WCCA, USSCo. Records, AF004:4:6, R. Crawford to Marine Superintendent Strang, 12 February 1909.
55 Mäenpää, 'Women below deck', 57–74.
56 *Fiji Times* (28 May 1884).
57 Lorraine Coons, 'From "company widow" to "new woman": female seafarers aboard the "floating palaces" of the interwar years', *International Journal of Maritime History*, 20: 2 (December 2008), 166–7.

58 Bullen, *The Men of the Merchant Service*, 193.
59 HC, Cameron Family Papers, MS 1046, Box 1, Jack Cameron to Angus Cameron, 4 November 1894.
60 Manning, *Below and Above the Water-Line*, 124.
61 USSCo., *General Instructions* (1895), 16.
62 USSCo., *General Instructions* (1910), 58.
63 Evidence of John Hughes, *Mercantile Marine: II – Minutes of Evidence*, 534.
64 USSCo., *General Instructions* (1895), 12, 32, 33.
65 *Nautical Magazine*, 88:1 (July 1912), 21–2.
66 HC, USSCo. Records, AG-292-005-001/002, Ford to Mills, 1 and 24 December 1884; AG-292-003-001/004, minutes of meeting of directors, 12 July 1886.
67 *Ibid.*, AG-292-005-001/023, Duncan to Mills, 23 October 1889.
68 *Ibid.*, Duncan to Mills, 15 November 1889.
69 WCCA, USSCo. Records, AF004:4:6, Captain Clift to Marine Superintendent Strang, 18 November 1909.
70 HC, USSCo. Records, AG-292-005-001/093, Holdsworth to Mills, 11 and 16 May 1909.
71 *Ibid.*, AG-292-003-001/023, minutes of meeting of directors, 30 March 1911.
72 Bullen, *Men of the Merchant Service*, 25.
73 WCCA, USSCo. Records, AF004:7:6, Strang to General Manager, 4 February 1908.
74 *Ibid.*, Box 13, McLeod to Mills, 8 May 1914.
75 HC, Cameron Family Papers, MS 1046, Box 5, Strang to Cameron, 22 December 1896.
76 HC, USSCo. Records, AG-292-005-001/080, David Mills to James Mills, 12 July 1905.
77 *Ibid.*, AG-292-005-001/090, W. R. Frey to Mills, 1 August 1905.
78 *Ibid.*, AG-292-005-001/046, Mills to Holdsworth, 7 July 1899.
79 *Ibid.*, AG-292-005-004/054, Williams to Mills, 8 September 1899.
80 HC, Cameron Family Papers, MS 1046, Box 11, J. R. Campbell to Mills, 21 December 1905.
81 HC, USSCo. Records, AG-292-005-001/086, Mills to Holdsworth, 3 April 1908.
82 *Ibid.*, AG-292-0005-001/101, Ritchie to Holdsworth, 29 July 1912.
83 Stanley, 'And after the cross-dressed cabin boys', 18.
84 Nayder, 'Sailing ships and steamers', 210–2; Dening, *Mr Bligh's Bad Language*, 81–3.

PART III

Abroad

CHAPTER SIX

The tropical challenges of the island trades

In the first months of 1907, unfavourable reports about the operations of the island steamer *Manapouri* began to filter back to Alexander Irvine, the Union Company's Auckland branch manager. He heard it was a common occurrence for native passengers travelling between islands to gain access to the holds in order to sleep amongst the cargo, 'using cases of spirits for pillows'. In island ports, business relations with traders and shippers were combative and frustrating. Pursers were faced with frequent requests for reimbursements and compensation because of inaccurate ship manifests and poor carriage of goods. Feeling irritated that none of the *Manapouri*'s senior crew had discussed any of their concerns with him personally, Irvine confronted the ship's purser, Mr McBurney, at Auckland wharf one afternoon in August, a few hours before the ship embarked for Apia.

After Irvine alluded to rumours about the freedoms enjoyed by indigenous passengers, the purser confirmed that it had indeed been going on, and for some considerable time. He flatly rejected Irvine's suggestions that the captain was culpable, for 'a better man for the Island trade could not be got'. The captain was 'badly supported' by an unsuitable mate and a third officer 'who was just as bad if not worse'. When pressed regarding why he had not mentioned the state of affairs earlier, McBurney retorted, 'Well Mr Irvine, it is evident you have never sailed as a ship's Officer or you would know the dog's life one would have if it became known that he had mentioned anything derogatory about any of his mates.' McBurney only said as much on this occasion as he had already decided to resign. If he remained on board now he would be called a 'rotten dog'. Things were 'even rottener' than shore-based management could imagine. There was 'nothing but growling' at every port in the run, and the purser copped the worst of it while those responsible escaped without challenge. Life had simply been 'a misery' to him at every island port. On hearing McBurney's concerns,

Irvine proposed appointing a travelling purser to oversee operations on all island steamers and report all matters of concern directly to managers in New Zealand. McBurney concurred, noting that this should have been done long ago.[1]

The *Manapouri*'s troubles were not unique. The company's island trades were challenging from their very inception. On a hierarchy of services they ranked below the more prestigious intercolonial and transpacific lines, but above the New Zealand coastal trades. They were popularly known as 'harassing', owing to the distances travelled, long hours of work, large crowds of indigenous passengers, carriage of perishable fruit cargoes and aggressive demands of traders and shippers in various ports.[2] Moreover, hazardous passages through uncharted coral reefs, the threat of violent storms in hurricane season and the tropical heat unsettled many shipboard workers and staff in port branch offices. The rigid black steamer lines mapped out in the company chart of routes at the start of this book can be animated by a closer consideration of the human stories circulating around and with the island trades. The mobile histories of European workers at sea and ashore reveal some of the attendant preoccupations and problems the USSCo. faced in moving men and conducting shipping operations at a tropical distance from New Zealand.

At sea: passages between regional ports

Steamships were widely celebrated for offering more predictable, regular and extensive services than vessels under sail, yet they were not able to eliminate or overcome all environmental frictions. Rough seas, high winds and the threat of severe storms in hurricane season could all delay or disrupt regional shipping services in the Pacific. The worst shipwrecks in the late nineteenth and early twentieth centuries occurred close to shore, around dangerous coastlines and difficult island passages. With particular respect to USSCo. vessels, the most serious incidents occurred along New Zealand's coastline, as seen with the loss of the *Tararua* off the Southland coast in 1881 when 131 people died, the *Wairarapa* wreck in 1894, and the wreck of the domestic inter-island ferry *Penguin* in Cook Strait in 1909 with the loss of seventy-five lives.

In the island trades there were no comparable tragedies for USSCo. vessels, but newspapers in this period document the routine hazards of navigation in Pacific waters. They are studded with reports of grounded or wrecked vessels. On occasion, cargo was lost in rough seas, as in the case of the *Arawata* in February 1890 on a passage between Auckland and Suva, when all livestock penned on deck, including sheep, horses, poultry and pigs, was washed overboard.[3] Some shippers were frustrated by the high rates of marine insurance in the Pacific. These rates were estimates, rather than determined on the basis of known risks, because underwriters had little correct data to go on and classed islands in the Pacific with the Torres Strait and the most intricate parts of the Great Barrier Reef.[4] In any case, coral reefs were, as Edward Reeves summated, a 'regular ship trap'.[5]

It is difficult to find any explicit engagement with the oceanic setting in USSCo. archival records. The sea itself appears to have gone missing. Correspondence more readily turns to the business concerns of shipbuilding, freight estimates and personnel. Yet it is still apparent that people did not understand the sea simply as a passive space; it was a dynamic, productive environment, which imparted a strong influence on the livelihoods and behaviour of the people who lived and worked on or close to this volatile resource.

Navigational challenges in the Pacific were a source of significant stress to USSCo. captains. One was 'an exceedingly nervous man', noted Fiji agent Alex Duncan, 'and on the coast often stood out half a mile or more when others would safely go nearer shore', while another was 'a big baby & held up to ridicule by everyone here – he has no pluck'.[6] In 1909 Captain R. G. Hutton fainted during a passage between Tongan ports. 'Doctor attributes to worry and run down. Two months [rest] at least absolutely necessary.' He was transferred to the Auckland–Fiji direct steamer so he could return home more often.[7] Observing in Apia harbour the German warship *Adler*, which had been wrecked in a storm in 1889, one USSCo. captain commented that anyone who let himself be caught by a hurricane 'would assuredly be fired by the company'.[8] Confident, skilful navigation demonstrated mature, competent manhood in the eyes of fellow Europeans and indigenous Islanders alike. There was a performativity involved in steering a vessel straight into port, for, as one captain was well aware, 'the natives are very critical as to how a boat is sailed and, if we go in zig-zagging, they will jeer at us for a parcel of land-lubbers, and they may not treat us with the proper respect'.[9]

The competency of white captains routinely rested on indigenous pilots who guided steamers through reef passages safely. The legendary seafarer Captain Richard Smith ('*Taviuni* Smith') recalled that because of the lack of reliable charts for the islands, the native pilots would swim out to the steamer *Taviuni* 'and when beside me on the bridge, would shout, "deep water here", "shallow there", "reef to the starboard", and so on'.[10] Yet some European commentators were also quick to dismiss the importance of this work. On an extended passage through the eastern Pacific, Reeves opined that 'the native pilot's office is a sinecure. Very important he looks, evidently blissfully unconscious that our captain could do better without him!'[11]

When the *Southern Cross* touched a reef in 1885, Ernest Ford hoped James Mills would not think the captain 'neglects his duties for he is most careful and attentive'.[12] Smith, who reportedly regarded the *Taviuni* as 'a playful toy', grounded the steamer on a reef at the entrance to Vavau Bay in Tonga in the 1890s. In 1907 the company's sugar steamer, the *Kilbride*, foundered at Suva notwithstanding the captain's thorough knowledge of reefs and shoals, for he had travelled in the region for forty-three years without an accident.[13] Such mishaps could temper over-confidence in taxing surroundings. Captain Holford, who had previously boasted he 'could take three P&O ships abreast' through a particularly narrow island passage, went on to ground the *Tofua* there in 1911. The incident 'will prove a very valuable lesson to him', reflected the Fiji manager, 'and the trouble and anxiety following it will impress him very considerably'.[14] Captain D. McColl believed remuneration should be higher in the island trades because of such risks and the associated anxiety of losing his master's certificate if he grounded a steamer. He was also of the opinion that no one should be posted to steamer work in Fiji for more than twelve months.[15]

In the face of these routine challenges, some captains turned to alcohol for escapism or relief. Following a severe hurricane in Fiji in January 1895, the *Ohau* nearly foundered. After the officers discovered the captain intoxicated and incapable, the chief officer superseded him in command.[16] The death of one crew member at sea in 1911 prompted the *Atua*'s chief engineer, W. McIntyre, to break his silence about the months 'of deceit and intrigue' on board. The captain spent most days locked in his cabin drinking and only appeared on the bridge when pulling into port, an appropriate display of authority for the island population lining the wharf. At sea he left the crew to navigate dangerous island passages and on one occasion did not attend to a seriously ill seaman or make an appearance at his sea burial.[17] The *Wairuna*'s chief officer also drank heavily, as one fireman reported to the Auckland Seamen's Union in 1912, and was 'subject to fits and has to be carried to his room'. On the last island trip, crew were 'treated like dogs . . . the meat was rotten and was washed in Condy's fluid before being cooked . . . for three days during our stay at the islands we had not bread'.[18] When the chief steward of another island steamer was dismissed for supplying alcohol to off-duty crew, he stressed that he did so to avert the likelihood of more trouble if men drank in island port town establishments: 'you know the trouble we have with these fellows round the group'. A few drinks on board kept things 'ever so much quiet'.[19]

The attractions of shore time also hampered captains in their work. Over-familiarity with island traders could be problematic. Captain Norman Beaumont had too many friends ashore. He was 'a really first-class man' for passengers, noted Duncan, but 'he does not attend to the work of his vessel in any way. You let his wife travel with him and he abuses the privilege . . . for pushing ahead we have no worse.'[20] One regular passenger believed that Captain Crawshaw had been too long in the island trades, an assessment based on his unpopularity with some island residents and his 'apparent want of delicacy in ladies' society'. But management also recognised that traders were 'a peculiar lot and I don't think the angel Gabriel would give them satisfaction. Crawshaw, not Gabriel, has certainly been very successful as regards navigating his vessel.'[21] As one provincial inspector in Fiji put it, 'continually moving about in Fiji in steamers is beyond words'. Moreover, 'to add to the joys of life' some of the people steamer crew had to deal with 'are stupid and lazy beyond description'.[22] Captain Jordon, reported for drunkenness and inappropriate contact with passengers on the Auckland–Fiji route, was also criticised for buying whisky for his Fiji friends, 'some of them not too desirable . . . who make a point of coming on board and expecting to be entertained'. Yet he was considered more popular in the islands than Holford, who was 'inclined to swelled head'. While Holford looked after 'special' passengers, he left the 'rank and file' to fend for themselves.[23]

Head office noted a level of ambivalence amongst crew of all rank in the island trades. Shore-based management were usually the last to receive reports of the unfavourable state of affairs, as seen with the concerns about the operations of the *Manapouri* in 1907. Reports indicated that another vessel, the *Navua*, was 'not well looked after'. Laxness prevailed among the crew, 'no one seems to take much interest in their work or in their ships', and [the purser] attributes it largely to the incessant changes', noted Mills. 'The men are in so many cases not long enough in a ship to know her well, and the feeling is growing among them that it is not worth their while in taking any trouble.'[24]

In 1907 there was a number of complaints from passengers. One prominent Christchurch businessman asserted that the steamer was 'the dirtiest ship he ever travelled in'. The stewards did not clean cabins thoroughly, merely washing round the carpet and not under it. The cooking was 'horrible', the porridge tainted with kerosene and the bread tasting of carbolic acid. Linen was only changed once a week and in bad weather urine from the adjacent toilets leaked into his cabin. Management acknowledged that it was getting harder to attract good stewards to the island trades as the tip money was so poor. A tropical allowance for island stewards was suggested along with a bonus paid to those who served more than three months.[25] Four years later the *Navua* still attracted criticism. One company director confirmed that information about the captain 'taking things rather easy is true for he goes very little about the ship and this being so when a Director was on board. I feel sure it would be more so at other times.'[26] Such revelations prompted the appointment of an island trades manager to make annual trips on steamers and visit port branches.

Not every captain shipping into the Pacific grounded a steamer on an island reef or broke down through stress or turned to drink, nor was every ship a dysfunctional workplace. But it was the case that this environment presented its own set of challenges for the USSCo. Port branch operations reveal a similar set of concerns.

Ashore: the politics of port town trades

The USSCo.'s first Fiji agent, appointed in 1881, was the Levuka resident Charles St Pinnock. He resigned in 1884 after investigations into fraudulent trading practices, leaving an outstanding balance of £575 in company accounts.[27] Ernest Ford from Russell in the Bay of Islands, New Zealand, was appointed as his replacement. On arriving in Fiji, Ford was instructed not to engage in trade. 'Above all things', Dunedin management noted, 'you should endeavour to attain a good social standing, and to do this you must relinquish much of your present free and easy style of manner and dress'. The agent for the ASNCo., the USSCo.'s main rival in Fiji, 'is a thorough gentleman, and welcome in every household in the Colony, you cannot do better, than endeavour to reach a similar standing yourself'.[28]

Ford wrote to Mills almost every week and hoped 'I do not bore you with my numerous letters'.[29] In these he presented himself as a steadfast, loyal and hardworking agent, bent on implementing 'systems'. He repeatedly assured Mills he had secured the confidence and 'good graces' of government officials who were all 'behaving like gentlemen to me'. With his commitment and focused attention on consolidating the company's position, he was certain 'you will yet find my forecast right that we shall have the whole of the Pacific trade in our hands & that we will come at the appointed time like a racehorse'.[30] Ford's upbeat tone and optimism were tempered by the Auckland manager's negative assessments of the state of the Fiji trade. It was precarious, irregular, unpredictable and costly, with the first decade overshadowed by unreliable freight estimates, poor returns and dissatisfied traders. In 1885 the Auckland manager despaired that the 'Fiji trade is heartbreaking. I do not see any course other than to put on a small boat. It is absurd to expect *Arawata* to keep running at such a serious loss.'

Five months later he related that 'the confounded Fiji trade is getting worse from here', and by the end of the decade concluded that 'there is something always going crooked there and the difficulty is no sooner overcome than another crops up'.[31] Back in Russell in 1889, Ford acknowledged that 'the island trades are certainly discouraging trades or more properly speaking difficult ones to know how to work for the best and at the same time necessary to be worked by the Union to keep others out'.[32] Such discouragement did not undermine the company's sense of entitlement and possessiveness over these routes.

One of Ford's contemporaries was Frederick Barkas, a commercial agent for the New Zealand Loan and Mercantile Company, who was posted to Levuka from Christchurch in 1888. On first arriving in Fiji, Barkas noted in his letters to his father and brother how pleasant it was to dine with the other white resident traders at the main hotel each evening. Yet within a few weeks his enthusiasm had waned. He witnessed some of Ford's early morning drunken pranks with other men about town. Barkas lampooned their activities, which he labelled 'The Boys' Fun', in a mock article for the *Otago Witness*. After showing his article to Ford, he and his wife were treated with 'icy politeness', yet Barkas was happily ostracised, for as he wrote to his brother:

> I appear to them like the old man near Margate who 'Never laughed and who never played' because I don't laugh at their childish jokes, such as sewing up the neck of Kerr's nightshirt, or dressing up a small shark in baby clothes and putting it in Ford's bed . . . I can not hang around the Pub, Bar, drink Lager when I don't want it, or grin at feeble jokes repeated for the twentieth time. I'm not built that way nor do I believe that the mystery of conducting 'Good Business' in Fiji is to lie on the edge of one perpetual Spree.[33]

Barkas's account of white sociability demonstrates the easy slippage between Ford's self-fashioning in letters to his superiors and his everyday entanglements with co-residents in port. Distilled from a myriad of experiences, Ford's letters were composed in relation to his own expectations about what the recipients wanted and needed to know. They served to reassure managers of his incremental progress, his loyalty and attention to their directives from afar.[34] Ford's less letter-worthy behaviour served as a form of release from the routine stresses and limitations of colonial life in this tropical port. In one sense, then, his letters were a way of writing out or over the messiness of business affairs in port.

Ford had no intention of staying in Fiji for more than a couple of years and thought 'it very doubtful if ever any of our men will take to the country very kindly'. His successor, the Suva resident Alex

Duncan, held the position for nearly two decades. Duncan's professionalism was continually questioned by New Zealand-based management. The USSCo. worked Fiji shipping in combination, rather than competition, with the ASNCo., Australia's largest coastal shipping company (incorporated as the Australasian United Steam Navigation Company (AUSNCo.) in 1887). Following ongoing hostilities, managers of both companies met in 1895 and agreed to carry cargo and passengers at equal rates between Fiji and Sydney. They used the deferred rebate system, where shippers secured a fifteen per cent rebate on goods shipped with either company. This was retained for twelve months and forfeited if traders chose to ship goods by other operators in that period. This combine practically excluded shipping interests in Fiji from running in opposition. Yet Duncan frequently jeopardised this alliance system by undercutting freight and passage rates and paying excessive refunds to shippers. In 1896 the USSCo. secretary, Thomas Whitson, requested that he 'try and be a little more stiff with shippers, as I assure you it is no pleasure to us to have to challenge any of your actions'. Whitson recognised that the Fiji trade was different from ordinary trades, but 'there is such a thing as being too easy in giving way to persistent claimants'.[35]

Pursers had considerable and onerous responsibilities in the island trades. As the Auckland manager noted, 'the work is so entirely different from ordinary pursers and it is absolutely necessary for them to know the people'. Building familiarity and trust with shippers and traders took time, so frequent changes in crew, routinely done to augment experience and enhance promotion prospects, were regarded as particularly disruptive. Pursers were also instructed to avoid claims by dealing 'firmly but fairly' with traders' demands. In 'nearly every instance', one circular outlined, claims 'can be traced to carelessness and neglect of ordinary precautions'.[36]

Duncan's over-zealous behaviour continued. He took important shipping matters into his own hands and disregarded instructions from New Zealand. His business letters document an ongoing struggle to assert the rightness of his actions: 'I want nothing but mere justice for I am not as bad as made out.' Without direct telegraphic communication to head office, for the Pacific Cable only connected Fiji in 1902, Duncan had to act without advice at times, particularly when circumstances changed rapidly and shipping decisions had to be made on the spot: 'If I make a mistake it should not be too hardly treated.'[37]

Letters were awkward instruments in building and maintaining company operations across regional ports. Duncan often complained that his correspondence was not even acknowledged by head office. The power of 'being there' was not lost on management, as seen in the appointment of inspectors in response to lax operations on board steamers. On visiting Duncan at Suva in 1898, Whitson observed that he was too intimate with traders. He ran business very informally, men walking in and out of his office as if it were their own.[38] Faced with further complaints about his outside trading interests, Duncan also glossed over conflict and boosted company prospects, arguing that 'the Fiji trade has increased wonderfully, and as you know I am responsible for that. . . . I have made mistakes (serious ones) which I do regret, and have offered to repay. To-day your trade in Fiji is progressing quietly and smoothly, while continuing to increase, until I can see ahead that you will have the lot.'[39]

By the end of the nineteenth century, four USSCo. steamers were running to Fiji each month from the ports of Melbourne, Sydney and Auckland. In 1883 the company stationed a steamer in Fiji to provide an inter-island shipping service and deliver mails free of charge throughout the group. The Fiji Government paid no direct subsidies for these services, but all USSCo. vessels were exempt from coasting licences, pilotage, light, wharfage and harbour dues, the total value of which was, in effect, an indirect subsidy.[40] Colonial officials soon regarded these concessions as excessive, the amount 'absolutely out of proportion to any service that the Company has rendered or could render. It is equal to one twenty-eighth of the whole revenue of the colony.' Their contract was amended in 1892, with the USSCo. to commute its use of the wharves to £300 per annum, remaining liable for any wharfage over and above that amount.[41]

The inter-island vessel served as a feeder for the steamers running to Australia and New Zealand, thereby boosting the remuneration of the island trades as a whole. It continually ran at a loss from disbursements in wages and victualling, coal, repairs, customs dues and other shipping fees, insurance, claims, trans-shipments and advertising.[42] Locals were dissatisfied with the steamers the USSCo. put on the route, for they were too small, slow and unbearably hot to travel in. Governor George O'Brien sought more competition in the trade. He was against the 'non-producing' classes in Fiji, including the shipping companies, who 'make incessant claims on the colony's revenue', unlike planters 'who have a real stake in the country and something to lose'. More importantly, indigenous Fijians, 'as owners of eleven-twelfths of the soil . . . have by far the largest interests in the colony'.[43] Following Duncan's advice the USSCo. withdrew from the running in 1903. On Duncan's letter informing the Government of their regret in having 'to withdraw after nineteen years' regular service', the colonial secretary underlined 'regular', and added a question mark and marginal note: 'very irregular and unsatisfactory'.[44]

When the Fiji Government then contracted the inter-island service to the AUSNCo. for a direct subsidy of £3,500 per annum, a figure greater than the USSCo. received in indirect subsidies (£2,600), Holdsworth believed Duncan had misrepresented the state of the trade.[45] The company could now not expect automatic exemptions from dues for their regular steamers trading to Fiji from Australian and New Zealand ports. Fiji's officials continued to look unfavourably on their operations, perceiving that, while they took more profit than anyone else out of the colony, they gave little back. What the company did contribute was earmarked for infrastructure, which directly benefited them, such as harbour lighting, pilot services and wharves.[46] So while steam was celebrated as a necessary boon to colonial development, as in the rhetoric explored in earlier chapters, the productive value of shipping was not automatically regarded in the same light as land-based industry. Moreover, the USSCo.'s operations in Fiji were increasingly constrained by wider political decisions about the allocation of limited colonial resources.

As Duncan argued, his relative isolation from New Zealand made it difficult for him to run the Suva branch office, but it also prevented his having a clear appreciation of the complexities involved in running a large-scale shipping enterprise out of Dunedin. He was encouraged to resign in 1907 after threatening the Fiji Government with the withdrawal of the transpacific Canadian Australian Line if it did not increase the company's concessions.[47] His account of affairs was ultimately deemed untrustworthy. As Whitson cabled from Suva in 1907, 'temperament incurable and might lead further troubles . . . I cannot recommend reinstate on the following grounds unreliability and elasticity of conscience'. Acknowledging Duncan's letter of resignation, Holdsworth replied, 'You have at all times been rather difficult to control.'[48]

Duncan's legacies confronted both of his successors to the Suva branch management. Charles Hughes and George Morgan had to redraw professional and social boundaries and worked to reform traders' unreasonable expectations. Hughes, Duncan's immediate replacement from Sydney, was reluctant to assume the posting. He feared 'he might be looked upon as side-tracked and not be available for any more interesting opening that might offer'.[49] He noted within a few weeks of arrival that 'I find the place terribly dull & the life a lazy one. People here think Suva the hub of the universe and that Fiji is responsible for the Union Coy's proud position today.' He was careful not to directly challenge them, 'but I must say I never have had such extraordinary requests or demands as they make'. Like Duncan, Hughes found it difficult to uphold the sanctity of his office: 'I know you will pardon my suggesting your not sending a "jolly good fellow". It's nothing but cards & liquor in and out of office hours. I haven't touched the former and find it a little difficult to dodge the latter.' It was also increasingly apparent that no one in Suva appeared to have a good word for Duncan.[50] Morgan, from the company's New Plymouth branch, replaced Hughes in 1908 and committed for a lengthy period. He aimed to 'gradually bring [traders] to see that they must do business in a businesslike way without continually threatening to force us to pay claims and give passages as they wish it'.[51]

The unsanctioned boundary-crossing between USSCo. agents and port traders, breaches of commercial and racial sovereignty, elicited much anxiety. The corrupting influence of intimacy with the 'wrong' crowd ashore also exercised others in the port community. Following the suicide of a settler from New South Wales in 1910, Reverend R. T. Mathews declared that this man came to Suva to a 'respectable position' but 'found the place full of temptation to evil and almost barren of any incentive to good'. He drank, gambled and 'lost his position'. This was no isolated case, for 'over and over again I have heard young men complain that they come here with letters of introduction which they present and which are ignored, and that failing respectable society there is nothing left for them but the hotel, the billiard table and cards'.[52]

Unlike New Zealand and Australia, from where many Europeans in Fiji had on-migrated from the 1860s, Fiji lacked a foundational settler narrative. It had no First Fleet, no New Zealand Company, no scheme of systematic colonisation. It was, as John Young concludes, 'the cultural terminus of a quarter-century of disorderly migration, chiefly by young men willing to risk much to make a quick fortune'.[53] As the first centre of European maritime and commercial activity in Fiji, Levuka gained a reputation as a lawless, booze-sodden, vice-ridden frontier community. A cotton boom in the early 1870s swelled the town's population, but the industry was short-lived and its collapse heightened social and racial tensions there. Britain's annexation of Fiji in 1874 was motivated by the desire to protect indigenous Fijians from the unchecked activities of Euro-American migrants. As self-styled King of Fiji, Ratu Seru Cakobau, put it: 'The whites who come to Fiji are a bad lot. They are mere stalkers on the beach.' He was certain that if Fiji were not ceded 'the white stalkers on the beach, the cormorants, will open their maws and swallow us'.[54] 'The Beach' was also a popular shorthand for the 'lower and uneducated class' of whites in port and continued to be used this way well into the early twentieth century.[55] The concerns aired in USSCo. correspondence about the threats to white prestige embodied by lower-class members of the port's European community also suggest something of the lingering influence of this earlier unsettled history. The frontier community appeared to live on as the 'bluffing bouncing' crowd of white traders in port. These internal class divisions can also be seen as a microcosm of tensions writ large across the colonial 'sisterhood' of Fiji, New Zealand and Australia over the course of the late nineteenth and early twentieth centuries.

Fiji's first Governor, Sir Arthur Gordon, informed settlers in 1874 that the new colony would not be a 'white man's country'. Many white residents bristled at the restrictions on settler access to land and indigenous labour embedded in Fiji's new status as a 'severe Crown colony'. Colonial official Edgar Layard was at pains to point out in the local press that 'severe' simply meant a 'pure' or 'perfect' form of government, signifying the Crown's 'absolute authority to rule with sense, spirit, and humanity', yet many Europeans understood severe as synonymous with 'tyrannous, oppressive, cruel'.[56] New Zealand commentators mused that, while Crown rule had no place in New Zealand, white settlers in Fiji would likely accept it as the island group was populated only by a few thousand whites who went there not to establish new homes, 'but simply to make money and get away'.[57] Many Fiji settlers rejected this distinction and insisted that colonists had always viewed life in Fiji in 'much the same fashion as in that of the adjacent colonies from which they originated'.[58] Continuing discomfort with Crown rule found its partial expression in movements for closer integration with the Australian and New Zealand colonies, as well as preoccupation with the impressions of outsiders. Imagined slights and ignorance about the colony aired in New Zealand and Australia were often reproduced and attacked in the local press, with the implicit recognition that distorted beliefs effectively pushed Fiji to the margins of Australasia and its resident Europeans to the margins of respectable whiteness.

When New Zealand achieved Dominion status in 1907, the *Fiji Times* regarded it as a rupture, for New Zealand was 'not a great time ago included as one of the various groups of islands comprising the "South Sea Islands"'.[59] For New Zealand this was an important rite of passage, a recognition of maturity and independence, for 'no New Zealander would wish his country to be confused with the Fijis, the Jamaicas, and the Sierra Leones of the Empire'. It set the nation apart from subordinate island colonies which were not responsible for making their own laws and 'where the Englishman is only an exile even though he is ruler and master'.[60]

Anxieties about the potential of Suva as a successful commercial base and home for 'respectable' whites circulated around the character of fellow white residents, port town sociality and restrictive Crown rule. It also encompassed the tropical environment. While the colony was widely reputed to be exceptionally healthy for the tropics, particularly given the absence of malaria, successful white settlement in the region was not a given. Dangers of 'demoralisation, degeneracy, depravity and debility', as David Livingstone puts it, exercised colonists across Oceania, Africa and Asia, inflecting debates about the specific form colonisation should and could take in tropical places.[61] USSCo. correspondence also provides insights into some of the routine struggles involved. Comments on the health of different individuals punctuate business letters. Employees often referred to Fiji as '*Malua* land', which captured the different pace of life in the island group. *Malua* translated as 'no hurry', 'plenty of time', 'don't fuss', and while many Europeans may have welcomed a more laid-back lifestyle, adherence to timetables and fast turn-around times in port underpinned company profitability. Ford prided himself on his work ethic. When much of the town was down with fever he declared, 'I have not time yet to spare to get sick.' Moreover, he informed Mills that one man 'remarked to me the other day he could not make out how I got the work I do out of white men as [he was] sure he could never do it'. General supervision of all matters was 'a very important thing to do down in Fiji otherwise human nature is prone to give way to the climate'.[62]

Yet white men could not evade the impact of ill health on daily business or the loss of colleagues who returned to more temperate branches. Low fever seemed to infect all, reported Ford in 1885, and the engineer of the company steamer 'whilst walking along with me to see after gear required, dropped down, but only for a few minutes, knowing that the work must be got through before he can really give way. It does not seem to last long, but leaves everyone *very weak*.' One of his co-workers, 'the Drs say, must never think of making Fiji his home again, in fact there are very few men that it does not eventually ruin in health'.[63] During his three months in Levuka, Barkas lost two stone. On returning to New Zealand his colleagues in Auckland were shocked at his 'yellow and shrunken appearance'. They insisted he stay in Auckland for a couple of days ostensibly to discuss business, 'but really that I should not frighten my wife too greatly by my livery and sweated-out appearance'.[64]

These concerns persisted into the twentieth century. A mother of one USSCo. employee, Gordon Gow, requested he not be sent to the Fiji branch office again, as 'the climate was beginning to tell on him. I don't think it would be at all wise for him to be there . . . I think anything almost would be better than Fiji.'[65] He was posted back to Suva. When Morgan took leave in 1912, he was reluctant to put Gow in charge for he was sure he could not manage alone: 'he may improve, but is easily "bluffed" by our sporting crowd here besides which he has no memory whatever'.[66] In the preceding months Morgan also reported that the weather had 'already found out the weak spots of the staff. J. A. Williams has been away with piles. Watson has had a fortnight's bed with mumps and fever while Hodge and Thompson who are just starting their second summer are all to pieces.'[67] Shipboard staff also succumbed to illness. In the year preceding McBurney's complaints, which opened this chapter, three island pursers were relieved in rapid succession. One died suddenly, another 'cracked up badly' and his replacement developed kidney stones and also proved 'unsound'.[68] While not making it formal policy as for the colonial bureaucracy or the Colonial Sugar Refining Company, the USSCo. did allow employees breaks to New Zealand and southern parts of Australia during the most oppressive months. New Zealand was framed as a 'natural sanatorium' in relation to its tropical neighbours, both in the Pacific and the Indian Ocean.[69]

The successive USSCo. agents and managers posted to Levuka, and later Suva, all struggled in some degree to make Fiji a permanent home; they felt stranded there, separated from their homes in Australia or New Zealand to which they always planned to return. At best the Fiji posting was understood as a temporary one, at worst it felt like exile. The 'pathologies of displacement' endemic to the colonial condition, as Penny Edwards puts it with reference to tropical colonies in South-East Asia, were in clear tension with the values invested in settled, stable and bureaucratised European occupation.[70] Ford, Duncan, Hughes and Morgan all emphasised their adherence to company protocol; they strove to fashion themselves as competent, efficient and loyal servants, and tried to present the company's prospects in the best possible light. But these men also narrated the colonial experience as one of personal discomfort, displacement and loss. They all felt head office should not overlook the human cost of company growth. As Ford reflected, 'I know that you will always bear me in mind for the inconvenience & lost [sic] I have undergone to serve our Company.'[71] Fearful of dismissal at one point, Duncan felt he had been in Suva too long seriously to contemplate a move. 'I have lost all touch with my former connections . . . I do not want to leave for I have nowhere to go to make another start.'[72]

The reproduction of white familial relations has been highlighted as a 'crucial prerequisite for the establishment of a viable settler community'. With the advent of regular steamship services, cheap tickets enabled women to travel to colonial outposts formerly accessible only to lone white men.[73] White women were valued for their contribution to moral uplift and the cultivation of the private interior. They played a prominent role in efforts to domesticate men in a familiar setting and in removing opportunities for sexual relations with indigenous women.[74] Their presence also helped fracture bonds of white male sociality. For Barkas, the 'boys' fun' was the result of men 'being without wives or home establishments'.[75] But Fiji was neither a white man's nor a white woman's country. Branch staff lamented the negative impact on domestic life. Ford and his wife left their children behind in Russell, as 'we think it would be cruel to bring them down here as the children here never seem like New Zealand ones'. Frequently ill, Ford's wife returned to New Zealand for recuperation but died shortly afterwards. When it was confirmed he would be posted back to New Zealand, Ford was 'very pleased to hear that there is a prospect of me getting out of Fiji alias Hell'.[76] Duncan, too, insisted that 'this place is no great attraction to anyone, the climate is bad and the work is difficult, added to that I have ruined the health of my wife so you can see it would not require much to take me away'.[77] Hughes, a widower, came to Suva alone, leaving his children in Sydney, while Morgan's wife and children relocated with him. He wrote of the difficulties in getting suitable female domestic help. Other Europeans in Suva had tried bringing out governesses from New Zealand but 'found it an absolute failure'. After six years in Suva, the doctor ordered Morgan's wife spend the summers away, preferably in Tasmania.[78] So, while this maritime transport revolution enabled white women to follow their men, it also made return trips to more familiar, temperate colonies easier and more frequent. This prevented the 'indigenisation' of whites, it averted their assimilation into a risky tropical environment, but in separating families for extended periods of time it also spoke to the failure of Fiji as a white settler colony.

Such difficulties in maintaining white domestic relations notwithstanding, there is little evidence of routine intimacy between port staff and indigenous women in the USSCo. records. What correspondence does exist, like most of the other letters I have explored here, was created to communicate concerns or resolve pressing problems. When Ralph Kearns, the purser on the inter-island steamer *Maori*, became involved with a Fijian woman and eventually married her in 1895, this provoked a strong response from his father, as well as Duncan and other company employees. Their collective reaction demonstrated the power of cultural prohibitions on such behaviour. Kearns's father accused Duncan of turning a blind eye to this state of affairs and insinuated it was common for USSCo. men to be involved with indigenous women. Duncan reacted keenly to this and wrote Mills a lengthy and impassioned letter, insisting that he should not have to monitor employees' private lives and, in any case, the 'men are not angels but the present officers are above touching the black women'.[79] He was concerned to locate the scandal squarely off the ship; Kearns had associated with the 'wrong crowd' ashore and no one else in the USSCo. was involved. He also emphasised that Kearns had an ingrained inclination 'to live with these people'. Before trading to Fiji he had intended to marry a young Samoan woman, yet fellow crew talked him out of it. At that time the captain had apparently warned the Auckland branch manager 'that to send this boy to the Islands would ruin him'. Duncan asserted that 'he always has apparently been soft with these women'.[80] Various attempts were made at all company levels to put him 'straight' and have him abandon her. Kearns refused and was subsequently dismissed from Fiji and transferred to the Auckland branch.

Four years later Kearns resigned after 'getting into trouble through his wife and other matters'. He left owing some passage money for her to and from Tonga. Later that year a prospective employer in Honolulu requested a character reference for Kearns. Management replied that he was no loss to the company, 'being of a low type and his general bearing and demeanour were objectionable'. His financial position was precarious and 'had he not left suddenly of his own accord (taking it is reported the wife of another man with him) I intended to strongly recommend that he be got rid of'.[81] In 1903 Kearns himself requested a free passage from Honolulu to Sydney. His application was declined given his debts and the fact he left Auckland 'taking with him the wife of a local Boarding House keeper'.[82]

The development of a Pacific world shaped by maritime transport operations clearly increased anxieties about family life. The establishment of a stable, permanent home in port was a tenuous project for most of the USSCo.'s Fiji branch staff. This prospect was even more challenging for sailors who lived and worked at a considerable distance from family, or remained unmarried with no permanent base onshore. Following the pioneering work of Ann Laura Stoler, scholars of colonialism readily treat domestic arrangements as clearly linked to public order, with sexual control 'both an instrumental image for the body politic – a salient part standing for the whole – and itself fundamental to how racial politics were secured and how colonial projects were carried out'. 'Renovated' imperial engagements in the latter part of the century placed increased emphasis not only on the presence of white women but also on the exclusion of colonists deemed 'unfit'. Only men of suitable character and class could safeguard the moral and physical integrity of the white colonial community, an integrity that would be undermined by interracial intimacy.[83] Kearns's restless regional mobilities were framed as particularly disruptive to the success of company operations in the Pacific, a success which came to be defined by the bearing and professionalism of its employees. Such fleeting glimpses of lives lived at the edges of this maritime industry provide some insight into the attendant messiness and interpersonal struggles that this project involved.

Adrift?

If the Pacific was overwhelmingly imagined 'as a place where whites were scarcely capable of living without losing their cultural and racial identity', as Nicholas Thomas and Richard Eves have concluded in their discussion of the letters of two island traders in the late nineteenth century, this Pacific did not embrace New Zealand.[84] The island trades were a separate category, sitting apart from the New Zealand coastal and trans-Tasman trades. Temperate New Zealand stood at the edge of unruly tropical space. It figured as headquarters and home, the site from which to account, to report misdemeanours to management, to reunite with wives and children, and to recoup and restore the integrity of the white body (from New Zealand, Ford typically wrote of going 'down' to the islands that lay to the north, mapping out a hierarchical regional relationship). While Duncan could assure Mills that his steamers 'have been as carefully watched over as if they were alongside the Dunedin wharf', concerns about discipline, order and control were magnified in trades that took men further away from the surveillance of senior management based in New Zealand.[85] The assessment of the fitness or otherwise of different men for the island trades filled up much of the correspondence between port branch agents and head office. There was a persistent concern with 'slippage', framed in the examples in various ways, whether through decline in physical and mental stamina, recourse to alcohol, or intimacy with the 'wrong crowd' ashore and an associated lax work ethic.

The USSCo.'s island shipping helps us chart the common history of the societies and individuals that were linked by maritime activity in the late nineteenth and early twentieth centuries. Even as modern transport networks stitched these communities together in ways not previously possible, new-found proximities under steam also highlighted what made these places distinct. As geographer Doreen Massey argues in her more general reflections on the meanings of space, the belief that efficient transport is the enemy of distance, and that the metaphor of speed evidences spatial and social control, removes much of the complexity and analytic potential of these processes. The seeming annihilation of distance, propelled here by the USSCo.'s web of steamer services, in fact raised new questions about the spatial configuration of social relations, multiplicity and difference.[86] And the very ocean itself, a metaphorical space of connection and affinity in the British Pacific, also continued to be lived and experienced as a difficult and hazardous space of separation.

Notes

1   HC, USSCo. Records, AG-292-005-001/082, Irvine to Holdsworth, 22 August 1907.
2   *Ibid.*, AG-292-005-001/034, Henderson to Mills, 25 October 1894; WCCA, USSCo. Records, masters' and officers' personal files, AF004:4:7, Marine Superintendent to R. G. Hutton, 26 August 1909.
3   *Fiji Times* (19 February 1890).
4   *Fiji Times* (2 May 1877).
5   Reeves, *Brown Men and Women*, 168.
6   HC, USSCo. Records, AG-292-005-001/032, Duncan to Mills, 9 February 1895; AG-292-005-001/022, Houghton to Mills (quoting Duncan), 8 September 1892.
7   WCCA, USSCo. Records, masters' and officers' personal files, AF004:4:7, Strang to Holdsworth, 20 May 1909 and Strang to Hutton, 26 August 1909.
8   ATL, MS-Copy-Micro 0670, Henry Hunter Brown, 'Reminiscences': Fiji, 1894–7.
9   ATL, MS-Papers-2491-05, Barkas Diaries, vol. 5: 'Some Memories of a Mediocrity', Frederick Barkas, article in *Weekly Press* (Christchurch) (24 January 1888).
10 Richard E. Smith, quoted in *Auckland Star* (16 November 1959), cutting in WCCA, USSCo. Records, AF004:7:11, masters' and officers' personal files.
11 Reeves, *Brown Men and Women*, 84.
12 HC, USSCo. Records, AG-292-005-001/002, Ford to Mills, 9 April 1885.
13 *Western Pacific Herald* (22 November 1907).
14 HC, USSCo. Records, AG-292-005-001/099, Morgan to Holdsworth, 12 July 1911.
15 *Ibid.*, AG-292-005-001/002, Ford to Mills, 21 February 1884; Cameron Family Papers, MS 1046, Box 1, McColl to Cameron, 1 October 1884.
16 HC, USSCo. Records, AG-292-003-001/009, minutes of meetings of directors, 22 January 1895.
17 *Ibid.*, AG-292-005-001/096, W. McIntyre to Smart, 24 March 1911.
18 UASC, FSU Auckland Branch Files, Box 1 – Correspondence General 1900–13, D-8, *Wairuna* fireman to Auckland Seamen's Union, n.d. [c. 1912].
19 HC, USSCo. Records, AG-292-005-001/104, Anderson to Holdsworth, n.d. [c. 1912].
20 *Ibid.*, AG-292-005-001/035, Duncan to Mills, 13 November 1895.
21 *Ibid.*, AG-292-005-001/027, Henderson to Mills, 25 April and 4 November 1892.
22 *Ibid.*, AG-292-005-001/057, Spence to Mills, 13 August 1899.
23 *Ibid.*, AG-292-005-001/093, Holdsworth to Mills, 16 May 1909; AG-292-005-001/096, Aiken to Holdsworth, 15 October 1910.
24 *Ibid.*, AG-292-005-001/086, Mills to Holdsworth, 27 April 1908.
25 *Ibid.*, AG-292-005-001/082, Sleigh to Holdsworth, 3 August 1907; AG-292-005-001/085, McLennan to Holdsworth, 7 August 1907.
26 WCCA, USSCo. Records, AF004:4:7, Masters' and Officers' Personal Files, C. M. McDonald to Strang, 15 May 1911.
27 HC, USSCo. Records, AG-292-003-001/003, minutes of meetings of directors, 13 October 1884.
28 *Ibid.*, AG-292-005-001/004, Houghton to Ford, 29 November 1884.
29 *Ibid.*, AG-292-005-001/002, Ford to Mills, 25 February 1885.
30 *Ibid.*, AG-292-005-001/002, Ford to Mills, 6 March, 8 July and 3 September 1885, 6 February 1886.
31 *Ibid.*, AG-292-005-001/001, Henderson to Mills, 2 September 1885 and 10 February 1886; AG-292-005-001/045, Henderson to Mills, 2 September 1889.

32 *Ibid.*, AG-292-005-001/012, Ford to Mills, 30 August 1889.

33 ATL, MS-Papers-2491-05, Barkas Diaries, vol. 5: 'Some Memories of a Mediocrity', Barkas to brother, 9 January 1888, 130.

34 My thoughts about the function of letters in this context have been influenced by Nicholas Thomas and Richard Eves, *Bad Colonists: The South Sea Letters of Vernon Lee Walker & Louis Becke* (Durham, N C: Duke University Press, 1999), esp. 6–7.

35 HC, USSCo. Records, AG-292-005-001/038, Whitson to Mills, 7 August 1896.

36 *Ibid.*, AG-292-005-001/056, Irvine to Holdsworth, 26 March 1901.

37 *Ibid.*, AG-292-005-001/035, Duncan to Mills, 15 April 1897; AG-292-005-001/037, Duncan to Mills, 7 May 1897.

38 *Ibid.*, AG-292-005-001/047, Whitson to Mills, 14 September 1898.

39 *Ibid.*, AG-292-005-001/044, Duncan to Mills, 5 May 1899.

40 For one contract see NAF, CSO, 88.3651.

41 NAF, CSO.92.514 [bound with 93.3726], Colonial Secretary, 19 February 1892.

42 HC, USSCo. Records, AG-292-005-004/054, 'Copies of Various Papers'.

43 *Fiji Times*, n.d., enclosed in HC, USSCo. Records, AG-292-005-001/062, Duncan to Mills, 9 April 1901.

44 NAF, CSO, 03.1904, Duncan, 16 September 1903.

45 HC, USSCo. Records, AG-292-004-003/001, Holdsworth to Mills, 28 September 1903.

46 NAF, CSO, 03.1904, 17 May 1904.

47 For more on the collusion between the USSCo. and AUSNCo., see Bruce Knapman, *Fiji's Economic History, 1874–1939: Studies of Capitalist Colonial Development* (Canberra: The Australian National University National Centre for Development Studies, 1987), 65–79.

48 HC, USSCo. Records, AG-292-005-004/082, Whitson to Mills, 7 February 1907; AG-292-005-001/081, Holdsworth to Duncan, 11 February 1907.

49 *Ibid.*, AG-292-005-001/081, Mills to Holdsworth, 8 February 1907.

50 *Ibid.*, AG-292-005-001/081, Hughes to Holdsworth, 21 May 1907; AG-292-005-001/087, Hughes to Holdsworth, 19 June 1907.

51 *Ibid.*, AG-292-005-001/087, Hughes to Holdsworth, 25 April 1907 and Morgan to Holdsworth, 26 March 1908.

52 *Fiji Times* (16 April 1910).

53 Young, *Adventurous Spirits*, 21.

54 ATL, Coleman Phillips Papers, 73-150-09, Correspondence respecting the cession of Fiji, Sir Hercules Robinson KCMG to the Earl of Carnarvon, 3 October 1874.

55 NAF, CSO, 13.104, Acting Sub-Inspector to Colonial Secretary, 7 January 1913.

56 E. L. Layard, letter to the editor, *Fiji Times* (9 September 1874) and anonymous letter to the editor (14 October 1874).

57 *New Zealand Herald* (24 September 1874).

58 *Fiji Times* (9 March 1898).

59 *Fiji Times* (28 September 1907).

60 *New Zealand Herald* (28 June 1907).

61 David N. Livingstone, 'Race, space and moral climatology: notes towards a genealogy', *Journal of Historical Geography*, 28:2 (2002), 172. For debates about New Guinea, see Richard Eves, 'Unsettling settler colonialism: debates over climate and colonization in New Guinea, 1875–1914', *Ethnic & Racial Studies*, 28:2 (2005), 304–30.

62 HC, USSCo. Records, AG-292-005-001/002, Ford to Mills, 8 July and 5 August 1885; AG-292-005-001/006, Ford to Mills, 27 January 1887.

63 *Ibid.*, AG-292-005-001/002, Ford to Mills, 20 July 1885 (emphasis in original); AG-292-005-001/008, Ford to Mills, 26 June 1887.

64 ATL, MS-Papers-2491-05, Barkas Diaries, vol. 5: 'Some Memories of a Mediocrity', 24 January 1888.

65 HC, USSCo. Records, AG-292-005-001/072, Gow to Holdsworth, 22 April 1902.

66 *Ibid.*, AG-292-005-001/108, Morgan to Holdsworth, 30 November 1912.

67 *Ibid.*, AG-292-005-004/120, Morgan to Aiken, 16 October 1912.
68 *Ibid.*, AG-292-005-004/133, Aiken to Holdsworth, 4 August 1906.
69 It had also been envisaged that New Zealand would serve as a retreat for 'invalid officers and civilians' from India. With the advent of regular steam transport New Zealand's invigorating climate would then be within 'easy distance'. Children would obtain sound education there and 'society certainly not to be met with else-where'. Here Indian colonists would 'recognise the parent country in embryo'. See 'Shall New Zealand have steam?', *Otago Witness* (5 March 1853) (reprinted from the *Commercial Daily List*), 4.
70 Penny Edwards, 'On home ground: Settling land and domesticating difference in the "non-settler" colonies of Burma and Cambodia', *Journal of Colonialism and Colonial History*, 4:3 (2003); http://muse.jhu.edu/journals/journal_of_colonialism_and_colonial_history/v004/4.3edwards.html (accessed 27 August 2007).
71 HC, USSCo. Records, AG-292-005-001/002, Ford to Mills, 5 August 1885.
72 *Ibid.*, AG-292-005-001/069, Duncan to Mills, 22 June 1903.
73 Lorenzo Veracini, '"Emphatically not a white man's colony": settler colonialism and the construction of colonial Fiji', *Journal of Pacific History*, 43:2 (2008), 192, note 20; Lewis H. Gann and Peter Duignan, *The Rulers of British Africa, 1870–1914* (London: Croom Helm, 1978), 242.
74 Edwards, 'On home ground'; Ann Laura Stoler, *Carnal Knowledge and Imperial Power: Race and the Intimate in Colonial Rule* (Berkeley: University of California Press, 2002); Claudia Knapman, *White Women in Fiji, 1835–1930: The Ruin of Empire?* (Sydney: Allen and Unwin, 1986); Margaret Jolly, 'Colonizing women: the maternal body and empire', in Sneja Gunew and Anna Yeatman (eds), *Feminism and the Politics of Difference* (St Leonards, NSW: Allen and Unwin, 1993), 103–27.
75 ATL, MS-Papers-2491-05, Barkas Diaries, vol. 5: 'Some Memories of a Mediocrity', 130, Barkas to brother, 16 September 1887.
76 HC, USSCo. Records, AG-292-005-001/002, Ford to Mills, 9 June 1885; AG-292-005-001/006, Ford to Mills, 16 March 1888.
77 *Ibid.*, AG-292-005-001/035, Duncan to Mills, 16 August 1895.
78 *Ibid.*, AG-292-005-001/087, Morgan to Holdsworth, 19 February 1908; AG-292-005-001/112, Hughes to Holdsworth, 4 November 1914. For more on white women and domestic life in colonial Fiji see Knapman, *White Women in Fiji*.
79 HC, USSCo. Records, AG-292-005-001/035, Kearns to Mills, 31 October 1895, Duncan to Mills, 21 October 1895, Duncan to Mills, 22 October 1895.
80 *Ibid.*, AG-292-005-001/035, Duncan to Mills, 21 October 1895.
81 *Ibid.*, AG-292-005-001/045, Henderson to Mills, 4 October 1899; AG-292-005-001/059, Aiken to Mills, 20 December 1899.
82 *Ibid.*, AG-292-005-001/072, Aiken to Holdsworth, 2 June 1903.
83 Stoler, *Carnal Knowledge and Imperial Power*, 78, 65.
84 Thomas and Eves, *Bad Colonists*, 88.
85 HC, USSCo. Records, AG-292-005-001/035, Duncan to Mills, 21 October 1895.
86 Doreen Massey, *For Space* (London: Sage, 2005), 9, 90–8; Massey, *Space, Place and Gender* (Cambridge: Polity Press, 1994), 137. The more conventional ideas about distance can be found in Blainey, *The Tyranny of Distance*, vii.

CHAPTER SEVEN

Sitima days in Suva: wharf labourers and the colonial port

On the wharf clusters a crowd of strange figures. How savage these Fijians look! The hair stiff, erect, and spreading in a huge mop above the dark faces: the features flat and negroid: the skin all shades from deep copper to actual black: the expression untamed and wild – all these alarm the timid traveller, and he says he will never go ashore among such savages! For all that we are in Suva, the European capital of Fiji, and a populous and busy town. And the 'horrible savages' are merely the peaceable labourers employed by the Union Steam Ship Company for cargo work, or else speculators from the native towns come up to sell coral and shells.

Beatrice Grimshaw, Three Wonderful Nations (1907)

In her narrative of a cruise through the South Pacific commissioned by the USSCo., the Anglo-Irish travel writer Beatrice Grimshaw's initial impressions of Suva echo moments of 'first contact' between indigenous Islanders and European explorers. Although Grimshaw writes from an early twentieth-century vantage point on board a steamship entering a colonial port town, these men staring back are unknown and, perhaps, forever unknowable. They are strange, dark and savage. Their appearance conjures up horrible visions of the likely harm that awaits the traveller on landing. Yet, on closer reflection, this is the European capital of Fiji, a 'populous and busy town'. The savages on the shoreline have in fact become peaceable, non-threatening wharf labourers through the transformative reach of imperial transport, communication and trading networks.

By the early years of the twentieth century, Suva was not simply the European capital, but also a growing multiracial and multicultural metropole in the western Pacific. People from the neighbouring provinces and outlying islands in Fiji were drawn to the port, whether for work at the wharf or for the attractions of an urban setting. Islanders from many other parts of the Pacific, Indians indentured to Fiji and

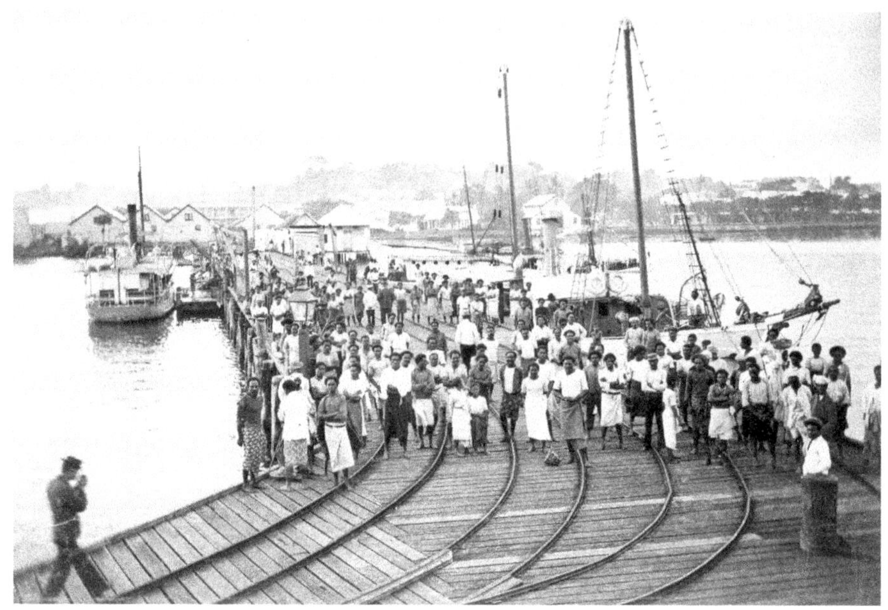

15 Suva wharf, 1900

Chinese all settled in and around Suva. The various European USSCo. branch staff and other white residents offered only one series of perspectives on the nature of business and social relationships in this colonial port. Turning to the circumstances of indigenous participation in this maritime industry opens a window on the fuller range of encounters that shaped the space of Suva. The port's early colonial history reveals some of the tensions inherent in managing this site as a crossroads of diverse people and influences.

Contesting port space

Across the Pacific, as Damon Salesa argues, harbours, anchorages, waterfronts and bays were typically the first indigenous spaces to be disciplined by imperial power.[1] From the late 1830s, the small beach-front settlement of Levuka, on the small island of Ovalau, was the first centre of European and American activity in Fiji. Suva, on the south-west coast of Fiji's largest island, Viti Levu, was also earmarked as a suitable site for white settlement. In 1860 Colonel W. T. Smythe visited Fiji to investigate Ratu Seru Cakobau's first offer of cession to the British. This offer, which was motivated by the desire to alleviate a debt of $45,000 to the United States Government incurred through damage to American property, included 27,000 acres of land around Suva Harbour. Yet Cakobau did not exercise authority over all islands in the Fiji group, or possess all of the land he proposed to cede. In his report to the Colonial Office, Smythe advised against acceptance of this offer, but did recommend moving the British consulate from Levuka to Suva 'so that a fresh start might be made with white settlement'.[2] Eight years later the Melbourne-based Polynesia Company purchased the land offered by Cakobau in the hope of profitable investment. This was a highly contentious charter, yet settlers were attracted to Fiji because of a depression in the Australasian colonies, the New Zealand Wars and the prospect of developing a cotton industry.[3]

James McEwan and Company acquired title to most of the land in the Suva area. After the formalisation of British imperial rule in Fiji in 1874, the company allotted the colonial Government every alternate block to encourage the removal of the capital from Levuka. The Government acquired more Suva land through the Native Lands Commission, set up in 1880 to register Fijian titles to land. It upheld settlers' Suva land claims if they could prove occupation and use. Any claims rejected by the commission remained in Government hands and were not returned to Fijian owners, as occurred everywhere else in Fiji under the commission. Moreover, the indigenous inhabitants of the area were displaced on the establishment of the new capital in 1882. Those living in Naqasiqasi or Old Suva Village, an area adjacent to the site of the proposed Government House, were relocated to land across the harbour. This village was named Suvavou (New Suva).[4]

The capital's early development was regarded as a fitting catalogue of imperial spatial control and transformation. As Chief Justice John Gorrie outlined to the Colonial Institute in 1883:

> We have seen the green knoll where a small wooden church once stood, levelled and rolled out into a pier; the native path along the beach raised to the dignity of Victoria Parade; the tidal swamp at the mouth of the creek reclaimed, and its square yards fought over as choice town sites. We have seen the value of the land rise, although the place has not yet cut its teeth, from two pounds an acre to even as much as a thousand pounds per acre near the shore; and the rivulets bridged, through which I have been obliged to wade to my waist before I could get back to my home after a tropical rain. Where a few years ago the native canoe alone was seen, or a solitary settler's boat coming up to the solitary store for a few tins of preserved meat and a case of gin, three (if not already four) first-class steamers per month from the Australian Colonies now load and unload cargoes.[5]

He also went on to note the periodical appearance of labour schooners from Melanesian islands and 'coolie ships' from India in Suva Harbour.

The littoral was transformed, the indigenous seascape and the markers of an earlier unsettled, frontier period in Fiji's history erased. While local and regional politics remained strong beyond Suva, particularly in the interior of Viti Levu where colonial officials met resistance, and in eastern Fiji where Tongan influence in the Lau Islands was marked from the early nineteenth century, the port was now increasingly locked into more durable and prestigious imperial networks, as the presence of the large steamships from the neighbouring colonies berthed at the wharf seemingly assured.

Despite the establishment of concrete structures of colonial rule, the port's development and appearance was an ongoing source of frustration and concern for civic leaders, and more so when Suva was included as a port of call on the prestigious transpacific mail routes. From the deck of a steamer entering Suva Harbour, the town might appear quaint and attractive, with lush tropical vegetation and tidy residences nestling in the hills, for the 'irritating defects, crooked streets, and the mixed races' were at a comfortable distance. Once the passenger disembarked, the 'grime and refuse of commercialism' became more apparent, lamented the *Western Pacific Herald*.[6] Suva's growing population regarded the wharf and foreshore as a rubbish dump. Animal carcasses, vegetable debris, night soil and refuse from shipping littered the muddy beach, and an effective sanitation programme was frustratingly slow to be implemented.[7] The citizens of 'this busy town, this rising port, this centre of ocean mail traffic' suffered long. The impressions of every visitor to the port could only be unfavourable. The post office was a 'dilapidated cowshed', a 'wreck of old times', a 'piece of flotsam from Levuka', remarked the *Western Pacific Herald*, and could hardly serve as a fitting home for the business 'which is so important that a great shipping company like the Union finds it worth its while to build noble steamers to cater for its necessities'.[8] The colonial Government struggled to finance urgent wharf improvements. By 1913 Suva was only able to accommodate one steamer at a time and the USSCo. contemplated landing cargo in the street.[9]

The physical appearance and unsanitary conditions of the wharf and surrounding streets were not the only cause for complaint. The social disorder on steamer days was also a target of reform. Steamer day (or mail day, beef day and ice day) stimulated a flurry of activity and excitement in port.[10] Crowds surged forward towards newly berthed vessels and blocked the gangway before passengers could safely disembark. White residents frequently disregarded requests from Fijian constables to stand back or move on, and ships' officers were instructed to exercise more control. Samoan washermen 'besieged' passengers and continued to hound them all the way to their hotels if they did not hand over their dirty laundry. 'Swarms of insistent blacks' competed for disembarking passengers, hoping to carry their bags to the nearest boarding houses. A government act was eventually passed to regulate the number of porters so as to remove this 'public nuisance'.[11]

Police supervision on Suva wharf increased in 1911 'for the protection of life and of government property, the latter being subject occasionally to rough treatment at the hands of inebriated sailors and firemen'.[12] But there were concerns that Suva's police force was not capable of managing the maritime crowd resident in the port on steamer days. Inebriated or not, sailors and firemen respected the authority of neither the native constabulary nor the white police officers. English, Scottish and Irish sailors and firemen were accustomed 'to a very different type of policeman', attested the inspector general of the constabulary. In the past, officers trained in Scotland had proved more than satisfactory in Suva. They already had experience of handling crowds 'of which the drunken riveter elements from the shipbuilding yards on the Clyde constituted a large element'. They were men 'of magnificent physique capable of dealing with the riotous firemen class'. Recent recruits from England, however, came to Fiji 'filled with weird information as to military expeditions'. One new appointee 'was told that he would have to train black troops to fight and would see active service in 6 months!!' He regarded the native constables as entirely unsuited to the work, with men falling asleep or drinking on the job. Firemen and beachcombers also subjected them to constant abuse.[13]

As larger and larger steamships were put in service, 'it became a matter of commercial necessity as well as of civic pride' to handle these vessels efficiently in port.[14] White commentators in Levuka had readily dismissed the image of indigenous men carrying passengers and packages to shore as inimical to the development of a civilised port town. In Suva, Europeans remained dependent on their work. Indigenous Fijians, as well as a number of Melanesian and Indian labourers, conducted most of the cargo handling.

Fiji's first Governor (1875–80), Sir Arthur Gordon, codified indigenous land tenure and restricted recruitment of indigenous labour. The development of Fiji's plantation economy rested instead on the exploitation of indentured labourers from neighbouring islands, particularly the New Hebrides and Solomon Islands, and of Indian men, women and children, 60,000 of whom were indentured to Fiji between 1879 and 1916. While labour regulations impeded 'unrestrained indigenous proletarianisation' and the decline of the subsistence village economy, Fijians could still find paid employment opportunities. The historian 'Atu Bain has probed the gap between official labour ideology and everyday practice. Rather than imposing 'labour embargoes on the able-bodied indigenous population', the colonial state in fact sought to regulate the flow of Fijian labour. By 1901 it is estimated that up to fifteen per cent of the adult male population, or about 2,850 individuals, worked away from their homes.[15]

Shipping companies regarded Fijian men, particularly the young and those of low status in chiefly lineages, as eminently suitable for heavy, difficult and exhausting manual labour. They were admired for their strong, muscular physique. The majority of waterside workers were drawn from Rewa, Suva's closest province, and shipping companies came to regard these men as skilled cargo handlers. Their proximity to the port reduced labour costs for employers and the state, as the domestic expenses of the labour force, including accommodation and food, would be met by their own villages. USSCo. branch manager, Alex Duncan, noted that they tried Indian men 'but they are too weak to handle sacks of sugar and are almost useless at shovelling coal'. Besides cargo work, indigenous workers also painted the steamers, chipped decks, cleaned the holds and did various other tasks. Their work saved the company significant expense, in a similar way to lascar seamen hired in the trades to Calcutta.[16]

For their part, villages in the provinces neighbouring Suva willingly sent groups of men to work at the wharf or other labour sites. Their wages, with earnings from cargo handling the highest, were used to purchase commodities or boats and to aid in house construction, and increasingly replaced agricultural produce as tax contributions. It appeared that Fijians valued wharf employment for its casual nature, in contrast to twelve-month plantation contracts. In this way it may have been regarded as an extension of the cyclical work of gardening and house construction, rather than a clear rupture in pre-colonial labour practices.

The USSCo. also employed Islander labour as general help. 'Instead of a black boy as an office boy', agent Ernest Ford had the services of Otto Vescey, the son of a failed Austrian planter and a Tongan woman, who was 'becoming very useful in the office . . . his Father gave him over to me to work him as we like'.[17] Ford also brought over a Melanesian boy from New Zealand who directed native labour on steamer days and he reported that the ships' officers 'are most pleased to have his services'. He also acted as a custom-house clerk for the company's inter-island steamer stationed in the group. Ford proudly informed James Mills that the boy refused to disclose information about the company's affairs when questioned about them in Ford's absence, retorting when asked how much he was paid that 'such matters we never mention outside the Coy's office'.[18]

Ford's reference to these 'boys' was typical of the infantilising language of colonialism, although he did recognise the incongruity of this label, noting to Mills at one point that he would receive a mat by the next steamer 'from Jim the boy or man I brought from NZ'.[19] The sketch by Joseph Lister (figure 16), drawn on his passage on the company steamer *Wainui* from Auckland to Fiji in 1888, most likely features the same individual Ford hired to work in the USSCo. office. This portrait is itself quite poignant, yet below the sketch Lister wrote: 'He is one of the labour people imported into Fiji. The septum of the nose and the lobe of the ear are perforated – iris brown.' Lister was more curious than fearful of this individual's imagined closeness to a barbarous past. His innate savagery, marked by the hole through his nose, could not be completely erased or disguised by the civilised shell of western clothing. Ford also domesticated and exoticised the spectre of Melanesian savagery in his midst. He often sent Mills various curios on the steamer to New Zealand, including clubs and spears, suggesting at one point that Mills's study 'ought now to present a warlike appearance'.[20] As an in between or liminal space, the port was a place where indigenous people were imagined to tread a line between primitivism and civilisation. This worked to quell or mitigate any threat to white residents or visitors, as also communicated by Grimshaw's opening vignette.[21]

On the expiration of plantation contracts, employers were expected (although many failed) to repatriate men to their homes within fourteen days. Many Fijians were hired illegally under the Masters and Servants Ordinances rather than the Labour Ordinance. The former imposed more lenient conditions on employers and did not require compulsory repatriation.[22] Steamer work did not carry the same expectation as plantation work and many Fijians did not return to their homes on non-steamer days. Provincial chiefs (*roko*) and district leaders (*buli*) began to complain of men 'bragging' that they had evaded communal work at home, while other men fled to Suva following domestic disputes, conflict with chiefs or episodes of fighting in their provinces.[23]

Those who left were not always the youngest men or those free of significant leadership responsibilities. In one case the head of a village clan in Namata, a district in Bau province, had escaped to Suva, complained Buli Namata to the colonial secretary. The people were left living 'like orphans' for there was now no one to lead them in delegating village work. On one occasion the clan leader returned to spread unease amongst the young men, telling them life in Suva was easier than cutting cane and better than living as a married man.[24] The *Lawa-i-taukei*, or Native Regulations, encoded strict obedience to chiefs and

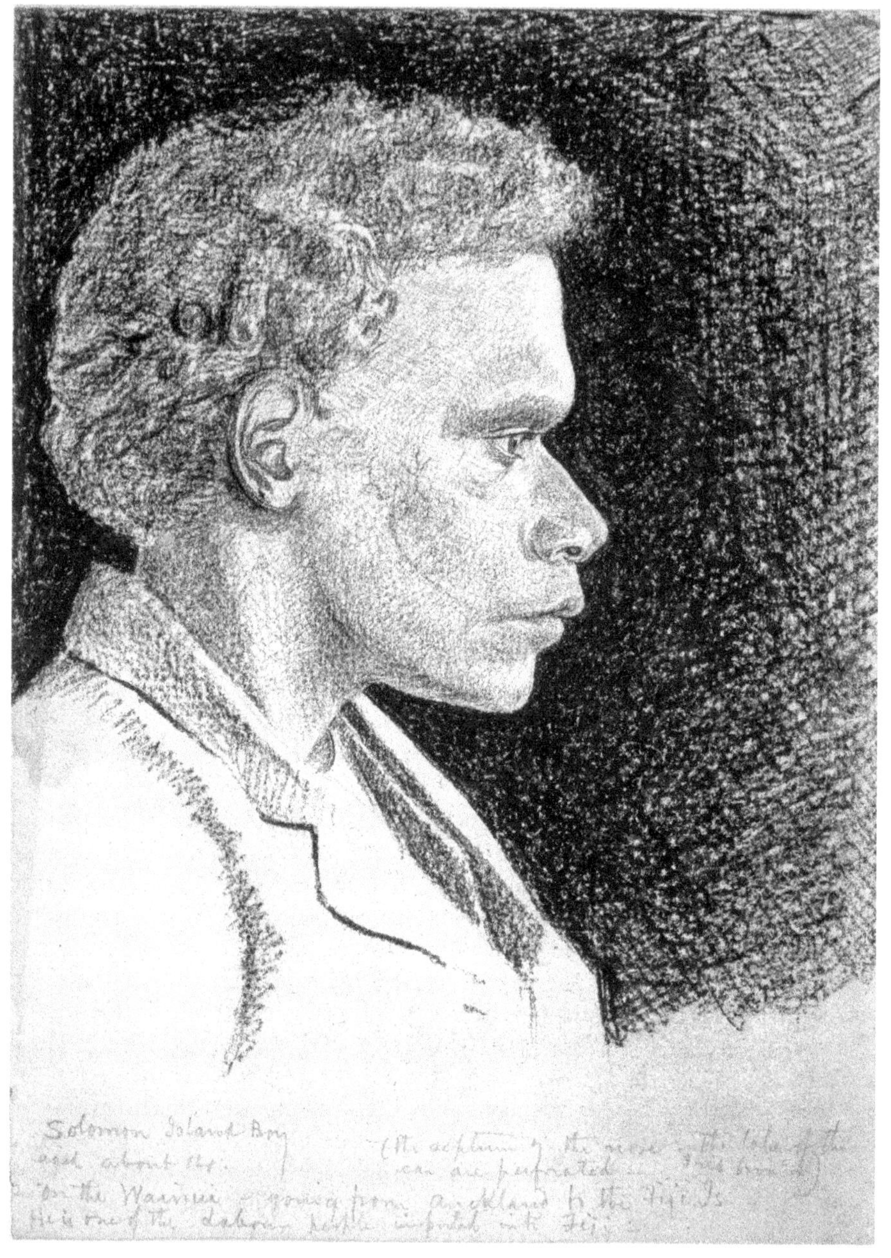

16   'Solomon Island boy aged about 14 on the *Wainui*', 1888

the debt of *lala* or labour service, which could include building houses, planting gardens, constructing roads, cutting wood, building canoes, fishing or any other work for the benefit of the community. Losing men permanently to the port town (and beyond) meant a loss of vital labour, familial support and communal contributions; it threatened the social fabric of village life.

As Governor of Fiji, John Bates Thurston (1888–97), who bolstered Gordon's foundational policies of benevolent protectionism towards indigenous Fijians, was concerned about emerging patterns of indigenous mobility following colonial rule. In the pre-colonial period, he argued, people only moved beyond their districts for feasting or fighting, with both practices circumscribed and controlled by custom and chiefly authority. Now Fijians were moving away from their home districts on an irregular and often permanent basis. He identified three main contributing factors: the influence of 'uneducated and unreflecting Europeans' who imparted a crude idea of 'liberty' to indigenous people; the 'evil influence' of Indian immigrants (meaning, presumably, the urban commercial activity of time-expired plantation workers); and Roman Catholic missionaries who valorised priestly authority and thereby undermined chiefly rule.[25]

The first of these was of long-standing concern. Intimacy with European men in urban places created what was derogatorily termed the 'white man's Fijian'. Many 'low-class' whites, it was felt, 'have some native, it may be only one favourite, who lives with them and attaches himself to them – men who never go near their chief or do any district work and whose absence is tolerated from fear of offending the white man'. Although chiefs sent for their men, 'such natives (encouraged and sheltered by Europeans who tell them that every British subject can do as he pleases), resist the messengers and defy the Chiefs'. Men from the native town at Suvavou were regarded as especially vulnerable. They were 'always in Suva picking up ideas from loafing low-class whites'.[26] The class dimensions of cross-cultural corruption were also mobilised around steamships. They were targeted as bearers of unwanted influences. In Tonga, for example, the Premier's secretary complained of Islanders procuring alcohol from second-class bars while steamers were alongside the wharf. Arrangements were made to close second-class bars while in port, there being 'no suspicion of the first-class bars'.[27]

Some missionaries were also concerned about patterns of interracial intimacy in port. The Methodist minister Reverend John G. Wheen argued that as Fiji became increasingly attractive for the tourist and the trader, both were content to stay in or near the port and their collective influence undid missionary work. The missionary's heart 'aches with sorry and shame' while he watched the corrupting actions of 'those who should be his allies'. As a result, the 'best type of Fijian character' could only be found 'in the more remote districts' where 'the native can follow a simple and natural life untrammelled by the pernicious example of a degenerate civilisation'.[28] Grimshaw, too, encouraged the adventurous traveller to venture beyond the port town and away from the cultural pollution the steamer brought with it in order to experience an 'authentic' Fiji.[29] So, while modern transport services were celebrated as reassuring markers of progress, the key to colonial development and prosperity, the benefits of speedier and more efficient connections with the wider world were not always so readily apparent. A steamer in port could as easily symbolise corruption as sophistication. The liminality of the port was a contestable state.

Many years after Thurston documented his concerns, indigenous leaders repeated similar complaints. While some were confident that young men continued to respect their authority – they could lecture absentees on their return 'and make them ashamed and they will thereafter remain with us' – others found the process entirely ineffectual. Buli Buresaga protested that while provincial and district chiefs were interrogated by officials at council meetings as to the state of their villages, absentees suffered no such humiliation:

> They defy the chiefs and officials. They have no respect for us or for our customs. They shirk all communal obligations and leave their villages to go to Suva to earn a little money with which they buy collars and neckties and coats! and save 2/- for a fine when they return home. Let them be whipped, then they will listen and take heed of us. If we attempt to assert our position and authority as Chiefs they go to Suva and say we are oppressing them: they lie and scheme and are becoming quite demoralized.[30]

Ultimately, however, officials saw little available remedy. While ordinances prohibited men from residing in districts other than their own unless under indenture, they could remain absent from their home village for up to sixty days without approval from chiefs before being fined. So a person could simply be absent from his district for fifty-nine days, return on the sixtieth, remain for a day and then leave again for another fifty-nine. If men remained absent for more than sixty days, were prosecuted under the Native Trespass and Vagrancy Ordinance and then duly paid their fines, nothing more could be said.[31]

This pattern of absenteeism also affected Rotuma, an island to the north of Fiji governed as an integral part of the colony after cession to Great Britain in 1881. A local chief, Tuifinau Faga, noted his concerns about the number of Rotuman women in Suva awaiting the return of their men who worked in the pearl shell industry in the Torres Strait. Every boat that left Rotuma for Fiji conveyed a large number of men and women, yet vessels returning to Rotuma brought none back. Rotumans were British subjects and enjoyed the right to remain in Fiji as long as they committed no offences. They could not be forced to return home. In response to these concerns, colonial officials proposed intercepting Rotuman men on the incoming Sydney steamers and persuading them to leave money with the Native Commissioner until they returned to Rotuma, rather than spending all their earnings in Suva.[32]

This absenteeism led to an increasing population of 'strangers' in Suva. The port population swelled around steamer days, as more people from outlying districts came to sell produce for shipment to the Australasian colonies or to earn money at the wharves. There was no suitable accommodation in town and men slept on shop verandas, at the native market or on the waterfront. There were no toilets or baths erected at the wharf for either Europeans or indigenous, with complaints about people defecating in the area at night.[33] While the colonial Government had a duty to provide for its subjects, it feared that erecting housing in town for those who slept about the streets could encourage a more permanent indigenous presence in town.[34] A number of women, both the young and the old and widowed, also left their home districts in order 'to see life' in Suva. A core group of women kept returning after successive arrests and 'deportations'. Some took up residence with European men but more, it seemed, lived with Fijian men or migrants from Melanesia whom, it was reported, the women favoured as they treated them better than their own countrymen did.[35]

Similar concerns about the regulation of labour, race and space were evidenced in other colonial ports. In Durban, for example, African *togt* (day) labourers were not tied to contracts. They were free to 'loiter' at the harbour until offered employment on steamer days. Stricter regulations were introduced to control their passage into Durban and regulate their conduct once there, including curfews and laws which forced labourers to register, pay a fee, wear a badge and find employment within five days of arrival in town.[36] Fiji's colonial officials did not resort to such extreme measures, but they passed a series of ordinances in an attempt to govern conduct in the urban setting and, in effect, to cushion white residents from close proximity to non-whites. A curfew was imposed between 11 p.m. and 5 a.m. for Indians and all Islanders, whatever their origin. They were prohibited from leaving their residences between these hours unless on sanctioned business. The construction of dwellings from native materials, rather than wood and iron, was outlawed, and alcohol consumption banned. In

1892 a Native Dances Ordinance prohibited all *meke* or ceremonial dancing and singing, which whites often dismissed as 'disorderly meetings' and 'drinking orgies', within town boundaries without a permit. This ordinance also made provision for the inspection of 'disorderly houses' in the event of a complaint 'by any two or more respectable householders'.[37]

Many Islanders resident in Suva and Levuka resented this ordinance. Some wrote seeking an explanation for the prohibition.[38] Others adopted different counter-strategies. In 1894, Aki, a Solomon Islander, protested against the *meke* ban by sitting in the middle of a track for a carnival foot race in full war dress. This led to a brawl with native police and he was arrested. On hearing of the disturbance the rest of the Solomon Islands community in Suva, about 400 people, refused to work at the wharf or the local stores for two days, and retreated into the forest on the outskirts of town to hold a lengthy meeting. Rumours circulated that they were planning to disrupt sports events on New Year's Day and 'take the head of at least one Fijian policeman'. This did not eventuate and it appeared their anger was also directed at some of the white men in Suva who taunted them, saying 'that the Fijians only regarded Solomon men as cats'.

In his report to the Colonial Office, Thurston denigrated the Solomon Islanders as 'the veriest savages that could be found in the Pacific', stating that the effect of missionary influence was merely superficial and when their passions were aroused 'the whole of their savage nature comes instantly to the surface and for the time they may be not unfittingly described as fiends incarnate and ready to kill or be killed with equal indifference'. He hyped up the threat of an attack by 'four hundred savages in the streets of Suva' and the 'latent dangers which must always exist in a colony such as this, the population of which is apparently governed by moral force alone'. In framing their actions as an innate savage reaction to excitement, rather than a reasoned response to the new pressures and stresses of urban life in a multiracial port, Thurston could sidestep the underlying grievances of the Solomon Islands community. He inspected all their homes and impressed on the headmen that they lived in Fiji under the protection of the Queen, and that they were privileged to work at the wharf earning good money and being able to build or lease houses. 'In fact as I showed them they made so much money and were getting so rich that they were becoming insolent and disorderly.' Following this incident new ordinances were passed to prohibit people entering town in improper dress, with blackened faces (done for customary reasons but regarded as a criminal disguise by some white residents) or carrying weapons.[39]

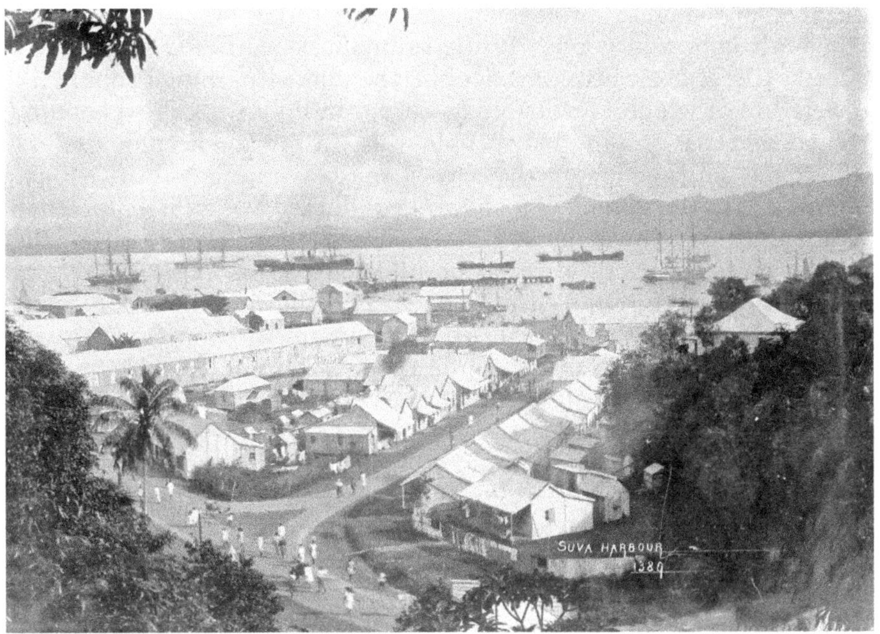

17   Suva Harbour, Viti Levu, c.1910

Meke continued, however, and it is clear that despite official attempts to demarcate and circumscribe racially coded spaces and activities in the port town these residents carved out their own spaces in Suva. Many men congregated around the wharf buildings in the evenings (figure 17). Near the pier, Cumming Street was colloquially known as 'All Nations Street', given the intermixture of people attracted by its shops, *kava* saloons, gambling houses and opium dens. As the non-European population was 'very properly debarred from the hotels', they had 'set up a *Quartier Indigène*, as it were, of their own'.[40] One attempt to shut down a gambling house in 1890 stalled, as the colonial secretary felt that the civic rights of Indians in Fiji were already severely curtailed. He argued that they should be more concerned about the Fijians and Melanesians who associated with them. The extent of this intermixture is reflected in the fact that many men indentured from the New Hebrides could speak Hindustani through their gambling contacts with Indians.[41] In 1904 a Solomon Islander named Saya was charged with keeping a common gaming house in Suva. Fifteen men present at the time, including Fijians, Polynesians and Indians, were also charged.[42]

Indigenous officials also petitioned the colonial secretary for reforms. As Savenaca Seniloli, the Assistant Native Lands Commissioner, noted in 1909, 'at the present time there are many things we see coming into Fiji, both men and goods'. While ordinances restricted many introduced evils, such as drinking alcohol, there 'is something I should like to tell you of which is worse than European liquor . . . this is opium'. He worried that opium made people 'waste away and become useless'. There was no urgency on the part of the Government to investigate opium use in the colony. An enquiry conducted two years later established that opium was more readily accessible in Suva than in other Pacific ports for there were no prohibitions on its sale or use (legal prohibitions were removed in deference to the findings of an Indian Opium Commission in 1895). An elderly Samoan woman reportedly ran one opium den in town. While there was some discussion about banning opium use to all but Indians, who would then be required to produce a medical certificate, a report in 1912 concluded that Suva's non-Indian population of opium smokers and eaters only consisted of sixteen Fijians, ten half-castes, six Chinese and one European.[43]

Others also petitioned colonial officials for assistance in regulating behaviour in port. In 1909 members of Suva's Samoan community held a meeting to discuss 'the bad conduct of some of our people'. One woman named Fou had left her husband to be with a man named Taesali, while another woman, Elena, had left home to live with Charles Grey, a Samoan man of mixed descent who worked for the Government. The community hoped the Government would deport them all 'so that the Samoans in Suva will see that they must live a clean life if they wish to stay in Fiji'. Officials replied that they were unable to interfere.[44]

Negotiating sitima *labour*

Regular steamer connections between Fiji and the southern white settler societies stimulated the trade in tropical fruit. This altered the meaning and value of island produce. Bananas and oranges became perishable export commodities and required new methods of handling and shipping. Indigenous communities readily engaged in this trade, which in turn bolstered the numbers of Fijians from outlying villages in the port. The traffic in banana boats was not well regulated and the evasion of wharfage payments by those who did not print names on their boats elicited complaints from Europeans, as did the lack of regulations to prevent workers deserting from European-owned banana vessels. Others complained that banana labour was poor, for the best men were attracted to the higher wages available on coal and sugar boats. Moreover, when profits from fruit were high, wharf labour was less forthcoming as villages were not in immediate need of cash.[45]

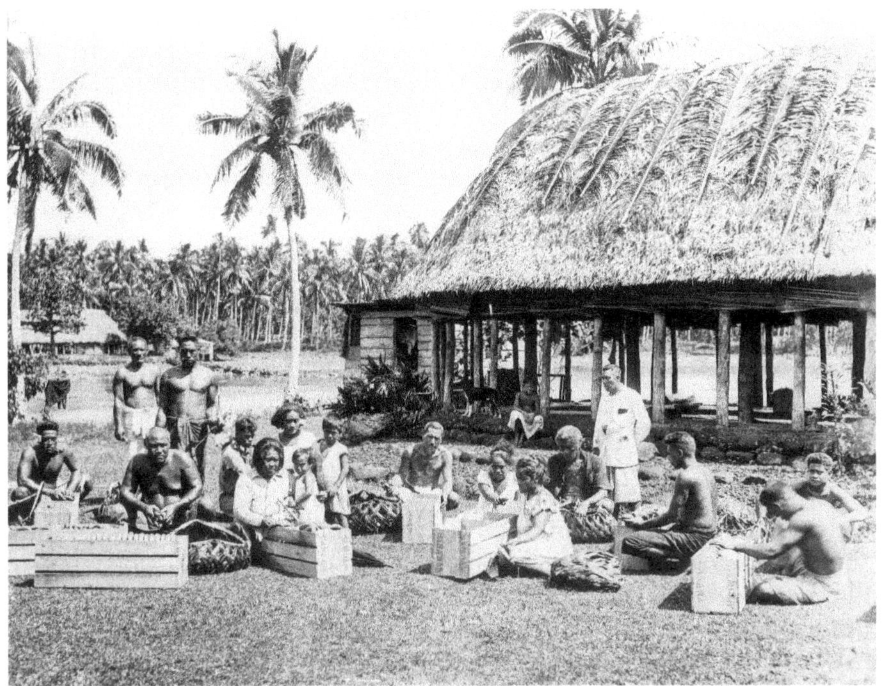

18   Packing bananas for New Zealand, Samoa, c.1890

Bananas were shipped green and initially sent as whole bunches. They were later packed in cases as separate 'fingers' and each case contained the equivalent of two bunches (see figure 18). Rough handling after picking, poor packing, inadequate shipping facilities, carelessness at overseas ports, delays to shipping through strikes, price variations, discriminatory tariffs and imposition of quotas by overseas countries, as well as pests, diseases and tropical storms, all affected the trade's progress. Hurricanes could flatten banana plantations, which took years to recover. The banana trade peaked in 1914 with the export of just over 1.7 million bunches.[46]

The USSCo. was beset by difficulties in this trade, as one captain's report in 1885 outlined. They landed the fruit 'in very bad order in fact had to throw the greater part over the side'. With no wind and hot weather the fruit overripe at shipment decayed on the voyage and 'the steam entirely cooked the rest of the fruit'. Steam from the sugar also assisted in the work of destruction and he concluded that neither fruit nor sugar could be carried during the summer months.[47] Twenty years later, the state of trade had not improved. Shippers protested that fruit

[185]

shipped by the *Navua* in August 1907 arrived 'in a boiled and baked condition owing to the fruit being stowed in the same compartment as copra and sugar and owing to the careless way the fruit is placed in the hold'.[48]

A government inspector was appointed in 1907 to oversee fruit handling in Fiji, and he frequently attacked the lading practices of indigenous labour. The USSCo.'s island inspector, R. K. McLennan, reported from Suva that 'it was disappointing to note the few punts, carrying bananas, that were provided with awnings to protect their contents from rain and sun . . . shippers' control of their labour is still lax; Mr Philpott [the government inspector] has on many occasions to check natives standing on the fruit while lifting it out of the punts'. There were many complaints about falsely packed cases where good fruit on top disguised bad fruit inside. One grower opined, 'it goes without saying that no European grower or shipper would "pack falsely" but when such does take place it is due to the fault and negligence of his labourers combined with insufficient inspection'. Another shipper suggested that since Fijians and Indians were always blamed for false packing, 'it might be advisable to compel all cases containing fruit to be branded grown and packed by "Fijians", "Coolies" or "Whites" as the case may be'.[49] Yet there were reports of poor handling in New Zealand too, with wilful mutilation and pilfering of bananas at Auckland, as well as lengthy delays trans-shipping fruit cargoes to southern ports.[50]

Europeans consistently denounced the work ethic of the indigenous people on whom they were so dependent and scorned their apparent inability to appreciate the challenges inherent in this new trade. But there was also evidence that labourers wilfully damaged produce in response to disputed land transactions and other political grievances. One observer on Suva wharf related that Fijian labourers enquired after the name of the shipper whose produce they were lading, 'and immediately afterwards several of the best bunches were deliberately dropped into the lower hold . . . I happened to know that the natives were unfriendly with the shipper owing to some dispute connected with the leasing or purchase of land.'[51] The most threatening instance of indigenous autonomy in response to perceived commercial exploitation was the rise of the Viti Company under the leadership of the commoner Apolosi Nawai in the decade from 1910. He encouraged Fijian growers to ship their bananas independently of European and Chinese middlemen. The company developed into a proto-national assembly and Nawai was eventually exiled to Rotuma in 1917 for seven years.[52]

In Rarotonga the USSCo. encouraged indigenous growers to engage in the fruit trade directly, much to the disgust of European shippers.

Edward Reeves felt the USSCo. had overstepped its role and should restrict itself simply to the carriage of fruit, contending that 'all natives understand profits, but it is doubtful if they will understand the losses that necessarily arise in the fruit trade sufficiently to continue shipping steadily'.[53] His reservations appeared to ring true a few years later when some indigenous shippers visited Auckland with a cargo of bad oranges in 1909. As a local fruit merchant noted, 'after paying their passages, freight, and incidental expenses, they will be in full enjoyment of the winter of their discontent. It was their intention to purchase goods to take home with them, all they can carry home to their people is an account of sales showing debit balance, they are heartbroken. This is only one instance, the rest of the natives who have consigned are in a similar position.'[54] The USSCo. recognised it had a duty to provide them with more support by carrying an inspector in each steamer to aid them in selecting and packing fruit.[55]

In any case, the fickleness of the fruit trade affected Europeans as much as the indigenous people who had invested in it. Mills ultimately believed all men involved in the trade needed to 'wake up', including McLennan and Duncan, for he was 'ashamed that after 20 years we didn't yet know how to handle fruit & that we wanted no excuses . . . pray excuse my impatient tone, but as you know I have always felt strongly that we do not do justice to the fruit trade & that we should not repeat our blunders year after year as we do'.[56]

Indigenous workers also influenced the course of this developing industry through demands for improved labour conditions. From the early 1900s, the USSCo., rather than the colonial state, met increasing demands for travel and food allowances to and from Suva and provided housing for men during their employment in town. In 1911 translated newspaper accounts, shipped to Fiji aboard Union Company steamers, detailed maritime labour unrest in colonial ports – a crucial instance of the port's function as a pathway for new ideas. This prompted Fijian wharf labourers to demand further wage increases. Wage rates for wharf labour in Tonga had recently increased from two to seven shillings per day. Fijian men now requested an increase from two to three shillings for day work and four to six shillings for night work.[57] In a report tabled to the Suva Chamber of Commerce, the USSCo. held that wage rates at the wharf regulated the price of labour in the rest of the colony. As the independence of men in seeking work was growing, which might soon cause problems, the company sought Government assistance to replace the casual nature of employment with an indenture scheme and 'further consider the question of freeing such men from their communal obligations as an encouragement for them to contract for permanent employment'. While the Deputy Governor argued that it was not the Government's role to interfere between employee and employer in labour questions, he accepted that the labour market was already restricted by current legislation. He alerted them to the impending Fijian Employment Ordinance of 1912, which would remove some restrictions and increase the supply of Fijian labourers.[58]

After many meetings between the Union Company and leaders of Rewa and Tailevu provinces, an agreement was drawn up to recruit 150 men, four or five from every village, for a one-year term. They would be free to return for village duties on non-steamer days, although a municipal tax would officially release them from communal work and would allow them to spend time planting solely for their families. An allowance would also be paid for travelling days to and from Suva.[59] Some Fijian leaders wanted further wage increases drawn into the contract, 'as the work was very hard and dangerous and several men had been disabled'. The Native Commissioner advised them 'not to embarrass the shipping coys, and cause them to raise freights which they themselves would have to help to pay through increased prices for the goods they had to buy'.[60]

Despite this arrangement, which dispersed recruitment evenly across villages, Rewa province again registered concerns about absenteeism a few years later. Chiefs requested the USSCo. to desist from employing men from their province for a few months while communal work was carried out. The company turned to men from other provinces already in Suva seeking paid employment. At other times, however, the USSCo. induced villages to forgo customary activities in order to continue working the steamers. In 1912, for example, *meke* practices to welcome the new Governor impinged on steamer days and a number of villages were persuaded to stand down from the practices.[61] The Fiji manager, George Morgan, complained at the 1913 Fiji Shipping Commission about these ongoing problems and the cost of native labour, but stressed they were 'very civil' and kind towards their workers.[62] This tension between communal and individualist activities impeded earlier maritime economies in Fiji, such as the bêche-de-mer trade, and continued to hamper successive governments in framing economic policy throughout the twentieth century.[63]

Following periodic labour shortages in other island ports, 'boys' were on occasion diverted from plantations to work at wharves on steamer days, although such labour was regarded as 'very "raw" at ship work'. The USSCo. had particular trouble in Rarotonga manning the lighters, as men appeared frightened of the fender belting (material which was lowered over the side of the steamers to prevent chafing against other vessels) and it had to be removed.[64] The captain of the *Talune* was frustrated by the time taken with lading work. They 'keep the work dragging all day. I cannot altogether blame them, but it's very annoying when one wants to get away at mid-day.'[65] Men were also shipped as wharf labour from Fiji to Samoa and Tonga to serve as strike-breakers in the face of excessive demands from local workers in those islands. One colonial official expressed concern about the company's routine requests to ship men out. While it prevented delays to steamer work, the men 'are sure to spend all of their earnings at Auckland and bring nothing back with them'. The colonial secretary only objected if the bulk of payment was made before the men returned to Suva, noting that they also earned a good deal indirectly by singing for the passengers.[66] This temporary arrangement was established on a more permanent basis in 1914 to save ongoing correspondence and inconvenience. The USSCo. lodged a £1,000 bond to carry twenty men every two weeks to Tonga and Samoa.[67]

Suva under steam

As was the case with earlier maritime industries in the Pacific, particularly the whaling and bêche-de-mer trades, interracial cooperation underpinned the success of the USSCo.'s island trades. Indigenous communities grew and transported fruit to the port and some also acted directly as shippers. Many men embraced cargo work at wharves on steamer days, an activity not entirely at odds with pre-colonial, cyclical labour practices. When they went to work for the USSCo., they also went to work *on* the company. Fijian communities incorporated wage labour into existing cultural practices and successfully negotiated the terms by which this would occur. District and village leaders sought to monitor and limit the disruption from new opportunities under colonial rule. When wharf labourers returned to villages on non-steamer days with wages in hand, ready and willing to perform familial and community duties, economic mobility was productive and valued as such. What was casual labour to white employers, to colonial officials and some white residents in Suva translating easily into 'casual living', was for indigenous workers, as Frederick Cooper has argued in the African context, 'part of a complex web of social relations and culture', a web connecting workplace, urban residence and rural home. Fijian chiefs wanted USSCo. employers to consider their men, not as 'so many interchangeable units of labour power, but as people for whom work was part of life and whose experiences over their life cycles affected the way they worked', as seen here in the case of crop planting, house construction and *meke*.[68] For its part, the USSCo. proved open to negotiation, prepared to periodically fracture and reset its terms of engagement.

Yet, for some men, work and life in the port of Suva represented an opportunity to refashion their obligations to kin and community. It provided an avenue of release from communal obligations now perceived as unnecessarily laborious and restrictive. New technologies of transport, communication and trade helped to reduce the power of rural villages to define personal and communal identities. New collectivities and ways of defining what it meant to belong were forming in port. Unrestrained urban economic mobility highlighted struggles over rank, age and gender in Fijian communities; ties to villages, respect for chiefly control and domestic relationships came under increasing strain.

Suva's 'mobile men' were situated differently within a racialised hierarchy constructed in the context of colonial labour relations. Many white officials and residents did not readily welcome the autonomy that young Islander men and women could achieve in this urban setting. They sought to buttress the port as the pre-eminent space for permanent white settlement by defining certain spaces and activities as disorderly, objectionable or criminal. In this respect Suva's early history as a port of call along USSCo. steamer lines reveals the ways in which modern shipping refashioned space and contributed to social problems in one particular colonial locale.

Notes

1 Damon Salesa, 'Contested oceans' (*The People of the Sea* book review forum), *Journal of Pacific History*, 43:1 (2008), 119.

2 R. A. Derrick, *A History of Fiji* (Suva: Fiji Government Press, 1946), 147.

3 For more on pre-cession Fiji, see Derrick, *A History of Fiji*, and Jane Samson, *Imperial Benevolence: Making British Authority in the Pacific Islands* (Honolulu: University of Hawai'i Press, 1998), 148–69.

4 See also Derrick, *A History of Fiji*, 138–55, 177–83; Hirokazu Miyakazi, *The Method of Hope: Anthropology, Philosophy, and Fijian Knowledge* (Stanford: Stanford University Press, 2004).

5 John Gorrie, 'Fiji as it is', *Proceedings of the Royal Colonial Institute*, 14 (1883), 160.

6 *Western Pacific Herald* (10 January 1912).

7 *Fiji Times* (17 September 1881 and 25 January 1890); NAF, CSO, 94.1091, Sanitary Inspector to Colonial Secretary, 8 March 1894.

8 *Western Pacific Herald* (11 October 1907).

9 *Fiji Shipping Commission*, 278.

10 Beatrice Grimshaw, *In the Strange South Seas* (London: Hutchinson & Co., 1907), 89.

11 *Fiji Times* (16 February 1907); *Western Pacific Herald* (12 July 1907).

12 NAF, CSO, 11.7567, Receiver General, 23 September 1911.

13 NAF, CSO, 13.104, Inspector General of Constabulary, 9 January 1913 and ensuing commentary.

14 Josef W. Konvitz, 'The crises of Atlantic port cities, 1880 to 1920', *Comparative Studies in Society and History*, 36:2 (1994), 301.

15 'Atu Bain, 'A protective labour policy? An alternative interpretation of early colonial labour policy in Fiji', *Journal of Pacific History*, 23:2 (1988), 122, 124, 135.

16   HC, USSCo. Records, AG-292-005-001/069, Duncan to Mills, 22 June 1903.

17   *Ibid.*, AG-292-005-001/006, Ford to Mills, 16 November 1886.

18   *Ibid.*, AG-292-005-001/002, Ford to Mills, 20 February 1885; AG-292-005-001/006, Ford to Mills, 5 June 1888.

19   *Ibid.*, AG-292-005-001/002, Ford to Mills, 17 March 1886.

20   *Ibid.*, Ford to Mills, 17 March 1886; AG-292-005-001/006, Ford to Mills, 23 December 1886.

21   See also the reflections about the framing of the primitivism of Aboriginal house-boys in Julia Martinez and Claire Lowrie, 'Colonial constructions of masculinity: transforming Aboriginal Australian men into "houseboys"', *Gender and History*, 21:2 (2009), 314–16.

22   See Bain, 'A protective labour policy?', 127.

23   NAF, CSO, 89.365, Roko Tui Ra, 19 December 1888; CSO, 89.2576, Josua Whingalau, 27 May 1889.

24   NAF, CSO, 99.4368, Buli Namata, 22 September 1899.

25   NAF, Despatches from the Governor of Fiji to the Secretary of State, vol. 8, despatch no. 20, Thurston, 2 May 1890.

26   NAF, CSO, 85.271, memo re Timoce of Rewa, 14 and 15 July 1884; CSO, 01.195, W. A. Scott, Native Officer, 3 January 1901.

27   HC, USSCo. Records, AG-292-005-001/093, McLennan to Holdsworth, 2 February 1909.

28   Reverend John G. Wheen, 'That which we have seen, or a chat about our work among the Fijians', *Australasian Methodist Missionary Review* (4 January 1910), 11.

29   Beatrice Grimshaw, *Three Wonderful Nations* (Dunedin: USSCO., 1907), 25–32.

30   NAF, Rewa Provincial Council Meetings, vol. 2, 1905–1918, Buli Buresaga, 1–2 October 1908.

31   NAF, Native Department, 2 November 1910.

32   NAF, CSO, 94.4206, 15 November 1894, and ensuing commentary. Earlier ordinances prohibited the wholesale emigration of sailors from Rotuma by placing age restrictions on those leaving. In 1939 a 'Rotuma Regulation' ensured that men could not ship out without the permission of the district officer and they had to make provision for their families, but once men emigrated to Fiji they were free to ship as they chose. Alan Howard, 'Rotuman seafaring in historical perspective', in Richard Feinberg (ed.), *Seafaring in the Contemporary Pacific Islands: Studies in Continuity and Change* (DeKalb: Northern Illinois University Press, 1995), 130–1.

33   *Fiji Times* (26 April 1890); NAF, CSO, 97.912, Duncan to Colonial Secretary, 10 March 1897.

34   NAF, CSO, 82.1495, Superintendent of Police, 17 and 24 June 1882; CSO, 83.3297, 17 December 1883.

35   NAF, CSO, 86.2166, Thurston, 10 November 1886; CSO, 88.1422, Buli Rewa, 27 April 1888.

36   Emil Jeffrey Popke, 'Managing colonial alterity: narratives of race, space and labor in Durban, 1870–1920', *Journal of Historical Geography*, 29:2 (2003), 248–67.

37   'No. 3 of 1892: An ordinance relating to native dances', *Ordinances of the Colony of Fiji* (Suva: Government Printer, 1914), 612–13.

38   NAF, CSO, 98.5061, Buli Levuka, 7 December 1898.

39   NAF, Despatch no. 9, Thurston, 18 January 1894; CSO, 94.536, Superintendent of Police, 1 February 1894.

40   *Fiji Times* (13 July 1910).

41   NAF, CSO, 90.2721, Police Sergeant, 2 September 1890; CSO, 96.3048, Sergeant Gostray, 7 September 1896.

42   *Western Pacific Herald* (27 May 1904).

43   NAF, CSO, 11.2420, Savenaca Seniloli, 28 May 1909, and J. McEwan, 29 March 1911.

44   NAF, CSO, 09.2871, 1 and 8 April 1909.

45   NAF, CSO, 88.1606, Robert Cocks to Collector of Customs, 11 May 1888; *Fiji Times* (27 August 1892, 7 September 1907).

46 Elsie Stephenson, *Fiji's Past on Picture Postcards* (Suva: Caines Jannif Group, 1997), 284–5.
47 HC, USSCo. Records, AG-292-005-001/014, Cromarty to Mills, 9 January 1885.
48 *Fiji Times* (10 August 1907).
49 NAF, CSO, 07.5017, R. K. McLennan, 8 October 1907, Lazarus, 16 November 1907, J. R. Turner, 20 November 1907.
50 *Western Pacific Herald* (2 March 1906). See also concerns about wharf labour stealing oranges at Picton: HC, USSCo. Records, AG-292-005-004/101, 'Pillage of fruit on board the *Wainui*, 11 November, 1902'.
51 NAF, CSO, 07.5017, A. R. Powell, 20 November 1907.
52 Alastair Couper, 'Protest movements and protocooperatives in the Pacific Islands', *Journal of the Polynesian Society*, 77:2 (1968), 268–71; James Heartfield, '"You are not a white woman!": Apolosi Nawai, the Fiji Produce Agency and the trial of Stella Spencer in Fiji, 1915', *Journal of Pacific History*, 38:1 (2003), 83.
53 Reeves, *Brown Men and Women*, 256.
54 HC, USSCo. Records, AG-292-005-001/090, Albert Glover to Holdsworth, 29 July 1909.
55 *Ibid.*, AG-292-005-001/107, Whitson to Mills, 6 September 1909.
56 *Ibid.*, AG-292-005-001/079, Mills to Holdsworth, 20 April 1906.
57 The 1890 maritime strike, which began in Sydney and spread to New Zealand, also found echoes in Fiji. A group of about forty Fijian workers from Suvavou struck for increased pay (a daily wage of four rather than two shillings) on 1 October. The strike was unsuccessful since the men failed to combine with other Fijian, Melanesian and Indian wharf labourers, all of whom continued to work the steamers, even when threatened with beatings. Timoce Nagusa of Ra province led the strike. He had been in Suva for one year, initially sent there with ten other men to earn wages to reimburse a European man for a cutter they had sunk. He maintained that he led the strike because Ratu Ambrose, chief of Suvavou, sanctioned it. Nagusa received a term of six months' imprisonment with hard labour, in default of a fine of £50: see NAF, CSO, 90.3088; *Fiji Times* (4 October 1890).
58 NAF, CSO, 11.9051, memo from Chamber of Commerce to Deputy Governor, 27 November 1911.
59 *Ibid.*, Morgan, 12 December 1911.
60 *Ibid.*, Native Commissioner, 19 December 1911.
61 *Western Pacific Herald* (12 July 1912).
62 NAF, CSO, 14.331, Native Commissioner, 26 March 1914; CSO, 14.3603, Morgan, 20 April 1914; *Fiji Shipping Commission*, 278.
63 R. G. Ward, 'The Pacific bêche-de-mer trade with special reference to Fiji', in Ward (ed.), *Man in the Pacific Islands: Essays on Geographical Change in the Pacific Islands* (Oxford: Clarendon Press, 1972), 91–123; Margaret Jolly, 'Custom and the way of the land: past and present in Vanuatu and Fiji', *Oceania*, 62:4 (1992), 331, 339.
64 HC, USSCo. Records, AG-292-005-001/096, McLennan to Holdsworth, 5 December 1910.
65 *Ibid.*, AG-292-005-001/107, Stevens to Holdsworth, 29 August 1909.
66 See ensuing discussion in NAF, CSO, 12.4668.
67 NAF, CSO, 14.818, 20 January 1914. Wharf labourers at Lautoka were also the first to attempt unionisation in 1916 in protest at the tendency of the USSCo. and the CSR to pay village headmen commissions to use traditional methods to recruit cheap labour: see Jacqueline Leckie, 'Workers in colonial Fiji: 1870–1970', in Clive Moore, Jacqueline Leckie and Doug Munro (eds), *Labour in the South Pacific* (Townsville: James Cook University, 1990), 53–4.
68 Frederick Cooper, *On the African Waterfront: Urban Disorder and the Transformation of Work in Colonial Mombasa* (New Haven: Yale University Press, 1987), 12, 248.

CHAPTER EIGHT

Indigenous maritime mobilities under colonial rule

In August 1892 a number of Samoan women arrived in Suva on board the USSCo. steamer *Upolu*. Governor John Bates Thurston believed they came to Suva for 'immoral purposes'. He wanted an end to the traffic and requested that the company prevent such women from boarding their ships. The company's agent in Fiji, Alex Duncan, could not see how this would be possible as they did not want to lose passage money. The Auckland branch manager was in Suva at the time and inspected the *Upolu*'s records. He found that there were thirty native passengers from Apia to Suva and another twenty for Tonga, but as the purser classed men and women collectively as 'natives', there was no way of knowing how many women had recently arrived in Fiji.[1] While Thurston considered a law change which would prohibit the migration of 'paupers and destitute persons' to Fiji, the 'tide of Samoans' was stopped two years later when permits for Samoans travelling beyond Samoa, to be issued by local authorities and the British Consul, were introduced.[2] Yet, the following year, Fiji's police superintendent reported the arrival of another fifty-eight Samoans on board the *Ovalau*. From discussions with the ship's purser it seemed that 'the steamer will take anyone who can pay passage money'.[3]

The USSCo.'s monthly round-trip service, which connected Fiji to Tonga and Samoa, reinforced Suva's status as a growing metropole in the western Pacific. Islanders made their way to Suva for a host of reasons related to broader regional patterns of labour migration, trade, kinship ties, rituals of feasting and exchange, religion, education and adventure, or, as in this case, perhaps for 'less salubrious reasons'.[4] This particular instance of indigenous travel exposed latent tensions between the interests of the colonial state and the steamship company. The USSCo.'s principal focus lay with making the island trades profitable. It was not overly concerned about the motivations of its paying passengers. Yet colonial officials in both Fiji and Samoa increasingly attempted to monitor and regulate the ways in which Islanders were leaving their homes and travelling about the region on steamers, both as seafarers and passengers. They sought to define ideal practices of mobility and policed the exceptions through measures such as travel permits, bonds to enforce return and restrictions on entry. The efficacy of these regulatory measures also rested on the USSCo. The company did not prevent people from boarding its vessels and, while it generally recorded the names of every European passenger, it did not individuate indigenous travellers, a practice that frustrated the documentary bent of the colonial state.

Previous chapters have explored the many ways in which the transport system set in motion by the USSCo. was a contested world of power and meaning. Examining the varied nature of Islander engagement in this industry as passengers and seafarers, as well as the official responses to their travelling practices, provides further insights into the cultures of maritime transport in the colonial Pacific. These mobile histories demonstrate that shipping operations were always much more than vehicles, routes and timetables; they also encompassed the modes of governance that mediated, ordered and controlled maritime infrastructure. These official interventions shaped the ways in which individuals and communities accessed and participated in the new mobility opportunities of the steam age.

Inter-island steamer travel

The origins of the dominant Western view of islands in the Pacific as small, isolated and marginal lie, as Epeli Hau'ofa argues, with the imperial partitioning of Oceania, which gathered pace at the close of the nineteenth century. European rulers turned their backs on the sea and confined Islanders to land.[5] Such a profound rupture in long-standing indigenous maritime networks and inter-island connectivities was neither immediate nor totally transformative. Imperial power was never as strong as Hau'ofa's account implies. Moreover, regular shipping services provided new opportunities for a greater number of people to travel, and to extend traditional pathways of social reproduction and forge new ones.

It is impossible to calculate the total numbers of Islanders travelling on steamers throughout this period, yet occasional commentary indicates that large groups routinely travelled between islands and that the USSCo. struggled to provide for their needs. In discussing a suitable steamer for Samoa in 1891, the company's Auckland manager noted that 'native passenger trade is large. This trip she carried 220 and had over 100 on board at one time.'[6] Two decades later the captain of the *Talune* complained that this vessel was insufficient for the island trades, for 'what with deck cargo from Auckland, there is barely room for the large number of native passengers, with their paraphernalia, boats, etc., who travel between the Islands'.[7]

We can gain some insight into how they travelled. Henry Hunter Brown took a voyage to Fiji in the late 1890s. He booked his passage by the Auckland–Fiji direct steamer, but missed his ship and was bumped on to an excursion steamer taking the island round-trip, 'so I had scored, and came in for a most interesting trip'. The steamer took on copra at Tonga, 'also a lot of native passengers going to visit relations in Samoa, or returning after a visit to their old homes in Tonga . . . our deck passengers brought their own food and bedding; they were a jolly lot, singing and dancing, and had a happy time'.[8] Similarly in 1891, Robert Paulin noted that there were over 100 native passengers between Tonga and Samoa, along with their pigs and some horses. They occupied the fore and after deck and 'spent most of their time eating, singing, and sleeping, nearly always lying down. The two decks were a picturesque medley of brown limbs, thick, shaggy hair, smiling dark eyes and faces, gaudy and varied rags and clothes, dirt, grease, oil, pigs, horses and sheep, with a smell that made one think we had a farmyard and oil factory on board.'[9] And taking the same round-trip passage later in the decade, Edward Reeves reflected, 'the Tongans, not being allowed to drink alcoholic liquors . . . spend their money on tinned meats and travelling'. As well as expeditions in their own catamarans and sailing vessels, by every steamer deck passengers either travelled to see friends at the different ports along the way, stopping for the next boat, or went the whole round without stopping, simply for the pleasure of the sea voyage. 'They sleep and eat, dance and sing on deck, laugh, talk, make merry, and thoroughly enjoy themselves.' They supplied their own provisions for the trip, including mats, kerosene lamps, yams, fruit, sewing machines, *tapa* cloth and pigs.[10] Preparation for a steamer trip clearly took some planning and mustering of resources. One group of Tongans travelling to attend a feast in 1910 assembled on the wharf in the early hours of the morning with vast quantities of yams and other produce, as well as pigs, horses and dogs, eight hours before the steamer was due to depart.[11]

Travelling from New Zealand to Rarotonga and Tahiti, a route newly established by the USSCo., Reeves noted that there were 'nothing like the big companies of jolly native tourists' that were common on the round-trip steamer between Fiji, Tonga and Samoa. In Tahiti crowds of indigenous people boarded the steamer: on the establishment of a new line it was necessary to give people an opportunity to look over the ships in order to popularise the idea of travelling on them.

Reeves predicted there would likely be less licence over time, and the strict rules and regulations governing shipboard access in island ports prevalent on the other route would prevail.[12]

Once the indigenous passengers were on board, the deck effectively became an indigenous space. Denied access to the cabins, saloons, smoking rooms and ladies' lounges, they made this open-air space their own. Reeves remarked that some European passengers sat amongst Islanders on warm evenings, rather than frequenting the stuffy smoking room below deck. One man in their party, he noted, 'leaned tight up against three pretty Samoan girls'. Some of the Island women seemed especially taken with a young European passenger and even crowded around her at night, striking matches to watch her closely while she sat on deck.[13] But it seems that on the whole, Europeans did not routinely mix with indigenous passengers although the confines of the ship brought them into close proximity. Those who recorded their travel experiences typically wrote as observers from a distance, framing Islanders as a collective mass, rather than a group of individuals, whose sensory impact was more remarkable than the opportunities steamer travel presented to mix freely with different people.

Steamer design for the island trades also demonstrated this underlying interest in keeping racial groups separate. The placement of toilets for native passengers on the *Tofua*, a steamer constructed in 1907, elicited concern. The island inspector proposed that native facilities be moved, as in their present position, twenty-two feet forward of the dining saloon windows, unpleasant smells were likely to drift back and offend passengers at meals. As native passengers travelled on the after deck, he proposed relocating their facilities to that end of the ship. These alterations would have been too complicated and, as indigenous passengers only travelled for a day or two each month, James Mills believed toilet location was not a major problem.[14]

Steamer circuitries not only brought whites and indigenous groups into new proximities, but also various Islanders. This did not always occur under ideal circumstances. 'Charlie', the Fijian boss of the USSCo.'s wharf-labour gang, was charged with assault after an incident on the *Atua* between Nuku'alofa and Vava'u in Tonga in 1907. As reported by the *Fiji Times*, Tonga's Judicial Commissioner 'remarked about the way native passengers generally are treated on the Union boats, and said he himself had seen many cases of it while travelling on the ships'. As the European pursers could not speak Tongan they usually asked Charlie to help collect fares. It seemed that if passengers did not hand over their money quickly enough he would resort to rough handling and kicking. He was fined in this case and it was hoped

Islanders would recognise that they had the protection of the courts and would have confidence enough to 'demand the treatment due to them from the company and its officers'.[15]

After disembarking from the big steamers, Islanders' journeys continued, for not all travellers were drawn to the colonial port. The USSCo. ships facilitated connections with the coastal or inter-island vessels, the second level of Pacific shipping. Some of these indigenous itineraries annoyed colonial officials. In one episode in April 1897, the USSCo. steamer *Ovalau* arrived in Suva with fifteen Tongans on board. Taking a provincial schooner from the capital, they headed to Lomaloma, an island in the Lau group in eastern Fiji. Lau was a historically significant region of contact, exchange and intermixture for Tongans and Fijians. From the late eighteenth century Tongans were drawn there for material goods that were rare in their own islands, including *vesi* wood canoes, parrot feathers, sandalwood for barkcloth, sennit, whale teeth, pearl shell and mats. During the nineteenth century Tongans also settled more permanently about the Lau group, offering their services to chiefs as warriors and canoe builders. By the 1860s the Tongan prince Ma'afu had gained ascendancy in the region.[16]

Fiji's Native Commissioner was displeased with these latest arrivals. The Tongans came to engage in *solevu*, a customary practice of feasting and property exchange, which he and other colonial officials regarded as synonymous with plundering and marauding.[17] With a recent scarcity of food in Lau, he was sure hosting new arrivals would place an unnecessary burden on the community. He hoped the Tongans could be restricted from travelling beyond Lomaloma, as the previous year they had made a tour of the whole province, returning home with hundreds of mats, bowls and dishes. The colonial secretary concurred, noting: 'It is from these people, more than from the Samoans, that we may expect this kind of trouble', but he was also concerned they would become 'a burden and a menace' in Suva if restricted from travelling to Lau. The Agent General of Immigration drafted a notice to the masters of native-owned cutters for publication in the Fijian-language newspaper *Na Mata*, instructing them not to give passage to Tongans to any part of the Lau group. Tongans who went would be prosecuted as vagrants, for 'they do incalculable harm wherever they go by spreading discontent amongst the Fijians, in addition to their plundering propensities'. If they were stopped he hoped it would show them 'that they cannot come here with impunity and foist themselves upon whoever they may wish'.[18]

This incident demonstrated the limits of official tolerance of regional mobilities. It also highlighted the crucial role of indigenous mariners in the colonial economy. Fijians dominated as boat owners and seafarers, ferrying people between islands in the various provinces. In 1890, for example, the Marine Board issued seafaring certificates to 269 indigenous sailors, eighty Europeans, seventy part-Europeans, five Indians and four others. The actual number of indigenous seafarers would have been far greater given that these certificates were only issued for registered vessels.[19] The activities of Fijian sailors were subject to a host of new regulations. In 1886 the Marine Board produced the 'Native Seamen's Book of Instructions'. It contained information 'for the better understanding on the part of these natives, of their own work and what is required of them by the law'. This pertained to the identification of vessels; seagoing certificates; unseaworthy vessels; sailing licences; rules of the road at sea; steering and sailing rules; collisions; signals of distress; signals for pilots; reporting casualties; harbour regulations; local light and signals; buoys and beacons; compasses; charts; lead line; log line; quarantine regulations; and customs regulations. The colonial secretary feared 'very much that the size of this code and the number of subjects dealt with will terrify and confuse the native seamen'.[20] These regulations were also likely to offend indigenous navigation traditions, knowledge and skills. There were occasionally complaints that mariners did not follow the new codes or understand their significance. In one instance they had ignored for five weeks a signal of distress at a lighthouse, announcing the ill health of the Indian lighthouse-keeper.[21]

Boat mania

It has been suggested that Fijians did not typically engage with new maritime technologies, as widely seen in New Zealand and Hawai'i where Islanders enthusiastically adopted schooners and cutters in both local and more wide-ranging trades.[22] While this may have been the case during the early decades of sustained European contact, early colonial Fiji provides ample evidence that this pattern had shifted. Villages made many requests for new boats and raised money to purchase or build them. Official attitudes towards these practices oscillated. Native Commissioner James Blyth was concerned that Fijians were unable to maintain the new vessels properly, particularly as paint, canvas, copper and cordage all had to be imported. This cast indigenous investment in new boats as being a wasteful and foolish activity. There were also reports of mixed-race men 'swindling' indigenous Fijians into spending inflated prices on western-style craft. In response to such reports, Governor William Des Voeux insisted in 1880 that 'this boat buying mania *must* be checked'.[23] A wide-ranging and influential report into the causes of native depopulation in Fiji published in 1896 (the Decrease Report) also regarded a perceived oversupply of new vessels as a source of impoverishment. Food normally grown to eat was instead sold to raise money to purchase a new boat. It appeared that 'much of this unnecessary expenditure is caused by the rivalry of tribes and chiefs as to the size of their cutters'.[24]

In his various official roles, and then as Governor, Thurston supported Fijians' acquisition of new vessels. Some European boat owners complained that Fijian-owned vessels were not subject to customs dues and wharfage charges. As they were not officially plying for trade they were exempt from these taxes, yet there were reports that they were trading surreptitiously.[25] Thurston was of the opinion that enforcing licences for the occasional paying passenger or freight delivery 'would greatly hamper their real usefulness'. European-style craft were welcome, 'saving as they do scores of lives annually and leading the natives [to] habits of industry'.[26] When he received complaints that the USSCo.'s inter-island vessel had displaced native-owned boats in carrying tax contributions from outlying areas to the port, Thurston argued that it was more important to support those who could ensure 'promptness, care and economy', even when it denied indigenous boat owners the opportunity. He thereby placed most emphasis on the values he believed such vessels represented, rather than on the class of people operating them.[27]

Yet the benefits of new boats were not inherently apparent. Local political and cultural contexts shaped their use. Indigenous communities put European technologies to unanticipated ends. They used them to strengthen communal and inter-tribal relations and to further some of the customary practices of travel and exchange that colonial officials had hoped to eradicate. Many communities requested new boats in order to visit neighbouring districts to maintain *solevu* traditions, as attacked in the earlier example from Lau. After the fourth such request from one district in 1903, the colonial secretary refused, for the vessel 'is only required for wandering about the group – or racing – a yacht is an expensive luxury for natives'. He decided the money was much better spent on their villages.[28] The Decrease Report maintained that *solevu* mobilities appeared to be on the increase with the introduction of European-style craft. Women's mobility was of special concern, for their activities 'interfere with the attention which mothers should give to their children'. Moreover, 'it is to be feared that the unbounded opportunity for lounging afforded by this increasing custom will so affect the food-supply, and consequently the chance of survival of infants, as to counterbalance any advantages of opportunity for marriage into distant tribes that may result from it'.[29]

New vessels were also used in the related custom of *kerekere*, a system of acquisition via requests made to a member of one's own kin group. One district chief wanted to contribute £100 to a neighbouring district so they could purchase a boat. The colonial secretary rejected this proposal as it would undermine the new values regarding money, work and time that the administration was attempting to inculcate. Relatives could only expect food, drink and shelter from one another, indigenous leaders were informed, not 'what you have earned by work. Then they will learn to work and earn what they want instead of relying upon getting it from you by *kerekere*.'[30]

In these cases of *solevu* and *kerekere*, new maritime technologies enabled older practices to be pursued on a more extensive scale. Fijians clearly reconstructed colonial knowledge about the meaning of new boats and their established maritime itineraries. They continued to pursue their own interests even as official regulations and patterns of surveillance began to monitor and restrict their activities in new ways. Despite the stakes involved in the regulation and control of mobility in the colonial period, Islanders, as Damon Salesa emphasises, 'were the people who articulated and gave meaning to island circuitry. Even with the new, "foreign" complexities, it remained a "Brown Pacific".'[31]

Travel to the white settler colonies

Islanders also boarded USSCo. steamers for passage to the Australian and New Zealand colonies. The company's Fiji schedule listed a hierarchy of fares between Fiji and Auckland for saloon (£8 single/£12 return), steerage (£4/£7) and 'Natives, Asiatics and Indian servants in attendance upon their employers' (£3/£4 10s.). European servants received a twenty-five per cent discount off saloon rates. Children under twelve paid reduced fares, as did schoolteachers and students travelling during vacation. Special saloon concessions were granted to theatrical parties, athletics teams, commercial travellers, naval officers on leave and their families, hospital nurses, missionaries, clergymen and their families, Sisters of Mercy and Salvation Army Officers. Native missionaries received a ten per cent discount off steerage.[32] This schedule indicates some of the motivations behind the routine circulation between New Zealand and Fiji in the early twentieth century. Along with many letters requesting discounted or favourable rates, it also reveals some of the ways in which ideas about race and class shaped expectations about mobility.

The comments of James Borron, a plantation owner in Fiji, are especially revealing. He wrote to Mills in 1902 for an estimate of costs for a six-month, round the world trip. The party also included his wife, their one-year-old child and a 'half-caste Fiji girl (Nurse) about 13 who can travel 2nd class or in the same cabin as we do'. But, he noted, 'of course a Fiji girl is not like a European and requires little comfort and should travel at a nominal rate'. He also drew Mills's attention to his membership of Fiji's Legislative Council, which entitled him to fare reductions.[33] Saloon and steerage accommodation constructed and affirmed ideas about race and class difference. Social identities were produced and performed through maritime travel. Borron's mobile practices and those of the Fijian nurse were bound up with the same logic, for the white planter family needed 'a Fiji girl' to make their round the world trip comfortable and to confirm their own mobility as free and leisured. As Cotten Seiler concludes, spaces and practices of mobility have long expressed 'the self-possession, national belonging, and social and economic capital of some people, and the dispossession, exclusion, and abjection of others'.[34]

But it was not as if the steamer company simply saw itself as confirming the status or self-possession of those who travelled in first class. Fare reductions were a sensitive matter. As noted, Duncan's superiors frowned upon his habit of granting excessive discounts on passage to members of Fiji's commercial community for it undermined the conference system with the AUSNCo in the Fiji–Australia trades. Moreover, senior USSCo. staff were annoyed that New Zealand politicians appeared to regard discounted passages as a right not a privilege. As one manager put it in 1909: 'If I thought that the concession of free travel would be *properly* appreciated by Members [of Parliament] I might be inclined to take a different view, but I cannot rid myself of the feeling that in a very short time the privilege would come to be regarded as a matter of course, without any thought of the generosity of the Company granting it.'[35]

In Fiji the state regulated the passage of 'Natives' and 'Asiatics' to New Zealand and Australia more tightly than the circulation of Islanders amongst Tonga, Samoa and Fiji. It is here that Hau'ofa's arguments about colonial interference are particularly relevant. Scholars have discussed the 'rewiring' of pre-colonial indigenous circuitries and the 'major re-orientation of linkages' that occurred with the advent of colonial rule and modern maritime transport systems in the Pacific. While remaining sensitive to the persistence of indigenous pathways, R. G. Ward reflects that the 'motives for movement' along these new networks 'were related less to the dynamics and mutual interactions between local indigenous communities and more to the attractions exerted . . . by outside pressures and external forces'. Different people, things and ideas now circulated within and between island groups, and centres were established along these paths, articulating new relations and regimes of power.[36]

Many European settlers took summer breaks in New Zealand for health, family or business reasons and often brought their domestic servants with them from Fiji. To do so, they generally lodged a £50 bond with the Fiji Government to ensure their safe and timely return. In 1903, for example, one USSCo. captain, Norman Beaumont, requested permission to take Tareinau, a Solomon Islander, to New Zealand as a domestic servant. She was fluent in English, had been there three times previously and was eager to go again. His request was approved, as was another from R. Caldwell for a woman named Wavidamu to accompany his wife to New Zealand.[37] In 1901, A. D. Carr's request to take a seventeen-year-old Indian girl, an orphan raised by his late parents, to New Zealand for six months was approved as he was a 'hardworking and successful banana planter'.[38] Others travelled to New Zealand independently, as was the case with Rarotongan fruit shippers in Auckland on a number of occasions. Travellers from one group in 1911 were given a small concession for the return trip as their Auckland agent complained that they would have to travel in steerage with Chinese passengers who were booked to Papaeete. This request suggested a 'common sense' hierarchisation of non-white passengers within steerage itself.[39]

Grounds for refusal appeared to rest on the length of the visit and perception of the political climate in New Zealand. Hugh Keith's request to take Michael Manau to New Zealand as a gardener for one year was rejected as 'the Government of New Zealand discourages the introduction of this class of labour'.[40] Indian transcolonial itineraries were particularly sensitive. There were growing fears in New Zealand of Indian labourers finding their way to New Zealand from Fiji after serving their term of indenture, displacing, to a certain extent, fears of Chinese immigration.[41] Yet others were keen to recruit free Indians to New Zealand as servants. Residents in Palmerston North engaged in lengthy correspondence with colonial officials in Fiji regarding the importation of free Indians for this purpose. The colonial secretary ultimately rejected their application 'in view of the feeling prevalent in New Zealand against the introduction of coloured labour' and the Governor 'is not disposed generally to encourage such introduction from Fiji'.[42] In another case, three Indians wished to return to Fiji as they found New Zealand too cold, as was often also the case with Polynesian servants. Their employers were expected to pay their passage back.[43] By 1911, there were fewer than fifty Indian settlers in New Zealand and immigration figures for 1907–16 revealed that a large proportion of Indians stayed in New Zealand temporarily, in transit to or from islands in the Pacific.[44] Clearly, as also reflected in protests against lascar crew, the fear and anxiety projected towards non-white migrants was out of all proportion to the total numbers of people who were actually crossing borders. But the underlying principles were big; 'drawing the global colour line' was an ongoing project of transnational exchanges and conversations about race, history and immigration across the white settler colonies of Australia and New Zealand, as well as South Africa and the United States, in the early twentieth century.[45]

Requests to ship indigenous Fijians to New Zealand temporarily as servants were approved from time to time, as they were for other Islanders. Fijians also travelled there for trade, education, sport and the church. When a Fijian cricket tour of New Zealand was mooted in the 1890s, the Governor feared it would 'unsettle a great many people and be productive of many inconveniences'.[46] Men might be exposed to alcohol or disease, and villages would be deprived of the essential labour of fit, young men. The cricket players who were members of the Armed Native Constabulary (ANC), referred to as 'young chiefs', were eventually allowed to travel if they had vacation leave owing and their crops were cut.[47]

Colonial exhibitions in the Australasian colonies also presented indigenous men with new mobility opportunities. Three Fijian men recruited from Levuka resided at the 'Fiji House' set up at the Sydney International Exhibition of 1879. This attraction soon closed as it did not pay, but the men were left stranded in Sydney. Thurston visited them and reported to the colonial secretary that they had run up debts at a native boarding house in the city and fell into the hands of a crimp at the wharf. He concluded:

> Nothing could tend more to degrade and debauch the Fijians than the life recently led by the men now under my charge. During the daytime they have been thrown into contact with the lowest order of whites. During the night, and to the strains of a barrel organ, they have been employed leaping and howling like a lot of maniacs for the amusement of people among whom the 'loafer' and 'larrikin' element chiefly prevailed . . . the hiring or engagement of Her Majesty's native subjects for places beyond the colony may as soon as possible be regulated by Legislative enactment.[48]

A more tightly regulated scheme was put in place for the International Exhibition of Arts and Industries held in Christchurch during the summer of 1906–7. Two groups of Fijian men proceeded to New Zealand. Ratu Ifereimi and the Assistant Native Commissioner, W. A. Scott, led one group of twenty-five men. In planning the trip Scott desired 'as many as possible to be ex-ANC members who have had the benefit of military training and who will be accustomed to discipline'. He hoped they would prove a 'unique attraction', demonstrating native skills such as house building, *meke* and *kava* ceremonies, but also that the exhibition itself 'should provide an instructive object lesson in all branches of manufacture'.[49] The men built a large, Fijian-style thatched house in the grounds of the model Maori *pa* (fortified village) where they resided during the exhibition. Another group of twenty-six firewalkers from the island of Bega arrived under the USSCo. agent Duncan's command shortly afterwards. He had to post a £300 bond with officials to ensure they would all return safely.[50]

Following the exhibition, it was reported that the Fijians earned 'golden opinions' from all those in authority 'by reason of their irreproachable good conduct under circumstances altogether novel and during a process of popular "spoiling" which might have turned the heads of men far less unsophisticated than these islanders'. They received numerous gifts from people in New Zealand, including clothing, travelling boxes, rugs and dogs. A number of European women and girls were criticised for being overly flirtatious towards the Fijians, as Scott also reported. 'I know of many instances of the men refusing liquor when it was offered to them . . . I expected the men to be spoilt by the attention they received from some of the women and I am glad to say they were not.'[51] A scurrilous account about the sexual misconduct of one man was written up in a 'gutter journal', but a Christchurch police inspector reassured colonial officials in Fiji that 'the lady referred to is now a grandmother, and long past the age of such conduct'.[52]

The trip was said to be a success at the time, yet when another exhibition promoter requested that a group of twelve Fijian men appear in a model village at the Panama Pacific International Exposition to be held in San Francisco in 1915, his request was declined. 'Previous experience has shewn', wrote the Native Commissioner, 'that the moral effect of a tour of this nature is bad. Moreover, out of the 25 men who went to Christchurch 3 have since their return died of phthisis [tuberculosis], though of course their stay in Christchurch may have had nothing to do with their contracting the disease.' He also alluded to 'several objectionable features in connection with the visit of the Fijians to Christchurch'.[53]

On occasion, labour circumstances also brought indigenous Fijians to New Zealand temporarily. Men who worked as crew on the USSCo.'s inter-island steamers in Fiji visited New Zealand when the vessels returned for their yearly overhaul and repairs. On an 1891 trip, the captain of the *Maori*, James Grey, requested that the men have the night for sightseeing in Auckland 'as such is one of the attractions the steamer has for them'.[54] A Fijian sailor from the government steamer *Ranadi* was injured by a tram while the steamer was in Auckland for repairs in 1907. Three years later, another *Ranadi* seafarer was run over by a tram in Sydney and lost both feet, while yet another sailor died of pneumonia.[55] Such incidents bolstered the colonial Government's concerns about unrestrained indigenous mobility.

Sailors' itineraries

In the wake of European exploratory voyages in the late eighteenth century, privately owned trading vessels were attracted to the Pacific by reports of maritime abundance. The sea otter, sealing, sandalwood, pearling, bêche-de-mer and whaling trades linked the region with the commercial centres of Europe, North America and China and the growing economy of the British penal settlement in New South Wales. Islander labour on shore and on ship underpinned the success of these maritime extraction economies. At the height of the whaling trade in the 1840s and 1850s, one-fifth of all crew on board Euro-American vessels were indigenous to the Pacific, with men recruited predominantly from Hawai'i, Tahiti and New Zealand.[56]

There was little formal regulation of labour recruitment in the first half of the nineteenth century. Thousands of men were absent from their home communities for considerable periods of time. As early as 1805, the number of Islanders discharged in Sydney without means to support themselves was great enough to move the Governor of New South Wales to order captains to provide for their welfare and to return them home. He also outlawed the engagement of Islanders along the Australian coast. Subsequent orders in 1813 and 1814 stipulated that seafarers must be paid fairly and could only be recruited with a chief's permission, and required ships calling at New Zealand or other islands in the Pacific to post a £1,000 good-behaviour bond.[57] Such regulations were notoriously difficult to enforce from Sydney. Further afield, the Church Missionary Society established the Strangers' Home for Asiatics, Africans and South Sea Islanders in London in 1856 in an attempt to provide for destitute foreign sailors in port. Estimates suggest that more than half of Island men shipping out in this period never returned.

By the end of the nineteenth century the socio-political climate was markedly different. Formal imperial rule in the islands, the clearer articulation of the respective regional identities of Australia and New Zealand, as well as the more aggressive politicisation of labour in these white settler colonies combined to exclude indigenous crew from foreign-going ships. The hostility directed towards Chinese and Indian recruitment demonstrated the extent to which ideas about race had assumed a new visibility. Seamen's unions found the employment of indigenous sailors on USSCo. steamers equally objectionable.

Although trading from Australia or New Zealand into the Pacific could not be classed as coasting, in these trades it became the norm to maintain coasting labour conditions and, hence, white labour. In 1884 the USSCo. removed all Islander labour from ships trading between Auckland and islands in the Pacific. The *New Zealand Herald* recommended that all other local companies follow suit. Indigenous crew were only deemed appropriate for inter-island steamers based in the Pacific, 'as the climate is not suited for Europeans'.[58] The USSCo. employed indigenous sailors, including Fijians, other Melanesians and Tongans, on its inter-island steamer in Fiji, retaining white men as senior crew.

Local shipping firms in Fiji were frustrated by the monopoly the USSCo. and AUSNCo. enjoyed in the island trades. They could not run a steamer in competition with them without applying the same wages and conditions that ruled in Australasian ports. As Walter Carpenter, manager of a Fijian shipping firm, noted at the Fiji Shipping Commission in 1914, 'if you registered the vessel here, you would have a fearful lot of trouble on the other side with penalties on crew and that, and the worry would wear you out'. If Islanders manned the vessels 'the unions would turn round and refuse to carry cargo handled by black labour'.[59]

Maori were positioned differently from other Islander seafarers. Their engagement on USSCo. steamers appears to have been minimal, despite their pronounced involvement in earlier local and regional maritime economies where they earned reputations as excellent seafarers. Yet the idea, at least, of increased Maori participation was welcomed by some. In his denunciation of steamship conditions in 1906 George Laurenson concluded: 'I know it has been asked why our native population are not in larger numbers taking up positions in our marine service. But how can we expect them to do so under the circumstances?' Although typical of the paternalistic attitude held by many *Pakeha* leaders towards Maori development at this time, his comments suggest that the recruitment of Maori crew was not entirely objectionable but something to be encouraged so long as shipboard conditions were significantly improved.[60]

Others regarded Maori men as a band of loyal workers to be deployed as strike-breakers when white and other indigenous crew disrupted steamer operations. The USSCo. established good relations with members of the Nga Puhi tribe in the Bay of Islands. Ihaka te Tai, a prominent Nga Puhi chief and, later, Member of the House of

Representatives for Northern Maori, presented Mills with a gift of mats in appreciation of the company's support of a regatta in 1882. When Ernest Ford served as the Fiji agent (1884–88), he maintained a correspondence with te Tai's son, Mita te Tai. In their letters they often discussed the 'Union Army' of forty-three men stationed in Russell. Ford shipped the army gifts of tropical fruit (they began requesting pineapples) and on one occasion te Tai travelled to Fiji to inspect the USSCo.'s operations. There is no record of this 'Union Army' elsewhere in company records so it is difficult to know exactly in what capacity they served the USSCo., but in 1885 Ford wrote to Mills of his trouble with customs officials over 'our native sailors'. He suggested that if the problems persisted 'our Union Army at the Bay would soon send me down good boys'.[61]

Again, in the context of labour troubles in Australia in 1888, Ford suggested arranging 'for a good body of Maories [sic] to proceed to Sydney with the boats & also that I can do it secretly without the Sailors Union knowing. The men could be sent out by launch to meet the Mail steamer off Russell Heads'.[62] The 1890 maritime strike caused the Melbourne manager's thoughts 'to turn again towards getting together a goodly band of Natives'. If a steamer took them from Russell to Wellington for distribution across the company fleet 'it would have a "huge" moral effect on the opposition'. He was not sure it would be wise to send them to Australia 'as they would probably come in for hard knocks and would be considered as "aliens" instead of "men and brothers"'.[63] White labour in New Zealand would be shamed by the loyalty of their indigenous 'brothers', those 'honorary members of the white tribe'. In Australia it would likely provoke more hostility because Maori were viewed as outsiders and a potent threat to the livelihoods of white men.[64] The meanings of race and racial difference were fluid and contested. As Laura Tabili discusses in the British context, the attachment of 'equal or inferior, mate or scab, union brother or threatening rival, comrade or class enemy' to particular groups at any time was 'shaped by domestic, labour and imperial politics, and by the simple pursuit of wealth'.[65] This instance also highlighted the limits of a shared 'white' maritime culture in the Australasian colonies.

That said, however, there is no evidence to suggest Maori were treated as brotherly equals on board company steamers. One isolated case provides some insight into shipboard discrimination. A Maori seaman named Ranohe served six months on an Auckland steamer in 1891. He wrote a letter of complaint to Mills in Maori after suffering abuse from the second mate, Murdoch Macpherson. Macpherson allegedly called him 'a black son of a bitch'.[66] Macpherson denied this specific charge, but indicated there was some tension between them on board, as 'owing to the man's stupidity and incapability I was afraid some accident would happen especially when approaching or departing from the wharf. This is my explanation of the charge made.' The Auckland branch manager confirmed his opinion: Ranohe appeared to be 'not very good' and in complaining to Mills he only further alienated himself from fellow crew. He was dismissed after his articles expired.[67] This incident reinforced the hold of informal shipboard power dynamics and the hazards associated with taking a refractory stance. It also indicated the normalisation of racial abuse and the differential treatment of white and indigenous labour, something that is supported, albeit fleetingly, in other correspondence. When the second officer of another vessel, Alan McDonald, sought a change of ship, his main complaint was the abuse meted out by senior officers. Since joining the ship, he asserted, 'I have been treated more like a native than an Officer'.[68]

When the New Zealand Shipping and Seamen's Amendment Bill was drafted in 1910 in a bid to discourage the lascar-manned P&O steamers from trading between Australia and New Zealand, Prime Minister Joseph Ward insisted, in response to concerns aired by the Maori Member of Parliament Tame Parata, that it did not target Maori or Pacific Islanders; they were not the 'coloured crew' to be excluded from ships.[69] A few years later the USSCo. engaged Rarotongan crew on its transpacific mail steamer when a number of white firemen deserted in the islands. The general secretary of the Federated Seamen's Union, Tom Young, accepted that 'the Rarotongan is a New Zealand citizen at law, but between him and the Maori there is no comparison as members of a community'. He was adamant that the USSCo. should not compel the union to enrol 'black labour' into its membership, for this would pull down wages, overtime and working conditions. There was no distinction, he asserted, between the 'coolie-manned ships' of British companies and a local vessel with an Islander crew.[70] Such arguments elevated Maori to a special status in the white colonial community, and demonstrated once again the unevenness of regional trades.

Legislative impediments in Fiji also prevented men from signing articles for foreign-going steamers. The various labour ordinances introduced after cession in 1874 were drafted without sailors in mind. Government officials and European shipowners were confused by the ambiguous position of labour afloat. Under the Imperial Merchant Shipping Act, the only legislation in Fiji that officially addressed seafarers, there appeared to be no restrictions on Fijian men shipping as crew on British vessels: they were British subjects and could be hired as such. This freedom of engagement conflicted with local statutes for the 'good government of the natives'. Some officials feared that the terms set out in the act favoured unscrupulous employers who could tie men for months to working conditions with which they were unfamiliar and which they might wish to leave after a few days. Moreover, these imperial regulations made no provision for the commutation of native taxes.[71]

Restrictions on the engagement of Fijian crew for vessels registered in Fiji and trading solely within the island group, such as the USSCo.'s inter-island steamer, were of less concern. These ships were more immediately within reach of local jurisdiction if abuse occurred. Larger vessels trading within the group generally took out articles upon which to hire crew. Any Fijian who wished to sign up required a permit of release from his district. For vessels trading beyond Fiji, the ship's master also had to lodge a bond to guarantee the safe and timely return of men. Permits of release and bonds were general regulations that applied to men leaving their districts or the colony for any reason.[72] Men of mixed European and Fijian descent and native crew from other islands living in Fiji were not subject to these regulations.[73] From time to time USSCo. agents and other shipping interests did request and receive special leave to ship men, but total numbers were small.

On one such occasion the survey vessel HMS *Penguin* applied to take a Fijian crew on a twelve-month trip to the Line Islands in 1896. A number of men applied for the position and after medical examinations six were chosen as deck hands. On his ship's return, the captain noted the men had been paid well and had no complaints to make. They lived with the European crew on 'friendly and cordial terms' and 'their departure is universally regretted by both officers and men'. The Fijians later requested leave for a return trip to Vava'u in Tonga in order to *solevu* the town that had shown them hospitality during their travels, an interesting instance of customary practices being furthered by engagement on foreign-owned vessels.[74] From the casual observations of travellers in other parts of the Pacific, it appeared men derived status from connections with foreign shipping companies. Many Rarotongan men that Beatrice Grimshaw observed, for instance, wore steamer caps and jerseys that they had acquired either from working as seafarers for different international steamer lines or through their connections with visiting ships.[75]

Within Fiji, racial groups were ranked on a hierarchy of seafaring skill. Indians indentured for plantation work were not regarded as seafaring people and 'usually have the sense to get Fijians to run their boats', quipped the *Fiji Times* on reporting one maritime accident.[76] European captains had long regarded Rotumans as particularly skilled seafarers and over the course of the nineteenth century many men left their homes to work on trading vessels or as pearl shell divers in the Torres Strait. One USSCo. captain suggested replacing white seamen and firemen on the Fiji steamers with Rotumans as the former 'were quite useless in the hot weather'. Rotuman men were 'splendid sailors and more like Europeans in there [*sic*] way'.[77]

In 1911, the government steamer's chief engineer had trouble securing firemen owing to labour shortages and high wages ashore. The colonial secretary commented wryly that 'the dissatisfied Fijian native workman has always many sick relatives'. He did not want increased wages paid to attract Fijians back to the work 'as I do not consider they are worthy of it as they are unreliable, lazy and careless'. He preferred Rotuman men as replacements, rather than Chinese or Indian workers, as the latter 'would be useless for boat work' and were not regarded as strong enough. Rotuman men were engaged in both steamer departments. Yet the captain soon reported that as firemen they 'have proved themselves utterly unfit for the work as they cannot stand the heat of the stokehold and are knocked up after an hour's firing'. The men subsequently complained that they were only fed rice when agreements stipulated native fare, and that work conditions were appalling, some men fainting on the job.[78]

As in the debates about the racial suitability of lascars for hot and dangerous work in the stokehold, Europeans were often quick to denounce the workers rather than the poor labour conditions on board ship. Assumptions about the maritime suitability or otherwise of certain racial groups tended to preclude improvements in the conditions in which such men were expected to operate. It seems that in this respect at least, the reluctance of colonial leaders to free up access to Islanders as crew on outbound steamers, where they would be expected to replace Europeans in the least desirable positions such as stoking the fires, was warranted.

Maritime mobility and colonial rule

The USSCo.'s steamship empire reordered the Pacific seascape into a structured system of steamer lines, which concentrated at specific ports. Yet we also need to look beneath and beyond the company's chart of routes (figure 3) to appreciate fully the different scales of maritime networking that took place during these decades. The concerns I have documented about Islanders moving freely amongst Tonga, Samoa and Fiji on *solevu* 'business' illustrate that the USSCo. was also hooked into maritime circuitries not of its own making, and company steamships were just one element of a maritime world made up of diverse transport technologies, including cutters and schooners, sailing between islands for a host of reasons not easily captured within a predominantly western understanding of seaborne commerce. Through the use of permits of release from home districts, passage orders and bonds, colonial officials attempted to give indigenous mobility more order and legibility so as better to delineate and contain it. But they could never fully comprehend the significance of indigenous patterns of circulation or effectively control them.[79] There were always many and different mappings of Oceania.

In abstract terms, company routes appeared to express a universal mapping of mobility, a commitment to freedom of movement and exchange. But these travelling opportunities were always more accessible to some than others. Some mobilities were sound, yet others were suspect. Modern mobility, as Tim Cresswell concludes, was both 'a central conduit of life' and threatening to social order.[80] Or, as historians of colonial India reflect, the 'conundrum of colonialism' centred on 'how to facilitate the development of the "right" forms of circulation and repress the "wrong ones"'.[81] The long-standing regional triangulation between Fiji, Tonga and Samoa, viewed now through a USSCo. optic, extended further south to Auckland and Sydney. Yet the traffic to these ports was regarded as a separate affair from the local inter-island passages that converged on Suva. Australian and New Zealand officials sought to secure a monopoly over the island trades in the face of foreign competition, yet they were also concerned about the regional mobility of non-whites, fearing indigenous circuitries in the Pacific might be routinely re-routed towards the white settler colonies. While the *Sydney Morning Herald* asserted that Australia's eastern seaboard 'should draw the island trade as naturally across the seas as the inland trade of Australia is drawn to the coast', the influx of goods was one thing, the influx of Islanders quite another.[82] Maritime transport infrastructure was overlaid with restrictive, racialised ideas about space, labour and national belonging. Steamer routes were both lines of possibility and lines of constraint.

Notes

1 HC, USSCo. Records, AG-292-005-001/022, Houghton to Mills, 8 September 1892.
2 *Ibid.*, Duncan to Mills, 24 August 1892.
3 NAF, CSO, 95.2868, 17 July 1895 and ensuing commentary. In 1892 the Malietoa Laupepa Government introduced a register of Samoans leaving the islands in order to track the overseas movement of Samoans: see Damon Salesa, '"Travel happy" Samoa: Colonialism, Samoan migration and a "brown Pacific"', *New Zealand Journal of History*, 37:2 (2003), 182.
4 Salesa, '"Travel happy" Samoa', 177.
5 Hau'ofa, 'Our sea of islands', 155.
6 HC, USSCo. Records, AG-292-005-001/027, Henderson to Mills, 23 July 1891.

7   *Ibid.*, AG-292-005-001/097, Mills to Holdsworth, 6 May 1911.
8   ATL, Ellinor Jane Hunter Brown Papers, 1839–1947, MS-Copy-Micro-0670, Folder 51, Reminiscences by Henry Hunter Brown 1894–1897.
9   HC, James Herries Beattie Papers, MS 582/F/25, Newspaper clippings album, no. 151, misc. newspaper cutting, 12 July 1891.
10 Reeves, *Brown Men and Women*, 81–2.
11 Harold Beauchamp, 'South Sea Islands: notes on a visit', *Evening Post* (27 August 1910), 15.
12 Reeves, *Brown Men and Women*, 199, 252.
13 Reeves, *Brown Men and Women*, 197.
14 HC, USSCo. Records, AG-292-005-001/085, McLennan to Holdsworth, 11 July and 19 December 1907, Mills to Holdsworth, 20 September 1907.
15 *Fiji Times* (26 January 1907).
16 Paul D'Arcy, *The People of the Sea: Environment, Identity and History in Oceania* (Honolulu: University of Hawai'i Press, 2006), 54–60; Derrick, *A History of Fiji*, 118–31.
17 Such attitudes were also marked in other islands: see Alastair Couper, *Sailors and Traders: A Maritime History of the Pacific Peoples* (Honolulu: University of Hawai'i Press, 2009), 145–6.
18 NAF, CSO, 97.1386, 21 April 1897 and ensuing commentary.
19 NAF, CSO, 91.2299, 'Return of British seamen employed in vessels registered in the colony of Fiji, 1891'.
20 NAF, CSO, 86.2360, C. Malau, President Marine Board, 8 and 9 December 1886.
21 *Western Pacific Herald* (6 May 1904).
22 D'Arcy, *The People of the Sea*, 142. For Hawai'i, see Peter R. Mills, '*Neo* in Oceania: foreign vessels owned by Hawaiian chiefs before 1830', *Journal of Pacific History*, 38:1 (2003), 53–67; Mifflin Thomas, *Schooner from Windward: Two Centuries of Hawaiian Interisland Shipping* (Honolulu: University of Hawai'i Press, 1983). For New Zealand, see Hazel Petrie, *Chiefs of Industry: Maori Tribal Enterprise in Early Colonial New Zealand* (Auckland: Auckland University Press, 2006).
23 NAF, CSO, 79.1806, James Blyth, 31 October 1879; CSO, 80.466, Des Voeux, 16 March 1880 (emphasis in original).
24 *Report of the Commission Appointed to Inquire into the Decrease of the Native Population* (Suva: Government Printer, 1896), 49; Couper, *Sailors and Traders*, 145–6, 158. In 1906, Fijians owned 122 registered vessels, Europeans forty-nine, Chinese twenty-three and part-Europeans eleven. For more statistics, see Couper, *Sailors and Traders*, 160.
25 NAF, CSO, 81.205, D. J. Chisholm, Audit Office, 29 January 1881; CSO, 82.347, 11 February 1882.
26 NAF, CSO, 82.347, Thurston, 3 February 1882.
27 NAF, CSO, 90.2831, Thurston, 19 September 1890; CSO, 92.2082, Thurston, 29 June 1892.
28 NAF, Rewa Provincial Council Minutes, vol. 1 (1892–1904), 20–21 October 1903.
29 *Decrease of the Native Population*, 48, 56.
30 NAF, Rewa Provincial Council Minutes, vol. 1 (1892–1904), 4 February 1897 and 10 October 1899.
31 Salesa, '"Travel happy" Samoa', 172.
32 HC, USSCo. Records, AG-292-005-004/082, Fiji Schedule 1907.
33 *Ibid.*, AG-292-005-001/071, Borron to Mills, 28 July 1902.
34 Cotten Seiler, 'Mobilising race, racialising mobility: writing race into mobility studies', in Gijs Mom, Gordon Pirie and Laurent Tissot (eds), *Mobility in History: The State of the Art in the History of Transport, Traffic and Mobility* (Neuchâtel: Alphil, 2009), 233. See also Tim Cresswell, *On the Move: Mobility in the Modern Western World* (New York: Routledge 2006), 43–4.
35 HC, USSCo. Records, AG-292-005-001/095, Kennedy [or Aiken?] to Mills, 4 December 1909 (emphasis in original).
36 Ward, *Widening Worlds, Shrinking Worlds?*, 14, 19.

37 NAF, CSO, 03.665, Beaumont, 6 February 1903; CSO, 04.4114, Caldewell, 12 October 1904.
38 NAF, CSO, 01.1906, William Allardyce, 7 May 1901.
39 HC, USSCo. Records, AG-292-005-001/107, Irvine to Mills, 16 March 1911.
40 NAF, CSO, 01.667, Hugh Keith, 15 February 1901.
41 O'Connor, 'Keeping New Zealand white', 41–65.
42 NAF, CSO, 98.979, William Allardyce, 15 December 1898.
43 NAF, CSO, 98.3386, n.d.
44 See *Census of New Zealand* (Wellington: 1916), 148–9. For more on this period and the interwar years, see O'Connor, 'Keeping New Zealand white', 41–65; Jacqueline Leckie, 'In defence of race and empire: the white New Zealand League at Pukekohe', *New Zealand Journal of History*, 19:2 (1985), 103–29.
45 Sekhar Bandyopadhyay, 'A history of small numbers: Indians in New Zealand, c.1890–1930', *New Zealand Journal of History*, 43:2 (2009), 150–68; Marilyn Lake and Henry Reynolds, *Drawing the Global Colour Line: White Men's Countries and the Question of Racial Equality* (Melbourne: Melbourne University Press, 2008).
46 NAF, CSO, 94.4251, Ratu Temesia, 17 December 1894 and ensuing commentary.
47 NAF, CSO, 94.4745, William Allardyce, 21 December 1894.
48 NAF, CSO, 80.550, 12 March 1880, Thurston to Colonial Secretary.
49 NAF, CSO, 06.2794, Scott, 26 June 1906.
50 NAF, CSO, 06.4625, bond between William Sutherland, Native Commissioner, and Alex Duncan, Leslie Brown and Alexander Joske, 5 October 1906.
51 NAF, CSO, 06.2794, Scott to Native Commissioner, 20 February 1907.
52 NAF, CSO, 06.2794, J. W. Dwyer to Scott, 6 February 1907.
53 NAF, CSO, 14.10046, Native Commissioner, 28 November 1914.
54 HC, USSCo. Records, AG-292-005-001/024, Grey to Mills, 26 December 1891.
55 *Fiji Times* (19 June 1907, 19 October 1910).
56 David Chappell, *Double Ghosts: Oceanian Voyagers on Euroamerican Ships* (New York: M. E. Sharpe, 1997), esp. chapters 3–6.
57 See 'Government and general orders', in Robert McNab, *Historical Records of New Zealand*, vol. 1 (Wellington: Government Printer, 1908–14), 257–8, 316–17, 328–9; Kelly K. Chaves, '"Great violence has been done": the collision of Maori culture and British seafaring culture', *Great Circle*, 29:1 (2007), 22–40.
58 *New Zealand Herald* (18 April 1884).
59 *Fiji Shipping Commission*, 187.
60 George Laurenson, 20 October 1906, *NZPD*, vol. 138 (Wellington: Government Printer, 1906), 726.
61 HC, USSCo. Records, AG-292-005-001/002, Ford to Mills, 20 February 1885.
62 *Ibid.*, AG-292-005-001/006, Ford to Mills, 23 July 1888.
63 *Ibid.*, AG-292-005-001/021, David Mills to McLean, 5 September 1890.
64 James Bennett, 'Maori as honorary members of the white tribe', *Journal of Imperial and Commonwealth History*, 29:3 (2001), 34–8.
65 Laura Tabili, 'The construction of racial difference in twentieth-century Britain: the Special Restriction (Coloured Alien Seamen) Order, 1925', *Journal of British Studies*, 33:1 (1994), 69.
66 Translated from the phrase as it appears in the letter: '*Tamaiti pango a te kuri wahine*', HC, USSCo. Records, AG-292-005-001/025, Ranohe to Mills, 1 June 1891.
67 HC, USSCo. Records, AG-292-005-001/027, Murdoch Macpherson to Crawshaw, 22 July 1891, and Henderson to Mills, 23 July 1891.
68 WCCA, USSCo. Records, AF004:6:2, Masters' and Officers' Personal Files, McDonald to Strang, 5 March 1909.
69 Joseph Ward, 27 October 1910, *NZPD*, vol. 153 (Wellington: Government Printer, 1910), 115.
70 ANZ, Marine Department Records, M-1-15/3/294, Engagement and Discharge of Coloured Seamen, Tom Young, letter to the editor, *New Zealand Times* (5 July 1917).
71 NAF, CSO, 93.861, Thurston, 3 June 1893.

72 NAF, CSO, 85.2659, 12 October 1885; CSO, 93.861, Attorney General, 23 May 1893.
73 NAF, CSO, 91.3885, Correspondence with Levuka Chamber of Commerce, 16 December 1891–14 January 1892.
74 NAF, CSO, 96.1659, 14 May 1896, Captain Field, HMS *Penguin*; CSO, 98.4660, 24 November 1898, Captain Field.
75 Grimshaw, *In the Strange South Seas*, 141.
76 *Fiji Times* (8 October 1890).
77 HC, Cameron Family Papers, MS 1046, Alex Cameron to Angus Cameron, 19 November 1890.
78 NAF, CSO, 11.2405, Chief Engineer, Ranadi, 18 March 1911 and ensuing commentary.
79 Salesa explores similar themes in the Samoan context, see '"Travel happy" Samoa'.
80 Cresswell, *On the Move*, 83.
81 Claude Markovits, Jacques Pouchepadass and Sanjay Subrahmanyam, 'Introduction: circulation and society under colonial rule', in Markovits, Pouchepadass, and Subrahmanyam (eds), *Society and Circulation: Mobile People and Itinerant Cultures in South Asia, 1750–1950* (Delhi: Permanent Black, 2003), 9, 13.
82 *Sydney Morning Herald*, reprinted in the *Western Pacific Herald* (5 February 1907).

Conclusion

The greatest of humanisers, that only perfect missionary, the regular steamship service, is bringing the far East every day more in touch with the luxuries, the aspirations, the morals of the West.
Edward Reeves, *Brown Men and Women* (1898)

This book has examined the nature and significance of steamship transport in the history of the colonial Pacific. It has drawn a wide range of people, spaces and experiences into an extended analysis of a new world of mobility and exchange. By approaching transport as a material culture and a cultural system, it has brought together questions about production and use in order to look more closely at the effects of human interaction – both at sea and ashore – on the development of this industrial subject.

Histories of the late nineteenth-century revolution in transport and communications systems have traditionally focused on the transformative promise of steamships, railways and the telegraph in an age of global empire. These imperial tools possessed an enlightening power and a civilising agency; they heralded the collapse of distance and a progressive universalism. Reeves's rhetorical flourish is common to the period. Throughout the book I have kept one eye on these more abstract political, economic and cultural investments in technology, but I have been wary of letting the promise of 'the regular steamship service' speak for itself. The meanings of transport systems and technologies were not stable across time and space, but had different meanings in different locations. In other words, the everyday texture of localised engagements with steam in particular colonial settings mattered.

To develop this argument, I have moved an analysis of steamshipping away from the imperial metropole and out into the Pacific. The USSCo. was not a small player in imperial shipping and it aspired to even greater things as it was absorbed into the Inchcape shipping empire in 1917. Yet the regional traffic in the western Pacific was a comparatively small trade, one that a focus on the superliners, prestigious mail routes and vertical links with the imperial metropole tends to obscure. The USSCo.'s shipping networks mapped out interrelationships that were not routinely tied into a centre–periphery exchange with Britain. Materialising these networks helps us to see the historical importance of a transcolonial arena in the western Pacific, one in which key ports in New Zealand and Australia, sites at the 'margins' of empire, held a sub-metropolitan status in their own right.

In destabilising one hierarchical model of imperial space, it might be tempting to adapt the older imperial method to a different setting. These networks and configurations can be read as evidence of New Zealand's growing regional power and influence. Predictions of the nation's maritime destiny as the Britain of the South held wide appeal during these decades; future political relations were imagined through the development of shipping services. Yet by looking below the nation, as we are encouraged to do by the organisation of the company archive by regional port branch, we can also chart the more particular, localised configurations of regional connectivity. What we might like to frame as national space was in fact divided by provincial debates about the placement of ports along steamer routes and the order of steamer calls. Not all ports were wired into modern Pacific networks in the same way.

Political leaders tended to fold the growing tonnage of the USSCo. fleet and the extension of new shipping services into a progressive narrative about nation-building. The steamship embodied white settler ascendency in the 'far-flung' Dominions, and New Zealand's regional influence in its island neighbourhood. Yet company management also came to regard the 'New Zealand' in their official title as more of a hindrance than an asset. Commentators across the Tasman Sea were ready to regard the USSCo. more as an Australasian enterprise than one centred on New Zealand. Looking across national space in this way also unsettles any neat framing of New Zealand as a regional centre to its island periphery. This was a shared transport culture and, in many ways, a shared culture of engagement in the western Pacific, even as the period in question was one of growing national sentiment on both sides of the Tasman. Imperial debates about proposed colonial laws to restrict maritime activity in the Pacific to local shipping interests also posed questions about what constituted national space. From a metropolitan perspective, the Australasian colonies were located in a wider British sea and were expected to defer to this maritime expression of imperial community before advancing an independent extra-territorial regionalism.

CONCLUSION

It matters, then, from where we narrate the impact of steam. Shifting the angle of vision to the Fiji end of the steamer lines that radiated out from Auckland and Sydney demonstrated again the vital part transport networks played in reconfiguring relations between colonies and in shaping the identities of specific nodes along these routes. Suva was refashioned as a regional centre of transport and trade in the western Pacific on its inclusion in the USSCo. port complex. Steamer services reduced the distance between New Zealand and Fiji by a number of days, stimulated the trade in tropical fruit and enabled more people to travel and to travel more often. Yet the benefits of steam were by no means immediate or evenly attainable. The provision of shipping services brought with it a series of ongoing challenges, such as building vessels more suited to a tropical trade; maintaining professionalism across multiple labour sites; negotiating for a steady supply of wharf labour in island ports; and improving the carriage of perishable cargoes. Working through these challenges meant engaging with a range of people whose own projects, ambitions and itineraries cross-cut those of transport managers and entrepreneurs. Resident traders regarded Fiji's capital as the 'hub of the universe' and vital to the USSCo.'s success, assertions some of the branch staff sent from New Zealand and Australia found implausible. They were often caught between the excessive demands of traders and shippers, who came to expect rebates and discounts as a matter of course, and colonial officials, many of whom were yet to be convinced of the company's productive value to the infant colony and unwilling to grant concessions and subsidies lightly. Looking more closely at operations in the port branches of Levuka and Suva has demonstrated that location still mattered, even as the power of colonialism and steam hooked these ports into more durable transoceanic networks.

Placing maritime space at the heart of colonial and imperial history goes some way towards bringing islands into a single interpretative frame, to see the ways in which a traditional, land-based historical method has artificially partitioned off a country like New Zealand from its regional setting and its regional pasts. The maritime geographies of shipping routes and vessels, the spaces in between, tend to get obscured in the newer approaches to imperial history that are attuned to the lateral or horizontal connections between colonies. Analysis more readily gravitates to the 'meeting up' of mobile people, objects, cultural practices and ideas onshore. Materialising the ship focuses attention on circulation, but it takes us further than that. The steamer was not only an engine of exchange, it was also a meaningful locale in these modern Pacific networks. It was a space where history was made.

In this book I have approached the history of the ship primarily through maritime working cultures. Working men and women have been hard to find in the connected archives of the shipping company empire. There are numerous photographs of individual ships, but few of crew. Journalistic descriptions of each new steamer that arrived in colonial ports from the Scottish shipbuilders accorded ample space to details of size, technical innovation and interior design, but paid comparatively little attention to the quarters of the everyday people who set these vehicles in motion. The company head, James Mills, began to insist that ship interiors were designed to keep workers out of the public eye by moving seamen's quarters further away from second- and third-class passengers, and ensuring workspaces were less visible when steamers were in port. Yet all the while seamen's union agitation, the rise of the state arbitration system, the work of charitable institutions and popular concerns about the declining appeal of the seafaring profession kept visible the working cultures at sea.

As a workplace undergoing technological change, new values of labour specialisation, hierarchy and discipline were developed, imposed and challenged here. The many menial tasks of shipboard work in the steam age appeared to compromise an older image of hardy, skilled and heroic maritime masculinity in the dying age of sail. At the same time, older stereotypes of the wayward, sexually promiscuous, hard-drinking sailor in port were attacked as part of a broader social project to domesticate the image of seafarers in national and imperial life. Broader realignments in cultural notions of masculine respectability and responsibility – as well as their limits – can be charted through maritime labour history.

The rise of modern managerial capitalism in shipping, with its rule books and regulations, also placed considerable emphasis on the routine flow of information between head office, ship and port branch. These correspondence networks could break down, as seen when managers were the last to know about shipboard misconduct, especially in the island trades. Widespread concerns about drinking also indicated something of the limits of official control and surveillance. Alcohol abuse – from captains sequestered in cabins too drunk to take command, to firemen failing to join ship – revealed something of the real hardships and pressures men faced in their daily work to keep this transport empire afloat. And seafaring, even in an age of timetabled, regimented shipping, could still foster a masculine independence and facilitate escape from domestic responsibilities, as seen in the purser Ralph Kearns's intimate entanglements in Samoa, Fiji, Auckland and Honolulu, or the first mate William Colquhoun's decision to abandon a lover and child in Sydney. Their lives moved to a different rhythm, one that was out of step with the expectations of employers, co-workers and family members.

Dominant cultural attitudes about women's engagement in paid work can also be accessed through maritime history. Women's working lives were more tightly circumscribed by prescriptive gender ideals. Rigid definitions of appropriate femininity, which encompassed physical appearance, marital status, age and behaviour, left only a narrow window of opportunity for those seeking employment as stewardesses. The protective, caring, maternal figure of the idealised stewardess held particular cultural appeal, especially in times of crisis at sea, such as the wreck of the *Wairarapa* in 1894. But in the everyday, messy dynamics of steamer operations, female workers were more often framed as disruptive and troublesome, upsetting the masculine order of this modern maritime enterprise.

Most powerfully, perhaps, maritime workers were thrust into the public eye through the highly politicised debates about labour recruitment in the imperial mercantile marine. Racialised definitions of national and imperial citizenship – and the fault lines that began to appear between them – were articulated through maritime working cultures. It was here that the stokehold, the most invisible space of all, assumed a potent visibility. Trade unionists and political leaders recruited these dark, dirty and dangerous spaces below the waterline, crewed by the 'unseen workers' of the steam age, as a kind of proving-ground for the racial strength of the self-governing Dominions. Stokeholds, they argued, were spaces for white men only and could not be sacrificed to lascars or other 'coloured' colonial labourers as some gesture of imperial goodwill. The ship was not apart or adrift from land-based society, but integral to its very definition in an age of assertive colonial nationalism. The *Aparima*, the only Union Company steamer manned by an Indian crew, was a stark reminder that business interests could ultimately trump nation-building rhetoric and visions of sub-imperial projection.

In other ways, too, the ship was a constitutive site. In both a symbolic and practical sense, shipowners invested considerable energy in fashioning spaces that projected a modern, mature image of colonial development and prosperity. Decisions about steamer names involved extended discussion at managerial level. Interior design was an exacting art, right down to the finer details of the tilt of a mirror in the women's bathrooms and the sound of a steamer whistle in port. Angus Cameron's more conservative attitudes about furnishings and fittings were particularly frustrating. Innovation and style mattered in such a competitive industry.

The cultural meanings invested in ships were not stable. Exquisite interiors had far less power when we consider the ways in which

Islanders travelled. The deck became the social centre of the ship and the smoking rooms, ladies' lounges and de luxe cabins receded from view. Islander passengers travelling between Tonga, Samoa and Fiji made the deck their own. They brought their own 'paraphernalia' on board ship, including mats, food and animals. They even brought their own boats. This image of indigenous boats sitting on steamer decks is a powerful one. It tells us something of the way steamers were hooked into histories not anticipated by the company or the new colonial rulers across the Pacific. While steamers brought 'the far East' (from Reeves's standpoint in New Zealand, this was Polynesia) more in touch with 'the West', these networks moved in both directions. European sailors and passengers were also thrust into more intimate contact with Islanders and indigenous cultural mores through the regular steamship service. These fleeting images point to the indigenous adaptations of new transport technologies, as well as the resilience of their established pre-colonial investments in the sea and maritime mobility, the cultural glue which held island communities together across vast oceanic space. Older ways to travel Oceania persisted into the steam age.

Labour ordinances, travel permits and immigration laws were some of the innovations that accompanied the rise of modern shipping. The 'collapse' of distance was not entirely friction-free. In an era of assertive nationalism in the white settler colonies of New Zealand and Australia, and a period of official commitment to the 'preservation of the race' in the Crown colony of Fiji, legislative measures were introduced to give maritime mobility more structure and definition. They were harnessed to police the racialised boundary order of the 'white man's country' and the 'indigenous village'. New Zealand's restrictive immigration policies were aimed more directly at Asiatics than Islanders, yet the free mobility of Fijians, Samoans and Tongans to the colony was discouraged, with the exception of temporary visits when accompanied by European employers or sponsors. Fiji's colonial rulers were unconvinced of the benefits of regional mobility, from the smaller-scale networks from village to port, to the more wide-ranging routes linking islands to the Australasian colonies. Young Fijian men residing or 'loitering' in Suva when their labour was required in their home districts, or Samoan women travelling to the port for seemingly immoral purposes, frustrated European and indigenous leaders. When the temptations of the port town became too great, steam's colonial boon was far less apparent. New proximities in a steam empire were as likely to be challenged as they were to be celebrated.

To chart these developments is not to reinscribe the power of the elite to determine the mobility cultures of those with less official power, influence or cultural capital. Evidence of these tools of sur-veillance and control is not the clear evidence of their immediate or seamless efficacy. Their introduction was often a reactionary response to the ways in which people were already making their own meanings from new transport opportunities. But opening up an analysis of shipping company history to these responses and experiences is to understand better the ways people used transport to redefine their own place and the place of others in the world. It provides rich insights into the negotiated and contested relationship between maritime space and social power.

Using the ship to connect a series of dispersed stories about sea transport and the cultures of colonialism has not resulted in an over-arching narrative or big-picture history of the 'story of steam'. This approach mirrors the kind of spatiality mapped out by inter-island steamer passages and port calls, but it does come with its own limita-tions. In emphasising movement and fluidity, there is an inherent une-venness in lingering only on a few ships and port spaces. The brief and fleeting snapshots of everyday life across a wide spatial canvas make it difficult to be certain how representative are the spaces and voices presented here. This is compounded by the fact that the experiences of most of the people in whom I have been interested – the stewardesses, the Islander seafarers and dock workers, the steerage passengers and firemen – were not self-authored, but filtered through the perspectives of commercial and political elites. All historians confront the archival challenges of silence, unevenness, fragments and dead ends to some degree. In a study like this, which attempts to give transport more visibility in the stories we tell about contested colonial spaces, these 'thinner' stories do have their own power. In setting this book against the narrower tradition of business and economic histories of ships and maritime enterprise, these stories hint at and point to a much richer and more complex, even if more partial, understanding of transport's cultural histories.

In its broadest sense, *Oceania under steam* is meant as a response to the growing calls to craft more wide-ranging, inclusive histories of maritime activity. By paying attention to the shipping company's complex of vehicles, routes, port branches and labour – some of the 'subjects', 'objects' and 'scapes' of a cultural transport history – we can begin to see the sea as a real space that was used by the people who worked on or lived near it. Bringing the histories of maritime workers together with the ocean-centred world that their work helped create, refines and sharpens our understanding of the ways in which these larger historical geographies – an otherwise abstract 'Oceania' or 'the western Pacific' – were lived and experienced. It demonstrates how the

micro-geographies of the ship were meaningful in the larger-scale political, economic and cultural constructions of maritime regionalism.

To craft less linear and inevitable – and more negotiated and complex
– histories of technology, imperial power and social change, I have
argued for a closer engagement of the histories of transport and empire
with those of New Zealand and the Pacific. These entwined perspectives open up an understanding of the complex cross-affiliations produced by maritime enterprise and, in turn, the connected and shared
historical experiences of a changing colonial world.

BIBLIOGRAPHY

I Primary Material

Alexander Turnbull Library, Wellington

Frederick Barkas Family Scrapbooks and Papers
  'Some Memories of a Mediocrity', vol. 5, MS-2491-05

Captain James Gerald Stokely Doorly Papers
  Selections from scrapbooks, MS-Papers-0687

H. L. Eliot Notebook
  MSX-4220

Federated Seamen's Union of New Zealand Papers
  Clippings re shipping, MS-Papers-0650-097A
  Correspondence to and from USSCo (1902–20), MS-Papers-0650-006
  Executive Council general correspondence (1896–1902), MS-Papers-0650-004
  Industrial and general scrapbook (1898–99), MSY-1030
  Industrial and general (1901–9), MSY-0131

Ellinor Jane Hunter Brown Papers, 1839–1947
  Reminiscences by Henry Hunter Brown 1894–97, MS-Copy-Micro-0670,
    Folder 51

Maurice Mayo, Letter to his mother, 29 November 1917
  MS-Papers-5742

Coleman Phillips Papers
  Correspondence respecting the cession of Fiji, 73-150-09
  Life history to 1924, qMS-1643
  Scrapbook, MSY-4803

H. O. Roth Papers
  Notes and clippings – seamen (1890–1903), 94-106-43/06
  Notes and clippings – seamen (1904–12), 94-106-43/07

Louisa Worsfold, 'Social history of Russell' (1946)
  qMS-2294

Archives New Zealand, Wellington

Marine Department Records
  'Amokura' – Transfer of Boys to Union S.S. Company's Training Ship
    'Aparima' – 1913–18, M-1-17/11/5
  Engagement and Discharge of Coloured Seamen, M-1-15/3/294

BIBLIOGRAPHY

City Council Archives, Wellington
USSCo. Records
  Classification of Steamers, 29 July 1887–9 Feb 1904, AF080:1:7
  Letterbook Private, July 1912 – June 1914, AF066:6:3
  Masters' and Officers' Personal Files, AF004
  Miscellaneous Files, AF080
  Operations – Cards and Invitations 1882–1975, AF077:6:1
  'Specifications of a Twin-screw Steamship for the USSCo of NZ Limited' (10
    November 1904), B97/6
  Steamers' Names, 6 December 1897 – 24 April 1913, AF080:9:12

Hocken Collections, University of Otago, Dunedin
James Herries Beattie Papers
  Notebook entitled 'Maori ethnology. Nondescript Maori topics', PC-0189
  Papers, MS 582/F/25

Cameron Family Papers
  MS 1046 series

USSCo. Records, c.1870–1914
  Annual Report and Balance Sheet, AG-292-002
  Holdsworth letterbooks, AG-292-004-003, AG-292-004-004
  Inwards correspondence files, AG-292-005-001, AG-292-005-004
  Management correspondence files, AG-292-005-001, AG-292-005-004
  Minutes of meetings of directors, AG-292-003-001
  J. Mills, private letterbook, AG-292-004-001/002
  Whitson subject files, AG-292-005-003

National Archives of Fiji, Suva
Colonial Secretary's Office correspondence (minutes)
  1875–1915

Despatches from the Governor of Fiji to the Secretary of State
  vol. 2 – vol. 10 (1880–94)

Native Department, Rewa Provincial Council Minutes
  vol. 1 (1892–1904)
  vol. 2 (1905–18)

Museum of City and Sea, Wellington
USSCo. ephemera miscellaneous files

Special Collections, University of Auckland Library
New Zealand Seamen's Union Papers, Auckland Branch Records
  D-8, Box 1 – Correspondence general, 1900–13
  91/3, Box 2

BIBLIOGRAPHY

Official publications

Appendices to the Journals of the House of Representatives. Wellington: Government Printer 1874, 1908, 1910, 1911.

Colonial Conference, 1907: Minutes of Proceedings. London: HMSO, 1907, Cd 3523.

Dominions Royal Commission. 'Minutes of evidence taken in New Zealand in 1913 (Cd. 7170)'. *Royal Commission on the Natural Resources, Trade, and Legislation of Certain Portions of His Majesty's Dominions.* London: 1913.

Lucas, Charles. *Dominions No. 1: Note on a Visit to Australia, New Zealand, and Fiji, in 1909.* London: HMSO, Colonial Office series, 1910, Cd 5100.

Merchant Shipping Legislation: Report of a Conference between Representatives of the United Kingdom, the Commonwealth of Australia, and New Zealand, 26th March–2nd April, 1907. Sydney: Government Printer, 1907.

New Zealand Parliamentary Debates. Wellington: Government Printer, 1896, 1906, 1910.

New Zealand Census. Wellington: Government Printer, 1916.

New Zealand Official Year Book. Wellington: Government Printer, 1893.

Ordinances of the Colony of Fiji. Suva: Government Printer, 1914.

Report from the Royal Commission on Ocean Shipping Service. Melbourne: Government Printer 1906.

Report of the Commission Appointed for the Purpose of Inquiring Into and Reporting Upon the Shipping Conditions and Facilities of the Colony, Having Reference More Especially to the Carriage of Passengers, General Cargo, Fruit and other Produce – Council Paper No. 111. Suva: Legislative Council, 1914.

Report of the Commission Appointed to Inquire into the Decrease of the Native Population. Suva: Government Printer, 1896.

Report of a Committee Appointed by the Board of Trade on the Question of Continuous Discharge Certificates for Seamen. London: HMSO, 1900, Cd 133.

Report of the Committee Appointed by the Board of Trade to Inquire into the Mercantile Marine: I – Report. London: HMSO, 1903, Cd 1607.

Report of the Committee Appointed by the Board of Trade to Inquire into the Mercantile Marine: II - Minutes of Evidence. London: HMSO, 1903, Cd 1608.

Report of the Postal and Telegraph Conference held in New Zealand in March 1894. Government Printer 1894.

Report of the Royal Commission on the Navigation Bill. Melbourne: Government Printer, 1906.

Report on the Supply of British Seamen, the Number of Foreigners Serving on Board British Merchant Ships, and the Reasons Given for their Employment, and on Crimping and Other Matters Bearing on Those Subjects. London: HMSO, 1886, C-4709.

Return of the Number, Ages, Ratings, and Nationalities of the Seamen

Employed on the 25th day of March 1896. London: HMSO, 1897, C-8579.
Shipping Safety: Loss of Life at Sea, 1887–1889, vol. 9. Reprinted Shannon: Irish University Press, 1970.
Statutes of New Zealand. Wellington: Government Printer, 1877.

Newspapers and periodicals

Advertiser (Adelaide)
Auckland Evening Star
Auckland Weekly Star
Christchurch Press
Evening Post
Fiji Times
Grey River Argus
Nautical Magazine
Nelson Examiner
New Zealand Herald
New Zealand Observer
New Zealand Times
Otago Daily Times
Otago Witness
Red Funnel
Sydney Daily Telegraph
Sydney Morning Herald
Western Pacific Herald

Published articles and books

Bathgate, Alex (ed.). *Picturesque Dunedin, or Dunedin and its Neighbourhood in 1890*. Dunedin: Mills, Dick & Co, 1890.
Berriedale, Keith, A. 'Merchant shipping legislation in the colonies', *Journal of the Society for Comparative Legislation*, 9:2 (1908), 202–22.
Bullen, Frank T. *The Men of the Merchant Service, Being the Polity of the Mercantile Marine for 'Longshore Readers*. London: Smith, Elder & Co, 1900.
Conrad, Joseph. *An Outcast of the Islands*. Oxford: Oxford University Press, rev. edn, 2002 [1896].
Cyclopedia of New Zealand: Otago and Southland Provincial Districts, vol. 4. Dunedin: The Cyclopedia Company, 1905.
Dexter, W. E. *Rope-Yarns, Marline-Spikes and Tar*. London: William Hodge and Company, 1938.
Gorrie, John. 'Fiji as it is', *Proceedings of the Royal Colonial Institute*, 14 (1883), 159–99.
Grimshaw, Beatrice. *In the Strange South Seas*. London: Hutchinson & Co., 1907.
Grimshaw, Beatrice. *Three Wonderful Nations*. Dunedin: USSCo., 1907.
Hursthouse, Charles. *New Zealand, or Zealandia, The Britain of the South*. London: Edward Sanford, 2nd edn, 1861.

Lawson, William. *Steam in the Southern Pacific: The Story of Merchant Steam Navigation in the Australasian Coastal and Intercolonial Trades, and on the Ocean Lines of the Southern Pacific*. Wellington: Gordon & Gotch, 1909.

Lawson, William. *Pacific Steamers*. Glasgow: Brown, Son & Ferguson, 1927.

Lort Stokes, J. 'On steam communication with the southern colonies (Australia and the Cape of Good Hope)', *Journal of the Royal Geographical Society of London*, 26 (1856), 183–8.

McNab, Robert. *Historical Records of New Zealand*. 2 vols. Wellington: Government Printer, 1908–14.

'New Zealand, Wellington, as a steam port', *Journal of the Society of Arts*, 12 (29 April 1864), 379.

New Zealand, the Wonderland of the World. Dunedin: USSCo., 1888.

Pember Reeves, William. *State Experiments in Australia and New Zealand*. 2 vols. London: Richards, 1902.

Protheroe, Charles. *Life in the Mercantile Marine*. London: John Lane, 1903.

Reeves, Edward. *Brown Men and Women; or, the South Sea Islands in 1895 and 1896*. London: Swan, Sonnenschein & Co, 1898.

'Seafarer' [Walter Manning]. *Below and Above the Water-Line*. Christchurch: Whitcombe and Tombs Limited, [1908].

Seeley, J. R. *The Expansion of England: Two Courses of Lectures*. London: Macmillan, 1883.

St Johnston, Alfred. *Camping Among Cannibals*. London: Macmillan and Co, 1883.

Tregear, Edward. *The Right Hon. R. J. Seddon's (the Premier of New Zealand) Visit to Tonga, Fiji, Savage Islands, and the Cook Islands*. Wellington: Government Printer, 1900.

USSCo. *General Instructions for Captains and Officers in the Service of the Union Steam Ship Company of New Zealand*. Dunedin: USSCo., 1895.

USSCo. *Instructions to Pursers in the Services of the Union Steam Ship Company of New Zealand, Limited*. Dunedin: USSCo., 1893.

Wheen, Reverend John G. 'That which we have seen, or a chat about our work among the Fijians', *Australasian Methodist Missionary Review* (4 January 1910).

II Secondary Material

Books, book chapters and journal articles

Adas, Michael. *Machines as the Measure of Men: Science, Technology, and Ideologies of Western Dominance*. Ithaca: Cornell University Press, 1989.

Ahuja, Ravi. 'Mobility and containment: the voyages of South Asian seamen, c.1900–1960', *International Review of Social History*, 51: Supplement S14 (2006), 111–41.

Ahuja, Ravi. 'Networks of subordination – networks of the subordinated: the ordered spaces of South Asian maritime labour in an age of imperialism (c. 1890–1947)'. In Ashwini Tambe and Harald Fischer-Tine (eds). *The Limits of British Colonial Control in South Asia: Spaces of Disorder in the Indian Ocean Region*. London: Routledge, 2009, 13–48.

Arnold, David. 'Europe, technology and colonialism in the 20th century', *History and Technology*, 21:1 (2005), 85–106.

Arnold, Rollo. *New Zealand's Burning: The Settlers' World in the Mid 1880s*. Wellington: Victoria University Press, 1994.

Atkinson, Neill. 'Against the tide: the Auckland Seamen's Union 1880–1914'. In Pat Walsh (ed.), *Trade Unions, Work and Society: The Centenary of the Arbitration System*. Palmerston North: The Dunmore Press Ltd, 1994, 69–90.

Atkinson, Neill. *Crew Culture: New Zealand Seafarers under Sail and Steam*. Wellington: Te Papa Press, 2001.

Bain, 'Atu. 'A protective labour policy? An alternative interpretation of early colonial labour policy in Fiji', *Journal of Pacific History*, 23:2 (1988), 119–36.

Balachandran, G. 'Circulation through seafaring: Indian seamen, 1890–1945'. In Claude Markovits, Jacques Pouchepadass and Sanjay Subrahmanyam (eds). *Society and Circulation: Mobile People and Itinerant Cultures in South Asia, 1750–1950*. Delhi: Permanent Black, 2003, 89–130.

Balachandran, G. 'Conflicts in the international maritime labour market: British and Indian seamen, employers, and the state, 1890–1939', *Indian Economic and Social History Review*, 39:1 (2002), 71–100.

Balachandran, G. 'Recruitment and control of Indian seamen: Calcutta, 1880–1935', *International Journal of Maritime History*, 9:1 (1997), 1–18.

Balachandran, G. 'South Asian seafarers and their worlds c. 1870–1930s'. In Jerry H. Bentley, Renate Bridenthal and Kären Wigen (eds). *Seascapes: Maritime Histories, Littoral Cultures and Trans-Oceanic Exchanges*. Honolulu: University of Hawai'i Press, 2007, 186–202.

Ballantyne, Tony. 'Mr. Peal's archive: mobility and exchange in histories of empire'. In Antoinette Burton (ed.). *Archive Stories: Facts, Fictions and the Writing of History*. Durham NC: Duke University Press, 2005, 87–110.

Ballantyne, Tony. *Orientalism and Race: Aryanism in the British Empire*. Basingstoke New York: Palgrave and Macmillan, 2002.

Ballantyne, Tony. 'Teaching Maori about Asia: print culture and community identity in nineteenth-century New Zealand'. In Henry Johnson and Brian Moloughney (eds). *Asia in the Making of New Zealand*. Auckland: Auckland University Press, 2006, 13–35.

Ballantyne, Tony. 'Writing out Asia: race, colonialism and Chinese migration in New Zealand History.' In Charles Ferrall, Paul Millar and Keren Smith (eds). *East by South: China in the Australasian Imagination*. Wellington: Victoria University Press, 2005, 87–109.

Bandyopadhyay, Sekhar. 'A history of small numbers: Indians in New Zealand, c.1890–1930', *New Zealand Journal of History*, 43:2 (2009), 150–68.

Banivanua Mar, Tracey. *Violence and Colonial Dialogue: The Australian-Pacific Indentured Labor Trade*. Honolulu: University of Hawai'i Press, 2007.

Belich, James. *Making Peoples: A History of the New Zealanders: From Polynesian Settlement to the End of the Nineteenth Century*. Honolulu: University of Hawai'i Press, 1996.

Belich, James. *Paradise Reforged: A History of the New Zealanders from the 1880s to the Year 2000*. Honolulu: University of Hawai'i Press, 2001.

Bennett, James. 'Maori as honorary members of the white tribe', *Journal of Imperial and Commonwealth History*, 29:3 (2001), 33–54.

Bennett, James, *'Rats and Revolutionaries': The Labour Movement in Australia and New Zealand, 1890–1940*. Dunedin: University of Otago Press, 2004.

Blainey, Geoffrey. *The Tyranny of Distance: How Distance Shaped Australia's History*. South Melbourne: Macmillan, 1975 [1st edn 1966].

Bose, Sugata. *A Hundred Horizons: The Indian Ocean in the Age of Global Empire*. Cambridge, Mass.: Harvard University Press, 2006.

Boyce, Gordon. *Information, Mediation and Institutional Development: The Rise of Large-Scale Enterprise in British Shipping, 1870–1919*. Manchester: Manchester University Press, 1995.

Bragard, Veronique. 'Transoceanic echoes: coolitude and the work of Mauritian poet Khal Torabully', *International Journal of Francophone Studies*, 8:2 (2005), 219–33.

Braudel, Fernand. *The Mediterranean and the Mediterranean World in the Age of Philip II*, trans. Sian Reynolds. 2 vols. London: Collins, 1972–73 [1966].

Brewer, N. H. *A Century of Style: Great Ships of the Union Line, 1875–1976*. Wellington: A. H. & A. W. Reed, 1982.

Brinnen, John Malcolm. 'The decoration of ocean liners: rules and exceptions', *The Journal of Decorative and Propaganda Arts*, 15: Transportation theme issue (1990), 38–47.

Broeze, Frank. 'Distance tamed: steam navigation to Australia and New Zealand from its beginnings to the outbreak of the Great War', *Journal of Transport History*, 10:1 (1989), 1–21.

Broeze, Frank. *Island Nation: A History of Australians and the Sea*. St Leonards: Allen & Unwin, 1998.

Broeze, Frank. 'Maritime history at the crossroads'. In Broeze (ed.). *Maritime History at the Crossroads: A Critical Review of Recent Historiography*. St Johns, Newfoundland: International Maritime Economic History Association, 1995, xiii–xiv.

Broeze, Frank. 'Private enterprise and public policy: merchant shipping in Australia and New Zealand, 1788–1992', *Australian Economic History Review*, 32:2 (1992), 8–32.

Buckley, Ken and Kris Klugman. *The History of Burns Philp: The Australian Company in the South Pacific*. Sydney: Burns Philp & Co, 1981.

Burgess, C. F. *The Fellowship of the Craft: Conrad on Ships and Seamen and the Sea*. Port Washington, NY: Kennikat Press, 1976.

Burton, Valerie. 'The myth of bachelor Jack: masculinity, patriarchy and seafaring labour'. In Colin Howell and Richard J. Twomey (eds). *Jack Tar in History: Essays in the History of Maritime Life and Labour*. New Brunswick: Acadiensis Press, 1991, 179–98.

Burton, Valerie. '"Whoring, drinking sailors": reflections on masculinity from the labour history of nineteenth-century British shipping'. In Margaret

Walsh (ed.). *Working out Gender: Perspectives from Labour History.* Aldershot: Ashgate, 1999, 84–101.

Byrnes, Giselle. '"A dead sheet covered with meaningless words?' Place names and the cultural colonisation of Tauranga', *New Zealand Journal of History*, 36:1 (2002), 18–31.

Carter, Paul. 'Travelling blind: a sound geography', *Meanjin*, 51:2 (1992), 423–45.

Casarino, Cesare. *Modernity at Sea: Melville, Marx, Conrad in Crisis.* Minneapolis: University of Minnesota Press, 2002.

Chappell, David A. 'Ahab's boat: non-European seamen in western ships of exploration and commerce'. In Bernhard Klein and Gesa Mackenthun (eds). *Sea Changes: Historicizing the Ocean.* New York: Routledge, 2004, 75–89.

Chappell, David A. *Double Ghosts: Oceanian Voyagers on Euroamerican Ships.* New York: M. E. Sharpe, 1997.

Chappell, David A. 'Kru and kanaka: participation by African and Pacific Island sailors in Euroamerican maritime frontiers', *International Journal of Maritime History*, 6:2 (1994), 83–114.

Chaves, Kelly K. '"Great violence has been done": the collision of Maori culture and British seafaring culture', *Great Circle*, 29:1 (2007), 22–40.

Churchouse, Jack. *Glamour Ships of the Union Steam Ship Company NZ Ltd.* Wellington: Millwood Press, 1981.

Conway, Mary. *From Jack Tar to Union Jack: Representing Naval Manhood in the British Empire, 1870–1918.* Manchester: Manchester University Press, 2009.

Coons, Lorraine. 'From "company widow" to "new woman": female seafarers aboard the "floating palaces" of the interwar years', *International Journal of Maritime History*, 20: 2 (December 2008), 143–74.

Coons, Lorraine and Alexander Varias. *Tourist Third Cabin: Steamship Travel in the Interwar Years.* New York: Palgrave Macmillan, 2003.

Cooper, Frederick. *On the African Waterfront: Urban Disorder and the Transformation of Work in Colonial Mombasa.* New Haven: Yale University Press, 1987.

Couper, Alastair. 'Islanders at sea: change and the maritime economies of the Pacific'. In Harold Brookfield (ed.). *The Pacific in Transition: Geographical Perspectives on Adaptation and Change.* Canberra: Australian National University Press, 1973, 229–47.

Couper, Alastair. 'Protest movements and protocooperatives in the Pacific Islands', *Journal of the Polynesian Society*, 77:2 (1968), 268–71.

Couper, Alastair. *Sailors and Traders: A Maritime History of the Pacific Peoples.* Honolulu: University of Hawai'i Press, 2009.

Creighton, Margaret S. 'American mariners and the rites of manhood, 1830–1870'. In Colin Howell and Richard Twomey, J. (eds). *Jack Tar in History: Essays in the History of Maritime Life and Labour.* New Brunswick: Acadiensis Press, 1991, 143–63.

Creighton, Margaret S. "Davy Jones' locker room: gender and the American whaleman, 1830–1870'. In Margaret S. Creighton and Lisa Norling (eds).

BIBLIOGRAPHY

Iron Men, Wooden Women: Gender and Seafaring in the Atlantic World, 1700–1920. Baltimore: Johns Hopkins University Press, 1996, 118–37.

Creighton, Margaret S. 'Review: Jack Tar fights back', *American Quarterly*, 43:1 (1991), 103–9.

Creighton, Margaret S. and Lisa Norling, Introduction. In Creighton and Norling (eds), *Iron Men, Wooden Women*, pp. vii–xiii.

Cresswell, Tim. *On the Move: Mobility in the Modern Western World*. New York: Routledge, 2006.

Curthoys, Ann. 'Conflict and consensus'. In Curthoys and Andrew Markus (eds). *Who Are Our Enemies? Racism and the Australian Working Class*. Neutral Bay, NSW: Hale and Iremonger, 1978, 48–65.

Damousi, Joy. 'Chaos and order: gender, space and sexuality on female convict ships', *Australian Historical Studies*, 104 (1995), 351–72.

D'Arcy, Paul. *The People of the Sea: Environment, Identity and History in Oceania*. Honolulu: University of Hawai'i Press, 2006.

DeLoughrey, Elizabeth M. *Routes and Roots: Navigating Caribbean and Pacific Island Literatures*. Honolulu: University of Hawai'i Press, 2007.

Dening, Greg. *Mr Bligh's Bad Language: Passion, Power and Theatre on the Bounty*. Cambridge: Cambridge University Press, 1992.

Denoon, Donald. 'Re-membering Australasia: a repressed memory', *Australian Historical Studies*, 34:122 (2003), 290–304.

Derrick, R. A. *A History of Fiji*. Suva: Fiji Government Press, 1946.

Deudney, Daniel. 'Greater Britain or greater synthesis? Seeley, Mackinder and Wells on Britain in the global industrial era', *Review of International Studies*, 27 (2001), 187–208.

Diamond, Marion. 'Queequeg's crewmates: Pacific Islanders in the European shipping industry', *International Journal of Maritime History*, 1:2 (1989), 123–42.

Dixon, Conrad. 'Lascars: the forgotten seamen'. In Rosemary Ommer and Gerald Panting (eds). *Working Men Who Got Wet: Proceedings of the Fourth Conference of the Atlantic Shipping Project*. Newfoundland: Memorial University of Newfoundland, 1980, 265–77.

Divall, Colin and George Revill. 'Cultures of transport: representation, practice and technology', *Journal of Transport History*, 26:1 (2005), 99–111.

Douglas, Bronwen and Chris Ballard (eds). *Foreign Bodies: Oceania and the Science of Race, 1750–1940*. Canberra: ANU E-Press, 2008.

Dyrenfurth, Nick and Marian Quartly, 'Fat man v. "the people": labor intellectuals and the making of oppositional identities, 1890–1901', *Labour History*, 92 (2007), 31–56.

Edwards, Penny. 'On home ground: settling land and domesticating difference in the "non-settler" colonies of Burma and Cambodia', *Journal of Colonialism and Colonial History*, 4:3 (2003).

Ethnic Labour and British Imperial Trade: A History of Ethnic Seafarers in the UK. Special issue *Immigrants and Minorities*, 13:2-3 (1994).

Evans, Raymond, Kay Saunders and Kathryn Cronin. *Exclusion, Exploitation and Extermination: Race Relations in Colonial Queensland.* Sydney: Australia and New Zealand Book Co., 1975.

Eves, Richard. 'Unsettling settler colonialism: debates over climate and colonization in New Guinea, 1875–1914', *Ethnic & Racial Studies*, 28:2 (2005), 304–30.

Farquhar, Ian J. *Union Fleet, 1875–1975.* Wellington: New Zealand Ship and Marine Society, 2nd rev. edn, 1976.

Fitzpatrick, Brian and Rowan J. Cahill. *The Seamen's Union of Australia, 1872–1972: A History.* Sydney: Seamen's Union of Australia, 1981.

Foucault, Michel. *Discipline and Punish: The Birth of the Prison*, trans. Alan Sheridan. New York: Vintage Books, 1979.

Foucault, Michel. 'Of other spaces', *Diacritics*, 16:1 (1986 [1967]), 22–7.

Fox, Stephen. *The Ocean Railway: Isambard Kingdom Brunel, Samuel Cunard and the Revolutionary World of the Great Atlantic Steamships.* London: Harper Perennial, 2003.

Gann, Lewis H. and Peter Duignan. *The Rulers of British Africa, 1870–1914.* London: Croom Helm, 1978.

Ganter, Regina. *The Pearl-Shellers of Torres Strait: Resource Use, Development and Decline 1860s–1960s.* Carlton, Vic.: Melbourne University Press, 1994.

Gibbons, Peter. 'Cultural colonisation and national identity', *New Zealand Journal of History*, 36:1 (2002), 5–17.

Gilliland, Jason. 'Muddy shore to modern port: redimensioning the Montreal waterfront time-space', *The Canadian Geographer*, 48:4 (2004), 448–72.

Gillion, Kenneth L. *Fiji's Indian Migrants: A History to the End of Indenture in 1920.* Melbourne: Oxford University Press, 1962.

Goffman, Erving. *Asylums: Essays on the Social Situation of Mental Patients and Other Inmates.* Harmondsworth, Middlesex: Penguin, 1968.

Goodall, Heather, Develeena Ghosh and Lindi R. Todd. 'Jumping ship – skirting empire: Indians, Aborigines and Australians across the Indian Ocean', *Transforming Cultures eJournal*, 3:1 (2008), 44–74.

Gordon, Keith. *Deep Water Gold: The Story of R.M.S. Niagara: The Quest for New Zealand's Greatest Shipwreck Treasure.* Whangarei: SeaROV Technologies, 2005.

Hamilton, J. H. 'The all-red route, 1853–1953: a history of the trans-Pacific mail service between British Columbia, Australia and New Zealand', *British Columbia Historical Quarterly* (January–April 1956), 20–26.

Hamilton-Paterson, James. *Seven Tenths: The Sea and Its Thresholds.* London: Hutchinson, 1992.

Harcourt, Freda. *Flagships of Imperialism: The P&O Company and the Politics of Empire from its Origins to 1867.* Manchester: Manchester University Press, 2006.

Hau'ofa, Epeli. 'Our sea of islands', *Contemporary Pacific*, 6:1 (1994), 148–61.

Headrick, Daniel R. *The Tools of Empire: Technology and European Imperialism in the Nineteenth Century.* New York: Oxford University Press, 1981.

Hearn, Mark and Greg Patmore (eds). *Working the Nation: Working Life and Federation, 1890–1914.* Annandale, NSW: Pluto Press, 2001.

Heartfield, James. '"You are not a white woman!": Apolosi Nawai, the Fiji Produce Agency and the trial of Stella Spencer in Fiji, 1915', *Journal of Pacific History*, 38:1 (2003), 69–83.

Howard, Alan. 'Rotuman seafaring in historical perspective'. In Richard Feinberg (ed.). *Seafaring in the Contemporary Pacific Islands: Studies in Continuity and Change*. DeKalb: Northern Illinois University Press, 1995, 114–43.

Howell, Colin and Richard J. Twomey (eds). *Jack Tar in History: Essays in the History of Maritime Life and Labour*. New Brunswick: Acadiensis Press, 1991.

Howe, K. R. 'Two worlds?' *New Zealand Journal of History*, 37:1 (2003), 50–8.

Huttenback, R. A. 'The British Empire as a "White man's country": racial attitudes and immigration legislation in the colonies of white settlement', *Journal of British Studies*, 13:1 (1973), 108–37.

Hyslop, Jonathan. 'Steamship empire: Asian, African and British sailors in the merchant marine, c.1880–1945', *Journal of Asian and African Studies*, 44:1 (2009), 49–67.

Jakobsson, Hakan. 'The warship in Swedish seventeenth-century society – a cultural construction?' *Scandinavian Journal of History*, 24:3-4 (1999), 225–43.

Jolly, Margaret. 'Custom and the way of the land: past and present in Vanuatu and Fiji', *Oceania*, 62 (1992), 330–54.

Jolly, Margaret. 'Colonizing women: the maternal body and empire'. In Sneja Gunew and Anna Yeatman (eds). *Feminism and the Politics of Difference*. St Leonards, NSW: Allen and Unwin, 1993, 103–27.

Jolly, Margaret. 'On the edge? Deserts, oceans, islands', *Contemporary Pacific*, 13:2 (2001), 417–66.

Jolly, Margaret, Serge Tcherkézoff and Darrell Tryon (eds). *Oceanic Encounters: Exchange, Desire, Violence*. Canberra: ANU E-Press, 2009.

Kelly, John. *A Politics of Virtue: Hinduism, Sexuality, and Countercolonial Discourse in Fiji*. Chicago: University of Chicago Press, 1991.

Kennerley, Alston. 'Stoking the boilers: firemen and trimmers in British merchant ships, 1850–1950', *International Journal of Maritime History*, 20:1 (2008), 191–220.

Knapman, Bruce. *Fiji's Economic History, 1874–1939: Studies of Capitalist Colonial Development*. Canberra: The Australian National University National Centre for Development Studies, 1987.

Knapman, Claudia. *White Women in Fiji, 1835–1930: The Ruin of Empire?* Sydney: Allen and Unwin, 1986.

Knowles, Richard D. 'Transport shaping space: differential collapse in time-space', *Journal of Transport Geography*, 14 (2006): 407–25.

Konvitz, Josef W. 'The crises of Atlantic port cities, 1880 to 1920', *Comparative Studies in Society and History*, 36:2 (1994), 293–318.

Kubicek, Robert. 'British expansion, empire, and technological change'. In Andrew Porter (ed.). *The Oxford History of the British Empire*, vol. 3. Oxford: Oxford University Press, 1999, 247–69.

Kubicek, Robert. 'The proliferation and diffusion of steamship technology and the beginnings of "new imperialism"'. In David Killingray, Margarette Lincoln and Nigel Rigby (eds). *Maritime Empires: British Imperial Maritime Trade in the Nineteenth Century.* Woodbridge, Suffolk: The Boydell Press, 2004, 100–10.

Lake, Marilyn. '"The brightness of eyes and quiet assurance which seem to say American" – Alfred Deakin's identification with Republican manhood', *Australian Historical Studies*, 38:129 (2007), 32–51.

Lake, Marilyn. 'From Mississippi to Melbourne via Natal: the invention of the literacy test as a technology of exclusion'. In Ann Curthoys and Lake (eds). *Connected Worlds: History in Transnational Perspective.* Canberra: ANU E-Press, 2005, 210–29.

Lake, Marilyn and Henry Reynolds. *Drawing the Global Colour Line: White Men's Countries and the Question of Racial Equality.* Melbourne: Melbourne University Press, 2008.

Lal, Brij V. *Girmitiyas: The Origins of the Fiji Indians.* Canberra: Journal of Pacific History, 1983.

Lal, Brij V. 'Veil of dishonour: sexual jealousy and suicide on Fiji plantations', *Journal of Pacific History*, 20:3-4 (1985), 135–55.

Lal, Brij V. (ed.). *Crossing the Kala Pani: A Documentary History of Indian Indenture in Fiji.* Canberra: Division of Pacific & Asian History, Research School of Pacific & Asian Studies, Australian National University, 1998.

Lester, Alan. 'Imperial circuits and networks: geographies of the British empire', *History Compass*, 4:1 (2006), 124–41.

Leckie, Jacqueline. 'In defence of race and empire: the White New Zealand League at Pukekohe', *New Zealand Journal of History*, 19:2 (1985), 103–29.

Leckie, Jacqueline. 'Workers in colonial Fiji: 1870–1970'. In Clive Moore, Jacqueline Leckie and Doug Munro (eds). *Labour in the South Pacific.* Townsville: James Cook University, 1990, 47–66.

Livingstone, David N. 'Race, space and moral climatology: notes towards a genealogy', *Journal of Historical Geography*, 28:2 (2002), 159–80.

Locker-Lampson, Steve and Ian Francis. *Eight Minutes Past Midnight: The Wreck of the S.S. Wairarapa.* Wellington: Rowfant, 1981.

MacKenzie, John M. 'Lakes, rivers and oceans: technology, ethnicity and the shipping of empire in the late nineteenth century'. In David Killingray, Margarette Lincoln and Nigel Rigby (eds). *Maritime Empires: British Imperial Maritime Trade in the Nineteenth Century.* Woodbridge, Suffolk: The Boydell Press, 2004, 111–27.

Mäenpää, Sari. 'Women below deck: gender and employment on British passenger liners, 1860–1938', *Journal of Transport History*, 25:2 (2004), 57–74.

Markey, Raymond. 'Race and organised labor in Australia, 1850–1901', *The Historian*, 58: 2 (1996), 343–60.

Markovits, Claude, Jacques Pouchepadass and Sanjay Subrahmanyam. 'Introduction: circulation and society under colonial rule'. In Markovits, Pouchepadass and Subrahmanyam (eds). *Society and Circulation: Mobile*

People and Itinerant Cultures in South Asia, 1750–1950. Delhi: Permanent Black, 2003, 1–22.

Marsden, Ben and Crosbie Smith, *Engineering Empires: A Cultural History of Technology in Nineteenth-Century Britain*. Basingstoke: Palgrave Macmillan, 2005.

Martinez, Julia and Claire Lowrie. 'Colonial constructions of masculinity: transforming Aboriginal Australian men into "houseboys"', *Gender and History*, 21:2 (2009), 305–23.

Massey, Doreen. *For Space*. London: Sage, 2005.

Massey, Doreen. *Space, Place and Gender*. Cambridge: Polity Press, 1994.

Maude, H. E. *Of Islands and Men: Studies in Pacific History*. Melbourne: Oxford University Press, 1968.

McConnell, M. L. "Cabotage and the colonial corset: the great Australian bind', *Maritime Law Association of Australia and New Zealand Journal*, 5 (1988), 3–18.

McKellar, Norman Lang. *From Derby Round to Burketown: The A.U.S.N. Story*. St Lucia: University of Queensland Press, 1977.

McLean, Gavin. *Captain's Log: New Zealand's Maritime History*. Auckland: Hodder Moa Beckett Publishers Ltd, 2001.

McLean, Gavin. 'Naming the "Niagara"', *New Zealand Marine News*, 36:2 (1986), 47–50.

McLean, Gavin. *The Southern Octopus: The Rise of a Shipping Empire*. Wellington: New Zealand Ship and Marine Society and the Wellington Harbour Board Maritime Museum, 1990.

Mellefont, Jeffrey. "Heirlooms and tea towels: views of ships' gender in the modern maritime museum', *Great Circle: Journal of the Australian Association for Maritime History*, 22:1 (2000), 5–16.

Mills, Peter R. 'Neo in Oceania: foreign vessels owned by Hawaiian chiefs before 1830', *Journal of Pacific History*, 38:1 (2003), 53–67.

Miyazaki, Hirokazu. 'Delegating closure'. In Sally Engle Merry and Donald Brenneis (eds). *Law and Empire in the Pacific: Fiji and Hawai'i*. Sante Fe: School of American Research Press, 2004, 239–59.

Miyazaki, Hirokazu. *The Method of Hope: Anthropology, Philosophy, and Fijian Knowledge*. Stanford, Ca.: Stanford University Press, 2004.

Moloughney, Brian and John Stenhouse. '"Drug-besotten, sin-begotten fiends of filth": New Zealanders and the oriental other, 1850–1920', *New Zealand Journal of History*, 33:1 (1999), 43–64.

Mom, Gijs, Colin Divall and Peter Lyth, 'Towards a paradigm shift? A decade of transport and mobility history'. In Mom, Gordon Pirie and Laurent Tissot (eds). *Mobility in History: The State of the Art in the History of Transport, Traffic and Mobility*. Neuchâtel: Alphil, 2009, 13–40.

Mongia, Radhika Viyas. 'Race, nationality, mobility: a history of the passport'. In Antoinette Burton (ed.). *After the Imperial Turn: Thinking With and Through the Nation*. Durham, NC: Duke University Press, 2003, 196–214.

Monin, Paul. *This Is My Place: Hauraki Contested, 1769–1875*. Wellington: Bridget Williams Books, 2001.

Moore, Clive. *Kanaka: A History of Melanesian Mackay.* Port Moresby: University of Papua New Guinea, 1985.

Mowbry Tate, E. *Transpacific Steam: The Story of Steam Navigation from the Pacific Coast of North America to the Far East and the Antipodes, 1867–1941.* New York: Cornwall Books, 1986.

Nayder, Lillian. 'Sailing ships and steamers, angels and whores: history and gender in Conrad's maritime fiction'. In Creighton and Lisa Norling (eds). *Iron Men, Wooden Women:* 189–203.

Norling, Lisa. *Captain Ahab Had a Wife: New England Women and the Whale-fishery, 1720–1870.* Chapel Hill: University of North Carolina Press, 2000.

O'Connor, P. S. 'Keeping New Zealand white, 1908–1920', *New Zealand Journal of History,* 2:1 (1968), 41–65.

O'Hara, Glen. '"The sea is swinging into view": modern British maritime history in a globalised world', *English Historical Review,* 124:510 (2009), 1109–34.

Ogborn, Miles. *Indian Ink: Script and Print in the Making of the English East India Company.* Chicago: Chicago University Press, 2007.

Omissi, David E. *The Sepoy and the Raj: The Indian Army, 1860–1940.* Basingstoke: Macmillan, in association with King's College, London, 1994.

Palmer, Sarah. *Politics, Shipping and the Repeal of the Navigation Laws.* Manchester: Manchester University Press, 1990.

Pearson, M. N. *The Indian Ocean.* New York: Routledge, 2003.

Petersen, Anna K. C. 'The European use of Maori art in New Zealand homes, c.1890–1914'. In Barbara Brookes (ed.). *At Home in New Zealand: Houses, History, People.* Wellington: Bridget William Books, 2000, 57–72.

Petrie, Hazel. *Chiefs of Industry: Maori Tribal Enterprise in Early Colonial New Zealand.* Auckland: Auckland University Press, 2006.

Popke, Emil Jeffrey. 'Managing colonial alterity: narratives of race, space and labor in Durban, 1870–1920', *Journal of Historical Geography,* 29:2 (2003), 248–67.

Prior, Richard (ed.). *Ocean Liners: The Golden Years.* London: Tiger Books International, 1993.

Quartly, Marian. '"Making working-class heroes: labor cartoonists and the Australian worker, 1903–16', *Labour History,* 89 (2005), 159–78.

Ralston, Caroline. *Grass Huts and Warehouses: Pacific Beach Communities of the Nineteenth Century.* Canberra: Australian National University Press, 1977.

Rediker, Marcus. *Between the Devil and the Deep Blue Sea: Merchant Seamen, Pirates and the Anglo-American Maritime World, 1700–1750.* Cambridge: Cambridge University Press, 1987.

Rediker, Marcus. 'The common seaman in the histories of capitalism and the working class', *International Journal of Maritime History,* 1:2 (1989), 337–57.

Rieger, Bernhard. *Technology and the Culture of Modernity in Britain and Germany, 1890–1945.* Cambridge: Cambridge University Press, 2005.

Ross, Angus. *New Zealand Aspirations in the Pacific in the Nineteenth Century.* Oxford: Clarendon Press, 1964.

Rüger, Jan. 'Nation, empire and navy: identity politics in the United Kingdom, 1887–1914', *Past and Present*, 185 (2004), 159–88.

Sager, Eric W. *Seafaring Labour: The Merchant Marine of Atlantic Canada, 1820–1914*. Kingston, Ont.: McGill-Queen's University Press, 1989.

Sager, Eric W. "Seafaring labour in maritime history and working-class history', *International Journal of Maritime History*, 2:1 (1990), 259–74.

Salesa, Damon T., 'Contested oceans' (*The People of the Sea* book review forum), *Journal of Pacific History* 43:1 (2008), 117–19.

Salesa, Damon T. 'Half-castes between the wars: colonial categories in New Zealand and Samoa', *New Zealand Journal of History*, 34:1 (2000), 98–116.

Salesa, Damon T., 'New Zealand's Pacific'. In Giselle Byrnes (ed.). *The New Oxford History of New Zealand*. Melbourne: Oxford University Press, 2009, 149–72.

Salesa, Damon T. '"Travel-happy" Samoa: colonialism, Samoan migration and a "brown Pacific"', *New Zealand Journal of History*, 37:2 (2003), 171–88.

Salmond, Anne, *Between Worlds: Early Exchanges Between Maori and Europeans 1773–1815*. Honolulu: University of Hawai'i Press, 1997.

Samson, Jane. *Imperial Benevolence: Making British Authority in the Pacific Islands*. Honolulu: University of Hawai'i Press, 1998.

Saunders, Kay. '"A new race, bred of the soil and sun": conceptualising race and labour, 1890–1914'. In Mark Hearn and Greg Patmore (eds). *Working the Nation: Working Life and Federation, 1890–1914*. Annandale, NSW: Pluto Press, 2001, 78–92.

Seiler, Cotten. 'Mobilising race, racialising mobility: writing race into mobility studies'. In Gijs Mom, Gordon Pirie and Laurent Tissot (eds). *Mobility in History: The State of the Art in the History of Transport, Traffic and Mobility*. Neuchatel: Alphil, 2009, 229–33.

Seymour, Michael. 'Warships' names of the English Republic, 1649–1659', *Mariner's Mirror*, 76:4 (1990), 317–24.

Shineberg, Dorothy. *They Came for Sandalwood: A Study of the Sandalwood Trade in the South-West Pacific, 1830–1865*. Melbourne: Melbourne University Press, 1967.

Sinclair, Keith (ed.). *Distance Looks Our Way: The Effects of Remoteness on New Zealand*. Auckland: University of Auckland, 1961.

Smith, Crosbie, Ian Higginston and Phillip Wolstenholme. '"Imitations of God's own works": making trustworthy the ocean steamship', *History of Science*, 41:134 (2003), 379–426.

Sorrenson, Richard. 'The ship as a scientific instrument in the eighteenth century', *Osiris*, 2nd series: Science in the Field. 11 (1996), 221–36.

Stafford, Jane and Mark Williams. *Maoriland: New Zealand Literature, 1872–1914*. Wellington: Victoria University Press, 2006.

Stanley, Jo. 'And after the cross-dressed cabin boys and whaling wives? possible futures for women's maritime historiography', *Journal of Transport History*, 23:1 (2002), 9–22.

Stanley, Jo. *Bold in Her Breeches: Women Pirates across the Ages*. London: Pandora, 1995.

Stephenson, Elsie. *Fiji's Past on Picture Postcards*. Suva: Caines Jannif Group, 1997.

Stoler, Ann Laura. *Carnal Knowledge and Imperial Power: Race and the Intimate in Colonial Rule*. Berkeley: University of California Press, 2002.

Streets, Heather. *Martial Races: The Military, Race and Masculinity in British Imperial Culture, 1857–1914*. Manchester: Manchester University Press, 2004.

Strong-Boag, Veronica and Carole Gerson. *Paddling Her Own Canoe: The Times and Texts of E. Pauline Johnson (Tekahionwake)*. Toronto: University of Toronto Press, 2000.

Tabili, Laura. '"A maritime race": masculinity and the racial division of labour in British merchant ships, 1900–1939'. In Creighton and Norling (eds). *Iron Men, Wooden Women*, 169–88.

Tabili, Laura. 'The construction of racial difference in twentieth-century Britain: the Special Restriction (Coloured Alien Seamen) Order, 1925', *Journal of British Studies*, 33:1 (1994), 54–98.

Tabili, Laura. *'We Ask for British Justice': Workers and Racial Difference in Late Imperial Britain*. Ithaca and London: Cornell University Press, 1994.

Teaiwa, Katerina Martina. 'Our sea of phosphate: the diaspora of Ocean Island'. In Graham Harvey and Charles D. Thompson Jr (eds). *Indigenous Diasporas and Dislocations: Unsettling Western Fixations*. London: Ashgate, 2005, 169–91.

Thomas, Mifflin. *Schooner from Windward: Two Centuries of Hawaiian Interisland Shipping*. Honolulu: University of Hawai'i Press, 1983.

Thomas, Nicholas. *Possessions: Indigenous Art / Colonial Culture*. London: Thames and Hudson, 1999.

Thomas, Nicholas and Richard Eves. *Bad Colonists: The South Seas Letters of Vernon Lee Walker & Louis Becke*. Durham, NC: Duke University Press, 1999.

Thompson, Roger C. *Australian Imperialism in the Pacific: The Expansionist Era, 1820–1920*. Carlton: Melbourne University Press, 1980.

Tinker, Hugh. *A New System of Slavery: The Export of Indian Labour Overseas 1830–1920*. London: Oxford University Press, 1974.

Tsokhas, Kosmas. 'Cartels, imperial relations and Australian shipping policy in the Asia–Pacific region, 1914–1939', *Journal of Contemporary Asia*, 27:3 (1997), 356–73.

Veracini, Lorenzo. '"Emphatically not a white man's colony": settler colonialism and the construction of colonial Fiji', *Journal of Pacific History*, 43:2 (2008), 189–205.

Ward, R. G. 'The Pacific beche-de-mer trade with special reference to Fiji'. In R. G. Ward (ed.). *Man in the Pacific Islands: Essays on Geographical Change in the Pacific Islands*. Oxford: Clarendon Press, 1972, 91–123.

Ward, R. G. *Widening Worlds, Shrinking Worlds? The Reshaping of Oceania*. Canberra: Centre for the Contemporary Pacific, Pacific Distinguished Lecture, ANU, 1999.

Waters, Sydney D. *Union Line: A Short History of the Union Steam Ship Company of New Zealand Ltd., 1875–1951*. Wellington: USSCo., 1951.

Wigen, Kären. 'Oceans of history: introduction', *American Historical Review*, 111:4 (2006), 717–21.

Williams, David M. 'Mid-Victorian attitudes to seamen and maritime reform: the Society for Improving the Condition of Merchant Seamen, 1867'. In Lars U. Scholl (ed.). *Merchants and Mariners: Selected Maritime Writings of David M. Williams*. St John's, Newfoundland: International Maritime Economic History Association, 2000, 229–52.

Williams, David, M. 'The quality, skill and supply of maritime labour: causes of concern in Britain, 1850–1914'. In Lars U. Scholl (ed.). *Merchants and Mariners: Selected Maritime Writings of David M. Williams*. St John's, Newfoundland: International Maritime Economic History Association, 2000, 273–92.

Winder, Gordon M. 'Seafarer's gaze: Queen Street business and Auckland's archipelago, 1908', *New Zealand Geographer*, 62 (2006), 50–64.

Worden, William. *Cargoes: Matson's First Century in the Pacific*. Honolulu: University of Hawai'i Press, 1981.

Yoon, Hong-Key. *Maori Mind, Maori Land: Essays on the Cultural Geography of the Maori People from an Outsider's Perspective*. Berne: Lang, 1986.

Young, John. *Adventurous Spirits: Australian Migrant Society in Pre-Cession Fiji*. St. Lucia: University of Queensland Press, 1984.

Young, John. 'Sailing to Levuka: the cultural significance of the island schooners in the late 19th century', *Journal of Pacific History*, 28:1 (1993), 36–52.

Unpublished Dissertations

Atkinson, Neill. 'Auckland Seamen and their Union, 1880-1922'. MA dissertation, University of Auckland, 1990.

Marshall, Peter. 'New Zealand's Trade with the Pacific Islands, 1870–1900'. MA dissertation, University of Otago, 1960.

Munro, R. J. 'Otago Interest and Intercourse with Fiji, 1870–73'. MA dissertation, University of Otago, 1967.

Werry, Margaret. 'Tourism, Ethnicity and the Performance of New Zealand Nationalism, 1889–1914'. PhD dissertation, Northwestern University, 2001.

Williams, H. E. 'Homosexuality: Aspects of the Problem Aboard Ships'. Preventive Medicine Dissertation, University of Otago, 1962.

INDEX

EU authorised representative for GPSR:
Easy Access System Europe, Mustamäe tee 50,
10621 Tallinn, Estonia
gpsr.requests@easproject.com

www.ingramcontent.com/pod-product-compliance
Ingram Content Group UK Ltd.
Pitfield, Milton Keynes, MK11 3LW, UK
UKHW021817150726
7214IPUK00016B/164